Fascism and resistance in Portugal

Aos amigos de Carcavelos
To my friends in Carcavelos

Fascism and resistance in Portugal

Communists, liberals and military dissidents in the opposition to Salazar, 1941–1974

D. L. Raby

Manchester University Press

Manchester and New York

Distributed exclusively in the USA and Canada
by St. Martin's Press Inc.,
175 Fifth Avenue, New York, NY10010, USA

Published by Manchester University Press
Oxford Road, Manchester M13 9PL

British Library cataloguing in publication data
Raby, D. L.
   Fascism and resistance in Portugal:
   communists, liberals and military dissidents
   in the opposition to Salazar, 1941–1974.
   1. Opposition (Political science) – Portugal
   – History – 20th century 2. Portugal –
   Politics and government – 1933–1974
   I. Title
   322.4'2'09469   DP680

Library of Congress cataloging in publication data

Raby, D. L.
   Fascism and resistance in Portugal: communists, liberals and
   military dissidents in the opposition to Salazar, 1941–1974/D. L.
   Raby.
      p.   cm.
   Bibliography: p. 270.
   Includes index.
   ISBN 0-7190-2514-1: $30.00 (est.)
   1. Portugal – Politics and government – 1933–1974.   2. Fascism –
   Portugal – History – 20th century.   3. Partido Comunista Portugês.
   4. Portugal – Armed Forces – Political activity – History – 20th
   century.   5. Salazar, Antonio de Oliveira, 1889–1970.   I. Title.
   DP680.R25   1988
   946.9'042 – dc19   87-32088
                                       CIP

ISBN 0 7190 25141 *hardback*

Typeset in Hong Kong
by Best-set Typesetter Ltd
Printed in Great Britain
by Biddles Ltd., Guildford and King's Lynn

Contents

Acknowledgements   page viii

Chapter I.   Fascism and resistance in Portugal and
elsewhere   1
Notes to Chapter I   15

Chapter II.   Resistance and unity: conflicting Opposition
strategies, 1941–57   17
1. The MUNAF: a broad resistance
movement on the European model   17
2. Free elections, 'as free as in free England'   22
3. Norton de Matos: the symbolic assault on
the centre of power   29
4. The MND: the Left goes it alone   33
Notes to Chapter II   38

Chapter III.   The rise of the Communist Party, 1941–47   41
1. The crisis of the Party in the late thirties   42
2. The reorganisation of 1940–41   47
3. The First Illegal Congress and the line of
national anti-fascist insurrection   55
4. The foundations of PCP hegemony
within the working class   68
5. The 'strategy of transition' defeated,
1945–46   90
Notes to Chapter III   100

Chapter IV.   The PCP from 1947 to 1962: crisis and
              renewal   107
              1. The Cold War and the 1949 crisis   107
              2. The line struggle of 1950–52   113
              3. The 'peaceful solution of the Portuguese
                 political problem'   116
              4. Working-class and popular struggles,
                 1949–62   123
              5. The PCP in crisis, 1958–59, and Cunhal's
                 'rectification' of 1960–61   129
              6. The revolutionary upsurge of 1960–62:
                 the end of the PCP's 'heroic era'?   133
              Notes to Chapter IV   144

Chapter V.   The emergence of military populism: Galvão
              and Delgado   150
              1. The background: military republicanism
                 and the populist tradition   150
              2. Henrique Galvão: the outraged honour
                 of a conservative idealist   152
              3. Delgado's origins and ideological
                 tendencies   159
              4. The crisis of the Opposition in the mid-
                 fifties and the search for a Presidential
                 candidate   166
              Notes to Chapter V   173

Chapter VI.   The populist whirlwind: Delgado's
              campaign and its aftermath   177
              1. The 'fearless general' takes the field   177
              2. The consequences of Delgado's campaign   197
              3. From the cathedral to the barracks: the
                 Juntas Patrióticas, Botelho Moniz and Beja 204
              Notes to Chapter VI   213

Chapter VII. Through war to liberation, 1962–74   219
              1. The colonial wars and the transformation
                 of Portugal   219
              2. The PCP and the Marxist–Leninists   223
              3. The exiles: factional strife and Guevarism 226

4. The Democratic Opposition: Socialists
   and Catholics   233
5. Caetano's false liberalisation: the
   beginning of the end   237
6. The Movement of the Captains and the
   'Revolution of Flowers'   244
   Notes to Chapter VII   249

Chapter VIII.   Resistance and liberation – the limits of
                change   254
                Notes to Chapter VIII   269

Sources and bibliography   270

Index   278

Acknowledgements

The research for this study was made possible by two University of Toronto Research Leave Grants, in 1976–77 and 1982–83. A smaller grant from the University of Toronto enabled the author to visit Portugal also in June–July 1978 and further grants assisted in typing and preparation of the manuscript. Research was carried out in the Robarts Library, University of Toronto; The British Library and Public Records Office, London; the Biblioteca Nacional, Lisbon; the archive of the Tribunal da Boa Hora; the archive of *O Século* newspaper; the Hemeroteca Municipal, Lisbon; and in several private collections. Thanks are due especially to Sr Carlos Ferrão, for facilitating access to his personal library; to Dr José Magalhães Godinho, for making available several documents from his personal papers; to Sra Maria Humberta Delgado Lourenço, for providing copies of some of her father's papers; to Dra Alcina Bastos, for access to papers from her personal collection; to Dr Manuel Sertório, for permission to consult his personal papers relating to General Delgado and the exile opposition; to Sr António Dias Lourenço for access to the *Avante!* archive; to João Arsénio Nunes, for material on the Communist Party; to the former staff of the *O Século* archive, especially Sr José Quitério; to Engineer Virgínia Moura and Dr Armando de Castro, for documentation on the MND; to Drs Francisco Sousa Tavares and Jorge Sampaio, for documentation on the student movements; to Dr Francisco Lino Neto, for materials on the Catholic opposition; and to the late Dr Luis Dias Amado, for information on the Masonic Order. Also very helpful were Dr Mário Murteira, the architect Nuno Teotónio Pereira, Dr Olívio França, the late Sr Oliveira Valença, Drs Ruy Luis Gomes and José Morgado, and the staff of the Gabinete de Investigacões Sociais (now Instituto de Ciências Sociais), notably Jaime Reis, Manuel Braga da Cruz and Luis Salgado de Matos. Acknowledgement is due also to all those who consented to be interviewed by the author, providing much valuable and otherwise inaccessible information. A word of thanks also to family and friends in Toronto and elsewhere, notably Beth, Chris, Brian and Penny; to my parents; and to Ana Lizón Alberro.

Finally, it should of course be emphasised that the author takes full responsibility for all opinions and interpretations expressed in the text.

D. L. Raby
Toronto, April 1987

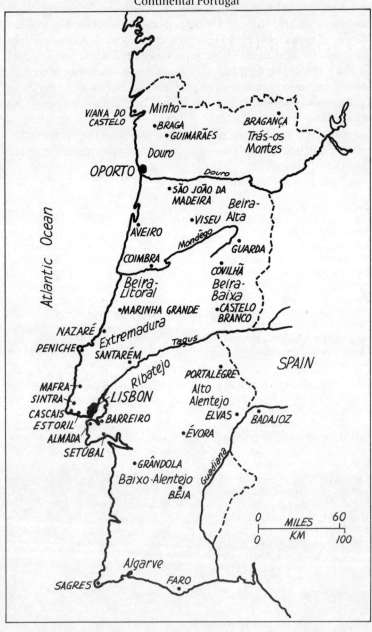

1

Fascism and resistance in Portugal and elsewhere

Honra a quem melhor souber ensinar a virtude, distribuir a sciência e a riqueza, entre um povo infeliz, digno de melhor sorte. Tratae d'elle, e vel-o-heis crescer e medrar-até ao dia em que dispense a tutella historicamente indispensável de classes privilegiadas, militares ou industriaes, aristocráticas ou burguezas. Então a democracia será uma verdade e não uma ficção; a liberdade um facto, não uma formula; a sociedade uma harmonia, e não um cahos. Mas, ai dos que não tiverem olhos para vêr! porque a marcha dos tempos, o andar das cousas não param; e se em vez de educar, seguirem destruindo; se em vez de proteger, explorarem o povo as classes que agora o dirigem, a democracia nem por isso deixará de vir. Mas virá com um brandão incendiário, um grito de guerra, uma foice, um chuço, um machado, vingar-se de quem não soube cumprir o seu dever . . .

Praise be to he who is best able to instil virtue, and distribute knowledge and wealth among an unhappy people, worthy of a better fate. Care for that people, and you will see it grow and thrive – until the day when it can do without the historically inevitable tutelage of privileged classes, be they military or industrial, aristocratic or bourgeois. Then democracy will be a reality and not a fiction; liberty a fact and not a formula; society a harmonious whole and not a state of chaos. But woe betide those who do not have eyes to see! For the onward march of time, the progression of things, will not stop; and if instead of educating they continue to destroy; if the classes which now rule over the people, instead of protecting them, exploit them; democracy will not on this account fail to arrive. But it will come with a flaming torch, a shout of war, a sickle, a pike, an axe, to punish those who did not fulfil their duty . . .

Oliveira Martins, *Portugal Contemporâneo* (1881)

The Portuguese regime identified with the name of Dr. António de Oliveira Salazar was the longest-lived right-wing dictatorship in Europe and possibly in the world. In power for almost forty-

eight years, from 28 May 1926 to 25 April 1974, it survived the
impact of civil war in its Spanish neighbour, of the Second World
War and the defeat of international fascism, and numerous *coup*
attempts and waves of domestic protest. Its architect and virtually
unquestioned leader from 1928 to his disablement in 1968,
Oliveira Salazar, was a shy, misanthropic economics professor
who shunned publicity and cultivated the image of a secular
monk, labouring behind the scenes to preserve traditional values,
the Catholic faith and the established social hierarchy against the
threats of Communism, Freemasonry and modernism. At times
the social stasis in Portugal seemed so complete that outsiders
were convinced of the validity of the official myth: that the *bom
povo português*, the simple Portuguese people, were content to
languish in stoic poverty and near-medieval isolation, with their
brandos costumes (gentle manners) saving them from political
passions and conflicts. When the régime was finally overthrown
by the Armed Forces Movement (*Movimento das Forças Armadas* or
MFA), it was the culmination of thirteen years of colonial warfare
in Angola, Guiné and Mozambique – a strain which would have
caused political ·upheavals in countries with much greater
resources than Portugal, as the example of France and the
Algerian war demonstrates.

All this has led many observers to overlook or minimise the
rôle of the anti-fascist resistance in Portugal itself. The regime's
remarkable longevity appears to lend credence to its claims to
have enjoyed extensive popular support, or at least to the idea
that opposition was limited in both numbers and vigour. There
was no civil war in Portugal, and after the first few years there
were no major acts of armed resistance as with the anti-fascist
resistance in Italy or Spain in the 1940's. The extent of direct state
violence (executions, deaths of prisoners while in detention,
killings of demonstrators and rioters by the police and the armed
forces) was much less than in Nazi Germany, fascist Italy,
Franco's Spain or Chile and Argentina under the recent military
regimes there. The total number of those killed in the notorious
Tarrafal prison camp in the Cape Verde islands, in gaol or police
custody, in the repression of strikes, demonstrations and popular
protests, and in armed uprisings against the dictatorship does not
exceed 1,000 at the outside.[1] It is therefore easy to conclude that
the Portuguese régime was not fascist, or that repression was mild

and highly selective, and that the attitude of the majority of the population was one of passive acceptance.

Such a benevolent analysis of Salazarism is not without foundation in comparative perspective; but it ignores the subtle and all-pervasive character of repression under the New State (*Estado Nôvo*), the term applied to the regime from 1933 onwards. The suppression of political parties and free trade unions, the systematic use of censorship and of the political police, the development of typically fascist institutions such as the official party, the paramilitary Portuguese Legion and Youth Movement (*Mocidade*) – all of this created a thoroughly repressive atmosphere and a comprehensive system of control over the population. If blatant physical repression was less pronounced or less extensive, this was because it was unnecessary; at moments of crisis, it tended to escalate rapidly. Once again, this raises questions about the opposition: if direct physical repression was less necessary, does this not also imply that opposition was much weaker than in other countries under fascist régimes? To some extent, this was indeed the case: Portugal's very low level of development by European standards, and its lack of major proletarian concentrations in mining or heavy industry such as existed in Spain and in some Latin American countries, inhibited the growth of organised mass resistance. But resistance did occur, and as the regime's contradictions deepened, mass discontent grew apace. It is a central theme of this work that popular resistance grew rapidly from the early 1940s onwards, and that Portugal experienced patterns of repression and resistance essentially similar to those found in more dramatic cases such as Franco's Spain or Chile under Pinochet. The longevity of the regime reflects not only the failures of the opposition but also, as in Spain, the extreme dificulty of dislodging such a regime once it has become institutionalised – and in the absence of foreign intervention.

Whether or not the Salazar regime should be characterised as 'fascist' has been the object of intense debate.[2] The classic Marxist-Leninist definition, advanced by Dimitroff at the VII Comintern Congress in 1935, is only of limited usefulness: to say that fascism is 'the open terrorist dictatorship of the most reactionary, most chauvinistic and most imperialist elements of finance capital'[3] is to ignore very basic aspects of the political

sociology of fascist movements. Such a definition may frequently describe accurately enough the economic policies of
fascist regimes, but it fails to identify the originality of such regimes and movements and the reasons for their great political
potential. More relevant in this respect is the analysis of Gramsci
and others, who see fascism as an 'attempt to make reaction
popular', to generate mass support for a reactionary political
project.[4] It represents therefore an alternative to traditional
conservative politics when conservatism as such is no longer
viable; when the popular classes have erupted on to the political
scene with too much force to be contained by traditional means.
Hence the crucial role of the fascist party or movement, and
the panoply of mass organisations which are both mobilisational
and instruments of control: uniformed paramilitary and youth
brigades, government-controlled unions and professional associations, the whole apparatus of the 'corporate state'.

It is this dual function of fascist mass organisations – both
mobilising and regimenting the masses – which is crucial to an
understanding of the Portuguese case. Several authors[5] have
argued that the Salazar regime was not fascist because it was not
mobilisational; because Salazar was not a flamboyant demagogue
like Hitler and Mussolini, because the regime rarely indulged in
mass rallies and marches, and in fact devoted considerable energy
to political demobilisation, propagating an ideology of submission
and depoliticisation. But this, in a sense, can be seen as the other
side of the coin of fascism; vigorous mobilisation is needed in
crisis situations, when the régime is faced with a powerful challenge from the Left or in preparations for a war effort. For most of
its long history, this was not the situation of the Portuguese
regime; it came to power in a context of disintegration of the
bourgeois republic; and of a vigorous but small and isolated
working-class movement – a potential threat for the future rather
than an immediate challenge to the capitalist system in Portugal.[6]
The apparatus of the corporate state was necessary therefore
mainly to ensure passive support for, or acceptance of, the
regime, and to suppress the limited challenge of the working-
class movement and the old bourgeois politicians. But mass
support, and mass support for reactionary policies, was nevertheless the *raison d'être* of the system.

There is a third aspect of fascism which also demands con-

sideration. Fascist regimes, while clearly and thoroughly reactionary in political terms, are not necessarily so in economic
terms; frequently they use the exceptional power of the corporate state to promote a developmental project, a modernisation of
capital favouring the growth of the more advanced sectors or the
transition to monopoly capitalism in an economy which has not
yet reached this phase. They are not, therefore, purely defensive,
as Dimitroff's definition implies – a last-ditch stand of capitalism
in extreme crisis. Even when originating in situations of severe
crisis for the system, they rapidly pass on to the offensive,
promoting the long- or medium-term viability of capitalism
through a forced modernisation of its structures. This was clearly
the case in Italy, and arguably so in Germany. The Portuguese
case, again, is not so clear; Salazar's vaunted ideology of ruralism
and self-sufficient poverty was the antithesis of modernisation,
and has to be seen as more purely reactionary, in a philosophical
and not merely a political sense. It has, however, been pointed
out that in practice Salazar did little to protect the interests of the
poor peasant smallholders whose way of life he professed to
admire, and much to benefit the big monopoly groups associated
with names like Melo, Champalimaud, and Espirito Santo.
Protectionist legislation, repression of labour and lucrative public
contracts were all beneficial to the big combines. But protectionist policies favourable to a few existing groups, and favouring
capital in general as against labour, do not costitute a developmental strategy. It was not until the 1960s, under the pressure of
colonial wars and European interests, that the régime adopted a
frankly expansionist project of rapid industrialisation. In this respect it reflected the extreme weakness of Portuguese capital,
and the fact that – as pointed out by the Guinean revolutionary
leader Amilcar Cabral – Portugal was simultaneously a colonial
power and a semi-colonial country.[7] The Salazar regime did not
adopt an aggressive autonomous industrialising policy because it
could not; the country lacked even the minimum preconditions
for such a strategy.

The Portuguese régime, then, undoubtedly exhibited several
fundamental characteristics of fascism; to describe it simply as
'authoritarian' or 'Iberian-corporatist'[8] is to evade the question. It
was a weak, semi-peripheral fascism, appropriate to the position
of a weak, semi-peripheral country; but its origins, functions

and structures were qualitatively similar to those of other fascist
régimes. Repression was generalised and systematic, if controlled
and selective in its more brutal forms (which tended to be applied
mainly to Communists, anarchists, striking workers and rebellious peasants). Ideological control was strict, through official propaganda, constant press censorship, and sporadic suppression
of books, theatrical productions and other forms of dissident
artistic expression. State control of employment opportunities
was systematically used to marginalise dissident intellectuals.
More significant in characterising the regime was the inculcation
of official ideology through the schools, the Church, the official
party, and the elaborate apparatus of the corporate state which
was designed to encompass the entire population: the Legion,
the *Mocidade*, the *sindicatos nacionais* (official unions), the *grémios*
(employers' associations) and *casas do povo* (rural community
organisations). The implications of this would become apparent
when mass protest and resistance developed on a larger scale,
as in the years 1942–49 and 1958–62: repression would then
become more open and less discriminate, less 'Portuguese' and
more fascist. *Brandos costumes* applied only so long as the people
kept their place.

  The history of the resistance to Portuguese fascism, though
perhaps less dramatic than in countries where repression was
more open and brutal, was essentially similar. Indeed, because of
its prolonged evolution without outside intervention, in conditions of repeated failure and constant frustration, it perhaps
illustrates with particular clarity some of the characteristics and
problems of resistance movements under fascist and crypto-
fascist régimes. Its history can be divided into at least six distinct
stages, reflecting changes in its structure, organisation and tactics,
and in its symbiotic relationship with the regime:

(1) 1926–31: the initial armed resistance and adjustment to
     clandestinity, coinciding with the consolidation of the
     regime.
(2) 1931–41: division, retreat and dislocation, with increased
     repression and the rise of fascism throughout Europe.
(3) 1941–49: the 'golden age' of anti-fascist unity, stimulated
     by the Second World War and the rise of resistance move-
     ments throughout Europe, and by the reorganisation of the
     Portuguese Communist Party (PCP) which becomes the
     dominant force of the opposition.

(4)   1949–57: Cold-War division and retreat, with the regime's recovery from the wartime and post-war crisis.

(5)   1957–62: the high point of the domestic anti-fascist struggle, revealing the emergence of vigorous new tendencies within the resistance: military populism, the Catholic Left and intense civilian-military insurrectionary activity ('Guevarism').

(6)   1962–74: the gradual restructuring of the opposition, determined by the failures of the previous phase, the neo-capitalist boom of the sixties, and (above all) the colonial wars in Africa – which would prove to be the decisive factor in the regime's final collapse.

In this study I have chosen to focus on stages (3) to (5), for three reasons. First, the story of the resistance before the Second World War is largely one of defence and retreat, and is in many ways a continuation of the development of the Republican and left-wing forces prior to 1926. Secondly, from 1962 onwards the entire political panorama was transformed by the impact of the colonial wars; my main concern in this work is to examine the dynamics of opposition and resistance within Portugal itself. Although external influences were never entirely absent, I have preferred to focus on the period when domestic factors were paramount: this is a history of the struggles, triumphs and disasters of the *Portuguese* opposition, not of the regime's collapse under the impact of colonial liberation movements. Thirdly, the two decades in question did witness the greatest waves of resistance and mass protest, especially from 1942 to 1949 (which could be considered the 'heroic era' of the PCP) and from 1958 to 1962 (when new forces, notably the leadership of military dissidents such as General Humberto Delgado, came to the fore). However, the course of events leading to the liberating *coup* of 25 April 1974 is briefly analysed in Chapter VII.

Analysis of resistance and opposition movements to fascist or institutionalised military régimes raises several important issues which are common to most experiences of this type. There is a certain distinction between 'resistance' and 'opposition', the former implying active struggle, the latter more peaceful or limited political activity which may be legal or at least 'tolerated'. Some ex-members of the underground resistance speak with contempt of the 'Democratic Opposition' (as it was often designated in Portugal) as a mere token manifestation of bourgeois intellectuals, contributing nothing to the real resistance of the Portuguese people against fascist oppression. Although, as we shall see, this criticism is not entirely without foundation, it fails to recognise the interconnection between different levels and types of opposition, and the value of legal or semi-legal work in rallying public opinion and testing the possibilities of public activity. A more serious issue, however, concerns the refusal of some sectors of the opposition to consider more direct and militant forms of action, and their encouragement of legalistic illusions: there were some who appeared to believe that the regime would fall or voluntarily abdicate its power simply in response to petitions, legal protests and participation in control-led 'elections'.

Related to this distinction is the problem of clandestinity: of adaptation to illegal and clandestine work, of clandestine security and the difficulties of combining underground with open or legal activities. Purely clandestine activity makes mass agitation and organisation impossible, leading to isolation and the politics of the conspiratorial sect; but open agitation going beyond mere petitions and symbolic protests exposes the clandestine organisation to the dangers of detection and repression. Underground activity of necessity breeds an atmosphere of mistrust and suspicion, inimical to political debate. There is no easy solution to this dilemma; parties which failed to develop a secure underground apparatus were doomed to extinction or to purely symbolic legal gestures. In fact, the PCP was the only party to maintain a permanent and effective clandestine apparatus, and this was an important factor in its hegemonic rôle within the resistance for most of our period.

If political parties must by definition be mostly clandestine in order to function under a fascist regime, the question is more complex with regard to trade unions and popular organisations. In Portugal, as in other such regimes, free trade unions were banned by the National Labour Statute of September 1933 – the application of which had provoked an attempted general strike and insurrection on 18 January 1934, under anarchist leadership and with Communist participation. For several years both anarchists and Communists – the main forces in the labour movement at the time – attempted to maintain illegal, underground unions, but they had little success. The PCP subsequently adopted the line favoured by its then General Secretary, Bento Gonçalves, which was to penetrate and use the official *sindicatos nacionais*. After a few years this tactic achieved considerable and even dramatic success, and while the regime could arrest individual union leaders on suspicion of being Communists or 'subversives', it could not dissolve the entire union structure without provoking serious trouble. The experience of working-class organisations in other countries has been similar: in Spain the Communist Party adopted a parallel solution with the organisation in the 1960s of the *Comisiones Obreras* (Workers' Commissions) functioning within the official *Organización Sindical*; and in Chile the Pinochet régime, having initially suppressed the CUT (United Workers' Confederation), has been forced to tolerate new unions which are in practice independent and largely Communist-led.[9] The Spanish *Comisiones Obreras* were technically not independent unions (which would have been illegal) but factory-based workers' committees; but as in Portugal their complete suppression (as opposed to the arrest of individual Communist activists) proved impossible.

What is true of trade unions applies in general terms to other types of mass organisations. To maintain openly independent, anti-régime associations was to invite repression; the alternatives were either to infiltrate official, pro-regime organisations, or to create 'non-political' bodies which would enjoy at least semi-legal status. In the Portuguese case, the former tactic was used not only in the trade unions but in the rural *casas do povo* and *casas dos pescadores*, and in the students' associations; the attempt to create 'non-political' associations was confined mainly to the electoral field, with the creation of non-party committeees and 'movements' to present opposition candidates in the official 'elections'. This raised further tactical issues for the anti-fascist forces: was participation or non-participation the best approach, given the fraudulent and even farcical character of the elections? Opinions on this varied dramatically, with some refusing to participate on any terms and others arguing for participation at any price; for several years the consensus of most opposition parties was to present candidates and take advantage of the propaganda opportunity offered by the official campaign periods, but to withdraw just before the ballot and denounce the electoral fraud. But in 1958 this changed, with General Delgado inaugurating an opposition policy of going 'right to the polls' and denouncing fraud afterwards. Positions on this question were not consistent with ideological orientation either: for many years the Communist Party advocated withdrawal before the ballot, but later it changed its position, while some sectors of the bourgeois opposition, previously favourable to full participation, began to advocate abstention!

The electoral issue was clearly a tactical one, however much some tried to present it as a matter of principle. If the regime allowed, or was forced to concede, enough room for political agitation for the opposition to have a mass impact, and if electoral fraud was blatant and demonstrable, then participation was surely beneficial to the opposition. But if restrictions on political activity were such as to prevent any real campaign and the ballot-rigging was subtle and well-concealed, then the only result would be to lend legitimacy to the regime while diverting opposition energies from more useful tasks and exposing opposition activists to further repression. The evidence suggests that the latter was the case with many of the elections under the *Estado Nôvo*, but not with the elections of 1945, 1949 and 1958, in all of which the opposition was able to mobilise massive public support such as to seriously embarrass the regime. Experience elsewhere also varies greatly in this area: Franco was blatant (or honest) enough simply not to hold elections except for the occasional plebiscite, and Pinochet's record in Chile is the same. But in Brazil the controlled elections conducted by the military from the mid-seventies onwards did allow for genuine, if limited opposition participation, and later (1985) culminated in victory for the opposition Presidential candidate. Similarly in Uruguay, the military regime's constitutional referendum of 1980 was administered in an honest enough manner to result in victory for the 'No' (opposition) forces – an extraordinary outcome, evidently unexpected by the regime which had underestimated the independence of the administrative and judicial officials responsible for conducting the ballot. In general, electoral boycotts are of value only where the fraudulent character of the vote is clear from the very beginning and where the function of the electoral process is transparently cosmetic, serving only to improve the regime's image.

The electoral issue and the problem of clandestinity versus

legal or semi-legal activity were only aspects of the global question of revolutionary strategy and tactics. The anti-fascist movement in Portugal was faced from the start with the classic issues of peaceful opposition versus armed struggle, military coup versus mass insurrection, class struggle versus broad democratic protest. Many of the old Republicans favoured military conspiracy, while some sectors of the bourgeois opposition adopted purely peaceful and legal activities; and the PCP, for most of our period, pursued a line of mass anti-fascist insurrection. But the variations on these fundamental lines and the interractions between them were many and complex. A mass demonstration or strike could be peaceful in conception but develop into armed confrontation in response to violent police repression; a military conspiracy combined with civilian actions could lead to mass insurrection. Protest against electoral fraud, initiated by bourgeois groups, could be overtaken by strikes in working-class areas which might rapidly change the class character and leadership of the movement. Or the reverse could happen: militant workers' and peasants' struggles might be diverted into purely electoral or legalistic channels.

The outcome of these crucial tactical differences would frequently depend on another basic issue, that of political alliances. As always, the goal of all anti-fascist parties and organisations – at least the nominal goal – was unity; but achieving unity in practice was quite another matter. Anti-communism was very powerful among many sectors of the bourgeois opposition, while for its part the PCP rejected some bourgeois oppositionists as traitors or collaborators. Even if these suspicions were overcome, the basis of unity had to be resolved: was the goal of the movement to restore the bourgeois Republic or to establish socialism – or what the Communists described as an 'advanced democracy'? Was there to be unity in action or merely symbolic unity? Was the main emphasis of the alliance to be on electoral activity, mass organisation or preparations for a military coup? What was to be the distribution of representatives in any coalition or broad-front committee that was set up? The achievement of unity from 1943 to 1949 and once again after 1958 was thus a great advance, just as the clear split of the opposition along Cold War lines from 1949 to 1957 was a major setback. The PCP gained an outstanding success in persuading the majority of the bourgeois opposition to commit themselves, at least in principle, to an insurrectional strategy from 1943 to 1949; and in the early sixties General Humberto Delgado and some of his associates achieved an equally remarkable success in persuading the PCP to prepare for immediate and specific armed actions, as opposed to long-term planning for an eventual mass insurrection.

The degree of unity which was achieved in Portugal should not be minimised: with the exception of resistance movements in occupied countries during the Second World War, anti-fascist or anti-dictatorial unity has proved very difficult to achieve. In Spain the anti-Franco opposition was deeply divided for long periods; in Chile the old Communist/anti-Communist split has prevailed again, with the recent formation of two major opposition coalitions, the *Alianza Democrática* (dominated by the Christian Democrats) and the *Movimiento Democrático Popular* (led by the Communists); in Argentina from 1976 to 1983 the old divisions between the middle-class Radical Party, the Peronists and the extreme left guerrilla groups were totally unresolved. In the Portuguese case, the chronic division which prevailed over the first fifteen years of the dictatorship was overcome in 1942−43 primarily by new initiatives from the Communist Party and from a group of independent socialists. But this was possible only because, first, the steady decline of the anarchists had resolved the bitter anarchist/Communist rivalry; secondly, the PCP's reorganisation from 1941 onwards had established the Party as a major force which the rest of the opposition could no longer ignore; and thirdly, the context of anti-fascist war in Europe inspired emulation in Portugal. Nevertheless, the maintenance of unity required constant struggle, and the practical implementation of a common revolutionary strategy proved very problematic.

In terms of the prospects of success for anti-fascist and anti-dictatorial movements, the Portuguese example is not encouraging. As a record of political frustration, the history of the Portuguese resistance has few parallels: a regime which survives for half a century, despite a major civil war in a close neighbour, a World War in which it faces potential threats from both sides, the international defeat of most regimes of similar ideology and structure, and repeated civil disturbances and military conspiracies, appears to lead a charmed life. There were several occasions when the Salazar regime appeared to be – very probably was – on the verge of collapse: August–November 1945, April 1947, May–July 1958, May–July 1962 – not to mention numerous other occasions when wishful thinking on the part of opposition conspirators convinced them that victory was at hand. But time and again the regime recovered, and the opposition forces were left to analyse their failures. Clearly, this pattern does raise serious questions about the orientation, strategy and tactics of the resistance: would a slightly different approach, slightly better coordination, or a more determined push have brought the regime down in 1945, or 1958, or 1962? Or was the strength of popular support for the opposition illusory? In fact, as we shall attempt to demonstrate, the regime was indeed in serious trouble on the three or four occasions mentioned; and divisions within the opposition, plus failure to appreciate the strength of the regime's reserves in the militarised state apparatus (armed forces and police) and its political will to resist, were crucial factors in its survival. The sobering conclusion to be drawn from the Portuguese case (reinforced by those of Spain and Chile and, in a way, Brazil) is that once a fascist or para-fascist regime becomes institutionalised, its overthrow becomes extremely difficult in the absence of external war or political reorientation within the regime itself (i.e. internal division or a process of gradual liberalisation and phased withdrawal from power). Domestic resistance may contribute to such divisions or to a decision to liberalise, but this process is far from simple. At least in the short term, militant resistance may only provoke greater repression, as recent experience in Chile demonstrates; but on the other hand counsels of restraint and moderation (on the grounds that aggressive tactics will undermine liberal elements within the regime) may simply castrate popular resistance and allow the regime a breathing space. This certainly occurred in Portugal on several occasions, when right-wing Republicans and liberal members of the opposition argued for the postponement of mass rallies and demonstrations.

In part such tactical questions depend on a correct assessment of the political conjuncture, of the state of the country's political economy and the international context. But they also depend on the political project for post-liberation society: if one's goal is no more than the restoration of parliamentary democracy, or even a 'limited democracy' based on the exclusion of Communists and the revolutionary left, then a strategy based on limited protest and compromise with liberal sectors of the regime is entirely logical. But for those who seek extensive social reforms, a more radical break with the existing regime is necessary, implying more open confrontation with the structures of repression. Finally, if the goal is socialism, or an 'advanced democracy' that will destroy not only the existing regime but the social roots of fascism and reaction, then the strategy must be one of revolutionary rupture based on mass mobilisation and insurrection. The first strategy – that based on moderation and compromise – would lead, as the Left warned in Portugal, to 'Salazarism without Salazar', or at best to a weak parliamentary regime incapable of confronting vested interests in the military, the police and the economy. In Portugal this was apparently the goal of certain Republican politicians who were manoeuvring in the late forties to obtain legalisation of political parties, but with the exclusion of the Communists. One suspects that in Chile today this is the goal of the Christian Democrats and their allies of the *Alianza Democrática*.[10] Even in post-Franco Spain, liberalisation was only possible once the Communist Party adopted an ultra-conciliatory, 'Eurocommunist' stand; and the result has been a relatively successful parliamentary democracy, but one in which the labour movement is in a weak position and neo-capitalist forces are very much in the ascendant.

Thus, fascist regimes – and the institutionalised military regimes of the Southern Cone of Latin America, which in this author's view are functionally similar – have generally been remarkably successful in 'making their countries safe for capitalism', even after their demise. Only where their overthrow has occurred through, or been closely followed by, mass insurrection, has this not been the case. Thus in Italy the resistance was revolutionary in character, and dominated by the Communist Party; and only the Allied occupation, assisted by the PCI's willingness to compromise, prevented a revolutionary outcome. The Portuguese case is also instructive in this respect: although liberation finally came about through a military coup, the revolutionary upsurge after 25 April did indeed threaten to destroy Portuguese capitalism, and while the threat was neutralised after 25 November 1975, the neo-capitalist order is rather less secure in Portugal than in its Spanish neighbour. This can be seen as belated testimony to the work of the Portuguese resistance over the decades: like Marx's mole, its burrowing had little visible effect for years, but it so undermined the foundations of the system that when the regime fell, mass revolt burst forth with unsuspected vigour.

Rather than a comprehensive history of all aspects of the resistance, what follows is a study of its most combative and effective sectors and the strategic and tactical dynamics of the movement as a whole. Close attention is therefore devoted to the Communist Party, the labour and peasant movements, the Republican military, and the populist dissidents from the regime such as General Delgado; less to the liberal, social-democratic and socialist intellectual groups, whose contribution was more in terms of testimonial protest and debate. But with regard to all classes, sectors and groups, I have attempted to convey a sense of the human reality of the resistance, its grandeur, tragedy and pathos, even its comic aspects – for they also did exist. We are not only examining the political structure and behaviour of a series of organisations and tendencies, but a large part of the lives of nearly three generations of the Portuguese people, their hopes, fears, frustrations and habits. When a regime lasts as long as this one, its values, practices and institutions become part of the national culture; and the values, practices and institutions of resistance become a part of that culture also. Portugal is Salazar, the Legion, the PIDE, tradition, submission and conformity; it is also the PCP, the Republican conspirators, Humberto Delgado, fraternity, protest and rebellion.

Notes to Chapter I

1   The total number of deaths in Tarrafal was thirty-two, out of a probable 293 prisoners who served time there. (See Acácio Tomás de Aquino, *O Segredo das Prisões Atlânticas*, Lisboa, 1978, A Regra do Jogo, pp. 283–98.) In anti-regime uprisings, by far the largest number of casualties occurred in the first such action, that of February 1927 in Oporto and Lisbon, which left 120 dead and 650 wounded (R. A. H. Robinson, *Contemporary Portugal: A History*, London, 1979, George Allen & Unwin, p. 42). There were several deaths in the insurrectionary strike of 18 January 1934 and the naval mutiny of

August 1936, and a few in later revolts (three at Beja on 1 January 1962). Repression of demonstrations left a steady toll of deaths, but rarely going into double figures on any one occasion.

2   See, especially, *O Fascismo em Portugal*, Actas do Colóquio realizado na Faculdade de Letras de Lisboa em Março de 1980, Lisboa, 1982, A Regra do Jogo; Manuel de Lucena, *A evolucão do sistema corporativo português, I: O Salazarismo*, Lisboa, 1976, Perspectivas e Realidades; Philippe C. Schmitter, 'The 'Regime d'Exception' that became the rule: forty-eight years of authoritarian domination in Portugal', in Lawrence S. Graham & Harry M. Makler (eds.), *Contemporary Portugal: The Revolution and its Antecedents*, Austin and London, 1979, University of Texas Press, pp. 3–46; Howard J. Wiarda, 'The corporatist tradition and the corporatist system in Portugal: structured, evolving, transcended, persistent', in *ibid.*, pp. 89–122.

3   Georgi Dimitroff, *The United Front: The Struggle Against Fascism and War*, San Francisco, 1975, Proletarian Publishers, p. 104.

4   Quintin Hoare & Geoffrey Nowell Smith (eds.), *Selections From the Prison Notebooks of Antonio Gramsci*, London, 1971, Lawrence & Wishart; Nicos Poulantzas, *Fascism and Dictatorship*, London, 1974, New Left Books; Arno J. Mayer, *Dynamics of Counterrevolution in Europe, 1870–1956: An Analytic Framework*, New York, 1971, Harper & Row; Peter R. Sinclair, 'Fascism and crisis in capitalist society', *New German Critique* IX, Fall 1976, pp. 102–7.

5   E.g. Wiarda, 'The corporatist tradition'; Robinson, *A History*, pp. 51–3; Hugh Kay, *Salazar and Modern Portugal*, London, 1970, Eyre & Spottiswoode.

6   The best treatment of the situation of the working-class movement towards the end of the First Republic is in Antonio José Telo, *Decadência e Queda da I Republica Portuguesa* vol. I, Lisboa, 1980, A Regra do Jogo, caps. 4, 10 and 11, and in Fernando Medeiros, *A Sociedade e a Economia Portuguesas nas Orígens do Salazarismo*, Lisboa, 1978, A Regra do Jogo, Segunda e Terceira Parte.

7   Amilcar Cabral, *Revolution in Guinea: An African People's Struggle*, London, 1969, Stage 1, pp. 63–4.

8   Wiarda, 'The corporatist tradition'; Robinson, *A History*, pp. 51–3.

9   On Spain, see Raymond Carr & Juan Pablo Fusi, *Spain, Dictatorship to Democracy*, London, 1979, George Allen & Unwin, pp. 141–6. On Chile, Carmelo Furci, *The Chilean Communist Party and the Road to Socialism*, London, 1984, Zed Books, p. 155.

10   See Furci, *The Chilean Communist Party*, pp. 163–4.

2
Resistance and unity: conflicting opposition strategies, 1941–57

Burgueses radicais, se a vossa republica não é mais do que a república do capital, assim como a monarquia dos conservadores não é mais do que a monarquia do capital, que temos nós, Proletariado, que ver com essa estéril questão de forma?

O you bourgeois radicals, if your republic is nothing more than the republic of capital, just as the monarchy of the conservatives is nothing more than the monarchy of capital, what do we, the Proletariat, have to do with that sterile question of form?

Antero de Quental (1880)

1 The MUNAF: a broad resistance movement on the European model

It was the Second World War which created the conditions for opposition unity, and also for some degree of effective resistance, within Salazarist Portugal. Wartime conditions gave rise to an intensification of strikes and popular protests, made possible the implantation of the Communist Party as a significant force, and also created a disposition favourable to united action against the regime among many sectors of the dispersed and demoralised opposition. The international climate of anti-fascist struggle, and especially the example of the resistance movements in occupied countries of Europe – of which some news filtered through despite the censorship – served as an example to all liberal and progressive forces in Portugal.

The practical initiative for unity came from two sources: first, the Communist Party, and second, a new grouping of socialist intellectuals. Beginning in 1942, the Communist Party began to

intensify its appeals for opposition unity (which it had favoured
in theory since 1935 and the adoption of the Comintern's
'Popular Front' line). Contacts were developed with all parties
and organisations – the Democratic Party (PRP), the remnants of
the old Socialist Party (SPIO), the newly-formed *União Socialista*,
the Freemasons, liberal sectors of the Catholic Church, the
anarchist *Confederação Geral de Trabalhadores* (CGT), and even the
Monarchists. In words which turned out to be prophetic, the
Party's clandestine newspaper *Avante!* warned against illusions of
easy liberation at the hands of the Allies:

> ... the military trend in favour of the Allies has ... had an effect which
> has to be opposed right away. This is the development in some anti-
> fascist circles of the idea that *Salazar will fall with Hitler, that the defeat of
> fascism in Portugal is absolutely dependent on the defeat of international fascism
> and that therefore we have to wait for the victory of the Allies to liberate the
> Portuguese people from the fascist yoke.* This trend has many supporters in
> the democratic and patriotic camp, and it leads to inaction, to the
> elaboration of impressive programmes for the period *after* the defeat of
> fascism and *to the absence of plans for struggle to overthrow fascism* ...[1]
> (Emphasis in original)

The Communist Party's line was to promote unity on a basis of
active resistance, through everyday popular struggles in factory
and field.

Among the many small and heterogeneous opposition groups
existing in the early 1940's, the most active and the most
interested in building a united anti-fascist movement (apart from
the PCP) was a circle of socialist intellectuals who were to create,
in late 1943, the Socialist Union (*União Socialista*). Dissatisfied
with the situation resulting from the collapse of the old Socialist
Party (SPIO) of Ramada Curto, the lawyers José Magalhães
Godinho and Armelim Moura Diniz, and an army officer, Major
Manuel Pires de Matos, began in the summer of 1942 to contact
many progressive lawyers, intellectuals and military figures in
order to develop a new socialist organisation. Together with the
eminent mathematician Bento de Jesús Caraça, they then contacted other sectors of the opposition, including the PCP, and
the result was a crucial meeting towards the end of 1942 or early
1943 which began the difficult process of negotiations to establish
a basis of unity.[2] Although agreement on the terms of unity and
form of organisation would take several months, it was this

initiative which led to the foundation of the *Movimento de Unidade Nacional Anti-Fascista* (MUNAF) towards the end of 1943.[3]

The structure of the MUNAF at national level was a dual one, combining a National Council with a broad membership and an Executive Committee of five or six members. Its President was the eminent republican General, Norton de Matos, who enjoyed widespread respect for his rôle in the First World War and his reformist administration of Angola. The Executive Committee – the key decision-making body – was composed initially of José Magalhães Godinho (Socialist), Fernando Piteira Santos (PCP), Prof. Jacinto Simões (Independent Republican), Major Moreira de Campos (Republican), Alberto Rocha and Manuel Duarte.[4] Despite its illegal and clandestine character, the movement grew rapidly, and within a year of its foundation it had acquired real national significance.

After further negotiations, the 'Emergency Programme of the Provisional Government' was finally adopted by the National Council in July 1944, and in the following month it was printed and distributed clandestinely throughout the country.[5] For the first time in eighteen years, the democratic forces had shown that they were capable of uniting and of proposing a realistic alternative. Salazar had reason to be concerned as the steady retreat of the Axis forces was accompanied by the rapid development of the anti-fascist movement in Portugal; in September he reshuffled the Cabinet, bringing in younger Ministers such as Marcelo Caetano, and continued to develop his relations with the Western Allies.[6]

With the successful publication of its Programme, the MUNAF could no longer avoid the intractable question of revolutionary strategy. The fundamental problem was simple: could an anti-fascist resistance movement, consciously modelled on those in occupied countries in Europe, be successful in an unoccupied country which was not even at war? This was the dilemma which the MUNAF never resolved, and which may in fact have been insoluble. The National Council, like the Communist Party, seized on every opportunity to brand Salazar's government as one of 'national betrayal', denouncing the continued exports to the Axis, the capitulation to the Japanese in Timor, or the privileges granted to the German and Italian legations; but this could not alter the fact that the regime's roots were domestic and that there were no foreign troops on Portuguese soil (strictly speaking, there were foreign troops in the Azores bases, but they were British and American, not Axis).

Within the MUNAF there were fundamentally two strategies on the question of armed struggle: that of the old Republicans and that of the Communist Party. The Republican strategy was that of the military conspiracy, leading to a *coup*, which would remove Salazar and his ministers and restore the Republican regime overthrown in 1926. As against this the PCP line was one of mass anti-fascist insurrection, to be developed by an intensification of popular struggles (strikes, bread riots, demonstrations) in combination with the preparation of armed groups of workers and the subversion or neutralisation of large sectors of the armed forces. It was of course theoretically possible to conceive of a combination of these two strategies, but in practice this was extremely difficult to achieve because they derived from radically different political conceptions. Where for the PCP the main protagonist was the working class, or the popular classes in general, and the goal of the movement was an advanced democracy which would imply a radical restructuring of Portuguese society, for the Republicans the protagonists were themselves, the bourgeois politicians of the First Republic or their successors, and the goal was essentially the restoration of the *status quo ante*, with some limited social reforms.

Towards the end of 1944 an important step in the direction of armed insurrection was taken by the National Council, with the decision to organise Anti-Fascist Combat Groups (*Grupos Antifascistas de Combate* or GAC's). The GAC's were directed especially towards 'those patriotic and anti-fascist Portuguese not affiliated to national political organisations' with the immediate aim of laying the basis of a fighting organisation for the coming struggle of national liberation.[7]

The movement to organise the GAC's was undertaken by members of the Communist Party and some of the Socialists and Republicans affiliated to the MUNAF, but in practice the results were disappointing. The efforts to organise these groups were confronted with two fundamental obstacles: the objective conditions in Portugal (which were not necessarily favourable to insurrection) and the inadequate political commitment of important sectors of the MUNAF. The PCP soon became impatient with the inaction of the bourgeois opposition; in February

1945 *Avante!* complained that the instructions issued by the National Council for the formation of GAC's were too vague, failing to specify their purpose, tasks and methods of organisation. The Communist Party as 'the vanguard force of the movement of National Unity', must take the initiative in creating these groups. The GAC's should become the armed detachments of the mass movement, intervening in defence of the workers and peasants in struggle; they must go into action right away.[8]

Where GAC's were formed, it seems they did attempt to obtain arms, and also to develop contacts with the military in order to win over or at least neutralise the troops.[9] But their activity did not go beyond this, and in reality the MUNAF never crossed the Rubicon of actually taking up arms against the regime. The fundamental reason for this was undoubtedly the fact that Portugal was a nation at peace and the internal social and political contradictions, though serious, had not reached the point of civil war. Nevertheless, if the anti-fascist resistance was to be effective, going beyond a merely testimonial presence, it must have a revolutionary strategy; and it is conceivable that armed resistance could have become a reality if the MUNAF as a whole (and not only the Communist Party) had encouraged the GAC's to go into action.

The preparation of a military conspiracy was the other side of the MUNAF's revolutionary strategy. The National Council created a secret 'revolutionary committee', also presided by General Norton de Matos, which was formally established at a meeting in the house of Professor Bento de Jesús Caraça. José Magalhães Godinho (whose father had been a prominent officer under the Republic) enlisted a number of military figures to participate in this committee, and they began to make plans. On more than one occasion, beginning early in 1945, it was said that groups of democratic officers were ready to act; but for one reason or another the movement was always postponed.

Thus, a major attempt was prepared for August 1945; with Norton de Matos as figurehead, the military leadership was under Brigadier Miguel dos Santos, and the conspiracy had connections among the militia officers mobilised during the War, in the police (PSP and GNR) and one or two garrisons of the Lisbon area. There was also a link with a separate conspiratorial network in the North organised by Captain Fernando Queiroga and centred in the Oporto Cavalry and Infantry Regiments.[10] But Salazar's

announcement of 'free elections' took the wind out of the
conspirators' sails, and action was postponed. In the view of
Fernando Rosas this was the last relatively autonomous attempt
of the liberal bourgeoisie to carry out a *coup* of its own –
independent, that is, of actual or potential dissidents from the
regime.[11]

Several other *coup* attempts were planned, but all came to
nought, through disagreements among the conspirators, pusil-
lanimous withdrawals at the last minute, or discovery by the
regime. It is tempting to dismiss them entirely as futile gestures;
but the *putschist* perspective cannot be completely ignored.
There was in fact a situation of almost constant military conspiracy from 1943 to 1947, stimulated by the regime's internal
crisis and international defeat of the Axis powers; and there
was a real possibility of a liberal *coup*, as in Brazil in 1945. Indeed, on certain occasions the PCP recognised as much; in
Cunhal's Political Report to the Party's first illegal congress in
1943 there were some very interesting observations on the
matter:

> It may happen that certain fascist leaders, at a given time, become
> interested in the overthrow of Salazarist fascism and even take
> initiatives towards – for example – a Portuguese 'Badogliada' [a re-
> ference to the movement headed by Marshal Badoglio which overthrew
> Mussolini]. We Communists could not ignore such a movement. On the
> contrary: we should take an active part in order to impose upon it a more
> democratic and progressive content.[12]

Thus the Communist Party's constant warnings against 'putschist
illusions' were not directed against the real possibility of a *coup*,
but against *putschism as a strategy*, in other words the tendency to
subordinate all political activity to a hypothetical *coup* which
never came. In this respect the PCP's criticism was clearly
justified; a military gesture by a few progressive officers would
only overthrow Salazarism if the regime's foundations had first
been weakened by a deep internal and/or external crisis (as
would finally happen in 1974).

2 Free elections, 'as free as in free England'

From mid-1944 onwards, as the impending defeat of the Axis
became clear, the Salazar regime began to prepare the ground

for survival in a non-fascist Europe. Already in June 1944, news of D-Day had caused spontaneous popular demonstrations in Lisbon; special editions of the newspapers with news of the Allied landings in France sold out within hours, and the next day the censorship prevented publication of any comment or description of the popular reaction to the news.[13] Symbols such as British and American (and even Soviet) flags began to appear, and liberal-minded companies displayed V-signs in their advertisments.[14] In May 1945, news of the German surrender was greeted with public celebrations throughout the country; there were massive demonstrations in the streets of Lisbon and other towns, as the people waved Allied flags and chanted democratic slogans: 'Free elections! Liberty! Democracy! Freedom for all political prisoners!' and, significantly, 'Down with fascism! Down with Salazar and the PVDE!'.[15]

Faced with such unprecedented public manifestations of opposition, and with the new international situation, Salazar recognised the need for a change of tone. In the following months the most openly fascist symbols were played down, while propaganda favourable to the Western Allies, especially Britain, was increasingly tolerated. This process was to culminate in Salazar's remarkable speech of August 1945 in which he declared, with astonishing candour, that 'it is not possible to govern against the persistent will of the people', and promised the celebration of free elections, 'as free as in free England'[16] – a declaration which was greeted with justifiable scepticism in some circles, but was taken by many as an indication that Allied pressure was indeed going to impose a return to democracy.

Although the opposition had every reason to distrust this sudden 'conversion' to democracy, there were some reforms which appeared to indicate that a genuine, if limited, liberalisation might be under way. In the circumstances the opposition resolved to test the Government's new democratic disposition in practice; a group of eleven Republican and Socialist intellectuals led by Mário de Lima Alves decided to submit a formal request to the authorities for permission to hold a public meeting to discuss the coming elections. This initiative led directly to the creation of the first legal expression of the opposition under the *Estado Novo*: the Movement of Democratic Unity (*Movimento de Unidade Democrática* or MUD).[17]

Somewhat surprised by the Government's swift authorisation of this request, the 'group of eleven' immediately convened a public session which took place on 8 October in the Centro Republicano Almirante Reis. At this meeting it was agreed to present the authorities with a series of demands for legal reforms in order to guarantee the democratic character of the elections: freedom of expression and assembly, legalisation of political parties, abolition of censorship, preparation of a new electoral register, etc. In addition – and this was in fact the first demand – they asked that the elections (scheduled for 18 November) should be postponed for six months, precisely in order to allow time for the above reforms to take effect. Finally, and most importantly, the meeting decided to publish the MUD's platform of demands throughout the country and to invite the public in general to sign lists indicating their support for this platform.[18]

The device of the lists was to be a crucial instrument for converting the MUD into a mass movement. Within days, MUD committees began to spring up throughout the country, often organised by local militants of the MUNAF, and thousands of signatures began to pour into the office of Mário de Lima Alves in the Rua do Ouro, which became the Movement's headquarters. In the words of Mário Soares, himself an active participant, the MUD was 'an overwhelming wave which swept the country in the space of a few days';[19] by 24 October Lima Alves was able to announce that they had over 50,000 signatures in Lisbon alone.[20]

It soon became clear that the Government was unlikely to concede most of the legal reforms demanded by the Movement; rather it began to indulge in a calculated game of cat-and-mouse, hinting at concessions and then applying selective repression and harassment. Tradesmen who had posted MUD lists in their shops for people to sign were called to the police and warned that this was not permitted, and some civil servants were told by their superiors not to sign the lists; veiled threats of a possible 'purge' were made by official spokesmen.[21] In fact, although there were probably some differences of opinion within the regime as to the extent of the concessions which might be necessary to prevent a popular explosion, there was never any intention of genuine liberalisation.

To most of the opposition the regime's intentions were suspect from the beginning, and as it became clear that no significant concessions would be made to their demands for electoral reform, the conviction grew that the MUD's only valid option was to advocate abstention, denouncing the elections as a farce. After much debate, all opposition candidates withdrew in protest shortly before the elections. But in two other matters the MUD's leadership displayed surprising ingenuousness: the decision to suspend public meetings and the surrender of the lists to the authorities.

The suspension of the MUD's public meetings came in late October, after a fortnight's intense campaigning, when the movement had generated enormous popular enthusiasm and was becoming a source of serious concern for the regime. To stop at this point seems so obviously counter-productive that all kinds of speculation has developed regarding the possible motives of the Central Committee. The most probable explanation is that given by Dr José Magalhães Godinho (who was a member of the MUD's Central Committee at the time). According to Magalhães Godinho, Lima Alves was approached by a group of Republican officers who requested the suspension of the MUD's public meetings and demonstrations 'so as not to prejudice a revolutionary movement which was going to occur within a few days with a great probability of success'. Their pretext was that while public opposition activities continued, all military units were being maintained in a state of alert, making it impossible for the democratic conspirators to act. In fact, there was no *coup*, and the only result was to destroy the growing momentum of the popular movement – the one form of pressure which, as Mário Soares has pointed out, might have obliged the regime to make further concessions.[22]

The second great error of the MUD, following closely on the suspension of activities, was the decision to surrender the lists to the authorities. The origins of this decision, which in retrospect seems quite extraordinary, was a manoeuvre by the regime in response to the Movement's claim to have more than 50,000 signatures in Lisbon alone and many more throughout the country. The Minister of the Interior, Botelho Moniz, questioned the authenticity of the figure, and requested the submission of the lists for official verification. In an atmosphere of considerable confusion and disagreement, Dr Mário de Castro handed over the lists of the Lisbon area to the Attorney General's office

(*Procuraduria da República*). Not surprisingly, the authorities did
not respect their promise to return the lists, but instead passed
them on to the police (PVDE) in order to begin reprisals, especially against civil servants. This action naturally aroused intense
controversy and indignation within the Movement, and bitter
accusations were voiced against Mário de Castro and others
responsible for the surrender of the lists. MUD Committees in
many other towns were less naïve; several members of the
Oporto District Committee (Prof. Ruy Luis Gomes, Dr Mário Cal
Brandao, Dr António de Barros Machado and Dr Olívio França),
who refused to hand over the lists, were arrested; and in Guarda
also the lawyer in charge of the lists was detained and the police
seized the lists by force. In Oporto the police had been unable to
find the lists, and the Committee members' arrest provoked a
vigorous popular reaction; they were held for about a week and
then released. On their return to Oporto, Dr Gomes and his com-
panions were greeted with a spontaneous demonstration of
support, whereas in Lisbon the leadership suffered a serious loss
of prestige which was reflected in the Movement's morale from
this time onwards.[23]

By the end of 1945, after the electoral farce, it was clear to all
that the *Estado Novo* was not about to dissolve itself peacefully;
those who had harboured illusions that a combination of
pressure from the Western democracies and popular agitation
would force Salazar to resign or to permit a genuine process of
liberalisation, now had to recognise that they had been mistaken.
Only force would change the regime – or at least, if there were to
be any process of more or less peaceful transition, it would be
slow and difficult. Nevertheless, despite a certain demoralisation,
the opposition had in the MUD a national organisation with a
massive following and a well-coordinated internal structure,
which still officially enjoyed legal status.

For the time being the MUD's main tactic was to continue
pressure on the regime by any means available for full democratic rights. In August–September 1946 the Government applied
for admission to the United Nations, so the MUD produced a
document arguing the case against Portuguese admission under
the existing regime; this was the pretext for the first arrest of the
MUD's Central Committee, accused of 'defamation' of the Head
of State, the Prime Minister and the country. They were released

on bail after a few days (the trial dragged on for years); intimidation was the regime's main purpose.[24] The Movement continued its activities, celebrating the anniversary of the proclamation of the Republic (5 October) and convening a large public meeting for 30 November 1946 in the *Voz do Operário* hall in Lisbon. But soon after this the Movement was subjected to further harassment, with the dismissal from their University positions of Azevedo Gomes and Bento Caraça, among others.[25]

The spring of 1947 witnessed an intensification of labour, youth and student struggles; student protests at Lisbon University, particularly in the Faculty of Medicine, were repressed with a large number of arrests.[26] The *MUD Juvenil* (the youth section of the Movement), after many fruitless requests to the authorities for permission to hold a public assembly, was finally authorised to organise a meeting in the *Voz do Operário* hall in March 1947; in fact this was to be the only legal meeting it ever held, for a month later (coinciding with the Lisbon workers' strikes) many of its leaders were arrested. The régime had reason to be concerned at the success of the *MUD Juvenil*, which was attracting large numbers of young people independent of class and ideology; students and young workers were attracted by the hundreds to illegal open-air meetings in wooded or isolated places around the country, some of which were discovered by the police and suppressed with considerable force (as at Beja in the Alentejo and Olhão in the Algarve).[27]

Although both the MUNAF and the MUD had, largely because of pressure from the Communist Party, maintained their commitment to mass mobilisation and their refusal to compromise with the regime, they were still also strongly influenced by other tendencies, notably those who favoured a *putschist* line. Scarcely a month passed without some rumour of a military conspiracy, either by genuine democratic officers or alleged fascist dissidents. Most never progressed beyond ambitious schemes, but there were occasional exceptions. The one significant uprising of the immediate post-war years, with extensive ramifications among progressive officers in the North and the more or less direct involvement of many civilians from the MUD/MUNAF, was the so-called Mealhada revolt of October 1946.

This was the culmination of a complex series of conspiracies and intrigues involving retired Republican officers linked to the

MUNAF, younger officers in active service, and discontented elements in the regime – including the ageing President Carmona. Among those involved were Admiral Mendes Cabeçadas (hero of both the 1910 and 1926 revolutions), General Norton de Matos and João Soares (father of the socialist leader).[28] Apparently Carmona and his cousin, Admiral Carmona, together with a number of high-ranking officers increasingly resentful of Santos Costa, made contact with the Republican conspirators through Mendes Cabeçadas. A compromise was reached by which operational command of the *coup* was withdrawn from Brigadier Miguel dos Santos of the MUNAF and entrusted to General Marques Godinho, and the centre of operations moved from Lisbon to the North. In the view of Fernando Rosas, this marks the definitive subordination of the liberal bourgeoisie to the dissident and 'modernising' elements of the regime.[29] In the event, on 10 October 1946 the only commander to move was Captain Fernando Queiroga, with the Sixth Cavalry Regiment of Oporto. Other units in the northern capital refused to move, as did key units in Tomar and Coimbra which were supposed to join him on the march south. Isolated, Queiroga surrendered to superior forces at Mealhada, north of Coimbra; he and several of his followers were tried and condemned (Queiroga himself got three years in gaol, and subsequently went into exile in Brazil).[30]

Queiroga's bold but futile attempt, however, was not the end of the *putschist* conspiracy – or network of conspiracies. The secret 'Military Junta of National Salvation' headed by Mendes Cabeçadas, continued its preparations. But the Government had some idea of what was going on (not surprisingly, in view of the large number of 'dissidents' involved, some of whom were undoubtedly lukewarm in their 'dissent'): and it acted to abort the movement by ordering the transfer of five of the leading military conspirators to commissions in the colonies or the Atlantic islands, effective 12 April 1947. This precipitated the new coup attempt, which took place on 10 April – exactly six months after the Mealhada fiasco. Once again, the top brass failed to deliver, and it was left to a few subalterns to risk their lives and careers; two mechanics at the Sintra air base managed to sabotage about twenty military aircraft, and then went underground when they realised that they had acted in isolation.[31]

One of these mechanics was the young Hermínio da Palma

Inácio, later to become famous as the organiser of the LUAR (League of Revolutionary Unity and Action) in the late sixties and early seventies. Significantly, heavy jail terms were imposed (in their absence) on these mechanics—twenty years in one case – while Admiral Cabeçadas, who had given the orders, received a twelve-month sentence commuted into a fine; a good example of class justice! However, this time the government did act against the leading conspirators; several of them were dismissed from the service and brought to trial, and one of them, General Marques Godinho, died in detention on Christmas Eve 1947 – an event which caused further malaise among the military establishment, who expected senior officers to be well treated even if they were politically dissident.

The government now intensified its offensive against all forms of dissent. On 31 January 1948, when the opposition was mobilising for its annual commemoration of the 1891 Republican uprising, the entire Central Committee and the Lisbon District Committee of the MUD were suddenly arrested, taken to police headquarters and then to the Aljube gaol, where they were held for over a month. Mário Soares declares that they spent 'a month's holidays' in the notorious gaol,[32] and it seems that they were not subjected to physical abuse as less distinguished prisoners might be. But this could not disguise the seriousness of the situation; the Government had clearly decided to outlaw the MUD and to reduce manifestations of dissent to the barest minimum. By mid-1948 opposition unity was effectively dead, with both MUD and MUNAF ceasing to function in any meaningful way. But at this point a present from the regime arrived to resuscitate the corpse of the MUD and to give it a brief but frenetic lease on life: the Presidential election of 1949.

3   Norton de Matos: the symbolic assault on the centre of power

Implicit in Salazar's promise of 'free elections' in 1945 was the possibility for the opposition to participate not only in the parliamentary campaign of that year, but also in the septennial 'election' of the President of the Republic. Although the Presidency was a purely ceremonial position devoid of any real power (there are many anecdotes about the political ignorance and

ineffectiveness of the ageing President Carmona), the opportunity for the opposition to contest what was nominally the seat
of supreme power was of great symbolic significance. The election
was not due until February 1949, but in March of the previous
year, given the outlawing of the MUD and the general increase
in repression, the opposition saw in the coming presidential
campaign the best available means of continuing its legal activity;
for this reason the candidacy of General Norton de Matos was
launched well before the start of the official campaigning period.

The prestige of the candidate was beyond dispute; in the words
of Mário Soares, he was 'the symbol of that Opposition which
never compromised on a matter of principle and which never
recognised the legitimacy of the dictatorial regime.[33] José
Mendes Ribeiro Norton de Matos was born in the North, at Ponte
de Lima, on 23 March 1987; on the date of the election he would
therefore be almost eighty-two. Having read mathematics at
Coimbra and surveying at the Military College, he had a
distinguished career as a diplomat and colonial administrator in
the last years of the Monarchy and under the Republic, becoming
Governor-General of Angola from 1912–15, Minister of War
1915–17 (and therefore responsible for organising the Portuguese
intervention on the Western Front in World War I), High
Commissioner in Angola from 1921–23 and Ambassador in
London, 1923–26.[34] Politically he could be described as a
patriarchal liberal, being a staunch member of the Republican
Party and a proponent of moderate social reforms; his administration of Angola was recognised as progressive by the standards
of the time (when Humberto Delgado visited the territory in 1938
he was told 'If you can see anything worthwhile you can be sure
it was Norton's work').[35]

Norton's campaign was formally launched in July 1948, with
the submission of his nomination papers to the Supreme Court of
Justice on 9 July and a press conference at his Lisbon home on
the 12th. Norton presented himself to some thirty Portuguese
and foreign journalists as a liberal Republican, 'neither Conservative, nor Socialist, nor Communist', although open to unity with
all opponents of the 'present regime'.[36]

Official harassment of Norton's followers had already begun
at this time. Several well-known opposition intellectuals who
wanted to sign his nomination papers found that their names

had been struck off the electoral lists, making it legally impossible for them to do so. Then the Supreme Court, with no valid reason, postponed its decision on Norton's eligibility until after the judicial recess, thereby imposing a delay of three months before public campaigning could begin.[37] There was every sign the regime intended to repeat the electoral charade of November 1945, so that for the opposition, participation in the elections could only be useful as a tactic forming part of a broader strategy. But such a strategy did not exist – or, what is worse, different sectors of the opposition had different strategies, barely papered over by the agreement to support a common candidate.

These differences were public knowledge from the beginning, and were already being skilfully exploited by the authorities. Despite the initial agreement to demand minimum democratic guarantees from the Government, in the absence of which the candidate would withdraw in protest shortly before the election, there were some in Norton's camp who wanted to contest the election anyway, even under conditions imposed by the Dictatorship. This was the tactic which would be followed ten years later by General Delgado (with considerable success, at least in terms of popular mobilisation and contestation of the regime). But in 1948 Norton had neither the bold style nor the active military connections of Delgado in 1958. To contest the vote on any terms would have made sense in relation to a *putschist* strategy, aiming to seize power immediately after the electoral fraud; but the long-rumoured coup seemed further away than ever.

The official campaign period did not begin until 1 January 1949, six weeks before the election. The tone of the campaign was that which had already, in the three years or so since the foundation of the MUD, become typical of the 'Democratic Opposition' (thus capitalised, this became the preferred designation of all the semi-legal movements which succeeded one another for the next three decades): indignant denunciation of repression, meticulous criticism of the Dictatorship's failings, and scrupulous moderation. Conscious of the ill-disguised tensions among his followers, the General insisted repeatedly on the need for unity and for the avoidance of partisan disputes: 'I told everyone that they must leave party politics behind at the door of my house, or at the entrance to the polling booths. Right now there is only one thing that matters: to overthrow the present

regime'.[38] But admirable declarations like this (pronounced
before thousands of enthusiastic supporters in the *Voz do Operário*
hall on 10 January) could not conceal the absence of any
concrete strategy to overthrow fascism. Everyone knew that
Norton had pledged himself to withdraw in protest if adequate
guarantees were not granted, and it was patently obvious that
they would not be.

Despite the agreement which had formed the basis of unity
around Norton's candidacy – i.e. to campaign on a platform of
minimum democratic demands, without which the candidate
would withdraw in protest and denounce the election as a fraud
– the right wing of the opposition had never abandoned the idea
of participating under any conditions. Norton himself, 'swayed
by bad advisors'[39] was tempted at the last minute to abandon his
abstentionist stand. Not only this, but prominent figures in the
campaign, influenced by the Government's anti-communist propaganda, began to argue openly for the abandonment of unity
and for a public break with the Communist Party by the
opposition candidate; only in this way, they maintained, would
the opposition obtain 'recognition' from the Government. In fact
there was little sign that the regime was prepared to recognise the
opposition under any conditions, but this did not prevent such
illusions from gaining credence in certain circles. This point of
view was defended particularly by the Lisbon District Commission of the opposition campaign, headed by Major Prestes
Salgueiro, an old Republican; and Norton himself was inclined
to accept this position at one point, although he was persuaded
against it for the time being. But the election was followed immediately by severe repression; Mário Soares recounts how his
house was assaulted by the PIDE, and in prison he found himself
in the company of many comrades from the democratic camp.[40]
The local pro-Norton Commissions, which in many cases tried to
carry on as representative organs of the opposition, were treated
as illegal by the authorities and subjected to systematic repression.

Furthermore, the definitive split in the Portuguese resistance
along Cold War lines, avoided at the cost of so much struggle and
with apparently positive results during the eighteen months
leading up to the election, was to become a reality during the
next few weeks. The organised opposition was about to enter a

phase, lasting almost a decade, of division, retreat and sterility, palliated only by the bold and determined stand of a principled minority: the group which now formed the MND (*Movimento Nacional Democrático* or National Democratic Movement).

4 The MND: the Left goes it alone

Norton's campaign and its aftermath demonstrated the practical bankruptcy of the liberal-Republican tendency within the opposition. Faced with the regime's persistent intransigence and the failure of military conspiracies, the established leadership of the 'Democratic Opposition' apparently had nothing more to offer than ineffective electioneering or dubious conciliatory manoeuvres. Having now also capitulated to Cold War anti-communism, it implicitly legitimised the regime's propaganda. The effect of this was to further discredit the liberal opposition in the eyes of large sectors of the Portuguese people, and to increase the prestige of the PCP as the only consistent force of resistance. Liberalism was also increasingly discredited in popular eyes, and for growing numbers of intellectuals, by the shameful rôle of the Western Allies in regard to Iberian democracy since the end of the Second World War; a betrayal which was confirmed in 1949 with Portugal's admission to NATO, indicating the primacy of anti-communism over democracy in the value-scale of the West.

The MND, which attempted to fill this void in the opposition camp, based its strategy on militant struggle to maintain and enlarge legal political rights, attempting to mobilise mass support for principled stands against the regime. But the MND had to struggle from the beginning against a widespread mood of demoralisation and apathy, the product precisely of official intransigence and of the capitulation of much of the democratic leadership.

Although the MND did not succeed in winning over most of the liberal intelligentsia, it did benefit from the participation of a distinguished minority, including a number of universally respected figures. In particular Dr Ruy Luis Gomes, a mathematician of international reputation; Virgínia Moura, the first woman engineer in Portugal and one of a select group of women who were beginning to earn public recognition in the face of widespread prejudice and official hostility; her husband, the

architect António Lobão Vital; Dr José Morgado, another outstanding mathematician; and the author Maria Lamas. Whatever accusations might be thrown at them by the regime (and
implicitly by certain oppositionists), their standing as men and
women of democratic principle and intellectual merit was such as
to command wide public respect.

The main emphasis of the MND's activity was to assume public
positions on events of symbolic significance, and to participate in
the regime's periodic 'election campaigns' in accordance with
now-established opposition tradition. One of the Movement's first
public acts was a tribute on 1 December 1949 to the Portuguese
physician Dr Egas Moniz, whose receipt of the Nobel Prize for
Medicine was conspicuously ignored by the Government because
of his democratic convictions.[41] The Movement celebrated (or
attempted to celebrate) all the traditional Republican festivals
such as 31 January and 5 October. But without doubt its greatest
impact, and its greatest innovation in relation to past opposition
practice, was in its critique of Salazarist foreign and colonial
policy; the MND was the first organisation to raise, however
cautiously, the question of colonial self-determination, and the
first (outside the Communist Party) to oppose Portugal's submission to the Atlantic powers.

Portuguese entrance into the Atlantic Alliance was approved
by Salazar's rubber-stamp National Assembly on 27 July 1949,
when the MND was only just beginning to become known as a
political force; but its criticism from this time onwards kept the
issue alive and helped to maintain a strong current of popular
opinion contrary to participation in military blocs. The Movement's campaign against the Alliance reached its peak in early
1952, when an important NATO Council meeting was to be held
in Lisbon. In a pamphlet entitled *Pacto de Paz, não Pacto do
Atlântico!* (A Treaty of Peace, not the Atlantic Treaty) the MND
denounced NATO as 'the expression of a bloc of powers whose
economy and social life are dominated by the policy of preparation for war' and as an instrument of foreign economic penetration, endangering national independence.[42] The statement had a
profound public impact, and resulted in the arrest of the Central
Committee and several other members of the MND.[43]

Even more important in the Portuguese context was the
MND's stand on the colonial issue. This came to a head over the

question of Goa in 1954, towards the end of the Movement's existence; when peaceful mass protests began in the Portuguese Indian outposts of Goa, Damao and Diu, to be met only with repression and warlike propaganda from the Lisbon Government, the MND's Central Committee published an historic 'official note' which was sent to Salazar and to the relevant authorities making a critical analysis of colonial policy and calling for a negotiated solution. Not surprisingly, publication of this statement was suppressed by the censors and its authors were arrested yet again, accused this time of high treason. The trial was not held until eight months later (from 26 April to 30 June 1955 in the Oporto Plenary Court), and once again it became a focus of democratic solidarity and general public repudiation of official repression. As on previous occasions, the regime's concern to maintain at least a minimal façade of legality made it difficult to obtain a conviction; the charges of treason and of membership in illegal organisations had to be dropped for lack of evidence, and the accused were finally sentenced to eighteen months' imprisonment on minor charges.[44] Nevertheless, they were in fact detained for over two years, and the effective existence of the MND came to an end at this time; not long after their release Ruy Luis Gomes and José Morgado went into exile in Brazil, their personal and professional life in Portugal having become impossible.

While the MND upheld the militancy of the Left, it was increasingly isolated from other political sectors. The same factors which alienated the progressive intelligentsia and most of the popular movement from the Western democracies, led the liberal, Republican and social-democratic 'notables' to draw closer to the Anglo-American camp. If the Western powers preferred Salazar to Communism, then the bourgeois opposition would repudiate any alliance with the Communists – even if this meant political castration in the struggle against Salazar. Thus no less a figure than Mário de Azevedo Gomes formed a 'Committee of Twenty-Four' with a strongly 'Atlanticist' ideology,[45] and also organised a rival movement to the MND – the *União Democrática Portuguesa* (UDP).[46] Continuing the same line of action, the philosopher António Sérgio was prominent in trying to organise a 'National Civic Organisation' which might attract American and British support.[47] In 1953 General Norton de Matos, formerly the living symbol of opposition unity, replied in humiliating terms to

an invitation from Virgínia Moura (on behalf of the MND) to
discuss a basis of unity: 'I believe that I cannot have any contacts
or political connections with national or foreign Communists;
and I give this advice to all Portuguese'. The MND denounced this
as a 'vile provocation' worthy of the police.

That many members of the MND (such as Virgínia Moura and
her husband Lobão Vital) were in fact Communists was virtually
public knowledge, and had it not been for the ferocious
repression directed against the PCP, they would no doubt have
been the first to proclaim their allegiance; but under a crypto-
fascist regime anti-communist rhetoric on the part of liberal
oppositionists could only be of benefit to the authorities. On the
other hand, the MND's errors must also be recognised: thus in
1952–53 it went so far as to denounce such eminent intellectuals
as António Sérgio and Câmara Reis as 'traitors' and 'provocateurs',[48] accusations which could only be regarded as sectarian
and counterproductive. These polemics demonstrated to what
extent Cold War tensions had succeeded in generating division
and sectarianism on both sides. It was in this climate of bitter
division that the opposition faced another election campaign for
the Presidency of the Republic, caused by the death of President
Carmona in 1951.

Salazar's replacement for Carmona was another pliant military
nonentity, Marshal Craveiro Lopes, whose campaign did nothing more than confirm the continuity of the regime. He was
opposed not only by Dr Ruy Luis Gomes but also by a third
candidate, retired Admiral Quintão Meireles, a dissident from the
system who was adopted by the right wing of the opposition,
notably Cunha Leal's group and the 'Atlanticists' led by Mário de
Azevedo Gomes and António Sérgio.[49] The rift in the opposition
ranks was thus dramatically confirmed, to the immediate
detriment of both sectors and of those (there were quite a few)
who did not identify with either candidacy. The appearance of
Quintão Meireles' candidacy did also confirm the existence of a
current of dissidence within the regime – a sign that the political
scene was not completely immobile – but it soon became clear
that this dissidence was not strong enough to cause any serious
threat to the 'Situation'. Meireles made it clear in his manifesto
that he represented a critical trend within the system, insisting
that it was not his intention 'to overthrow a regime, provoke a

disturbance, agitate a new ideology, or even open up a solution dangerous to the continuity of the Country's public life'.[50] This fascinating attempt to 'square the circle' – to be both a defender and an opponent of the Salazarist regime – was naturally unsuccessful, and Quintão Meireles did not receive anything like fair and equal treatment from the authorities; on the other hand, his campaign did not attract much support among the opposition or among the people in general, many of whom no doubt considered, as the MND declared on 8 July, that his was 'a candidacy of the Situation' which represented 'a rift in the governmental camp and not a rift in the democratic camp'.[51]

In contrast to that of Quintão Meireles, Ruy Luis Gomes's campaign posed as never before (in terms of public, legal activity) the question of opposition as resistance: not merely verbal criticism of anti-democratic abuses, corruption and inefficiency, but the political expression of popular struggle for democracy at all levels of society, for social and economic protection of workers and peasants and for true national independence. But severe repression from the very beginning made Dr Gomes's campaign practically impossible; the campaign was not allowed (or was unable) to develop into a real mass movement, and soon was brought abruptly to an end. On 3 July a campaign meeting for Dr Gomes had been organised at the Victoria Cinema in Rio Tinto (Oporto). The cinema was surrounded by an impressive contingent of police, and after speeches by Dr Gomes, Virgínia Moura and José Silva, the fourth orator (Dr José Morgado) was interrupted and the authorities closed the session. As they left the building the leading figures of the campaign, including Dr Gomes himself, Virgínia Moura, José Morgado, Lobão Vital and Lino Lima, were violently assaulted by the police, having to receive hospital treatment for severe bruising and bone fractures.[52] After this it was clear that the campaign would not be allowed to develop further, and shortly afterwards Dr Gomes was disqualified as ineligible by the Council of State.[53] If proof were needed that a truly democratic and principled election campaign was impossible under the *Estado Novo*, it had now been provided.

When in 1953 there were further parliamentary elections, the MND from the beginning adopted an abstentionist position, proclaiming that it would not even present candidates unless its 'minimum conditions' – an honest electoral register, freedom of

propaganda, and independent supervision of the polls – were first
conceded. Those who did contest the 1953 elections – the right-
wing liberals of Cunha Leal, who presented lists in Lisbon, Oporto
and Aveiro – once again suffered humiliating defeat, receiving
(officially at least) only ten per cent of the vote.[54]

Although the MND had significant support in some areas, it
never achieved the same degree of massive popular mobilisation
as the MUD or the Norton campaign. Its failure to develop into
a broader and more powerful movement was interpreted by
the liberal opposition as a demonstration of its sectarianism and
inflexibility. This was also the subsequent judgement of the PCP,
which in 1956–57 underwent a political re-orientation that was
decisive in putting an end to the Movement; although the MND
was not merely an instrument of the Communist Party, it could
scarcely survive once abandoned by its main source of organised
support. But there may well have been other factors involved
in the Movement's failure to generate a mass following; in the
opinion of Ramiro da Costa, 'The MND's failure was due more
than anything to the retreat of the labour movement and not so
much to the position of the liberal bourgeoisie'.[55] The early- to
mid-fifties were years of relative calm in the class struggle after
the great strikes and protests of the forties, and this could not be
changed by the idealistic stand of the democratic vanguard; all
they could do was to maintain the spirit of resistance and prepare
the ground for the inevitable future upsurge. But first, before
looking at the dramatic developments which took place from
1958 onwards, it is necessary to look more closely at the crucial
rôle of the Communist Party during the previous two decades.

Notes to Chapter II

1 *Avante!*, VI Série No. 25, 2a. Quinzena de Janeiro de 1943.
2 José Magalhães Godinho, *Como surgiu a União Socialista* (mimeographed document, consulted by courtesy of the author), pp. 1–3.
3 *Avante!*, VI Série No. 46, 1a. Quinzena de Janeiro de 1944.
4 Author's interview with Dr José Magalhaes Godinho, Lisbon, 22
January 1977. Mário Soares (*Portugal Amordaçado: depoimento sobre os
anos do fascismo*, Lisboa, 1974, Arcádia, p. 52) gives the membership of
the Executive Committee as including Bento Caraça and Manuel Serra,
but this seems to be an error.
5 Magalhães Godinho, *Como surgiu*, p. 5.
6 *O Século*, 6 & 7 September 1944; *Diário de Noticias*, 6 &7 September
1944.

7 *Avante!*, VI Série No. 68, 2a. Quinzena de Dezembro de 1944, quoting a statement of the National Council of Anti-Fascist Unity.
8 *Ibid.*, VI Série No. 72, 2a. Quinzena de Fevereiro de 1945: 'Os GAC's devem agir desde já'.
9 Author's interview with Dr José Magalhaes Godinho, Lisbon, 22 January 1977.
10 Fernando Rosas, 'Putschismo e Oposiçao nos anos 40', *História*, 50, Dezembro 1982, pp. 42–3.
11 *Ibid.*
12 *A Luta pelo Pão, pela Liberdade e pela Independência do Povo Português: Informe Politico ao 1o. Congresso Ilegal do Partido Comunista Português.* Informante: Camarada Duarte. Fasciculo IV, pp. 1–2 (In Tribunal da Boa Hora, Processo 16, 016-C, 1961, 3o. Volume, fls. 231–4).
13 *O Século*, 7 June 1944 (with material cut by the censorship; in *O Século* archive, Lisbon).
14 *Ibid.*, 12 December 1944; in an advertisement for 'Pasta medicinal Couto' the image of a hand raised in the V-sign was cut by the censor.
15 *Avante!*, VI Série No. 77, 2a. Quinzena de Maio de 1945.
16 Soares,*Portugal Amordacado*, pp. 86–7, 95–6.
17 *Ibid.*, pp. 95–9. Details of the formation of the MUD were also given to the author by Dr José Magalhaes Godinho in an interview on 22 January 1977.
18 *Seara Nova*, No. 948 (*loc. cit.*).
19 Soares, *Portugal Amordaçado*, pp. 99–100.
20 *Seara Nova*, No. 949 (Supplement), 26 October 1945: report of the press conference given by the MUD Central Committee on 24 October 1945.
21 *Seara Nova*, Nos. 949 (Supplement), 26 October 1945, and 950, 27 October 1945.
22 José Magalhaes Godinho, 'Historia que tem de ser feita. – IV: O desenvolvimento da Farsa', in *República*, 16 October 1974; and author's interview with Dr José Magalhães Godinho, Lisbon, 22 January 1977.
23 José Silva, *Memórias de um Operário*, Porto, 1971, Convergência, 2o. Volume, pp. 90–1; author's interview with Profs. José Morgado and Ruy Luis Gomes, Oporto, 30 June 1977.
24 Soares, *Portugal Amordaçado*, pp. 131–3.
25 *Ibid.*, pp. 133–7; and *A Sessão de 30 de Novembro de 1946 do Movimento de Unidade Democrática* (Edição da Commissao Central do MUD, Lisboa, 1946), *passim.*.
26 Soares, *loc. cit.*; *Avante!*, VI Série No. 103, 2a. Quinzena de Junho de 1947.
27 Soares, *Portugal Amordaçado*, pp. 120–1; *Avante!*, VI Série No. 103, 2a. Quinzena de Junho de 1947; *Aos Camaradas do Comité Central (Circular No. 3)*, clandestine document in the archive of the Tribunal da Boa Hora, Processo No. 16, 016–C, 1961, 3o. Volume, fl. 240; p. 4.
28 Richard Robinson, *Contemporary Portugal: A History*, London, 1979, George Allen & Unwin, p. 69.
29 Rosas, 'Putschismo', pp. 46–7.

30 *Ibid.*, pp. 46–8; *O Século Ilustrado*, 22 February 1975; Soares, *Portugal Amordaçado*, p. 137.

31 Ministry of War communiqué, in *Diário de Noticias* of 20 April 1947.

32 Soares, *Portugal Amordaçado*, pp. 139–41; see also *Avante!*, VI Série No. 114, 1a. Quinzena de Fevereiro de 1948.

33 Soares, *Portugal Amordaçado*, pp. 147–9.

34 Norton de Matos, *Os Dois Primeiros Meses da minha Candidatura á Presidência da República*, Lisboa, 1948, Edicão do Autor, pp. 7–8.

35 Humberto Delgado, *The Memoirs of General Delgado*, London, 1964, Cassell, p. 86.

36 Norton de Matos, *Os Dois Primeiros Meses*, pp. 31–9.

37 *Ibid.*, pp. 27 & 44–5.

38 *República*, 11 January 1949.

39 Silva, *Memórias*, 2o. Volume, pp. 122.

40 Soares, *Portugal Amordaçado*, pp. 157–62.

41 Silva, *Memórias*, 2o. Volume, pp. 288–90.

42 Movimento Nacional Democrático, *Pacto de Paz e não Pacto do Atlântico!*; pamphlet issued in January 1952. Consulted by courtesy of Engineer Virgínia Moura.

43 MND. Commissão Distrital de Lisboa, *Aos Democratas – Aos Defensores da Paz – Aos Portugueses*; leaflet dated February 1952, consulted by courtesy of Engineer Virgínia Moura.

44 *Jornal de Notícias*, 30 November 1974, 'Uma Carta Notável de Rui Luis Gomes e José Morgado no Plenário do Porto'; Silva, *Memórias*, 2o. Volume, pp. 420–8; and Soares, *Portugal Amordaçado*, p. 314.

45 Soares, *Portugal Amordaçado*, pp. 169–71.

46 *Unidade!*, Boletim da Commissão do MND, July-August 1953, Nos. 5–6 p. 3. Consulted by courtesy of Engineer Virgínia Moura.

47 *Ibid.*, p. 4.

48 *Ibid.*, pp. 1 & 3; and Ramiro da Costa, *Elementos para a História do Movimento Operário em Portugal, 1820–1975*, Lisboa, 1979, Assírio e Alvim, 2o. Volume, p. 104.

49 Soares, *Portugal Amordaçado*, pp. 187–92.

50 *Uma proclamação do candidato á Presidência Sr. Almirante Quintão Meireles*; pamphlet reproduced from the *Diário de Norte* of 5 July 1951. Consulted by courtesy of Engineer Virgínia Moura.

51 Silva, *Memórias*, 2o. Volume, pp. 403–4.

52 *A Agressão de Rio Tinto*; illustrated leaflet published by the MND in 1951 (with photographs of the victims after the event). Consulted by courtesy of Engineer Virgínia Moura. See also Silva, *Memórias*, 2o. Volume, pp. 380–2 and 389–95; and author's interview with Profs. José Morgado and Ruy Luis Gomes, Oporto, 30 June 1977.

53 Soares, *loc. cit.*; Silva, *Memórias*, 2o. Volume, p. 405.

54 Da Costa, *Elementos*, 2o. Volume, p. 105.

55 *Ibid.*, 2o. Volume, p. 106.

3

The rise of the Communist Party, 1941–47

Há, efectivamente, um grande combate travado: há dois exércitos e duas bandeiras inimigas: dum lado o Trabalho, do outro o Capital: dum lado aqueles que, trabalhando, produzem: do outro lado aqueles que, sem esforço, e só porque monpolizaram os instrumentos do trabalho, terras, fábricas, dinheiro, vivem da pesada contribuição que impõem a quem, para produzir e viver, precisa daqueles instrumentos, daquele capital.

There is indeed a great battle formed: there are two armies and two hostile banners: on the one side, Labour, on the other, Capital: on the one side those who, by working, produce: on the other side those who, without effort, and only because they have monopolised the instruments of labour, lands, factories, money, live from the onerous tax which they impose on those who, to produce and to live, have need of those instrument and that capital.

Antero de Quental (1871)

Although the Portuguese Communist Party (PCP) had begun to supplant the anarcho-syndicalists as the main force in the working class from the mid-1930's onwards, and in many respects had also begun to assume a leading rôle in the anti-fascist resistance during those years, it was only in the early and middle years of the following decade that it rose to a position of undisputed hegemony in both spheres. In the late thirties the PCP went through a severe crisis provoked by police repression and political confusion within the Party, from which it emerged as a result of a thoroughgoing process of reorganisation led by Alvaro Cunhal, José Gregório and a few others during 1940–41. This reorganisation created for the first time an extensive and disciplined clandestine party network encompassing most of the important urban and some rural areas of the country, with a clear and realistic political line and a capacity for effective political intervention and leadership in different areas of national life. By 1945 the PCP appeared to offer a real revolutionary alternative, dominating a popular movement which posed a serious threat to the survival of clerical-fascism; it was widely respected among middle-class and intellectual circles, as well as being clearly hegemonic in the labour movement. It continued to enjoy this dominant position right down to the liberation of April 1974, although it passed through serious organisational crises in 1949–51, 1958–60 and 1962–65, and its revolutionary leadership was increasingly questioned from 1958 onwards.

1   The crisis of the Party in the late thirties

The PCP in the 1920s had never really been more than a small sect, but after 1929, under the leadership of Bento Gonçalves, José de Sousa and Júlio César Leitão[1] it began to achieve influence in the working class, disputing the leadership of the anarcho-syndicalist CGT. The Party gained prestige in the resistance to the imposition of the fascist union structure from 1933 onwards, collaborating with the CGT (despite serious differences) in the insurrectionary general strike of 18 January 1934[2] and subsequently arguing (against the anarchists) for penetration of the official 'national unions' as the most effective tactic of working-class resistance. The Communists had also begun to penetrate the rank and file of the armed forces, being responsible for the Revolutionary Organisation of the Navy which in August 1936 attempted to hijack three Portuguese warships in order to support the Spanish Republic.[3] During these years the Party also achieved significant successes on the intellectual front; thus in 1934 the student representatives elected to the four Faculty Councils of Lisbon University were all (unofficially, of course) Communists, among them Alvaro Cunhal who became the single student representative on the University Senate.[4]

But these successes did not last; in November 1935, shortly after returning clandestinely from the VII Comintern Congress in Moscow, Bento Gonçalves was arrested in Lisbon along with José de Sousa and Júlio Fogaça, and deported to the Tarrafal concentration camp in the Cape Verde Islands.[5] Other leading cadres were arrested shortly afterwards, and during the next three years the Party organisation was decimated as successive Central Committees and other clandestine structures were dismantled by the police one after another. The Party's history in these years is obscure, partly because of confusion and destruction of records resulting from police repression, and partly because of internal conflicts. Thus very little is known, or is likely to become known, about the rôle of Francisco Paula de Oliveira, 'Pavel', who was one of the Portuguese delegates to Moscow in 1935 and, according to some sources, filled Bento Gonçalves' place as Secretary-General on returning to Portugal in 1936. Arrested in 1937, 'Pavel' escaped shortly afterwards and reportedly went to Paris to re-establish contact with the International, but he was denounced on suspicion of collaboration with the police, and ceased to play any rôle in the Party.[6] The case of 'Pavel' is far from clear – there are indications that he may well have been a victim of intra-party rivalries – but a couple of years later, as we shall see, there was little doubt that the Party leadership was infiltrated by the police. Describing the crisis of those years in a report of 1964, Alvaro Cunhal pointed out that from 1935 to 1940 the Secretariat of the Central Committee was dismantled by the police five times; he attributed this vulnerability to the lack of an extensive clandestine organisation – 'the central leadership consisted in practice only of the Secretariat, and the central clandestine apparatus was virtually limited to the Secretariat and the printing presses ...'.[7] Elsewhere he also suggested that the Party had set itself over-ambitious targets in 1936, thus exposing its militants to further repression.[8]

The PCP's political line during this period was, in theory, that of the Popular Front, as adopted by the Comintern in 1935. Several manifestoes and appeals were launched calling on all democratic and anti-fascist forces to unite in a Portuguese version of the Popular Front, but the Party never succeeded in converting the slogan into a political reality. Successive Popular Front 'programmes' issued by the Party had little value because they neither reflected effective unity with other opposition forces nor proposed a meaningful strategy for the overthrow of the regime.[9] This was recognised by *Avante!* in April 1937, in an article declaring that the Programme had erred in speaking only of the measures to be taken after the formation of a people's government, ignoring the immediate struggle and specific concerns of the masses.[10] This recognition was followed a year later by the publication of a detailed and well-reasoned statement of strategy and tactics, *Objectives and Tactics of the Popular Front*, which showed, for a Party in the midst of a profound political and organisational crisis, a surprising capacity for coherent analysis.[11] Although this document was published as an anonymous Party statement, it bears all the marks of Alvaro Cunhal's vigorous and direct style, and defends many of the same themes which would form the basis of Party policy under his leadership after 1941. Given the Party's weakness at this time, it had little immediate impact, but it shows clearly that the political basis of the PCP's subsequent orientation already existed in embryo in 1938.

Objectives and Tactics of the Popular Front posed with admirable clarity the major problems facing the Portuguese resistance. Recognising that some steps in the direction of anti-fascist unity had been taken, it insisted that this unity would never be effective unless there was agreement on two fundamental questions: first, how to overthrow fascism, and secondly, how to prepare the necessary preconditions for that overthrow. Regarding the first point, it said that there was tacit agreement among all opposition groups that the regime could only be overthrown by force; except in very special circumstances, which seemed unlikely to occur, a peaceful transition to democracy could not be expected. But on the form of armed insurrection, on its timing, leadership, support and tactics, there was no agreement. Most of the old Republican politicians continued to put their trust in a military *putsch*, a classic barracks revolt under democratic officers. But this tactic was no longer viable, as was apparent from the failures of 1927, 1930, 1931, etc.; and it was not viable because the enemy – the fascist regime – was a much more formidable target than the weak governments which had been made and unmade by military *coups* in the nineteenth century or the First Republic.[12] Moreover, the goal of the anti-fascist insurrection – a popular democratic government – could not be achieved by an isolated movement of well-meaning officers. As for the idea favoured by some, of a military *coup* with popular participation (through the distribution of arms to civilian partisans), this still implied leaving the key decisions on timing and tactics to the military. For the Communist Party, insurrection was a political

question, and could only succeed when the political conditions –
of crisis for the regime and mass mobilisation – had been created.
What the Party proposed was a classic Leninist strategy:

It is through struggle that the masses, coming into conflict with
fascism, perceive clearly who and where is their real enemy and how he
must be fought . . .
It is through the position that they take up in struggle that revolutionary organisations win the confidence of the masses. A Party or
revolutionary organisation which does not constantly occupy the front
line in the struggle for the defence of the general interests of the masses,
cannot expect them to follow it at the decisive moments.
MASS STRUGGLE IS, THEN, THE ONLY METHOD WHICH ON THE
BASIS OF THE EXISTING OBJECTIVE SITUATION, CAN AND MUST
CREATE THE REVOLUTIONARY SITUATION WHICH WILL ASSURE
THE TRIUMPH OF THE INSURRECTION AGAINST FASCISM.[13]
(Capitals in the original)

The document also addressed itself to the second fundamental
question it had posed, namely how to prepare the preconditions
for popular insurrection. Here it entered into a detailed refuta-
tion of certain theses which were strongly defended both by the
anarchists and by many Communists, notably by José de Sousa.
Where the latter defended the need to maintain illegal, clandestine unions, the new document (following the lead of Bento
Gonçalves) argued for participation in the official 'national
unions' created by the regime. Where the anarchists and old-line
Communists denied the possibility, or the convenience, of
struggling for workers' everyday material demands under fascism
(arguing that the regime would not permit any such demands to
be met or alternatively that the concession of some demands
would create illusions about the regime among the workers), the
new document insisted that struggles for minor reforms were
both possible and necessary, and would help to build up a mass
movement with political consciousness. It pointed out, correctly,
that the illegal unions had failed because they had to maintain
rigorous secrecy and thus could not be mass organisations; they
became like revolutionary political parties but without the
political perspective of such a party. The document quoted
examples of workers' struggles which had already taken place,
more or less spontaneously, taking advantage of the legal institutions of the corporate state, although without showing any
illusions about the benevolence of these institutions; the masses

were well aware that the State had granted concessions reluct-
antly, as a result of their militancy.[14]

The line proposed in this document was not applied in practice
at this time, partly for organisational reasons – arrests, lack of
resources – and partly because of political differences. Cunhal's
arrest was followed by others, such as those of Manuel Guedes
and Alberto Araújo; another leading militant, Joaquim Pires
Jorge, was seized by Franco's troops in Spain and handed over to
the Portuguese authorities, who deported him to the prison-
fortress of Angra in the Azores.[15] In April 1939 a new Secretariat
was created consisting of Francisco Miguel, Dr Ludgero Pinto
Basto and Alvaro Cunhal (now out of gaol), but it only lasted
a few months before the first two were arrested.[16] During
1938–40 the Party leadership alternated between those who
followed the Popular Front/legal union line, and others who
pursued a line tending towards military *putsch*ism and reliance on
the Republican bourgeoisie. The former consisted of working-
class militants such as Francisco Miguel and Manuel Guedes,
with one or two intellectuals such as Cunhal; the latter of those
who were to be excluded from the 1941 reorganisation and
subsequently denounced as the 'Provocative Groupuscule'
(*Grupelho Provocatório*), in particular the Engineer Vasco de
Carvalho, the ex-student Cansado Gonçalves and the Doctor
Vélez Grilo. The accusations against the 'groupuscule' will be
examined later, but it does seem to be demonstrated that while
they were in control, police agents penetrated to high positions
in the organisation, leading to its virtual collapse.[17] A Party
document of 1942 paints a grim picture of the situation in
1939–40:

> Towards the end of 1939 the Party was in complete crisis; its leading
> cadres had fallen one after another under the claws of the fascist police;
> the individuals who were in charge of the Party had been disowned by its
> cadres and the majority of militants no longer had any confidence in
> them. The 'Avante!', a newspaper of revolutionary traditions dear to
> Portuguese workers, had been replaced by 'Em Frente', an unfamiliar
> mimeographed sheet with no revolutionary traditions, which in its last
> issues revealed the political ineptitude of its editors.[18]

Allowing for possible rhetorical excesses, and without attempting to assign responsibility for the situation, there can be no
doubt that the PCP was at one of the lowest points in its history.

Having a few years earlier made great strides in terms of political influence among the masses, the Party had regressed to the level of the early thirties and was in serious danger of disintegration. The leadership's political inconsistency and the increasing evidence that it was infiltrated at a high level by police agents led the International to suspend relations with the Portuguese Party in 1939.[19]

2   The reorganisation of 1940–41

Although for obvious reasons many details of the process of reorganisation are unknown, most sources agree on the essential aspects. The process was begun in 1940 by a group of leading militants who returned from deportation in Tarrafal and Angra as a result of the 'Amnesty of the Centenaries' (commemorating the foundation of the kingdom of Portugal in 1140 and the restoration of independence from Spain in 1640); together with others who were at liberty (although in varying degrees of clandestinity), they laid the foundations of a new Party organisation.[20] Their initiative was disputed by what remained of the old leadership of Cansado Gonçalves, Vasco de Carvalho and Vélez Grilo, but they soon succeeded in winning the allegiance of the majority of militants and regional structures of the old Party, and Cansado Gonçalves's group was condemned as the 'Provocative Groupuscule' (*Grupelho Provocatório*). For a while there were in effect two parties, each publishing its own *Avante!*, and each accusing the other of betrayal, provocation and Trotskyism. Both evidently sought the recognition of the International (or, after the dissolution of the International in 1943, of Moscow), but as José Pacheco Pereira points out,[21] the struggle between them seems to have been conducted without any direct intervention by the International.

The reorganisation imposed new, rigorous norms of clandestine security, and undertook the development of an extensive network of Party cadres (professional revolutionaries living in illegal conditions) at regional as well as national level. The new leadership also put into practice the new line proposed in the 1938 document *Objectives and Tactics of the Popular Front*, a line which would be ratified in substance (although no longer under this title) at the Party's First Illegal Congress in 1943. *Avante!*

began to be published regularly once again, the Party began to enjoy successes in recruiting workers and organising in factory and field, and despite some arrests in August 1942 (Fogaça, Pedro Soares, Pires Jorge),[22] it succeeded in preserving its essential structures from police repression or infiltration. The success of the Party's reorganisation was reflected in the Party's leading rôle, increasingly recognised, in the waves of strikes and popular protests which broke out from 1942 onwards, and in the inability of the police for several years even to get a clear picture of how it functioned. The ex-PIDE agent Gouveia was forced to admit as much in his *Memoirs*:

> ... no one could understand how it was possible in Lisbon to carry out the great strikes of Barreiro in October-November 1942 and Juiy–August 1943, and on 8–9 May 1944, not only in Lisbon but also in the industrial zone along the Lisbon-Vila Franca de Xira railway line. Only in the course of the last strike did the Police realise that it was the work of Communist agitators and that everyone talked openly about the Communist Party, attributing to it the organisation of the strikes ...
>
> They arrested hundreds of strikers, but it was not possible to find one who would admit to being a member of the Party. Yet, as we would find out later, among those released for lack of evidence there were some who were 'responsible cadres' and others who were members of 'factory cells' and 'Local Committees' of the affected regions, who managed to conceal the organisation's functioning ...
>
> There was arrested in Lisbon, if I am not mistaken, in the early months of 1944, an individual who lived in clandestinity and who declared himself a Communist Party agitator; however, nothing was found out, because this individual, whose surname was Ferreira Marques, preferred suicide to betrayal ...[23]

This was a far cry from the conduct of some of the Central Committee in the late thirties, and is impressive testimony to the change in morale which had occurred since the reorganisation.

In the 1930's Party cells were often organised on a street or neighbourhood basis, and meetings would take place in streets or public squares; after 1941, the transition was made as far as possible to factory or enterprise cells, and meetings were as few as possible, the norm being individual contacts which would arouse less suspicion. The use of pseudonyms was much more extensive and rigorous than before, and cell members were not permitted to know either the name, profession or place of residence of their 'controller'. New contacts must always be confirmed by passwords and other devices, and any failure of a contact to appear must be immediately reported to higher authority. Many documents were encoded, and archives, except those of the Central Committee, were reduced to a minimum. Cadres were strictly forbidden to frequent cinemas, taverns or other places of recreation, and often lived in conditions of extreme isolation except when directly involved in mass activity.[24]

It seems fairly clear that the principal architects of the 1941 reorganisation were Alvaro Cunhal and Júlio Fogaça, who clearly stood out among their colleagues for intelligence, culture and political sophistication. Fogaça had entered the PCP in the early thirties, soon rising to become a member of the Central Committee and then in 1935 of the Secretariat, the key leadership group. Soon afterwards he was arrested and deported to the Tarrafal concentration camp, but in 1940 was among those released in the 'Amnesty of the Centenaries'; his prominent rôle in the Party's reorganisation would appear to be confirmed by documentation which has recently come to light concerning his attempts to contact the International on behalf of the PCP, and also by the hostile rhetoric of the 'Provocative Groupuscule' who referred to the reorganised Party as the 'Frango group' – 'Frango' apparently being Fogaça's pseudonym at this time.[25] But in 1942 he was again arrested and sent to Tarrafal, returning in 1945 after another amnesty; and from that time onwards his leadership rôle was compromised by his identification with a dissident reformist line, the 'policy of transition'.

Certainly by 1942, even before Fogaça's arrest, Cunhal seems to have been in the ascendant as the principal party strategist. The son of a Lisbon lawyer, Adelino Cunhal, the young Alvaro followed in his father's footsteps, reading law at Lisbon University and completing his legal training in 1940, leaving gaol under special permit to sit his final exams. Although suspect to some, in the 'workerist' atmosphere of the Communist movement at the time, for his intellectual and petty-bourgeois origins, this slight, wiry and eagle-faced young man, twenty-seven years old at the time of the reorganisation, had proved himself the equal of his proletarian comrades in determination and discipline. Even his political enemies and rivals are obliged to recognise Cunhal's exceptional qualities; Mário Soares described him as 'a remarkable personality in every respect',[26] and Francisco Martins

Rodrigues (who led the Marxist-Leninist schism from the PCP in 1963) writes with regard to Cunhal's rise to domination of the Party at this time that 'he displayed exemplary conduct when under arrest, and rapidly distinguished himself by his political ability'.[27] Cunhal had joined the Communist Youth on entering the Law Faculty of Lisbon University in 1931, and rose rapidly to prominence, first in the Youth section and then in the Party itself. Although only one of several Central Committee members, and from August 1942 one of three members of the Central Committee's Secretariat (along with Manuel Guedes and José Gregório), Cunhal clearly provided the political lead on most issues, and was in effect Secretary-General from this time onwards (a post which theoretically remained vacant after the death of Bento Gonçalves in Tarrafal in 1942 until 1961, when Cunhal's pre-eminence was finally recognised by his election to the position).[28] The key political rôle played by Cunhal is evident from the fact that in the Party's First Illegal Congress in 1943, it was he who presented both the Political Report and the all-important Report on the Activities of the 'Provocative Groupuscule'.[29]

Inevitably, the work of reorganisation involved friction and conflict. It is quite possible that members of the previous Central Committee may have been unjustly treated, and the accusations against them of being 'Trotskyists' and 'provocateurs' can probably be dismissed as part of the traditional lexicon of the Communist movement at the time. But what cannot be denied is that under their direction the Party had reached a historic low, whereas under the new leadership it rapidly advanced and gained the respect of broad masses of workers as never before. If the sudden and total exclusion of Vasco de Carvalho, Vélez Grilo and their colleagues seems sectarian and inquisitorial, it has to be remembered that the methods used were necessitated by the conditions of clandestine security: no organisation which is systematically persecuted by the authorities and threatened by police infiltration can afford to have free and open discussions with those suspected of collusion with, or weakness towards, the enemy. Contrary to the all-too-frequent pattern of character assassination, slander and exorcism typical of Stalinist purges, the Party's explanations for the exclusion of Vasco de Carvalho and his group were well-reasoned and quite plausible. Cunhal's report on the subject to the 1943 Party Congress described the situation thus:

> ... the militants realised that, at a certain point, the Party leadership consisted of only two persons [Vasco de Carvalho and Sacavém] who, long before the reorganisation, were under suspicion of compromise with the class enemy, and that the closest collaborators of these persons were also individuals of irregular revolutionary activity ...
>
> It was precisely the activity of these individuals which led to the mistrust which weighed upon them. Even admitting, as some comrades did, that certain events which seemed to indicate the connivance of these individuals with the police were 'unfortunate coincidences', 'poor [political] work' and 'mistakes', nevertheless these 'coincidences', 'poor work' and 'mistakes' were such as to lead all sincere militants to the conclusion that, in the Party's interest and for its security, it was absolutely necessary that these two individuals and their closest collaborators should be excluded from Party activity; also that in continuation of the struggle against provocateurs which led to the discovery of police agents inside the organisation, such as Pinto Loureiro and Armindo Gonçalves, there should be carried out a *radical purge* of the Party, that its ranks should be cleared of suspect elements, café gossips, undisciplined intellectuals, and individuals lacking in commitment and self-sacrifice ...[30] (Emphasis in original)

Cunhal admitted that there were comrades who had expressed doubts about the methods used in the reorganisation, for example the fact that the reorganisation was not discussed with the members of the former leadership, or that a number of local militants had been excluded from the reorganisation. But he argued that experience had since shown that any information about the reorganisation which did by one means or another reach the ears of the former leaders, was passed on by them to 'known provocateurs' and thus to the police. This had unfortunately been proven the hard way in the case of the Beja region, where contacts and negotiations with sympathisers of the 'Groupuscule' had led in 1942 to the police discovery and arrest of the regional Party committee and the temporary extinction of the regional organisation.[31]

It is clear that the reorganisation restored the confidence of many rank-and-file militants in the Party; in several regions it seems that the new leadership was able to re-establish contacts with old militants from the 1930s, or even entire local committees, which had lost contact with the Central Committee during the organisational crisis, or who had refused to have dealings with the former leaders because of a total lack of confidence in them. According to the PIDE agent Gouveia, when in 1945 the police finally began to form a picture of the new PCP organisation, they discovered that throughout the northern region of the country, the reorganised Central Committee had managed to link up with the clandestine organisation of the old Communist Party, isolated since the successive 'disasters' of the late thirties.[32] Although Gouveia takes it upon himself to shed crocodile tears for the former leaders of the Party, he is forced to recognise the success of the new organisation:

Consolidating connections in some places and developing their structure further with the collaboration of those who were afraid to lose contact, and recruiting new elements, at the end of almost three years' activity they had managed, in fact, to set up a fully operative apparatus, as we discovered when, after the 'fall' of the three 'illegal houses', we attacked and dismantled it.[33]

This last claim was slightly exaggerated, since while it is true that the 1945 arrests and the police discovery of valuable Party documentation at this time did constitute a serious blow, the Party was able to recover and continued to progress until the arrest of Cunhal and other leading cadres in 1949.

The Party structure from the time of reorganisation onwards consisted of a Secretariat of three – Alvaro Cunhal ('Duarte'), José Gregorio ('Alberto') and Manuel Guedes ('Santos') – a Central Committee of about a dozen, Regional Committees in the major areas of the Country (Lisbon, the South Bank of the Tagus, the Alentejo, the Algarve, the Ribatejo, the 'West' – the littoral north of Lisbon – and the North), and rank-and-file cells constituted by workplace or by profession. There were also normally at least two clandestine printing presses and other specialised technical units (for example, for communications over the border with Spain). It is not possible to be precise about membership of the Central Committee, but those who participated in it at the time of the reorganisation or within the next few years (until 1946) included (with their most commonly used pseudonyms) Júlio Fogaça ('Ramiro'), Sérgio Vilarigues ('Amílcar'), Joaquim Pires Jorge ('Gomes'), António Dias Lourenço ('João'), Alfredo Diniz ('Alex'), Miguel Pereira Forjaz de Lacerda ('Pinheiro'), Fernando Piteira Santos ('Fred') and António

Guedes da Silva ('Augusto'), Pedro Soares and Francisco Ferreira Marques, plus of course the three members of the Secretariat. There was an approximately equal balance between those of proletarian origin (Gregório, Guedes, Vilarigues, Pires Jorge, Dias Lourenço) and petty-bourgeois intellectuals (Cunhal, Fogaça, Forjaz de Lacerda, Soares, Piteira Santos).[34] All the Central Committee members and a number of other cadres were paid Party functionaries, living in rigorous clandestinity; residing in 'illegal houses' in groups of two or three, usually in small towns or villages with little political activity, they kept contacts with local inhabitants to a minimum, justifying their seclusion on medical grounds, or alternatively – if their tasks required frequent travel – presenting themselves as travelling salesman. Those most directly involved in working-class agitation and organisation naturally had to live in the main cities and industrial towns. Domestic tasks were carried out by women militants, one to each 'illegal house', normally the wife or *companheira* of one of the men living there. All were armed, although with strict instructions to use their arms only in an emergency, to prevent arrest or discovery of Party archives and printing presses. The life of the Party cadre was one of constant vigilance, since it was necessary to watch constantly for any sign that he was being observed or followed; yet there could also be long periods of boredom or time-wasting, as he engaged in useless activities purely in order to maintain his 'cover', or awaiting a contact which failed. Any failed contact had to be reported to higher authority and investigated at once, since it might mean that a comrade had been arrested who could, willingly or not, pass on information to the police leading to the discovery of units of the clandestine apparatus.

Clandestinity undoubtedly had undesirable consequences in terms of excessive secrecy within the Party, suspicion, lack of debate, and dogmatism; but under conditions of illegality and dictatorship there was clearly no alternative. It was only this rigorous system of security which enabled the Party to continue its activities so successfully year after year, and with a consistency unmatched by any other organisation. In fact, no other opposition political group or tendency had any organisation to speak of during most of the Salazarist period; the Republicans, Socialists and others lacked either the desire or the discipline necessary to

build an effective underground apparatus. A partial exception
was the Masonic Order, with its pre-existing semi-clandestine
structure, and which for this reason sometimes served as a
vehicle for Republicans and Socialists; and in the 1960s there
emerged a series of Marxist-Leninist and 'New Left' groups which
attempted, with limited success, to create underground organisations. But the PCP was the only Party or tendency with an effective clandestine organisation maintained for a period of decades,
and this impressive achievement was one of the main foundations
of its success in becoming the hegemonic force in the anti-fascist
resistance. Despite serious blows by the police at times (as in 1949
and the early sixties) the PCP's organisation remained intact in
essentials from 1941 until the liberation in 1974, and throughout
these years *Avante!* was published regularly (normally once a
fortnight) with only one brief interruption. Contrary to the
practice of opposition parties in many countries under dictatorial
regimes, including some Communist Parties, the PCP generally
kept its main leading nucleus in Portugal, and produced its
newspaper and other propaganda inside the country – a circumstance which did much to increase its popular prestige.[35]

Despite the crucial importance of the creation of this clandestine apparatus, the reorganisation of 1940–41, like the crisis
which preceded it, was not only organisational but also political.
Without unity around a clear political line it would scarcely have
been possible to find the drive and discipline necessary to rebuild
the Party, or to win a mass following to support the clandestine
structure and prevent it from becoming a mere secret society. The
new Secretariat of Cunhal, José Gregório and Manuel Guedes
led the Party in applying , for the first time in a practical way, the
strategy of anti-fascist unity which in theory had been Party
policy since the beginning of the Popular Front period several
years earlier; both in terms of mass propaganda and political
contacts with other sectors of the opposition, a process was begun
which would bear fruit a couple of years later with the formation of the Movement of National Anti-Fascist Unity (MUNAF).
Similarly, on the proletarian front the tactic of working within
the official corporate unions, advocated by Bento Gonçalves
since 1935, was systematically applied for the first time, and with
considerable success. These policies, for which the new leaders
had fought against both Vasco de Carvalho's group and some old

militants such as José de Sousa, were fully elaborated and given formal recognition at the Party's Third (but First Illegal) Congress held in 1943.

3 The First Illegal Congress and the line of national anti-fascist insurrection

The PCP's Third Congress (the first held in clandestinity) took place in the late summer or early autumn of 1943 (between late August and the beginning of October) in a private mansion in fashionable upper Estoril, where the Party had made use of its bourgeois contacts to obtain the use of what was surely one of the least likely venues for such an event. The attendance was very small for reasons of security, and the very fact that a Congress had been held at all was not announced publicly (in *Avante!*) until a couple of months later. But it was rightly presented as a symbolic event of great importance, indicating the resurgence of the Communist Party as a major force in the anti-fascist resistance.[36]

At the Congress, the all-important Political Report was presented by 'Duarte' (Alvaro Cunhal). Entitled 'The Struggle for Bread, for Freedom and for the Independence of the Portuguese People', it argued systematically for the strategy of working within the official unions and building broad anti-fascist unity – the strategy the Party was already following, but to which there was still some resistance. It condemned Salazar's Government as one of 'national betrayal', and advocated a great movement of national unity to overthrow fascism, a movement which would potentially include almost the entire nation since all but a 'handful of traitors' were interested in the defeat of the regime. Portugal had to choose between democracy and fascism; there was no third way. The Party had already proposed (in March of that year) its 'Nine Points' of unity for the anti-fascist movement, and it was necessary to propagate this position as widely as possible. The government which would replace that of Salazar, said Cunhal, would not be a proletarian one; conditions in Portugal were not ripe for socialist revolution. Rather, the entire nation should be united behind a 'government of unity of all progressive and patriotic forces', in which the Communists might or might not participate, but which would implement an emergency programme to dismantle the fascist state apparatus and convene free elections.[37]

The 'Nine Points' in essence simply enumerated the basic measures necessary for a full democratisation of the country's institutions. But Cunhal now insisted on the need to be more precise; for instance, with regard to freedom of association and the abolition of corporativism, he argued that following the overthrow of the regime the official unions ('sindicatos nacionais') and village associations ('casas do povo') should not simply be dissolved but rather be democratised through free union elections – otherwise it would be very difficult 'to build new working-class organisations'. Another thorny point in the programme was the eighth, dealing with rights of the colonial peoples; where the colonies were concerned, said Cunhal, the Communist Party 'does not abdicate from the goal . . . of the right to independence', but it realised that other anti-fascist organisations were not willing to go so far, and therefore proposed a vaguer formulation which spoke of 'the establishment of a free alliance with the colonial peoples'.[38] Cunhal's position on this question, developed more fully elsewhere in his report, was particularly interesting, and perhaps helps to explain the excellent relations the PCP was later to develop with the African liberation movements, despite its public compromises with the scruples of the bourgeois opposition in Portugal:

> We Communists recognise the right of the colonial peoples to establish themselves as independent states, although the peoples of the Portuguese colonies, under-developed in all respects, cannot alone, in present circumstances, guarantee their own independence. It is not a question of 'granting' an independence and separation for which the colonial peoples would not be ready. In the present circumstances such a 'concession' would mean that the Portuguese colonies would fall under the domination of another imperialist power . . .
> The front of anti-imperialist struggle of the Portuguese people and the colonial peoples is only possible if the Portuguese proletariat gives effective support to the national resistance movements against exploitation and violence in the Portuguese colonies, against the Portuguese imperialist bourgeoisie . . .[39]

For its time this was a remarkably explicit and realistic position on the colonial question, and although in its public statements the PCP remained more cautious, this goes a long way towards refuting charges made in more recent years by representatives of Trotskyist and left-Catholic groups to the effect that the Party never overcame a colonialist mentality.

With regard to the labour movement, Cunhal argued that the struggle to maintain illegal democratic unions had proved largely ineffective and that the organised working class was increasingly found in practice inside the official unions. The Party should go where the workers were, and not waste time and effort maintaining artificial structures with no mass following. Bento Gonçalves had long ago pointed out that 'the illegal unions do not carry out any serious mass work' and that their activity was often limited to publication of an occasional newspaper; but Gonçalves's arrest in late 1935 and the sectarian attitudes of many comrades had prevented until recently a real application of the new line.[40] But since the 1941 reorganisation this had begun to change, and many workers were in any case participating in the *sindicatos nacionais*. In several cases workers had succeeded in electing leaderships representing rank-and-file opinion, and if these leaders were disqualified by the authorities, the workers had elected new representatives also enjoying their confidence. This tactic of 'boring from within' was proving so successful that, in Cunhal's opinion, it was no longer a matter of winning over sections of the rank and file or gaining control of a few leadership positions; rather, conditions were ripe for 'the large-scale assault' on the fascist unions, to 'turn the *S[indicatos] N[acionais]* into militant organisations of the working class'. Communists should encourage all workers to enter the official unions and should organise mass pressure on the leaderships to take up the workers' demands, while simultaneously organising independent Unity Committees to take action if the union bureaucracy failed to do so.[41] This approach was further emphasised by 'Santos' (Manuel Guedes) who presented the organisational report to the Party Congress: while the recent strike movements demonstrated the PCP's success in this field, he urged more consistent efforts combined with greater tactical flexibility:

Some of our militants have not yet learnt to work with the necessary flexibility within the unions. In some cases there has been too much haste in the struggle against the leaderships, giving rise to State intervention with nomination of administrative commissions, thus denying us the possibility of infiltrating honest elements into the union leaderships. In other cases our militants have put forward [as candidates] elements

who are too 'burnt' [i.e. well-known as anti-regime], thus jeopardising
official approval of the leadership slates elected in mass meetings . . .[42]

On the other hand, said Guedes, when popularly-elected union
leaderships were denied official recognition, it was important to
continue a campaign among the workers to force the authorities
to recognise the popularly-elected leaders or else expose completely their anti-democratic stand. In order to assure that these
tactics were effectively applied, the Party must strengthen its
factory cells and also set up cells of union cadres within the
sindicatos nacionais themselves. The Congress Resolutions particularly stressed the importance of setting up a co-ordinated
leadership of the Party's union cadres at national level.[43] This was
nothing short of a blueprint for the complete takeover of the
union structure, just as Cunhal had advocated.

No less important for the Party than building a solid base in
the working class was winning over the peasantry, 'the most
powerful ally of the proletariat' in Cunhal's words. Somewhat
optimistically, he affirmed that the fascist regime had not
succeeded in winning over the vast masses of the peasantry, who,
on the contrary, were actively joining in the revolutionary
movement of national unity. He cited recent actions of peasants
in the North in resistance against the Government's policy of
requisitioning grain for export to the Axis: in several villages
'thousands of peasant men and women' had taken direct action
to prevent 'the theft of maize, flour and other staples', in at least
one case overcoming the authorities' attempts to remove the
crops by force, and in other cases causing serious embarrassment
to the repressive forces.[44] There had also been important
struggles by the agricultural labourers in the Ribatejo against a
wage cut imposed by Government decree; striking workers in
several places had forced the landlords to restore wage levels,
ignoring the Government's orders. In this struggle the Communist Party had played a significant rôle, both through the activities
of its local cells and by distributing 20,000 copies of a leaflet
entitled 'Let no one accept starvation wages!' – the biggest
distribution of a pamphlet since the Party's reorganisation. But
Cunhal had to recognise that the Party's influence among the
peasantry was weak; many of the protest movements were
spontaneous and occurred without any leadership or even

participation by Communists. One of the reasons for their inability to mobilise the peasant masses was 'the rigidity of the organisational forms which we have tried to impose on them, [and] ... our failure to understand properly the differences of lifestyle and temperament of the peasantry and the industrial proletariat'.[45] Here Cunhal touched on a fundamental problem, which the Party never really succeeded in overcoming; right down to 1974 it remained very weak among the smallholding peasantry (as opposed to landless rural labourers, whose class situation was quite different).

The peasant question was also addressed quite frankly and directly by Manuel Guedes in the organisational report. The Party's work among the peasants continued to be weak, he said, and in the absence of close ties to the peasantry, its understanding of their problems remained superficial. The Party must find a way of dedicating much more attention to peasant issues; experienced cadres must be sent into the rural areas to devote themselves full-time to local issues, they must receive adequate organisational support and be in a position to train peasant militants. But also, organisational structures must be simplified: 'given the nature of their economic activity, the peasant classes adapt themselves with difficulty to complex organisational forms'; structures devised for an urban milieu could not be imposed on rural society. The Congress resolution on the peasant question also stressed that 'the organisational forms of the industrial proletariat' must not be 'schematically applied' to the peasantry, who needed 'less rigid' structures which would make less demands on their members. The resolution suggested collective readings of the Party press and other small informal meetings as appropriate means of action. Some progress had been made since the reorganisation, and 'principally in two regions' – we are not told which, but one of them must have been the Ribatejo – the beginnings of a mass organisation of peasants under Party control had been created. It would be interesting to know more of the concrete measures taken by the Party in this sphere following the Congress; the sensitivity of the question is shown by the fact that three points of the resolution on peasant organisation were deliberately left blank in the version of the Congress Resolutions published clandestinely in 1943.[46]

The most important aspect of this Third Party Congress (which

some writers describe as the first real congress the Party had ever
held, since the two held in legal conditions in the 1920's were
so disorganised and faction-ridden),[47] apart from reaffirmation
of the line of penetration of the *sindicatos nacionais*, was the
ratification of Cunhal's strategy of National Anti-Fascist Unity. By
overcoming sectarian opposition to a tactical alliance with the
Republican bourgeoisie, and yet simultaneously insisting upon
the PCP's independence and refusing to compromise with the
regime, Cunhal made possible the emergence of the first effective
democratic front in the history of the Portuguese resistance, the
MUNAF. Some comrades feared that this might be a betrayal of
revolutionary purity, quoting Stalin to the effect that 'the liberal
bourgeoisie of a capitalist country cannot cease to be counter-
revolutionary' and arguing that the Party should form 'Workers'
Defence Committees' rather than 'National Unity Committees';
but Cunhal insisted that Portugal must be analysed as a country
with a dual, and contradictory, character: both dominant and
dominated, imperialist and imperialised. The alliance with the
liberal bourgeoisie was correct because 'in the present stage of the
revolution, while viewing Portugal as an imperialist country, we
must see [it] fundamentally as a *dependent country, a semi-colonial
country*. The present stage of the revolution in Portugal is that of
a national-democratic revolution, against foreign domination
in our country, against the political, economic and diplomatic
subservience of Portugal ....' Even some sectors of the bourgeoisie had an interest in fighting against the 'policy of betrayal' of
Salazar's government.[48]

   To gain acceptance for this line within the Party had not been
easy; in fact it had been a principal factor in the internal strife
from which the Party was only just emerging. A strenuous
opponent of the new line was none other than José de Sousa, the
veteran Communist imprisoned in Tarrafal along with Bento
Gonçalves since the end of 1935. Already at that time De Sousa
was known for his opposition to Gonçalves's tactic of working
within the *sindicatos nacionais*, and in prison he continued for
years to defend the idea of organising illegal underground
unions. Because of his prestige he continued to be accepted as a
Party member and – at least in theory – as a member of the
Central Committee, like Gonçalves (although they clearly could
not exercise practical leadership from the prison camp in the

Cape Verde Islands). But De Sousa was more and more openly in disagreement with the Party line on several issues, and when news of the 1939 Nazi–Soviet pact reached Tarrafal, he publicly (i.e. to non-Communist prisoners as well as Party members) accused the Soviet leaders of betraying the cause of the working class. His ideas found an echo among other prisoners, particularly the anarchists, but also among dissident or expelled Communists, so that from the Party's point of view his position was not only heretical but also divisionist.[49] Following various disputes, the Communist Prisoners' Organisation in the camp formally expelled José de Sousa, Alvaro Duque da Fonseca and nine others, for divisionism and anti-Party activities. The Secretariat of the Central Committee subsequently made one last appeal to De Sousa to mend his ways, in a letter appealing to him as an historic leader; but the schism had evidently become insurmountable, and hence in November 1943 the Secretariat published a circular letter confirming De Sousa's expulsion.[50]

Beyond all the polemics and sometimes petty disputes which arose within the prison camp, it is clear that José de Sousa was a partisan of a fundamentally different line, one which harks back to Rosa Luxemburg and the 'Council Communists' of the 1920s: a 'workerist' reliance on the rank and file (refusal to enter the *sindicatos nacionais*), rejection of diplomatic compromises (the Nazi–Soviet pact), and refusal of alliances—even when consistently anti-fascist – with the liberal bourgeoisie. In the circumstances the Party's treatment of De Sousa was relatively restrained: two years passed before his expulsion was confirmed, and he was not at first subjected to the kind of character assassination all too common in the international Communist movement. His cause was taken up back in continental Portugal by the members of the 'provocative groupuscule' of Vélez Grilo, Vasco de Carvalho and their associates, and indeed De Sousa did come to join them after his release from Tarrafal in 1946. In fact the 'groupuscule' offered the only clearly formulated alternative strategy for the Party, and in this sense there is no doubt that their exclusion was the result of a political, and not merely a disciplinary and organisational, struggle for control.

The 'groupuscule' went to great lengths to present itself as an orthodox Communist Party, publishing an *Avante!* of its own with the same format and symbolism, and using the same polemical

jargon. It denounced the reorganised PCP as 'Trotskyite provocateurs', as a 'sectarian-opportunist group of informers' and as
'traitors to the working class'. Its publications were full of
quotations from Lenin and Stalin and articles in praise of the
USSR. After 1942 it too claimed to favour a tactic of national
unity, but criticised the reorganised Party as being too conciliatory:

We will never support JUST ANY government, for the simple reason of
having overthrown the Dictatorship (in appearance or in reality), we will
never support JUST ANY GOVERNMENT OF NATIONAL UNITY simply
because that government calls itself one of national unity . . . [51] (Capitals
in original)

– and it pointed out the hypocrisy and opportunism of many
monarchists and members of the clergy, Generals and Legionnaires, long-time supporters of the regime, who were now in
time of crisis conspiring against Salazar. This was a clear reference
to Cunhal's position in his Political Report, advocating openness
to tactical alliances with many different groups, even ex-fascists
and Legionnaires in certain circumstances.

Although initially the situation was confused and it was
understandable that many Party militants should doubt the
new leadership led by Cunhal, Guedes and Pires Jorge, by 1943
the superiority of the reorganised Party's line was clear to any
unbiased observer. As the reorganised Party made steady progress
during 1943 and 1944 in building a solid working-class base and
developing effective broad anti-fascist unity, the 'groupuscule's'
criticisms became manifestly opportunist or worse. Where previously it had criticised the new Party leadership for being too
conciliatory towards the regime, it now condemned the great
strike movements of October 1942 and July–August 1943 as
'destabilising' the Portuguese situation when Salazar was
negotiating the concession of the Azores bases to the British and
Americans! It also condemned the Party's support for and
stimulation of the popular assaults on granaries owned by
speculators and resistance to the authorities requisitioning grain
for export to the Axis; yet these were some of the most clearly
spontaneous and potentially revolutionary actions ever undertaken against Salazarism, and the PCP's support for them undoubtedly won it sympathy among workers and peasants in the

small towns and villages of the Ribatejo and the North where these incidents occurred.[52] By condemning the broadest and most militant mass struggles to have occurred since the beginning of the Dictatorship, the 'groupuscule' lent credence to PCP accusations that it was a tool of the police. It certainly ceased to be a serious threat to the PCP which was coming to be recognised as the dominant force in the anti-fascist resistance.

Cunhal's report to the 1943 Congress also devoted considerable attention to the importance of political work among youth, women and the Armed Forces. He made scathing criticisms of the Party's youth wing, which he said 'does not at present constitute a nation-wide organisation' and whose activity in factories and workshops was 'extremely weak'; its leadership showed 'lack of initiative and of enterprising spirit', a tendency to rely on 'ready-made formulae' and 'an almost total lack of imagination'. Although Cunhal did find some words of praise for the Youth Federation's leadership, especially 'comrade Amilcar [Sérgio Vilarigues] who is present here in his capacity as a member of the leading cadre of our Party', this could only be taken as an abrupt rebuke for Vilarigues and his comrades.[53] In the next few years the Party would greatly intensify its activity among working-class youth and students, and several future politicians such as Octávio Pato, Salgado Zenha and Mário Soares had their political baptisms in the Communist Youth. The *MUD Juvenil* (created in 1946), the opposition's most successful broad-front youth movement, would owe its existence largely to PCP initiative; and in this way the Party laid the foundation of its future strength for two or three decades to come. As in other aspects of Party activity, the orientation proposed by Cunhal's 1943 report was decisive; he insisted that Communist youth work should be broad and non-sectarian, but also that it should combine legal and illegal forms of activity, thus creating youth organisations capable of resisting repression.

What Cunhal had to say about the rôle of women was at this time brief and not very significant. Much more important were his remarks about the Armed Forces, although this also remained a serious weakness of the Party's work. Since the remarkable progress of the ORA (Revolutionary Organisation of the Navy) in the mid-30s, culminating in the August 1936 mutiny of sailors in solidarity with the Spanish Republic, PCP activity within the

Armed Forces had been minimal. Although in theory the Party
had always maintained that fascism could only be overthrown
by force of arms, little had been done to translate this strategic
perspective into practical terms. Cunhal now claimed that the
arms which would serve to overthrow fascism were 'the very
arms which fascism has placed in the hands of soldiers and
sailors'; for the resistance to triumph it was necessary to win over
'the workers and peasants in uniform and the progressive and
patriotic section of the naval and military officer corps' – a task
for which, he said, conditions were ripe.[54] Referring to growing
discontent among the rank and file because of low pay and poor
rations and resentment against their employment in the repression of 'popular protests, and anti-Axis feeling among many
officers, Cunhal argued that many troops could be won over to
form 'Committees of National Defence' and to refuse to repress
workers and peasants. Manuel Guedes, in his Organisational
Report, referred to unspecified recent incidents in which troops
or militarised police (GNR) had refused to obey superior orders to
use force against the people, revealing their unreliability for the
regime. But he also admitted that very little was being done to
resolve the problem of revolutionary organisation within the
Armed Forces, a situation which demanded urgent attention. All
the Party militants or sympathisers called up for military service
must contact the Party's military committee and must attempt to
organise broad anti-fascist committees within their units, and
Communists outside the Armed Forces must cultivate contacts
and friendships with troops and officers and attempt to persuade
them to side with the people against fascism, or at least to remain
neutral in the event of civil strife.[55] It was resolved to form
'Committees of National Unity' – this was the title now adopted-
within the military; although Communist Party cells might also
be formed, this was regarded as less urgent than the creation of
broad unitary committees. These nuclei should respect the
existing military hierarchy, with separate committees for officers,
NCOs and other ranks; and the Party must immediately establish
a central body responsible for directing its military activities,
under the direct control of the Central Committee's Secretariat.[56]

In the development of a broad anti-fascist front, general
declarations of intent were clearly insufficient; it was necessary
to define clearly the forces and organisations with whom it was

desired to establish unity, and to formulate specific tactical proposals. The most significant potential allies were the anarchists and the Republicans; in relation to both of these the PCP had committed serious errors in the past. But the anarchists were no longer the force they had once been; as Cunhal pointed out, six or seven years previously the CGT had an effective underground organisation, a functioning leadership, and a regular illegal press – all of which it had now lost. The question was no longer one of structured relations with the CGT, but rather winning over individual anarchists or small groups, and of recognising the ideological importance of libertarian thought: 'Anarchism still has an ideological influence on the working class, and sometimes, comrades, it even appears in various forms in our own Party.'[57] The best anarchist militants had moderated their previous sectarianism and had learnt the need for anti-fascist unity, above all through the experience of the Spanish Civil War; the PCP must therefore appeal to 'all sincere anarchists, to all anarchists of the school of Mário Castelhano (the great anarchist leader who had recently died in Tarrafal, like 'our own unforgettable Bento Gonçalves').[58] But not all anarchists were like this; Cunhal warned against 'certain former anarchist militants who have gone over to the side of the class enemy', and quoted the example of one prominent ex-anarchist (no name is given) who used his influence to sabotage the strikes of October–November 1942, or of an 'anarchist' organisation in Oporto which was in the pay of an (unspecified) foreign secret service. It is undeniable that in both Spain and Portugal there were anarchists who collaborated with fascism, or in a few cases actually became fascists; but the Communist movement could not claim innocence in this respect either, and Cunhal had to recognise that the emphasis should be on reconciliation and unity, not on further sterile polemics.

The situation with regard to the Republicans, 'presently . . . the strongest anti-fascist tendency after the Communists', was quite different. The Republican movement was the principal representative of the petty-bourgeoisie, enjoying the support also of some elements of the bourgeoisie proper; and in the absence of an effective Socialist Party, Republicanism was the main opposition force to the right of the Communists. The main problems of the Republican movement were those which had plagued the

PRP (Republican Party) before 1926: chronic factionalism and division, and a tendency to rely on behind-the-scenes arrangements and intrigues rather than mass politics. Cunhal repeated the Communist criticism of Republican *putschism* – the eternal faith in a military *coup* which never succeeded – and the rooted anti-communism of many Republicans. But he recognised that this was beginning to change and that some Republicans were willing to consider unity with the PCP under certain conditions.[59] This was to be the basis for the formation of the MUNAF and Cunhal's strategy was in practice based above all on seeking an alliance with the Republicans; it was this alliance which broke the isolation of the PCP and constituted the biggest change in opposition politics since 1934.

Within the PCP the most controversial aspect of the new line was the question of defining the limits of anti-fascist unity. All but a few dogmatists were won over by Cunhal's arguments for collaboration with anarchists and Republicans, but it was a different matter when it came to dealing with Catholics, monarchists and dissidents from the ranks of the regime itself. Already in December 1942 the Central Committee had spoken of 'holding out a hand [of friendship] to the Catholics', recognising that many practising Catholics were out of sympathy with the regime; but there was clearly opposition to this within the Party, given the extent to which Cunhal felt obliged to justify it in his Political Report. This is not surprising in view of the strength of the Iberian anti-clerical tradition, and in fact opposition to such a policy was not confined to the Communist Party; anti-clericalism was powerful among the anarchists and Republicans as well. Cunhal found it necessary to explain that the Party was in no way wavering in its adherence to dialectical materialism, that it continued to regard religion as 'the opiate of the people'; but he pointed out the sterility of dogmatic anti-religious campaigns and the counter-productive nature of attacks on popular Catholicism – 'For us the struggle against religion emerges from the political struggle. It is the bourgeoisie and not the proletariat which benefits from diverting the proletariat from the economic and political struggle to the religious one'.[60] Today, in the aftermath of Vatican II and with the emergence of the 'revolutionary Church' in Latin America, this may seem self-evident; but in the Portugal of the 1940s it was far from being so. To separate class struggle from ideological anti-religious struggle was very difficult.

The problem of how to deal with actual or potential dissidents from the regime has plagued anti-fascist and anti-dictatorial movements everywhere. In this respect, as in others, Cunhal did not hesitate to assume potentially unpopular positions. After specifying certain categories of Salazarist agents who were completely beyond the pale – the PVDE (Secret Police, later PIDE) with all its agents, the 'Germanophile' commanders of the Portuguese Legion, those involved in hoarding grain for export to the Axis, etc. – he went on to affirm that 'we Communists do not want to bind every man inexorably to the errors of his past':

We accept that there may be men who yesterday were fascist collaborators and today are sincerely convinced of their errors and sincerely desire a regime of freedom and democracy in Portugal. We see the participation of these men in the Movement of National Anti-Fascist Unity as possible, provided that their anti-fascist spirit and their fighting spirit are demonstrated in action. But the evolution of the national and international situation may bring us even greater surprises . . .[61]

Cunhal argued that the Party should be open to collaboration with individual members of even such a fascist institution as the Portuguese Legion; although the Legion as such 'embodies more than any other organisation the true policy of Salazar's fascist government',[62] those Legionnaires who were unwilling recruits or who had seen the errors of their ways could potentially participate in the anti-fascist movement. Workers in certain industries were obliged by their employers to join the Legion; and others, while seduced by the regime's propaganda, were nevertheless drawn by their objective class situation into strikes and protest movements. Their struggles, which would tend to weaken the regime, should be encouraged.

It is ironic that Cunhal, who would later acquire such a reputation as a hardliner, should have gone to such lengths at an early stage of his political career to defend a conciliatory line. But he was not advocating conciliation and collaboration at any price. Rather, in arguing at this point against the dogmatic Left of the PCP, he was striving to establish a coherent line which would avoid the pitfalls of both left sectarianism and right opportunism. As would rapidly become apparent, there were some in the Party who wanted to go much further in seeking a peaceful and voluntary dissolution of the regime, rather than simply advocating tactical flexibility in taking advantage of divisions and dissidents within its ranks. Cunhal's line, which was to be pursued with remarkable consistency right down to 1974 (with the exception of a brief period in the late 1950s when he was in gaol), was to maximise the camp of anti-fascist unity, incorporating elements of the liberal bourgeoisie and even fascist dissidents, while rejecting any illusions about the benevolence of the régime itself or the probability of its voluntary or peaceful dissolution. The theoretical basis for this, stated explicitly in this 1943 report, was that Portugal was not yet ripe for the conquest of power by the proletariat; the present phase of the struggle was that of a national democratic revolution. 'In Portugal power is concentrated in the hands of the great landlords, the great capitalists and financiers, the great industrialists and traders, and part of the medium bourgeoisie linked to German imperialism. Power must be taken by an alliance of the following classes: the proletariat, the peasantry, the small and medium bourgeoisie . . .'[63] The problem here – and on this Cunhal was not clear – was which class should have hegemony within this democratic front, and what kind of regime should follow the eventual downfall of the fascist regime. This question was to lie dormant for twenty years, because of the persistence of Salazarism and the repeated resurgence of liberal illusions regarding a peaceful transition of the regime. But the PCP's line on the class character of the revolution would come under attack during the Marxist-Leninist schism of the 1960s and the revolutionary crisis of 1974–75.

4   The foundations of PCP hegemony within the working class

Whatever the limitations of the new Party line in terms of revolutionary class analysis, in terms of political organisation and practical work in the short or medium term it was remarkably effective. Following its reorganisation the Party for the first time began to apply systematically the tactic of penetrating the official unions, and the impact was startling. Within a few years the PCP was unquestionably the major force in the union movement, was playing a leading role in a series of great strike movements without precedent under the *Estado Novo* and was electing militant workers to the leadership of the *sindicatos nacionais*. By

1945 although its actual membership was still limited by the conditions of clandestinity, it had become for the first time a true mass party.

The basis of this spectacular advance was the reorganised Party's consistent and militant agitation among rank-and-file workers in all the major industries. There can be little doubt also that the line of working within the official unions was now in accord with the mood of most workers, who were increasingly active in the *sindicatos nacionais* and were coming to regard any attempt to maintain illegal clandestine unions as irrelevant. Wartime inflation and shortages contributed to an upsurge of popular discontent, first manifest in the strikes and demonstrations of 1942. If the PCP did not cause the strikes, it was certainly the only effective organisation taking a prominent rôle in the movement and giving it direction. Already in the summer of 1942 the regime was showing signs of alarm at the breakdown of 'social peace'; as *Avante!* proclaimed with satisfaction in June:

More than the bankruptcy of corporativism, it is the influence of the Communist Party among the masses which alarms the men of the Corporate State; it is the leaders of the *sindicatos nacionais* who reveal this when they talk to Salazar 'of the most intense Communist propaganda being carried on among them, which right now is meeting with very rapid acceptance'; or when they say that the Communists 'in serried ranks, more and more numerous and intense, are carrying out their offensive, and gaining ground in an alarming way among those whose life is spent working'; or the distinguished *Diário de Notícias* when it speaks of 'harmful propaganda' which 'intensifies the discontent of the working class' ...[64]

Given the objective situation, there was little the regime could do to combat this tendency. It had little room for concessions to the working class, and police repression against the PCP was proving much less effective since the Party's reorganisation had tightened up its conspiratorial security. The practical failure and tactical sterility of anarcho-syndicalism, together with the continued absence of an authentic Socialist party, meant that the PCP was the only significant organisation in the working class, and official propaganda was of diminishing efficacy.

The rapid deterioration of the situation, from an official point of view, was fully revealed with the strike wave of October–November 1942 in Lisbon and elsewhere. For the first time in the

history of the regime, what seemed like a co-ordinated series of
mass strikes spread through several industries and threatened to
become a general strike. The action was not openly insurrectionary as in 1934, but it involved larger numbers of workers and
persisted over a period of weeks despite repression. Beginning in
the Lisbon shipyards and docks, the movement spread rapidly
and was estimated to involve some 20,000 workers in such
industries as flour milling, textiles, chemicals, the railways, the
Lisbon Tramways and Gasworks, and the Telephone Company.
The *Avante!* of early November described the increasingly determined actions of different groups of workers in the face of
repression:

This was the case of the stevedores, porters and clerks of the port of
Lisbon who refused to work overtime if family allowance contributions
were discounted from their pay. This was the case of workers in
important firms such as the National Construction Company, Parry and
Sons, CUF, etc., who categorically refused to work overtime unless they
received double pay and without family allowance deductions. This was
the case of the brave and heroic workers of the Lisbon Tramways who,
seeing that their just demands were not being met, began a sit-down
strike. In the Tramway workshops all work came to a halt and many
trams went out of service: many conductors stopped collecting fares.
And the government, finding itself impotent despite making nearly
2,000 arrests in an attempt to make the Tramway workers submit, finally
gave way and released them ...[65]

The government subsequently decreed the militarisation of
public services and made further mass arrests, but the effect was
to provoke further solidarity strikes until the authorities were
forced to grant concessions. It was perfectly true, as affirmed by
official propaganda, that the Communists were deeply involved;
indeed, their influence was growing almost daily. Among those
who were prominent in the organisation and co-ordination of
the struggle was Alfredo Diniz ('Alex'), a worker in the Parry &
Sons shipyard in Cacilhas on the south bank of the Tagus; a
Communist since 1936, he would be elected to the Cental
Committee in 1943 at the age of twenty-six, in large part because
of the leadership qualities he showed at this time.[66]
    Although the outburst of strike activity in October was in part
spontaneous and took many people (including the Government)
by surprise, it was the culmination of a long period of preparation

in which the PCP played a central rôle. Since early in the year the Party had been campaigning in the *sindicatos nacionais* for a general wage increase, but when this pressure finally led to public expressions of concern by the official union leaders, Salazar's response was simple: 'I cannot indicate any other solution but to work and produce more and to limit oneself to consume less' – and this response was translated into action by a decree increasing hours of work and instituting a kind of family allowance (*abono de família*) to be financed in part by workers' contributions.[67] The unpopularity of this can be imagined, and consequently the Party was 'swimming with the tide' when (in late August) it launched the slogans 'For a wage increase without compulsory overtime!' and 'Against the family allowance deduction!'. It urged workers to form broadly-based factory committees to campaign publicly against the unpopular decrees – a proposal which was successfully implemented in several factories. In his Political Report to the 1943 PCP Congress, Cunhal described this strike wave as the first great offensive of the proletariat against the Salazar regime (in contrast to 18 January 1934, the last great defensive action during a period of working-class retreat). In the 1942 struggles, 'Communists and anarchist workers, Republicans and those without party, Catholics and Legionnaires, all united in the struggle against capitalist and fascist exploitation'.[68]

This movement was, however, far from being a total victory for the workers or for the PCP. Important concessions were wrung from the authorities, but many grievances were not resolved and in some cases repression increased. The police offensive against the PCP's clandestine organisation intensified and it was precisely around this time that the reorganised Party suffered its first setback with the arrest of four leading militants (Militão Ribeiro, Joaquim Pires Jorge, Pedro Soares and Júlio Fogaça).[69] The Party also had to admit that it had been taken by surprise in several cases by the spontaneous outbreak of the strikes and by the extent of their success, with the result that it was unable to provide adequate tactical leadership and coordination.[70] But these deficiencies were only to be expected in a movement and a Party which were barely emerging from a long period of retreat and disorganisation. What was most significant, demonstrating that the struggles of 1942 were not just a flash in the pan and that

the Portuguese labour movement was entering a new phase, was
the resurgence of militancy in the following year.

A growing cause of discontent was the shortage of essential
foodstuffs in urban markets, at least in part caused by the
regime's policy of exporting grain, cooking oil and other products
to Germany. Protests against this were already starting to have an
impact; in January 1943 *O Século* reported that the Lisbon City
Council had made 'temporary concessions' because of 'certain
abnormalities' in the supply of produce to the markets.[71] During
the spring and summer the PCP maintained a persistent campaign against shortages of basic staples, denouncing cases of
speculation, hoarding and exports to the Axis:

> The shortage of staples for the workers and the poorer classes
> continues to grow alarmingly. Staples are in short supply because
> Salazar's corporative system has organised the pillage of the country
> by the *grémios*, by the 'regulating' boards and organisations. In the
> corporative organisations the great proprietors, the great wholesalers,
> the great speculators and the great exporters to the 'Axis' are able to
> gorge themselves. Staples are in short supply because large quantities are
> stored in speculators' warehouses and because further large quantities
> are sent, with the government's protection or by its orders, to Spain and
> Germany . . .
>
> Thus for example, every day a goods train runs along the Douro line in
> the direction of Spain. On each wagon there is a sign with the word
> 'Bloco'. When it reaches the border the signs are replaced with others
> which say 'Portuguese surplus'. Salazar condemns the people to hunger
> in order to send staples to the Hitlerite bandits, and on top of that he tries
> to make the world believe that Portugal lives in abundance, since
> 'Portuguese surpluses' are sent out of the country . . .[72]

That same article denounced specific cases, such as a German
agent, Bruno Lesser, who was alleged to have negotiated the
export of more than two million cans of sardines; a cork
merchant in northern Portugal, H. Macedo, whom it accused of
the clandestine export of sugar, coffee, codfish and rice concealed
in cork shipments to Germany; and F. F. Joaquim Pereira da
Silva, an influential customs official who sent two big shipments
of foodstuffs to Spain. These were just a few cases among many
which seriously undermined the Government's paternalistic
image.

That real and widespread hardship was being experienced is
clear from the wave of hunger marches and food riots which

swept the country at this time. In many small towns and villages peasants gathered to prevent grain requisitions or oil shipments for export, or assaulted granaries or warehouses. In a village near Gaia angry women broke into storehouses full of flour said to be destined for export to the Axis, and proceeded to sell it to the public at the official price; a GNR detachment sent to restore order was said to have sided with the people, refusing to take repressive action. In Oliveira de Azeméis about fifty women from the nearby village of Feijões went to the town hall to denounce a certain Sra. Baptista who was said to be hoarding maize for sale to the Axis; they intimidated the local officials who gave orders for all grain in Feijões to be registered and sold to the public for regulation prices. But in a similar case in Macinhata do Vouga, the peasants' initial success in preventing the removal of grain from the town was broken by the arrival of twenty-three GNR, who in this instance, far from siding with the people, opened fire on the crowd, wounding two of them and making arrests.[73] An element of *opéra bouffe* was not lacking in some of these incidents; in Trevões a wealthy proprietor accused of hoarding olive oil for export, 'while in workers' homes there has been no oil for months', narrowly escaped with his life when the population *en masse*, having forced the town councillors to go with them in order to distribute the oil to the people, discovered that the owner had adulterated the oil so that it was suitable only for industrial use; he made a quick exit while the people began stoning his house. As always in times of scarcity and in the absence of effective public inspection of food processing and distribution, adulteration was widespread; in Lisbon a group of women assaulted a grocery which was selling *chouriços* (garlic sausages) filled with sawdust, and destroyed all the produce in the full view of the police.[74]

The gravity of the situation is underlined by the reaction of the authorities, who while reinforcing police patrols and displays of force, also began to take well-publicised measures against speculators and to regulate food distribution. Individual merchants were brought to court on charges relating to black market practices and evasions of regulations, and a special anti-speculation section of the PSP made public appeals for retailers of sugar and potatoes (two of the commodities most affected by the problem) to observe the regulations. Olive oil was another commodity actively traded on the black market, and twenty-three oil producers and merchants were arrested in mid-July in Bragança, Tomar, Santarém and elsewhere.[75] Later in the same month the Government tried a different tactic, appealing to the 'good sense' and 'foresight' of the Portuguese housewife to help overcome the 'difficulties of the present hour' by limiting consumption, but the futility of this approach was implicitly recognised a few days later with the creation (by decree) of a new General Inspectorate of Supply ('Intendência Geral dos Abastecimentos') within the Ministry of the Economy.[76]

Popular discontent over shortages and speculation – and real hunger for some – continued to find vigorous and sometimes violent expression throughout 1943 and in fact until the end of the Second World War and beyond. In June 1945 the Ministry of the Economy increased the subsidy for growing wheat and created a subsidy for the use of fertilisers, while freezing the price of bread to the public;[77] and in October 1946 there were reports of several more trials of merchants accused of speculation in foodstuffs.[78] The Government's efforts to regulate trade in basic staples and its willingness to punish some of the worst black marketeers seems to have had some effect – if it had not been for this, the food riots might have got completely out of hand – but they could not resolve the problem in any fundamental way. The chronic inefficiency of Portuguese agriculture and the privileges accorded to wealthy landowners and traders through the *grémios* and *juntas de lavoura* ensured that food supplies would be precarious, especially in a wartime situation which brought inflation and disrupted grain imports. Much of the peasant and working population clearly saw the problem as one of power and wealth rather than natural scarcity, and acted accordingly against the most obvious culprits. From the Government's point of view there was an evident danger that they would come to see it in broader political terms and would blame the regime rather than a few individual *caciques* and speculators; a radicalised peasant movement under Communist leadership was not necessarily such an impossibility as it may appear with the benefit of hindsight. The pages of *Avante!* for 1943–44 are full of accounts of hunger marches, protests against hoarding and assaults on granaries, often in small towns of the Centre and North – the regions where the PCP had always been weakest.

As forms of pressure on local authorities to enforce the law on rationing and price regulation, or simply to distribute stock-piled goods, *Avante!* urged the people in demonstrations to carry black banners and posters with slogans saying 'We are hungry!', 'We want bread!', 'We want food!' and to form Popular Committees to Control Supply.[79] This was apparently precisely what happened in July 1943 in Vila Real (Trás-os-Montes), in the most remote and backward province in continental Portugal. Since olive oil had become virtually unobtainable there, and the town's deputy mayor was said to be hoarding the product and selling it at high prices to outsiders, a group of women went to the local Board of Trade (Commissão Reguladora do Comércio) to protest. Having been promised action within a few days, they returned several times but without success, until finally on 12 July over 150 women with black banners marched on the town hall to demand the oil; after a brief confrontation the authorities gave way and put the oil on sale at the regulation price. Similarly in Régua – also in the rural North – the consistent failure of the local authorities to enforce price regulations on oil and other staples, and in fact evidence that the mayor and other officials were themselves hoarding these products and selling ration coupons at inflated prices, provoked the natural popular protest – once again led by the women. However, in this case the authorities refused to make any concessions.[80] In Braga also – an industrial town but once again in the Catholic North – a large group of women with a black banner marched on the city hall demanding bread.[81] Dozens of similar protests throughout the country, but especially in the Centre and North, bear witness to widespread discontent among sectors of the population not normally involved in opposition activities; and the PCP, as the only organised force supporting these protests and giving them publicity through its clandestine press, was beginning to acquire influence there.

If the regime was prepared to take at least partially effective action concerning rationing and food distribution, it was much less willing to grant any concessions with regard to wages. Strikes were inevitably met with severe repression, and only after bitter struggle did the workers win significant wage increases. This had been the case in October–November 1942, and it was equally true in the even greater strike wave of July–August 1943. As in the previous year, this was in essence a spontaneous movement of resistance against increasing exploitation and hardship in the main industrial zones, but even more than in 1942 organisation and leadership was assumed by the PCP. From early in the year the Party, determined to overcome the weaknesses of its intervention in the previous movement, had been working in factories and offices to create broadly-based workers' committees through which it could exercise political leadership of the struggle, winning rank-and-file support for its view of the tactics and goals of the strikers. Thus the strike leadership should combine 'the dissemination of the Party's slogans' with 'the clarification, in each enterprise, of the demands which are of particular interest to the workers of that enterprise, and in particular, a decision on how much wages should be increased'. Co-ordination of the movement between different factories and between different towns and regions should be assured.[82] It seems that these preparations were successfully implemented by Communist militants in many workplaces, with the result that PCP leadership and direction of the movement was a reality – to the extent that any such mass movement can be politically directed and controlled.

The movement was preceded in May and June by local struggles of agricultural workers in the Ribatejo and Alentejo for higer wages, and one or two isolated industrial stoppages also (in the Covina glassworks at Póvoa de Santa Iria and the Tejo cement plant, Alhandra).[83] The success of these strikes apparently convinced other workers (and the PCP leadership) that the time was ripe for broader action. On 21 July the Party issued a manifesto calling for a general strike in the Lisbon region in support of demands for a generalised wage increase, double pay for overtime, against deductions for family allowances, against speculation and food shortages.[84] On 26 July the first walkouts occurred in some of the shipyards and other enterprises on the South Bank of the Tagus, followed the next day by the 5,000 workers of the CUF chemical plant in Barreiro and by other shipyards and a soap factory. On the 28th the movement spread rapidly throughout the industrial zone of the south bank and in Lisbon, and soon there were 50,000 workers on strike in a movement without precedent in the history of the dictator-ship.[85] Large demonstrations occurred as well, demanding action from the authorities to provide bread, oil and other staples at reasonable prices. In Barreiro on the 28th the CUF workers marched to the railway sheds and convinced the railwaymen to join them, and so on to other factories; soon there were over 6,000 demonstrators marching on the town hall when they were stopped by police with baton charges and machine-guns which were fired 'into the air' (although several protesters received bullet wounds). Other demonstrations went to Lavradio, Alhos Vedros, and nearby localities, recruiting workers from the cork processing plants, stopping a train on the main Alentejo railway line and cutting telephone and telegraph wires to prevent the summoning of police and troop reinforcements. Some of the local police had refused to use force against the population, and it was only the arrival of large numbers of heavily-armed GNR commanded by regular officers which finally brought the situation under control.[86] In other words, the movement was acquiring an insurrectionary character, and if it were not stopped soon there was no telling what might happen.

Official alarm was revealed, although in muted form, in the censored press. On 29 July the *Diário de Notícias* reported that on the previous day, 'as if it were all following a previously established plan', a number of work stoppages occurred in Lisbon, Barreiro and Almada and 'groups of men and women tried to disturb the peace'. The paper admitted that demonstrators had assaulted certain commercial establishments 'with the pretext that inside there were hoarded foodstuffs', although those involved in the disturbances were people 'who do not have much reason for complaint within the context of the general difficulties'[87] – an implicit recognition of the gravity of the situation. The same report also confirmed the authorities' determination to take firm action with the nomination of Major Jorge Botelho Moniz as 'Special Delegate of the Ministry of War for Industrial Mobilisation' – a measure which clearly contradicted the Minister of the Interior's statement that the work stoppage was not 'a monster strike, in the old style' and was limited to a few shipyards and cork factories 'and one or another factory of lesser importance' on the other bank of the Tagus.[88] Moreover, this attempt to minimise the extent of the strike was totally contradicted by an official statement a couple of days later which listed those factories authorised by the Ministry of War to resume production, and those ordered to remain closed pending further investigations: the first list named fifteen plants, some of them very big, and the second ten, as well as others which were not named. Moreover, another similar announcement over three weeks later revealed that even at this late date there were at least nineteen factories (mainly cork processing plants in Almada, Seixal, Amora and Caramujo) which had not been 'authorised to reopen'.[89] The reason for the 'authorisations' was the Government's desire to purge the labour force in those plants where the most serious disturbances had occurred – and in some cases, to punish employers who did not display sufficient zeal in persecuting strikers.

After the surprise of the first two or three days, the Government dealt with the strikes and demonstrations by massive repression. As well as the use of heavily-armed troops against demonstrators, there were hundreds of arrests and hundreds of workers dismissed by Government order. Botelho Moniz tried to form forced labour battalions, and there were rumours (which do not seem to have been confirmed) that hundreds of workers were going to be transported to the colonies. On 4 August the PCP, deeply divided on how to respond to this huge official counter-offensive, issued a call for a 'tactical retreat', proposing a gradual return to work in order to avoid further repression, confirming whenever possible the concessions granted by employers in the course of the strike. Discussions at the Party Congress later in the year revealed that some comrades concluded subsequently that the signal for retreat should have been given as early as 29 July, immediately after large-scale repression began, or at least on 1 or 2 August; while some workers wanted to continue the strike even beyond 4 August, despite the increasingly difficult conditions.[90] From the Party's point of view, the problem was how to call a halt without losing all that had been gained through the workers' offensive, and how to retain the confidence of the masses and their willingness to launch such an ambitious struggle again in the future, despite the experience of massive repression.

Although the Government did regain control after a week or so and did impose widespread reprisals, the movement could be considered a qualified success both for the workers and the Communist Party. Many employers did make concessions on wages, and the Government did take further measures to improve food distribution and combat speculation. But most important was the increased confidence of the working class and the blow to the myth of the regime's invincibility; the extent and combativity of the strikes and demonstrations took everyone by surprise. There were some defections, although only at local level, from the ranks of the regime: the mayor of Almada and the chief administrator of Seixal both resigned, and quite a few Legionnaires resigned rather than participate in the repression.[91] Cunhal claimed that the Lisbon 'July Days' were a major advance for the PCP:

The first really new aspect ... is that it was a movement prepared, organised, unleashed and directed by a single leadership, namely our Party. No longer [did we experience] surprise at the rapid maturation of the objective conditions. No longer was the Party leadership experiencing difficulty 'as in October–November' in getting information on what was happening. No longer [was there] a Lisbon Regional Committee uncertain about what to do. No longer was the Party losing control of the movement and trailing in the wake of events after a certain point ... In July–August, we witnessed something different. We saw the Party's leading organisations analysing the situation, studying plans and taking measures for the success of the movement. We saw the decisive rôle of the Party in the preparation and unleashing of the strike. We saw the Party's guiding action throughout the movement.[92]

According to Cunhal, the Party even succeeded in persuading the workers to accept its decision on the order in which different factories should enter the strike. Even anarchist workers in practice accepted the Party's leadership, and in one factory the workers insisted that they would only join the movement if it were under Communist leadership.

Even allowing for some exaggeration by Cunhal, it is indisputable that the PCP had now established itself as the dominant force in the Portuguese labour movement. The issue at stake now was whether it could use that dominance to create a mass revolutionary movement capable of overthrowing the regime – a task which was to prove far more difficult, if not impossible. In this, the next four years would be decisive: if World War II and its immediate aftermath did not bring revolutionary conditions, then a further opportunity was likely to be a long time in coming. A crucial issue was the need to strengthen the Party's influence in other regions; it was obviously weak beyond Lisbon and the south bank of the Tagus. In this context, it should be recognised that the July–August strikes were not confined to the Lisbon region; very significantly, there was also an upsurge in the North, in São João da Madeira (a centre of the boot and shoe industry some twenty miles south of Oporto). Local PCP militants evidently took advantage of growing discontent to start a movement which began a week later than in Lisbon; rank-and-file workers' commissions were elected on 3 August, and the strike began on the 5th. The demands were certainly precise and relevant to local concerns: a minimum wage of twenty escudos a day for factory workers and twenty escudos after expenses for domestic workers (important in the shoe trade); an end to piece-work; against the big cattle breeders and for an improved supply of hides and leather – as well as the usual demands for an end to family allowance deductions and for improved food supplies.[93] Some employers were apparently willing to meet these demands, but others, backed by the politically decisive *grémio*, were not; thus on the 5th some 2,000 workers downed tools, and were immediately joined by another 2,000 from the neighbouring industrial villages of Couto, Arrifana, and Nogueira do Cravo. A large demonstration took place and was met by a heavily-armed force of GNR; about eighty workers were arrested, but many were immediately released when the women blocked the road to prevent them being taken to Oporto. On 9 August Botelho Moniz travelled north to coordinate the repression, and during the following weeks large numbers of militant workers, including most of the Communist Party's members in the region, were arrested and beaten or tortured. The repression was so bad that some PCP members concluded that it had been a mistake to launch the São João strikes; Cunhal admitted that the Party organisation suffered a severe blow – 'no other local organisation was so hard hit' – although he defended the action, quoting Lenin to the effect that temporary setbacks and repression have to be expected in civil war.[94] Nevertheless, in his Political Report he was very critical of this organisational failure, and also of the Party's failure to penetrate the Armed Forces; if there had existed a well-organised PCP network among the troops, he said, it would have been possible to save both the Party and the workers in general from such severe repression. Moreover, 'All conditions exist to begin the formation of a national revolutionary military organisation on a large scale' and the Secretariat should take immediate measures to begin this task.[95]

Despite this local setback, and the generalised repression which followed the July-August strikes throughout the country, the Party continued to consolidate its position among the workers and its infiltration of the *sindicatos nacionais*. The working class and peasantry also recovered from the effects of repression, and further localised strikes and protests occurred during the next few months culminating in May 1944 in a third great upsurge of mass struggle against the regime. This time the movement was concentrated in the industrial zones on the northern outskirts of Lisbon, in the Ribatejo (Vila Franca de Xira, Alhandra, Santa Iria) and the *saloio* area: a coordinated series of work stoppages and demonstrations broke out on 8–9 May, involving several thousand workers in construction, cement, stone quarries, glassworks, transportation and shipbuilding (in the capital itself).[96] Once again the movement was heralded by a manifesto of the PCP Secretariat calling on the people to take to the streets demanding bread and staple foodstuffs; in the words of *Avante!*:

> The people must demand bread supplies from the bosses, they must *assault* the buildings (whether stores or private houses) where staples are hoarded and *distribute them among the people*.
> Those who do not eat cannot work. *We must go and find foodstuffs wherever they may be.*[97] (Emphasis in original)

Already in the preceding weeks there had been many local hunger marches and invasions of granaries and bakeries in the Ribatejo and *saloio* areas; and the situation was evidently becoming critical.[98]

Once again the movement was extensive and well coordinated, and the regime's lame attempts to minimise its significance were ineffective and even self-defeating. On 10 May the *Diário de Notícias* carried an article headed 'An Unsuccessful Attempt at a Work Stoppage' in which on the one hand it claimed that the authorities had prior knowledge of the planned strikes, but decided to take no action until after the event, and on the other hand reported what appear to be drastic emergency measures-massive arrests of workers and even managers, compulsory closing of certain factories in order to purge the labour force, etc. As in 1943 also, it claimed that there were very few work stoppages, but then proceeded to give a long list of factories which were affected.[99]

Although the May 1944 strikes were quite extensive and combative, they were not as big as those of the previous year. There is evidence of division within the Party leadership; Alfredo Diniz ('Alex'), a young shipyard worker from the south bank who had been elected to the Central Committee at the 1943 Party Congress, apparently urged that the strike movement should have an openly insurrectional character, whereas Alvaro Cunhal argued that the time was not ripe for this. After the event also, some leading cadres evidently thought that the movement had been a failure – this opinion is attributed to Dias Lourenco – and as in 1943, some thought the strikes had been pushed too far whereas others thought they should have been taken further.[100] It was only to be expected that such tactical differences should arise, and that the Party would make mistakes in its leadership of mass movements; this, however, was less important than the basic issue of consistency in developing and applying a general revolutionary strategy.

With regard to the 1944 movement, there is evidence of weakness in the Party's coordination and leadership of the strikes, but not such as to justify the conclusion of one recent critic, that 'the strikes occurred precisely in those places where the Party had done least to organise them'.[101] The movement did on the whole take place at the time and in the areas for which the Party had prepared; if it failed at all, it was in guiding and developing the strikes once they had begun. But even this failure was only relative; the fact was that once again a massive strike wave, involving tens of thousands of workers and affecting a broad geographical region, had occurred when the PCP had given the signal, in an open and direct challenge to the regime. The Party had shown considerable tactical sensitivity; aware of the dangers of 'adventurism' (of which it was accused, for example, by the 'provocative groupuscule'), it had resisted pressure from militant workers to call the strike as early as February or March. In the words of a Party propaganda sheet issued in March:

WORKERS! SONS AND DAUGHTERS OF THE WORKING CLASS!
In you there lives the will to struggle and triumph which astonished the fascist regime in July–August. Many of you see as the only immediate solution, the resort to strike action ... This inclination is growing among the working masses. Why then does the Communist Party wait to give the word of command? What is the Communist Party waiting for to call the workers out on strike?

Workers! The Communist Party does not lead you into adventures . . . The Communist Party has an exact idea of its responsibility to the working class and will do everything to continue deserving your trust. A correct orientation will lead the working class to victory. A mistaken slogan by the Communist Party can ruin many efforts and sacrifices by the workers. The situation is maturing for another great strike. But at present the conditions are still not ready for it to be carried out successfully . . .[102]

The very fact that the Party issued such a statement shows that its voice was listened to, and that it was striving to maximise the workers' chances of success. Its position as the leading force in the struggle was evidently accepted by large numbers of workers in Lisbon, the south bank of the Tagus, and the Ribatejo.

The lower Ribatejo, an unusually rich and varied area combining both large- and small-scale agriculture and industry, had witnessed an effective PCP organising drive during the previous two years. The region was characterised by that social and economic mix which is often most favourable to radicalisation: recent industrialisation along the main railway line from Lisbon to the north and east; large-scale agriculture in the *lezírias* (rice paddies and cattle pastures) of the Tagus flood-plain, where thousands of underpaid and casually-employed labourers eked out a precarious living in stark contrast to the aristocratic *latifundiários* who raised fighting bulls and thoroughbred horses; small peasant agriculture on the right bank of the Tagus, a wine-producing and market-gardening area serving the Lisbon market; and of course the proximity of the capital, itself, with its traditions of labour militancy and intellectual radicalism. The aristocratic world of the great cattle breeders was vividly portrayed by the great realist novelist Alves Redol: a life of rural hierarchy, paternalistic *bonhomie*, blood-sports and family vendettas. This world was fighting a vigorous rearguard action under the Salazar regime – so favourable to its traditional values-against the encroaching threats of industrialisation and proletarian militancy.[103] Poles apart from this, both materially and ideologically, was the life of the emerging working class in the jumble of factories and workshops, large and small, which stretched from the eastern suburbs of Lisbon to Vila Franca; the wretched living and working conditions of this population are revealed in harrowing detail in the works of another Portuguese neo-realist writer, Soeiro Pereira Gomes. Periera Gomes, who became a prominent member of the Communist Party's local organisation at this time, was chief clerk of the Tagus Cement Co. and as such was one of the numerous group of white-collar and managerial personnel in several companies whose arrest was ordered by the Ministry of War in May 1944 for leniency or complicity in the strike.[104] He escaped by going underground, dedicating what remained of his short life – he died in 1949 at the age of forty – to organising the people whose lives he had described: 'boys who looked like men and who never knew childhood', whose whole existence since infancy had been a struggle for survival.[105] Tuberculosis, bronchitis, diarrhoea, constant hunger and thread-bare clothing, living in miserable shanties which were suffocating and mosquito-ridden in summer, cold and damp in the winter, surviving on casual jobs in tile- and brick-works or at harvest time in the orchards, with long periods of idleness which drove them to petty theft – this was the fate of the band of urchins who are the heroes of Pereira Gomes's best-known work, *Esteiros*, published in 1941. Conditions of skilled or semi-skilled workers with regular jobs in the larger factories were certainly better, but the picture of chronic hardship and insecurity described by this young intellectual romantic (for, despite his bitter neo-realism, a pronounced streak of romanticism runs through Pereira Gomes' works) is not far removed from the reality faced by most Portuguese workers in the 1940s.

Working closely with Pereira Gomes in the preparation and coordination of the Ribatejo strikes was another young Communist militant, Octávio Pato. Only nineteen years old in 1944, Pato came from a family of small peasant proprietors near Vila Franca, and had begun to work in a small shoe factory at the age of fourteen; with other young workers he had very quickly become involved in discussions of socialist ideas and in production of a clandestine news-sheet, and was recruited by Dias Lourenço (PCP organiser in Vila Franca) into the Communist Youth.[106] Described by Mário Soares – with whom he was to work closely a year or two later in the *MUD Juvenil* – as being 'of a very lively intelligence, with an extraordinary sense of organisation and a limitless devotion to the cause to which we dedicated our-selves',[107] Pato plunged into intense and ceaseless activity building a network of contacts and sympathisers throughout the lower Ribatejo, travelling constantly by bike and on foot to distribute propaganda and hold small clandestine meetings. The Party's intervention, whether conducted in total secrecy or with some degree of openness, covered a wide range of activities: not only union issues and building workers' committees, but organising local committees of the MUNAF, promoting community groups independent of the regime, organising sporting and recreational clubs, and so on. In terms of preparation for the strike, for some time before the event the Party was encouraging the formation of workers' unity committees in each factory or among rural workers on each estate; then as the time approached, strike committees were to be formed in each enterprise, mainly if not exclusively of Communist militants or sympathisers; there were also agitation brigades responsible for distributing propaganda, painting slogans on walls, etc.[108] Only this degree of involvement in the everyday life of the local communities would guarantee a mass response when the Party gave the signal; only this degree of coordination would make possible defensive actions to protect the clandestine apparatus from repression when it came. It 1944 the police knew that Communists were very active in the strike movement, but were unable to pinpoint most of the key Party militants involved in the struggle;[109] it was at this time that the Party functionary, Ferreira Marques, mentioned by the PIDE agent Gouveia, was arrested but died in custody without providing any information (supposedly he 'committed suicide'). Also at this time Octávio Pato's brother was arrested and died under torture at PIDE headquarters in Lisbon.[110]

As before, reaction by the authorities to the strike movement was drastic. Large detachments of the GNR were concentrated in the affected districts, together with Legionnaires, and several hundred strikers and demonstrators were arrested and herded into the Vila Franca bullring. Those regarded as 'ringleaders' were transferred to other gaols and detained for long periods, often being tortured; the rest were gradually released. As in 1943, several factories were ordered to remain closed pending investigations to purge the labour force; on 17 May a communiqué of the War Ministry's Industrial Mobilisation Service (Botelho Moniz' office) declared that in no circumstances could strikers be readmitted to work without written permission from the Ministry, and that the affected factories would remain closed for thirty days, or more if necessary.[111] Evidently political and social order was a higher priority than production in the Government's eyes.

Following this third great wave of labour unrest centred in the Lisbon region, the PCP's next priorities were to broaden its support in other classes and regions – above all the peasantry of the north and centre – and to develop a military organisation. These were the Party's main goals during the next few years; and the fact that it ultimately failed in both of these tasks should not lead us to conclude that serious attempts were not made. Regarding the peasant question, as early as May 1942, in one of the key documents to emerge from the reorganisation, it was recognised that the Party had neglected the struggle among the peasantry, the 'principal ally' of the proletariat. Undesirable 'traditions' had grown up which led Communist cadres in rural areas to avoid serious work among the peasantry and in practice to concentrate their efforts on the rural petty bourgeoisie. This implied imposing strict supervision on Party cadres in rural areas, making it obligatory for them to undertake systematic work among the peasants:

Without this general reorientation of the whole activity of Party cadres in rural centres towards the peasant sector, all the guiding slogans and all the activity of the Party's central cadres will be futile, will be no more than impotent gesturing. This firm decision of the Party's C. C. to make a definite shift towards work in the peasant sector *implies punishment of those comrades responsible for rural organisations who do not try to put into effect the Party's instructions,* who remain tied to sectarian work in the commercial and petty-bourgeois milieu of the towns and cities and make no contact with the peasant class.[112] (Emphasis in original)

The long-term goal must be to recruit cadres of peasant origin, but in the meantime it was essential that existing cadres of urban origin should immerse themselves completely in peasant society. These cadres should be workers, not intellectuals, and should base their activity on careful study of specific local conditions.

Party policy recognised that the peasantry was far from being one undifferentiated mass; to begin with, a clear distinction was made between the rural proletariat, especially in the Alentejo – 'the shock brigade' of the peasantry – and the small proprietors and tenants of the centre and north. It was among the latter that the Party's influence was weakest, and therefore greatest efforts must be made. Policies and slogans were proposed to appeal to as many sectors of the peasantry as possible. These included general proclamations against taxes and other government levies or against harassment by the GNR and the forest guards, and specific programs relating to the distribution of rural property, credit problems, State grain requisitions and pricing policies: 'Against the *fintas-braçais* (a kind of labour-due for road maintenance, sometimes commuted into a cash payment) and other municipal impositions!' – 'Abolition of small proprietors' debts to the Caixa Geral dos Depósitos and the Caixas de Crédito Agrícola (official credit institutions)!' – 'For the division of uncultivated land from the great estates!' – 'For freehold possession of uncultivated land sharecropped from the great landlords!' – 'Against grain requisitions by the fascist authorities!'[113]

Undoubtedly these were in general appropriate slogans; peasant resentment of taxation is always a powerful factor; credit problems, be they with private or public sources of funds, are a perennial peasant grievance; rental and sharecropping arrangements would often give rise to friction and the regime's compulsory crop requisitions (of wheat, maize, olive oil and other crops) were extremely unpopular, especially given wartime inflation and scarcities. We have seen how this last issue had indeed begun to destroy social peace in the northern villages, and physical resistance by peasants to crop requisitions was beginning to link up with bread riots by urban workers: both could attribute their problems to Government requisitions, exports to the Axis, and speculation by wealthy merchants. The 1944 Ribatejo disturbances showed this convergence of peasant and worker protests; as the Communist Party proudly proclaimed in a manifesto of June 1944, evaluating the results of the strikes:

The struggle of 8 and 9 May was a great movement of unity of the working people ... Guided by the Communist Party, thousands and thousands of workers and peasants came together as brothers and understood that their interests are the same and that their struggle is the same. The fighting alliance of workers and peasants was sealed for the future ...[114]

This was particularly true in the Ribatejo, where conditions were most favourable to this convergence of worker and peasant struggles; it was less so in the north, but even there the PCP was

making headway. The Central Committee member responsible
for this sector – the 'Douro Regional Committee' – was Joaquim
Pires Jorge, a key figure in the reorganisation.[115] Under his
direction the Party had apparently made significant progress in
developing a network in the Upper Douro and Trás-os-Montes –
precisely one of the areas in which it was to be weakest in
subsequent years. A cadre who confessed under police torture in
October 1945, Miguel Pereira Forjaz de Lacerda, estimated that
during a period of four months (May–August 1944), as courier
responsible for delivering the Party's press to Oporto for the
whole of the northern region, he had transported a total of
12,000 copies of *Avante!* and 1,000 of *O Militante* (this in five
trips). Later (in spring 1945), when Lacerda was responsible for
political supervision on a more local level, he regularly delivered
fifty *Avantes!* and fifteen *O Militantes* to the comrade responsible
for the municipalities of Póvoa do Varzim and Vila do Conde
(north of Oporto), and one hundred *Avantes!* and fifty *O Militantes*
to a series of towns in Trás-os-Montes.[116] In an area of isolated
rural settlements and under clandestine conditions, this is quite
impressive, especially since each newspaper would be read by
several people, often in small groups for the benefit of those who
were illiterate or semi-literate. Until much of it was destroyed in
successive blows by the police between 1945 and 1951, the PCP
had apparently begun to develop a solid organisation in the
northern interior, with a genuine peasant following; where it
failed was in rebuilding this after the disasters of the late forties
and early fifties.

The experience of the destruction of the Party's apparatus in
large areas of the North, despite evidence pointing to an
extensive organisation with strict clandestine discipline, under-
lines the importance of the conspiratorial secrecy imposed on
militants. Party organisational documents lay great stress on
questions of security; a key manual on building factory cells
insisted that no more than five individuals should meet at one
time (and preferably only three or four); that each meeting
should begin with a 'conspiratorial minute' in which those
present agreed on an alibi to which they would all stick if
interrupted and questioned by bosses or police; that written
records should be kept to an absolute minimum, never mention-
ing names of comrades, places and times of meetings, or other

compromising details.[117] The crucial problem, of course, was how
to reconcile these precautions with mass political work – to
make the Party's presence known among the workers, to explain
its line and win their sympathy. It was frequently the difficulty of
reconciling these two needs which led to the discovery and arrest
of Communist cadres by the police; in the last resort, only if broad
support for the Party already existed in a given factory or locality
could mass agitation be carried out without serious risk of
discovery.

The next great wave of workers' struggles did not come until
April 1947, and it was to be the last for a number of years. A
major cycle of militancy was coming to a close, to be followed by
a long period of working-class retreat and retrenchment until the
emergence of a new period of conflict and crisis after 1958. In
1947 it was the turn once again of workers in Lisbon, in the docks
and shipyards, to lead the movement of resistance. It was the
imposition by the Minister of the Navy of compulsory overtime,
beginning in March, which sparked discontent in the shipyards,
and the strike began in the CUF yards on 5 April. On the 7th the
PCP called for a general strike in the Lisbon region, and the
movement spread throughout the shipyards but not to other
sectors.[118] The Ministry of the Interior announced on the 9th the
imposition of measures to 'repress severely' any disturbances
caused by workers failing to report for work because of threats
by 'Communist agitators';[119] the measures imposed were indeed
severe, including the deportation of dozens of workers to
Tarrafal.[120] The PCP emphasised that the Lisbon strike was 'a true
national struggle' with 'national and international repercussions';foreign commentators, including the BBC, had criticised
the extent of repression, thereby embarrassing the Government
which was just at that moment seeking further international
approval.[121] On 26 April the Party urged a return to work after
eighteen days of the strike; in fact on the 15th the attempt to
spread the movement to the Naval Arsenal had failed, and many
workers had returned to work by the 19th. One writer, Ramiro
da Costa, argues that the PCP was over-ambitious in attempting
to spread the strike beyond the shipyards, and seriously out of
touch in waiting so long to call for a return to work; and the
Central Committee did recognise that its manifesto of the 26th
was 'somewhat tardy'.[122] In fact, precisely on 26 April the

authorities announced that the shipyards would reopen 'the day after tomorrow',[123] and although the strike did coincide with some struggles in other sectors – the Lisbon student movement, and labour conflicts among cork workers in the south and textile workers in the North – it was not as successful as previous movements. Clearly the time had come for the Party to reconsider its tactical line for the labour movement.

5 The 'strategy of transition' defeated, 1945–46

It was not only experience on the terrain of mass struggle which was leading some to question the PCP's tactical, and even strategic line. In the Tarrafal prison camp several leading members of the Communist Prisoners' Organisation – Júlio Fogaça, Pedro Soares, João Rodrigues and others – developed from 1943 onwards what they called the 'policy of transition' advocating a peaceful and non-revolutionary change of regime. Influenced apparently by the wartime climate of anti-fascist unity and collaboration between the Western Allies and the Soviet Union, they advocated active involvement in Republican *putschist* conspiracies, efforts to win over dissidents from the fascist camp, and a substantial muting of the revolutionary and class-conscious tone of Communist propaganda (including for example the removal of the hammer and sickle from the masthead of *Avante!*).[124] It is not clear how far they were aware of international developments or even Portuguese events outside the confines of the camp – whether for example they were directly influenced by 'Browderism', the liquidationist tendency in the international Communist movement named after Earl Browder, Secretary-General of the US Communist Party, who advocated dissolution of the Party and its simple incorporation into the broad democratic movement. In any case they did not have to look so far for inspiration: none other than Bento Gonçalves, the former Secretary-General of the PCP who died in Tarrafal in September 1942, had in his final years adopted very right-wing positions, even advocating collaboration with the Salazar regime in the event of a German invasion of Portugal. This 'new policy' (*política nova*) of Gonçalves seems to have been a direct influence on those who now proposed the 'policy of transition'; indeed, as leaders of the Communist Prisoners' Organisation (OCPT) they had worked closely with him in elaborating the *política nova*.[125] Moreover, it appears that they were later explicitly influenced by the Italian example: the 'Badogliada' in which Mussolini was ousted by a bourgeois *coup* led by Marshal Badoglio.[126] Unfortunately they overlooked the fact that Italy at the time was a defeated nation, partially occupied by Allied troops: a situation which scarcely applied to Portugal.

The 'strategy of transition' acquired greater influence in the Party when several of its advocates were among the beneficiaries of the amnesty which in October 1945 allowed many prisoners from Tarrafal to return in freedom to continental Portugal.[127] Fogaça, Soares, Rodrigues, Alvaro de Araújo, Manuel Rodrigues da Silva and others immediately assumed their positions within the PCP apparatus, and began to exert pressure in favour of the new line. Some, such as Fogaça, were experienced and respected comrades who had occupied leadership positions in the thirties or during the reorganisation (and Fogaça was re-elected to the Central Committee at the Second Illegal Congress in August 1946). Their line did not win the Party – there was too much opposition from 'hard-liners' such as Cunhal, José Gregório and Pires Jorge – but it undoubtedly had an influence; this was only to be expected given the rapidly changing international situation and the confusion caused in Portugal by Salazar's astute 'democratic' manoeuvres in 1945.

In August–October 1945 events in Portugal did lend credence to the idea of a gradual and peaceful liberalisation of the regime (although one might have expected greater scepticism and caution from experienced revolutionaries just emerging from prolonged internment in a concentration camp). Salazar's famous 'as free as in free England' speech, the liberalisation of the electoral law, the partial relaxation of censorship, and the amnesty itself – freeing ninety-eight of the two hundred political prisoners in Tarrafal and Peniche;[128] these reforms could be seen as the timid beginning of a real liberalisation such as we have seen in more recent times in Spain or Argentina, or – of more immediate relevance to Portugal in 1945 – as a prelude to the type of process which forced Getúlio Vargas to abandon power in Brazil in that very year. The spirit of 'national reconciliation' which prevailed in recently-liberated countries such as Italy and France, with Communists participating in government alongside liberal bourgeois and even conservative parties, reinforced these visions of peace and harmony.

That the 'policy of transition' did not win a majority on the PCP's Central Committee or in the 1946 Party Congress is testimony to the consistency and class-consciousness (some would no doubt call it dogmatism) of the bulk of the Party leadership. The Party had after all consistently warned against illusions that 'Salazar would fall with Hitler', or with the opening of the Second Front, or with a Labour victory in Britain, etc.; and its scepticism regarding the 1945 'liberalisation' was also proved absolutely correct. Leftist critics have argued that, despite the public statements, the Party did in practice share such illusions. Thus Fernando Rosas has recently produced evidence of secret contacts during the war between the PCP and the British secret service, and on the basis of this and of a textual analysis of the Party's statements on the international situation from 1939 to 1945 he argues that the PCP in practice functioned 'essentially as a pressure group keeping watch on the Salazarist government, in accordance with the interests of the Western Allies and of England in particular':

To prevent Salazar's entry into the War, first – these are the several variants of the 'policy of neutrality'; to oblige him to take decisive actions in support of the Allies (Azores, the wolfram question, etc.), later – this is the phase of militant support for the U. N.. The promised reward would be the PCP's participation in a future government to emerge from elections which were guaranteed to be free. But the illusions then propagated and encouraged by the PCP and the oppositionists in general to wait for a miraculous redemption to be effected by the Western allies, these illusions were swept away by the wind and by the allies themselves, who had after all other allies here, reliable, tried and trusted.[129]

This interpretation seems manifestly tendentious and exaggerated: whatever the PCP's contacts with British (or other) secret services – only to be expected in a war situation when all kinds of eventualities had to be anticipated – its public statements always manifested caution (and at times open hostility) towards the Western Allies; and it is stretching credibility to suggest that the PCP could have influenced Salazar in regard to the Azores bases or the wolfram shipments to Germany. Moreover, to lump the PCP together with 'oppositionists in general' as guilty of spreading illusions about a 'miraculous redemption' at the hands of the

Western Allies, when from 1942 onwards *Avante!* had repeated *ad nauseam* explicit and vigorous warnings against such illusions, is gross distortion of the evidence. The PCP's line, both publicly and in its clandestine organisation, was and continued to be one of popular insurrection; its problem was its inability to bring about the promised insurrection, not any secret proclivity to favour the reformist or *putschist* illusions of the liberal opposition.

The proponents of the 'policy of transition', although defeated within the Party, were not expelled. According to Cunhal this was because they did not go so far as to constitute a 'fraction', but accepted Party discipline and submitted when their line was defeated at the Second Clandestine Congress; indeed, once the issue was resolved, four of them were elected to the Central Committee at that Congress.[130] The Marxist-Leninists argue that this was a serious mistake which facilitated the later ascendency of the opportunist and revisionist tendencies. They see Cunhal's rôle as being ambiguous and conciliatory, and the Second Clandestine Congress as representing a step backwards in the Party's political line; although his political report condemned the 'policy of transition' as opportunist, his emphasis on unity – 'the unity of all honourable Portuguese' – is criticised as having subordinated the proletariat to the liberal bourgeoisie within the anti-fascist movement:

... From this line of Unity there follow concessions to the liberal politicians which allow them to capture the leadership of the MUD, the dissolution of the Communist Youth [substituted by the *MUD Juvenil*], the dissolution of the GAC's, the abandonment of the 'excessive class language' used in the 1941–1945 period.[131]

There is some validity in these criticisms – the dissolution of the GAC's clearly represented a step away from the insurrectionary line in practice, even if it were only tactical; but the question of hegemony in the leadership of the MUD was a thorny one. To insist on Communist control of the key positions in a broad electoral front of this kind could only lead to its destruction as an unitary opposition organisation; it might be different in countries which had just emerged from a process of liberation through armed struggle (as for example, in their different ways, Greece, Yugoslavia and Albania), but in Portugal the liberal bourgeoisie was too strong to be simply pushed aside. If the PCP insisted on such a policy, it would merely isolate itself in a sectarian ghetto.

There were other issues raised or implied at the 1946 Party Congress which were of greater potential significance for the Party's future. The question of the peasantry was discussed again, and it had to be recognised that little progress had been made on this front. It was decided to begin publication of a special clandestine newspaper for the peasantry, *O Camponês*; but time was to show that this paper was oriented primarily towards the rural proletariat of the Alentejo and Ribatejo (where the Party was already making progress) rather than the smallholding peasantry. It is also essentially true, as Francisco Martins Rodrigues argues,[132] that the Party's policy of anti-fascist unity placed greater emphasis on unity with the liberal bourgeoisie of the MUNAF and the MUD than with the peasantry. A second major problem was that of the development of the mass movement and its relationship to the famous 'national anti-fascist uprising'. The Party's success in stimulating and leading mass strikes and protests had reached an impasse, in that the simple repetition of the same type of struggle could only become futile and frustrating after a while; the very success of these movements posed the need to pass on to a different and higher level of struggle, moving closer to the political goal of armed insurrection. But this was precisely what the Party seemed incapable of doing, and in the lack of any such clear perspective, popular militancy could only decline – as would begin to become apparent with the 1947 strike.

This Second Illegal Congress, held in August 1946 in an elegant country house on the outskirts of Lousã (near Coimbra), occurred at a crucial moment in the Party's history, when it had more members than at any other time during the dictatorship (except possibly in 1961–63), and at a time of crisis for the regime, faced with internal dissension and external pressures (the question of Portuguese admission to the United Nations raised embarrassing problems for the Western powers, who would undoubtedly have welcomed at least a partial liberalisation in Lisbon).[133] It is very difficult to be precise about the Party's actual membership, but Manuel Garcia and Lourdes Maurício, apparently basing themselves on PIDE records, give an estimate of 'about seven thousand' for 1945–47: 'a truly extraordinary number, taking into account the conditions of repression at that time and the size of the Portuguese labour force; extraordinary in relation to the membership of other Communist Parties in similar circumstances'.[134] No other opposition Party or group was even remotely comparable in either size or organisation. The Party had achieved this stature despite increasing police harassment; from 1945 onwards the PIDE maintained a special brigade- that of José Gonçalves – exclusively for hunting down Communists.

The intensified police vigilance did cause problems for the PCP. In June or July 1945 PIDE agents arrested two Party cadres who were disembarking in Lisbon from the trans-Tagus ferry: Joaquim António Campino, responsible for the Party's network in the Alentejo, and Orlando Juncal da Silva, an Oporto lawyer in charge of the Party's intellectual sector in that city. On the basis of Campino's or Juncal's diary notes they were able to intercept Alfredo Diniz ('Alex') at a clandestine meeting just outside Lisbon, shooting him rather than allowing him to escape; and the diary notes of 'Alex' in turn led to the location of the clandestine house where Guy Lourenço and Piteira Santos lived.[135] But worse than this, some arrested cadres inevitably confessed under police interrogation, with serious consequences.

Whatever the circumstances which led to the confessions of certain Party cadres – and it takes little imagination to envisage the torments they endured, which in some cases at least have been widely reported- the consequences for the PCP were potentially catastrophic. Court records containing transcripts of PIDE interrogations show that if and when a cadre did crack, the confession that followed was extensive and detailed; and there is in general little reason to question their authenticity. This was the case of Dalila Duque da Fonseca, a thirty-four-year-old woman from the Cape Verde Islands whose brother, Alvaro, had been expelled from the Party because of differences relating to the reorganisation. Dalila was arrested in the summer of 1945 at the Party's clandestine HQ for the whole northern region, the house in São Romão do Coronado where she was living with Joaquim Pires Jorge and Francisco Inácio da Costa. This house was discovered through information given by Da Costa, recently arrested while travelling at Monção, near the Spanish frontier. When the police arrived at São Romão do Coronado, Pires Jorge was not present but Dalila was captured along with a large quantity of documentation.[136] Under interrogation in Lisbon in

September 1945, Dalila gave a full and apparently frank account of her clandestine activities. She explained how she had been contacted in Lisbon on 2 December 1944 by 'Alex' (Alfredo Diniz) and persuaded to live and work in clandestinity with Pires Jorge (whose _companheira_ she had been before, in 1941–42). She described the contact with Pires Jorge in Oporto, the beginning of her clandestine work with him at a Party house in Maia (near Oporto), and the move from that house to São Romão do Coronado on 27 January 1945. Using the pseudonym of 'Maria', she was responsible for the housekeeping, for typing internal reports and memoranda, for translating foreign documents, and for keeping accounts of Party dues collections and donations to the Party from sympathisers. She gave names and psuedonyms of other comrades who at different times shared the house with her and Pires Jorge, and of other cadres with whom she had contact. She knew little of the higher-level Party organisational and political work carried on by Pires Jorge, since all the relevant documentation was in code and was not discussed with her. She also revealed that, in effect, her arrest and the discovery of the precious archive was a result of over-confidence on the part of Pires Jorge: when Da Costa's unexplained absence was noticed, Pires Jorge had not taken the normal precaution of moving all comrades and all important documents to another location so as to prevent detection by the police. He apparently did not believe that Da Costa would inform, and concluded that there was no urgent need to move.[137] In one sense his confidence may have been justified; according to Gouveia, Da Costa did not at first give information voluntarily (or, one may surmise, under torture); rather, it was extracted from him by a ruse. The PIDE planted an agent in his cell, masquerading as 'Rafael' (João Lopes dos Santos), another Party cadre recently arrested in Lisbon; Da Costa did not know Dos Santos personally, although he was aware (through the Party network) of the latter's arrest. The police had prepared their 'plant' well enough to convince Da Costa that he was genuine, and to draw Da Costa into a lengthy conversation about his own work, revealing abundant information which was then passed on to the fake prisoner's superiors.[138]

This entire tragic episode underlined for the PCP the absolute necessity to apply strictly, even rigidly, the norms of clandestine secrecy. Obviously Da Costa should not have confided in another

'Party cadre' whom he did not know personally, however convincing the imposter appeared; and Pires Jorge should have applied immediately the rule that clandestine installations should be moved when any cadre who knew of their location was arrested, regardless of the trust he placed in Da Costa. It was for this reason that Pires Jorge was censured by the Secretariat of the Central Committee, and Da Costa was subsequently expelled. Although it was understandable that some cadres should crack under duress, the Party could not afford to relax on this issue.

Among those arrested in 1945, others who gave abundant information to the police were Miguel Forjaz de Lacerda and his wife Armanda. We have already seen that the husband's confession revealed a great deal about the PCP network in Trás-os-Montes and the Minho coast. His wife Armanda, who like Dalila Duque da Fonseca had performed a combination of domestic chores and clerical duties, had less detailed knowledge of names and organisational links, but her statement certainly helped the police to piece together information extracted from other informants.[139] Similarly, statements obtained from other militants arrested at this time gave the authorities detailed knowledge of the PCP network in the North, on the south bank of the Tagus and the coastal area of the Alentejo, and also of its military contacts and the intimacy of its work with the MUNAF. This had consequences outside the Party as well: information was given of the membership of local MUNAF committees, with names of Republicans, Socialists, Freemasons and independents – often local notables who could not take refuge in clandestinity. Thus the membership of the Oporto Committee of the MUNAF was revealed by Juncal da Silva who had served as PCP representative on this committee.[140] It is more than possible that the police already had this information, given the lack of clandestine security characteristic of liberal professionals; but we do not know this for sure, and it was regrettable that details of the broad anti-fascist resistance should be leaked by a member of its most militant and dedicated organisation. Potentially even more damaging was the information about the Party's military contacts: in Piteira Santos' archive the police found various documents relating to the military networks of both the Party and the MUNAF, as well as plans of military barracks and installations in the Lisbon area, Abrantes, Penafiel, Ota, Vila Franca and else-

where.[141] The Party, then, had evidently been doing serious work
on the military front – work which was rendered completely
useless by this breach of security.

The expulsions, sanctions and new rigorous precautions
imposed by the Party leadership in late 1945 and 1946 did
temporarily 'stop the rot', so that at the time of the Second
Clandestine Congress the Party was still in a strong position.
Cunhal's Political Report to the 1946 Congress was bold and
confident, defending essentially the same line put forward in
1943. He rightly emphasised once again the futility of expecting
the regime to fall through external pressures or gradual liberal-
isation- given the current situation – and criticised once again
the *putschist* solution. Even with civilian participation, he said, a
putsch was a *putsch*, and offered no solution in the Portuguese
context:

There are in history, it is true, examples of victorious military coups.
This becomes possible when governments have neither a solid base of
support, nor a strongly organised repressive apparatus, nor trustworthy
military commanders; when the rulers themselves are already hesitant,
or when it is not a question of a profound change in national politics. In
such situations victorious military coups were possible during the 1910
Republic.

Today the situation is different. Despite the democratic spirit of many
honourable officers and of our soldiers and sailors, fascism has
trustworthy commanders, it has a vast spy apparatus in the armed
forces, it can count on the desperate support of a handful of unpatriotic
exploiters and of individuals who are criminally complicit with fascist
policies. In these conditions, either the conspirators do not succeed in
getting enough supporters to have the courage to take action, or, having
committed themselves too far to withdraw, they decide to act and are
then defeated. The history of the anti-fascist struggle in our country is
full of examples of one or the other of these alternatives.[142]

More than once, Cunhal pointed out, such illusions had come to
predominate within the National Council of Anti-Fascist Unity,
whose members would begin to talk as if freedom and legality
had already arrived – illusions against which the PCP had to
struggle in virtual isolation. More than once, he insisted, the PCP
had saved the opposition from dangerous adventures. The Party
had been asked to participate in *coup* attempts, either by using its
clandestine military network, by mobilising the workers in support of a coup, or by using its underground technical apparatus;
but it had always refused to fall into the trap.[143]

The alternatives to *putsch*ism, Cunhal maintained, were two. The first, which as in 1943, he did not exclude, was the possibility of a *pronunciamento* by leading figures in the regime; in a sense, another type of *putsch*, but one which was totally out of the control of the opposition. Cunhal still maintained that if this were to happen, the Party should welcome it by mobilising the masses in order to radicalise the situation. However, this was clearly no basis for a revolutionary strategy. The other alternative, and the only correct one, was the 'national uprising': the mass insurrection against fascism which the Party had been advocating since the reorganisation. But to insist on the 'national uprising' did not mean that conditions were ripe for it to occur. As Cunhal admitted, 'An insurrection cannot be decreed' – and to attempt to bring it about by decree would be to apply to popular insurrection the principles of the *putsch*. Rather, the Party's duty was to work constantly to bring about a revolutionary situation, to contribute by its mass agitation and propaganda to creating the 'general national strike' in which insurrection could occur, to raise the fighting spirit of the masses and give them experience of active resistance to the fascist regime, to draw new groups and sectors into the popular movement.

Such a strategy, however, was difficult to apply in the absence of concrete indications that progress was being made in 'creating the conditions' for the future insurrection. Unless the mass movement maintained a steadily increasing momentum, or the Party could point to specific advances in the preparation of its political and military network, scepticism and discouragement were bound to set in. Clearly the PCP itself was not immune to such scepticism; Cunhal had to admit that:

Caricaturing the Party's orientation, there was one comrade who said that the Party had put the question in the following way. 'The national uprising will come one day, until then we will continue to organise reformist struggles'. Naturally, comrades, this is a caricature in bad taste. We regard partial struggles precisely as the road towards the national uprising, and in this respect our Party's error was, at most, to insist too much.[144]

But it is by no means clear that many Party militants, let alone those outside the Party, found this argument convincing. To continue to insist that insurrection was around the corner, or at the end of a relatively short and visible road, when conditions were if anything becoming less revolutionary, was to invite disbelief and disillusionment. This was not yet happening on a large scale – in 1946–47 the momentum of the war years was still close and the popular movement still vigorous, even if showing signs of having reached a plateau – but in the late forties and early fifties this trend would affect the morale of many in the anti-fascist movement. And if the Party did not modify its line to take account of this, it was bound to lose support except among the hard-core minority. The 'line of transition', the reformist strategy proposed by the Tarrafal group, might not be the answer; but some modification of the Party's line was clearly necessary to take account of the changing national situation. A really new and effective strategy was never devised, and the PCP never entirely escaped from its vacillation between the Scylla of abstract insurrectionism and the Charybdis of liberal reformism.

Notes to Chapter III

1 Bento Gonçalves, a lathe operator at the Naval Arsenal in Lisbon, is described in PCP documents as having been mainly responsible for the reorganisation of 1929 and as Secretary-General of the Party from that time until his death in 1942. Other sources suggest that a more important role in 1929 and subsequently was played by José de Sousa and Júlio César Leitão (e.g. José Pacheco Pereira, 'Problemas da história do PCP', in *O Fascismo em Portugal: Actas do Colóquio realizado na Faculdade de Letras em Março de 1980*, Lisboa, 1982, A Regra do Jogo, p. 276).

2 On the '18th of January', see L. H. Afonso Manta (ed.), *O 18 de Janeiro de 1934: Do movimento de resistência proletária à oftensiva fascista*, Lisboa, 1975, Assírio e Alvim; Edgar Rodrigues, *Breve História do Pensamento e das Lutas Sociais em Portugal*, Lisboa, 1977, Assírio e Alvim, pp. 245–56;and *Estudos sobre o Comunismo*, No.2, Janeiro a Abril de 1984, publicado em Agosto de 1984, pp. 5–60.

3 R. A. H. Robinson, *Contemporary Portugal: A History*, London, 1979, George Allen & Unwin, p. 66; Tom Gallagher, *Portugal: A Twentieth-Century Interpretation*, Manchester, 1983, M. U. P., p. 86.

4 Author's interview with Alvaro Cunhal, Lisbon, 26 June 1978; and *Biografia do Camarada Alvaro Cunhal*, 1954, Edicões 'Avante!' (In 3o. Juizo Criminal de Lisboa, Processo No. 14499 de 1949, Apenso (1956), 1o. Volume, fl. 31).

5 Francisco Martins Rodrigues, *Elementos para a História do Movimento Operário e do Partido Comunista em Portugal*, Lisboa, n. d., Edições Militão Ribeiro, p. 25; Fernando Gouveia, *Memórias de um Inspector da PIDE: 1. A Organização Clandestina do PCP*, Lisboa, 1979, Roger Delraux, p. 109.

6 Francisco Ferreira ('Chico da C. U. F.'), *26 Anos na União Soviética,*

Lisboa, 1975, Ed. Fernando Ribeiro de Mello / Afrodite, pp. 69–70 and 168; Gouveia, *Memorias*, pp. 117–21; João Arsénio Nunes, 'Da Política 'Classe contra Classe' às origens da estratégia anti-fascista; Aspectos da Internacional Comunista entre o VI e o VII Congressos (1928–1935)', in *O Fascismo em Portugal*, p. 68, note.

7 Alvaro Cunhal, *Rumo à Vitória: As Tarefas do Partido na Revolução Democrática e Nacional*, Lisboa, 1975, Edições 'A Opinião', p. 274.

8 Alvaro Cunhal, *Relatório da Actividade do Comité Central ao VI Congresso do PCP*, Lisboa, 1975, Edições 'Avante!', p. 191.

9 See the programmatic documents quoted in L. H. Afonso Manta (ed.), *A Frente Popular Antifascista em Portugal*, Lisboa, 1976, Assírio e Alvim, pp. 49–76.

10 *Avante!*, II Série No. 32, 1a. Quinzena de Abril de 1937, quoted in Afonso Manta (ed.). *A Frente Popular*, pp. 163–5.

11 *Objectivos e Táctica da Frente Popular*, Abril 1938, Edições 'Avante!' (In 3o. Juízo Criminal de Lisboa, Processo No. 14499 de 1949, 6o. Volume, fl. 399). The document was seized from Cunhal's archive when he was arrested in March 1949. Cunhal's authorship is uncertain, since among other things he was in gaol from July 1937 to June 1938; but it could have been drafted before his arrest, or for that matter written in prison and smuggled out. In any case, whoever was responsible for the actual text, its significance lies with its correspondence with the line adopted by the Party leadership after 1941.

12 *Ibid.*, pp. 3–6.

13 *Ibid.*, p. 9.

14 *Ibid.*, pp. 10–15.

15 Martins Rodrigues, *Elementos PCP*, p. 26; *Biografia do Camarada Alvaro Cunhal*.

16 Francisco Miguel, *Uma Vida na Revolução*, Lisboa, 1977, A Opinião, pp. 81–2; Gouveia, *Memórias*, p. 364.

17 'Duarte' (Alvaro Cunhal), *Sobre a Actividade do Grupelho Provocatório*, Informe presentado no I Congresso Ilegal do PCP, 1944, Edições 'Avante!', pp. 5–11 (In 3o. Juízo Criminal de Lisboa, Processo No. 14499 de 1949, 6o. Volume, fl. 393).

18 *Temas de Estudo*, Maio de 1942, Partido Comunista Português, p. 2 (In 3o. Juízo Criminal de Lisboa, Processo No. 14499 de 1949, 6o. Volume, fl. 371).

19 Martins Rodrigues, *Elementos PCP*, p. 26.

20 *Ibid.*, p. 30; *Biografia do Camarada Alvaro Cunhal*; Gouveia, *Memórias*, p. 128.

21 Pacheco Pereira, 'Problemas', p. 284.

22 Martins Rodrigues, *Elementos PCP*, p. 30; *Biografia do Camarada Alvaro Cunhal*. Another source (Carlos da Fonseca, *História do Movimento Operário e das Ideias Socialistas em Portugal, I. Cronologia*, Lisboa, n. d., Publicações Europa-América, p. 196) gives the date of these arrests as October 1942.

23 Gouveia, *Memorias*, p. 175.

24 *Ibid.*, pp. 131 & 137–48.

102 *Fascism and resistance in Portugal*

25 *Estudos sobre o Comunismo*, No. O, Julho de 1983, 'Uma carta de Júlio Fogaça ao jornal "Primeiro de Janeiro"', p. 32, and No. 1, Setembro a Dezembro de 1983, 'Documentos sobre uma tentativa de contacto entre o Bureau Político do PCP (Júlio Fogaça) e a IC em 1941'.
26 Mário Soares, *Portugal Amordaçado: depoimento sobre os anos do fascismo*, Lisboa, 1974, Arcádia, p. 23.
27 Martins Rodrigues, *Elementos PCP*, p. 31.
28 *Ibid.*, p. 62.
29 *Avante!*, VI Série No. 44, 2a. Quinzena de Novembro de 1943.
30 Cunhal, *Sobre a Actividade do Grupelho Provocatório*, pp. 5–6.
31 *Ibid.*, pp. 6–7.
32 Gouveia, *Memorias*, p. 171.
33 *Ibid.*, p. 172.
34 *Ibid.*, pp. 223–4; Martins Rodrigues, *Elementos PCP*, pp. 30–2; and various PCP sources.
35 The summary of PCP clandestine organisation is based on a variety of Party sources, including the author's interviews with members of the Central Committee, and also on the accounts of Gouveia, Silva Marques and others: J. A. Silva Marques, *Relatos da Clandestinidade: O PCP visto por dentro*, Lisboa, 1976, Edições Jornal Expresso.
36 *Avante!*, VI Série No. 44, 2a. Quinzena de Novembro de1943: 'Mais uma Grande Vitória – O I Congresso do Partido Comunista'.
37 *A Luta pelo Pão, pela Liberdade e pela Independência do Povo Português*, Informe Político ao lo. Congresso Ilegal do Partido Comunista Português, Informante: Camarada Duarte, lo. fascículo, pp. 2–3 (In Tribunal da Boa Hora, Processo No. 16, 016–C, 1961, 3o. Volume, fl. 231).
38 *Ibid.*, lo. fascículo. pp. 4–5.
39 *Ibid.*, 2o. fascículo. pp. 11–12.
40 *Ibid.*, 2o. fascículo, p. 2, quoting Bento Gonçalves' report to the VII Comintern Congress.
41 *Ibid.*, 2o. fascículo, pp. 4–5.
42 *Tarefas de Organização*, Informe do Secretariado do Comité Central sobre a questão de organização, lo. Congresso Ilegal do Partido Comunista Português, Informante: Camarada Santos, pp. 14–15 (In 3o. Juízo Criminal de Lisboa, Processo No. 14499 de 1949, 6o. Volume, fl. 395).
43 *lo. Congresso Ilegal do PCP: Resoluções*, 1943, Edições 'Avante!', pp. 8–9 (In 3o. Juízo Criminal de Lisboa, Processo No. 14499 de 1949, 6o. Volume, fl. 397).
44 *A Luta pelo Pão*, 2o. fascículo, pp. 5–6.
45 *Ibid.*, 2o. fascículo, pp. 6–7.
46 *Tarefas de Organização*, pp. 12–13; *lo. Congresso Ilegal do PCP: Resoluções*, pp. 7–8.
47 Martins Rodrigues, *Elementos PCP*, p. 31; Ramiro da Costa, *Elementos para a História do Movimento Operário em Portugal, 1820–1975*, Lisboa, 1979, Assírio e Alvim, 2o. Volume, p. 64.
48 *A Luta pelo Pão*, 2o. fascículo, p. 8.

49 *Circular aos Comités Regionais, Locais e de Zona e aos responsáveis de célula,* November 1943 (signed by the Secretariat of the PCP's Central Committee), p. 1 (In 3o. Juízo Criminal de Lisboa, Processo No. 14499 de 1949, 6o. Volume, fl. 378).

50 *Ibid.,* pp. 1–2.

51 'A nossa posição', in *Avante!,* IV Série No. 11, Janeiro de 1944. Capitals in original. I wish to thank Alex Macleod of the University of Quebec in Montreal for making this material available to me.

52 'Basta! Os Comunistas não são terroristas!', in *Avante!,* IV Série, Número Especial, Maio de 1944; and 'Provocação e Traição' in *ibid.,* Julho de 1944 (no number).

53 *A Luta pelo Pão,* 2o. fascículo, pp. 13–15.

54 *Ibid.,* 3o. fascículo, pp. 2–3.

55 *Tarefas de Organização,* pp. 19–20.

56 *1o. Congresso Ilegal do PCP: Resoluções,* pp. 9–10.

57 *A Luta pelo Pão,* 3o. fascículo, p. 4: 'O anarquismo continua tendo influência ideológica na classe operária e, por vezes até, camaradas, manifesta-se, sob formas variadas, no nosso próprio Partido.'

58 *Ibid..*

59 *Ibid.,* 3o. fascículo, pp. 6–9.

60 *Ibid.,* 3o. fascículo, p. 10.

61 *Ibid.,* 4o. fascículo, p. 1.

62 *Ibid.,* 4o. fascículo, p. 4.

63 *Ibid.,* 4o. fascículo, p. 10.

64 *Avante!,* VI Série No. 11, Junho de 1942.

65 *Ibid.,* VI Série No. 20, 1a. Quinzena de Novembro de 1942.

66 Da Fonseca, *História do Movimento,* p. 196; Da Costa, *Elementos,* 2o. Volume, p. 66; *Avante!,* VI Série No. 81, Outubro de 1945

67 *A Luta pelo Pão,* 1o. fascículo, p. 9.

68 *Ibid.,* 1o. fascículo, pp. 9–10.

69 Da Fonseca, *História do Movimento,* p. 196.

70 *A Luta pelo Pão,* 1o. fascículo, pp. 10–11.

71 *O Século,* 6 January 1943.

72 *Avante!,* VI Série No. 30, 1a. Quinzena de Abril de 1943. See also *Avante!,* VI Série No. 24, 1a. Quinzena de Janeiro de 1943; VI Série No. 27, 2a. Quinzena de Fevereiro de 1943; VI Série No. 31, 2a. Quinzena de Abril de 1943; and VI Série No. 32, Maio de 1943.

73 *Ibid.,* VI Série No. 31, 2a. Quinzena de Abril de 1943.

74 *Ibid.,* VI Série No. 32, Maio de 1943.

75 *Diário de Notícias,* 14 July 1943.

76 *Ibid.,* 23 & 29 July 1943.

77 *O Século,* 1 July 1945.

78 *Diário de Notícias,* 29 October 1946.

79 *Avante!,* VI Série No. 39, 1a. Quinzena de Setembro de 1943; VI Série No. 38, 2a. Quinzena de Agosto de 1943; and VI Série No. 31, 2a. Quinzena de Abril de 1943.

80 *Ibid.,* VI Série No. 39, 1a. Quinzena de Setembro de 1943.

81 *Ibid.,* VI Série No. 33, 1a. Quinzena de Junho de 1943.

82   *A Luta pelo Pão*, 1o. fascículo, pp. 11–13. Cunhal was quoting the directions given in an *Avante!* article of January 1943, and arguing that these directions had in the main been successfully implemented.
83   *Avante!*, VI Série No. 33, 1a. Quinzena de Junho de 1943; VI Série No. 34, 2a. Quinzena de Junho de 1943; and VI Série No. 35, 1a. Quinzena de Julho de 1943.
84   *Ibid.*, VI Série No. 38, 2a. Quinzena de Agosto de 1943.
85   *Ibid.*; Martins Rodrigues, *Elementos PCP*, pp. 28–9; and Da Fonseca, *História do Movimento*, p. 196.
86   *Avante!*, VI Série No. 38, 2a. Quinzena de Agosto de 1943; and VI Série No. 39, 1a. Quinzena de Setembro de 1943.
87   *Diário de Notícias*, 29 July 1943.
88   *Ibid.*, 30 July 1943.
89   *Ibid.*, 31 July; 1, 2, 3 and 24 August 1943.
90   *Avante!*, VI Série No. 39, 1a. Quinzena de Setembro de 1943; VI Série No. 40, 2a. Quinzena de Setembro de 1943; and VI Série No. 46, 1a. Quinzena de Janeiro de 1944; and *A Luta pelo Pão*, 1o. fascículo, pp. 15–17.
91   *Avante!*, VI Série No. 39, 1a. Quinzena de Setembro de 1943.
92   *A Luta pelo Pão*, 1o. fascículo, p. 14.
93   *Avante!*, VI Série No. 40, 2a. Quinzena de Setembro de 1943.
94   *A Luta pelo Pão*, 1o. fascículo, pp. 17–18.
95   *Ibid.*, 1o. fascículo, p. 19.
96   Da Costa, *Elementos*, 2o. Volume, pp. 68–9.
97   *Avante!*, VI Série No. 53, 1a. Quinzena de Maio de 1944.
98   *Ibid.*, VI Série No. 52, 2a. Quinzena de Abril de 1944; and VI Série No. 53, 1a. Quinzena de Maio de 1944.
99   *Diário de Notícias*, 10 May 1944.
100   Pacheco Pereira, 'Problemas', pp. 272–3.
101   *Ibid.*.
102   *Trabalhadores! Este é o Caminho que o Partido Comunista Indica!* (PCP clandestine pamphlet), March 1944, pp. 2–3 (In 3o. Juízo Criminal de Lisboa, Processo No. 14499 de 1949, 6o. Volume, fl. 374).
103   For a vivid description of this, see António Alves Redol, *Barranco de Cegos*, Lisboa, 1983, Publicações Europa-América (first published 1961).
104   *Diário de Notícias*, 14 May 1944.
105   Soeiro Pereira Gomes, *Esteiros*, Lisboa, 1979, Edições 'Avante!', p. 184.
106   *Conversando com Octávio Pato*, Lisboa 1976, Edição da SIP do PCP, pp. 3–4.
107   Soares, *Portugal Amordaçado*, pp. 118–9.
108   Author's interview with Octávio Pato, Lisbon, 4 March 1977.
109   Gouveia, *Memórias*, p. 175.
110   On Ferreira Marques, see Gouveia, *Memórias*, p. 175; on Carlos Pato, see Soares, *Portugal Amordaçado*, pp. 118–9.
111   *Diário de Notícias*, 17 May 1944.
112   *Temas de Estudo*, p. 13.

113 *Ibid.*, p. 16.
114 *Operáros e Camponeses!* (PCP pamphlet), June 1944, p. 1 (In 3o. Juízo Criminal de Lisboa, Processo No. 14499 de 1949, 6o. Volume, fl. 376).
115 Gouveia, *Memórias*, pp. 158 & 171.
116 *Auto de Perguntas de Miguel Pereira Sarmento Forjaz de Lacerda* (In 3o. Juízo Criminal de Lisboa, Processo No. 14499 de 1949, 8o. Volume, fls. 487–494).
117 *A Célula de Empresa*, Edição revista e actualizada, Julho 1947, pp. 4–5, 7–8 and 26 (In 3o. Juízo Criminal de Lisboa, Processo No. 14499 de 1949, 6o. Volume, fl. 391).
118 Da Costa, *Elementos*, 2o. Volume, pp. 70–1.
119 *Diário de Notícias*, 9 April 1947.
120 Da Costa, *Elementos*, 2o. Volume, pp. 70–1; and *Aos Camaradas do Comité Central – Circular No. 3* (internal PCP document), pp. 1–2 (In 3o. Juízo Criminal de Lisboa, Processo No. 14499 de 1949, 6o. Volume, fl. 240).
121 *Ibid.*.
122 *Ibid.*; and Da Costa, *Elementos*, 2o. Volume, pp. 70–1.
123 *Diário de Notícias*, 26 April 1947.
124 Da Costa, *Elementos*, 2o. Volume, pp. 79–80.
125 Martins Rodrigues, *Elementos PCP*, pp. 32–3; and Fernando Rosas, 'O PCP e a II Guerra Mundial', in *Estudos sobre o Communismo*, O, Julho de 1983, pp. 7–8.
126 Martins Rodrigues, *Elementos PCP*, pp. 32–3; and *A Luta pelo Pão*, 4o. fascículo, pp. 1–2.
127 Martins Rodrigues, *Elementos PCP*, p. 35.
128 Manuel Braga da Cruz, 'A Oposição Eleitoral ao Salazarismo', in *António Sérgio: Número especial da Revista de História das Ideias* (Faculdade de Letras, Coimbra), 5o. Volume, 1983, p. 705.
129 Rosas, 'O PCP', pp. 13–14.
130 Author's interview with Alvaro Cunhal, Lisbon, 26 June 1978.
131 Da Costa, *Elementos*, 2o. Volume, p. 81. Essentially the same criticism is found in Martins Rodrigues, *Elementos PCP*, pp. 36–8.
132 Martins Rodrigues, *Elementos PCP*, pp. 36–8.
133 *Ibid.*; and Da Costa, *Elementos*, 2o. Volume, p. 80.
134 Manuel Garcia and Lourdes Maurício, *O Caso Delgado: autópsia da 'Operação Outuno'*, Lisboa, 1977, Edições Jornal Expresso, p. 251.
135 *A Todas as Organizações e Militantes do Partido Comunista Português* (internal PCP document), July 1945, p. 1 (In 3o. Juizo Criminal de Lisboa, Processo No. 14499 de 1949, 9o. Volume, fl. 590); and Gouveia, *Memórias*, pp. 198–201 & 203.
136 Gouveia, *Memórias*, pp. 153–8 & 162–8.
137 *Auto de Perguntas da Dalila Duque de Fonseca*, (In 3o. Juízo Criminal de Lisboa, Processo No. 14499 de 1949, 8o. Volume, fls 480–4).
138 Gouveia, *Memórias*, pp. 154–7.
139 *Auto de Perguntas de Armanda da Conceição Silva Martins Forjaz de Lacerda e de Miguel Pereira Sarmento Forjaz de Lacerda* (In 3o. Juízo

Criminal de Lisboa, Processo No. 14499 de 1949, 8o. Volume, fls. 484–98).

140   *Ibid.*; and *Auto de Perguntas de Orlando Juncal da Silva* (In 3o. Juízo Criminal de Lisboa, Processo No. 14499 de 1949, 8o. Volume, fl. 500).

141   *Ibid.*; and *Auto de Perguntas de Fernando António Piteira Santos* (In 3o. Juízo Criminal de Lisboa, Processo No. 14499 de 1949, 8o. Volume, fls. 515 & 517–8).

142   *O Caminho para o Derrubamento do Fascismo: Informe Político do Comité Central (Relator: Duarte) ao 2o. Congresso Ilegal do Partido Comunista Português; 1946* (Documento dactilografado, no arquivo do *Avante!*), pp. 4–5.

143   *Ibid.*, p. 7.

144   *Ibid.*, pp. 10–11.

4

The PCP from 1947 to 1962: crisis and renewal

... o mesmo Cristo Favoreceu a Pedro e amimou a João, e eram doze os apóstolos. Um dia se averiguará que Judas traiú por ciúme e abandono.

... even Christ gave precedence to Peter and made John his favourite, when there were twelve apostles. One day it will be discovered that Judas became a traitor through jealousy and neglect.

José Saramago, *Memorial do Convento* (1982)

1 The Cold War and the 1949 crisis

It was not only the dynamics of the class struggle in Portugal which made life more difficult for the PCP from 1947 onwards. The beginning of the 'Cold War' encouraged the régime to intensify repression, especially against Communists, and it also made many members of the liberal and socialist opposition reluctant to collaborate with the Party. These tendencies were to culminate in the rupture of opposition unity in March–April 1949, immediately following the presidential election of that year, but they had been maturing for at least eighteen months before that. In the growing climate of Cold War anti-communism, many liberals, socialists and Republicans assumed that by demarcating themselves from the PCP they might win a degree of tolerance from the regime.

The PCP went to great lengths to maintain unity while rejecting *putschism* and reformism; the dissolution of the Communist Youth and the creation of the *MUD Juvenil* as a broad youth organisation – basically a decision of the 1946 Party Congress, although of course implemented with the agreement of the MUD – was an example of this. The early presentation of

Norton de Matos's candidacy for the Presidency – in March 1948, almost a year before the election – was also a concession to the Republicans. But this achieved little more than to paper over the cracks, as we have seen; large sections of the bourgeois opposition were simply no longer willing to collaborate with Communists. These unfavourable political trends in society at large tended to lower Party morale, and in conjunction with a series of breakdowns in clandestine security, they led in 1949 to the ultimate catastrophe: the arrest of Cunhal and Militão Ribeiro, surrounded by the police in a Party house near Luso in central Portugal, on 25 March 1949.

The wave of arrests of leading Party cadres at this time, which almost destroyed the PCP's clandestine apparatus, began in late 1948 with the capture of António de Almeida, a glassworker from Marinha Grande who controlled the Western Regional Committee. In January 1949, according to the PIDE, Almeida 'committed suicide' in his cell in the Aljube; but the general belief was that like Germano Vidigal and Ferreira Marques, he had died as a result of police brutality.[1] Then in March the GNR, possibly through an informant, located the house in Macinhata do Vouga where Militão Ribeiro was living with his wife, Luisa Rodrigues; Militão managed to escape but Luisa was captured along with a significant quantity of documentation. Militão sought refuge in the house near Luso which served as Alvaro Cunhal's hiding-place, but it was here that they were both captured shortly afterwards, together with Cunhal's *companheira* Sofia de Oliveira Ferreira. Still in March, the PIDE captured in Lisbon Jaime dos Santos Serra, a leading figure in the Party organisation in the capital, followed by one of his subordinates, Augusto de Sousa.[2] Next to 'fall' was a household of Party cadres in Coimbrão (near Leiria) along with a clandestine printing press: António Bastos Lopes, Mercedes de Oliveira Ferreira (sister of Sofia), José Augusto da Silva Martins and Casimira da Silva.[3] Then in November came another Central Committee member, António Dias Lourenço and his *companheira* Georgette Oliveira Ferreira (the third sister).

The collapse continued through 1950 and into 1951, to such an extent that the PIDE claimed that the Communist Party had been completely destroyed. It was not destroyed, but the recovery was to be a long and difficult process.[4] Among those arrested was José

Moreira, responsible for the coordination of the Party's underground printing presses; he became another victim of a PIDE
'suicide', probably because the police were aware of the crucial
nature of his responsibilities but were unable to extract any
information from him on the exact location of the presses.[5] A
Central Committee member with a leading rôle in the Lisbon area
organisation, Manuel Rodrigues da Silva, was detained along
with one António Saboga when the two were engaged in a
clandestine encounter in the Campolide district of Lisbon.[6] José
Magro, an outstanding working-class militant, was captured
early in 1951. According to most accounts, entire regional Party
organisations were destroyed, in the Minho, Algarve, the West
(Marinha Grande – Leiria – Caldas da Rainha), parts of the
Alentejo, and major sectors of the Lisbon organisation. The Party
was virtually reduced to the South Bank of the Tagus, some areas
of the Alentejo, and non-working-class sectors in Lisbon.[7]

The extent and rapidity of the collapse, and the way a PIDE
source (Gouveia) describes the discovery of key Party installations as having come about virtually by chance,[8] raises forcefully
the possibility that the chain of events may have been triggered
by police infiltration or deliberate betrayal. This is what Party
(and some non-Party) sources have always maintained: the
name of Mário Mesquita is given, as a cadre who in gaol did not
simply confess under torture but actively collaborated with the
police; and Manuel Domingues, a Central Committee member,
was denounced as a spy and provocateur.[9] Octávio Pato says that
the betrayal of Mário Mesquita, responsible for the Southern
region, led to the destruction of dozens of Party organisations;
Pato speaks of the arrest of 'hundreds of Communists' in the
whole Alentejo and Algarve region, in part due simply to a
massive police offensive, but aided by Mesquita's betrayal.[10]
Regarding Domingues, his rôle was evidently considered more
sinister; Ramiro da Costa, quoting a clandestine pamphlet of
1952, *Lutemos contra os espiões e provocadores* ('We must struggle
against spies and provocateurs'), says that the arrests of Cunhal
and Militão Ribeiro, as well as many others, were attributed to
Domingues's actions.[11] It is not surprising, if Domingues was
considered responsible for such catastrophic events in the Party's
existence, that he was subsequently murdered, very probably by
Party members; his body was found on 4 May 1951 in the Belas

pine-forest, just north of Lisbon, having it seems been shot. Mário Soares, who suggests – although without evidence – that the accusations of betrayal against Domingues were 'apparently groundless', simply says that the body was found 'in rather strange circumstances'; Gouveia attributes the murder directly to Central Committee members; the Party, as might be expected, has never admitted anything, although condemning Domingues in no uncertain terms as a traitor and provocateur.[12]

The regime was predictably ecstatic about its triumph over the Communist foe. The press at the end of March 1949 was filled with headlines about 'The Enemies of the Nation in the Service of Moscow' having been captured; 'the secretary-general of the Portuguese Communist Party and one of his most active collaborators were discovered and arrested after a sensational investigation', proclaimed the tabloid *A Voz*. Detailed accounts of Cunhal's career were published, with emphasis on his petty-bourgeois origins and good education, and moralistic comments on how, 'despite all the beneficent influences' which might have kept him on the straight and narrow, he had preferred 'the life of ups and downs he has been leading for ten years, today here, tomorrow there', with no regular family life and no means of support except for Party funds.[13]

An important factor in maintaining the morale of what was left of the Party was undoubtedly the exemplary conduct of these leading cadres under interrogation. Not even Cunhal's worst enemies have been able to deny his heroic resistance while in gaol; although at the time the details could not be publicly known, some indications did leak out – if only in the form of the authorities' obvious frustration at their inability to obtain a confession. The same applies to Militão, although in his case he paid with his life for this dignified attitude: he died on 3 January 1950 from the combined effects of torture and a hunger strike which he and Cunhal had both undertaken in order to demand better treatment.[14] Cunhal could very well have died also; it is possible that the police, aware of his importance, did not push him quite to the limit, but the evidence indicates that at times his health was very precarious. PIDE records give impressive confirmation of his unshakeable resolve: the official transcript indicates that in his first interrogation (the day following his arrest) he totally refused to reply to any questions; and in the second, when asked why he still would not respond, he simply stated that 'as a member of the portuguese communist party,* he had nothing to say to the police ...'[15] More than a year later – still in solitary confinement in the Lisbon Penitentiary – Cunhal, accused of contempt of court, gave his lawyer a formal statement in the following categorical terms:

I am accused of 'in the PIDE Sub-Directorate of Oporto, on being interrogated by the respective Sub-Director, having refused to reply to the question of whether I had previously been arrested, when and why, and whether I had ever appeared as a defendant in court'.
This is not correct. That question was asked of me, not by the aforementioned Sub-Director but by a subordinate officer of the same police force.
I should explain that if the same question had been asked of me by the aforementioned Sub-Director, I would similarly have refused to reply. But it was not ...

Cunhal then insisted on setting down for the record that this was only one of many questions to which he had refused to reply; in fact, he had refused to reply to any question relating to his political activity. He concluded with a defiant proclamation of his Communist faith:

In the 'notes' and 'articles' published by the PIDE in the newspapers after my arrest, it is said (among numerous inexactitudes, lies and slanders) that the silence of imprisoned Communists (and, hence, my own silence) is due to 'the Party's rigorous discipline' and to 'the fear of sanctions' ...
On this point the PIDE almost said the truth. A Communist who is arrested prefers torture or death rather than make any statements prejudicial to his Party. Many Communists have been tortured, many have died in solitary confinement, for refusing to make statements.
Those who act thus do so because they believe it to be their duty; because they are defending their cause with honour; because they want to keep an honourable name and the confidence of the Party and the people; because terror of the Police (as the PIDE 'note' says) does not overcome their spirit and their resolve as good citizens and good patriots.
There is, in fact, a discipline in the Portuguese Communist Party. And those who weaken in the face of the enemy suffer sanctions as a result. What sanctions? Criticism, public censure, reduction of their responsibilities or expulsion ...[16]

---

* In lower case in the original; the PIDE would never capitalise this subversive organisation!

In fact, as we saw in the case of Manuel Domingues, Party sanctions may sometimes have been more drastic than this; but it remains true that Cunhal's declaration was a fine moral statement of Party honour and dignity in the face of police intimidation and torture.

That Cunhal and Militão Ribeiro were held under very harsh conditions is confirmed by a statement of the official defence counsel, Mário Ferreira. Expressing serious concern for the prisoners' health, Ferreira said that the conditions under which they were detained were 'worse, much worse' than those of common criminals. They were in solitary confinement, with the right to only one weekly visit of fifteen minutes by family members (and in the presence of a PIDE officer); they were denied recreation, were not allowed to read and write, and sometimes went as long as three weeks without a bath or change of clothing. Alvaro Cunhal was suffering from vitamin deficiency and intercolitis, and Militão Ribeiro was so ill that it seemed doubtful if he would survive (and indeed, he only lasted another two months).[17] Despite this apparently genuine concern of the official defence counsel, Cunhal demanded a new lawyer, and was allowed to have his father, Dr Avelino Cunhal, as counsel. By the end of January 1950 Avelino Cunhal was close to despair, and in view of Ribeiro's death and the reported suicide attempt of another political prisoner (Dr Silva Martins), addressed an anxious plea to the judicial authorities expressing urgent concern for his son's life.[18] In fact the PCP leader was held in solitary confinement for nearly fourteen months before being brought to court (on 2 and 9 May 1950). He was of course found guilty and condemned to four years and six months' imprisonment or six years and nine months' exile, with loss of political rights for fifteen years – a sentence which was subsequently increased by the Supreme Court to four years' imprisonment followed by eight years exile and one year of 'security measures'.[19] He was actually held in the Lisbon Penitentiary until 27 July 1956, when he was transferred to Peniche – where he stayed until a spectacular escape in January 1960. The régime of solitary confinement had come to an end in late 1953, when a seriously ill Cunhal was transferred to the Penitentiary's sick ward for treatment – although Party sources indicate that the treatment he received was totally inadequate that his health remained poor.[20]

While Alvaro Cunhal and many other Communist cadres were languishing in gaol, the few Central Committee members who remained at large were struggling to pick up the pieces. The Central Committee was reduced in 1950 to five full members (José Gregório, Joaquim Pires Jorge, Manuel Guedes, Júlio Fogaça and Sérgio Vilarigues) and two non-voting members (Octávio Pato and Soeiro Pereira Gomes, who died a few months later anyway).[21] The crisis called for a thorough reassessment of the Party's discipline and political line; inevitably there were differences and recriminations. After several years of cautious reconstruction, the Party would adopt a new and fundamentally reformist strategy, but only after intense internal debate.

2   The line struggle of 1950–52

In the wake of the disaster of 1949–50, a defensive reaction set in: retrenchment was deemed essential to save the Party. The reformist tendency which would triumph in 1956 was very much in the minority in the early fifties. Information is very scant on the inner-party debates of this period, but the Marxist–Leninists have always maintained that first Militão Ribeiro (before his death in January 1950) and then José Gregório ((before being incapacitated by illness in 1955) began a revolutionary critique of the Party's errors in the late 1940s. It was the removal of these two veterans, in this view, which made possible the revisionist 'turn' which triumphed in 1956; it has even been suggested that Gregório's illness was used as a pretext to get him out of the way by shipping him off to Czechoslovakia in 1955.[22] The present Party leadership has vigorously denied this, maintaining that there was always fraternal unity between Ribeiro, Gregório and the rest of the Central Committee, and that Gregório's departure was entirely due to his deteriorating health.[23] Certainly, there is little evidence to suggest that Gregório's position differed significantly from that of Cunhal, who after his escape from Peniche in 1960 would lead the attack on the 'right-wing deviation' of 1956–59. That is to say, there undoubtedly was a difference of opinion between the advocates of the 'peaceful solution' (Júlio Fogaça, Sérgio Vilarigues and others) and the 'hard-liners' (José Gregório and the imprisoned Cunhal); but there is little to suggest that Gregório defended anything resembling the Marxist–

Leninist stance of later years, rejecting even Cunhal's line as conciliatory and revisionist.

Militão Ribeiro did apparently express dissatisfaction with the Party's tendency, as he saw it, to make excessive concessions to the liberal bourgeoisie in the MUD and MUNAF. In a report to the Central Committee in January 1949 – one month before the Presidential election in which Norton de Matos was opposition candidate – Ribeiro criticised the Party's tendency to take orders from the bourgeois democrats and to 'bow down before them'. He emphasized the revolutionary role of the proletariat and insisted that the Party must not allow its vanguard position in the anti-fascist struggle to be usurped by any other force, for the movement would then serve only the interests of the bourgeoisie and petty-bourgeoisie.[24] This was certainly a revolutionary marxist clarion-call for demarcation from bourgeois tendencies within the opposition; but there is little reason to suppose that it was not supported by Cunhal and one or two other members of the Central Committee later condemned by the marxist-leninists as 'revisionists'.

Following the arrest of Cunhal and Ribeiro and the other disastrous events of 1949–50, the surviving leaders did undertake a critique of lax discipline and opportunism within the Party – a critique which did not spare some members of the Central Committee. One of the Party's best-known figures, Júlio Fogaça ('Ramiro') – a veteran from the thirties and a prominent participant in the 1941 reorganisation – was forced to make an extensive self-criticism for his participation in formulating the 'policy of transition'. In fact, it seems that this was his third self-criticism on this account; the document, dated March 1951, refers to his previous two letters to the Central Committee, in November 1948 and May 1950, neither of which was considered satisfactory. Its ideological content is very explicit and very revealing concerning the internal debate in the Party from the return of the Tarrafal group in 1945 down to 1951.

In his self-criticism Fogaça admits that the advocates of the 'policy of transition', himself included, had been guilty of a grave 'under-estimation of the revolutionary róle of the working class' and a corresponding 'under-estimation of the role of the Party' in national life. This had led them to propose such policies as the removal of the hammer and sickle from the masthead of *Avante!*, or even the complete abandonment of the Communist organ and its replacement by the MUNAF's news-sheet, *Libertação Nacional*; to conceive of a political strategy based on the support of the Western powers for a 'palace coup' against Salazar and a gradual transition to democracy; to attribute the PCP's prestige in Portugal mainly to Soviet victories in the war.[25] On their return from Tarrafal, many comrades had refused to undertake clandestine work, preferring to carry out exclusively legal tasks in the MUD and other unitary opposition organisations. They had avoided participation in mass movements such as strikes and hunger marches.[26] Fogaça now admitted that all of these positions had been gravely mistaken and opportunistic. Yet even this self-criticism did not really satisfy the Secretariat of the Central Committee; Fogaça failed (they said) to recognise the deep roots of the group's errors, the fact that they had evolved in Tarrafal long before the return to the mainland and that they reflected not merely an ignorance of the real situation in Portugal, but a fundamental lack of confidence in the working class and the Party.[27] Probably the only reason that Fogaça and his comrades were not expelled was that, unlike a number of other dissidents, they accepted Party discipline and submitted to the official line when criticised.

The purge which did occur in 1950–51 embraced not only those accused of outright treachery, such as Manuel Domingues, but also several intellectuals who were said to have manifested 'social-democratic' and 'Titoist' tendencies, including Mário Soares and Fernando Piteira Santos. Mário Soares had by the late forties clearly ceased to be a Communist – if indeed he ever really was one except in name – and his expulsion merely confirmed his *de facto* separation from the Party.[28] The case of Piteira Santos is more interesting. A student friend of Alvaro Cunhal, he had entered the PCP in the early forties and by late 1943 was co-opted to the Central Committee. Among other responsibilities, he was put in charge of the Party's military organisation (together with José Magro). It was indeed Piteira Santos who had recruited the young Mário Soares into the Communist Youth in April 1944;[29] he evidently enjoyed great prestige among progressive students at the time. An interesting assessment of Piteira is given by Manuel Garcia and Lourdes Maurício in their book *O Caso Delgado*:

Piteira Santos was, it seems, an indefatigable and dedicated militant, plunging into all kinds of activities ... Intellectually brilliant –

something of which he was well aware – his virtues were overshadowed by an insufferable pride and a terrible tendency to intrigue, defects which were difficult to reconcile with the new style of work imposed by Gregório, Cunhal and others after the 40/41 reorganisation.[30]

When arrested in July 1945, Piteira apparently made extensive declarations to the PIDE;[31] in any case he had already been demoted from the Central Committee for indiscipline, although he remained in the Party until his expulsion in 1950. In the end he was expelled for further (unspecified) acts of indiscipline, and also for ideological divergences – he was accused of 'Titoism' and 'Browderism':

Piteira Santos defended 'Browderism', he defended the idea that we ought to go right through to socialism with a government of national untiy. He considered that the MND and the MUD had become closed, sectarian movements, without the preconditions for a legal existence, and attacked the Central Committee of the MND . . .[32]

Although outside the PCP, and isolated of several years, Piteira was to have a long and interesting career as an independent leftist, becoming a key figure in the FPLN (*Frente Patriótica de Libertação Nacional*) in Algiers in the sixties – where he worked closely with both the PCP and General Delgado – and then editor of the *Diário de Lisboa*. Given his individualism and disciplinary infractions, it is not surprising that the Party expelled him – but this did not prevent him from making a valuable contribution to the anti-fascist resistance in a less structured and disciplined milieu. His case is perhaps typical of many intellectuals who were unable to adjust to the Party's demands.

3   The 'peaceful solution of the Portuguese political problem'

The Secretariat's offensive against what were seen as rightwing deviations continued through the early fifties. In 1954 a special plenary meeting of the Central Committee criticised and dismantled what was described as a 'right-wing fraction' whose leaders argued for the dissolution of the MND; one of them, João Rodrigues, was expelled from the Party. The same fifth plenary meeting of the Central Committee witnessed an explicit ideological statement of the revolutionary position, with the proposal of the first fully elaborated Draft Programme of the Party; it put forward a strategy based on 'popular democracy' as the goal of the revolution in Portugal, implying expropriation of the big monopoly capitalist groups, of the latifundists and of imperialist capital, agrarian reform and independence for the colonies. The Programme also called for preparation of the masses for the road of popular insurrection, and while accepting the need for alliance with the liberal bourgeoisie, warned against the 'inconsistencies and betrayals' of this class.[33]

But the adoption of the Draft Programme soon revealed itself to be a pyrrhic victory for the hard-liners; it never became the Party's official ideological basis, and within less than two years was replaced by the frankly reformist line of the 'Peaceful Solution of the Portuguese Political Problem'. The Marxist–Leninists attribute this *volte-face* to the departure of José Gregório and the return to the Central Committee (actually in 1952) of Júlio Fogaça, and the promotion of other cadres with reformist ideas. In one sense this interpretation is clearly valid – there were significant leadership changes – but there were also new developments in the domestic and international situation which help to account for the Party's reorientation. One of these developments, recognised by marxist-leninist critics, was the XX Congress of the Communist Party of the Soviet Union in February 1956 with Khruschev's denunciation of Stalin. But also the years following the Korean War witnessed an international retreat of revolutionary movements, and in Portugal itself the consolidation of the regime following the upheavals of the forties was apparent to all.

Already in 1955 the sixth plenary meeting of the Central Committee revealed a change of emphasis: the main concern was the struggle against sectarianism and the need to develop broad mass work, reaching out to the less advanced strata of the working class in legal organisations such as the *sindicatos nacionais*. Within the Party, the emphasis was to be on collective leadership, internal democracy and criticism/self-criticism.[34] The new line became consolidated during the next few months: in October 1956 a manifesto of the Central Committee proclaimed for the first time the 'possibility of a peaceful solution', and in 1957 the V Party Congress (III Illegal) confirmed and extended this analysis. The Central Committee's 1956 manifesto began by quoting the classic lines of Camões – 'Mudam-se os tempos, mudam-se as vontades . . .', and announced boldly that:

The Central Committee of the Portuguese Communist Party, having analysed the evolution of the national and international situation and the growing disintegration which is occurring among the Salazarist ranks, concluded that it is possible today to find a democratic and peaceful solution for the national political problem, that it is possible to expel the government of Salazar from Power without civil war and without violence.[35]

There was – it continued – a line separating the entire Nation (capitalised in the original) from the 'Salazarist clique', and the unity of all anti-Salazarist groups would be sufficient to bring about a change in government. The first and decisive step was to create a 'vast anti-Salazarist electoral front' to participate mass-ively in the forthcoming elections, which could force the regime to grant political representation to the opposition. In support of this, the document quoted the example of Greece, where the opposition had recently won 135 out of 300 seats in the Lower House, 'despite the violence and gerrymandering of the Karamanlis government'.[36] Such an electoral advance would open the way to many and varied popular struggles which would further weaken the government's position, and 'We should not discount the possibility that internal and external political events, favourable to the anti-Salazarist forces, may speed up the development of the situation and bring about a quicker solution of the national political problem.'

The Central Committee statement did recognise that this scenario might seem over-optimistic to some, and therefore included a ritual *caveat* about the violence which might occur if the classes which had hitherto supported the Salazar regime persisted in upholding a government 'divorced from the great mass of the Nation'; but the desire was growing among all sections of the population for 'the reconciliation of the Portu-guese family' and for an end to fratricidal divisions.

In proposing such a conciliatory line the Central Committee could scarcely ignore its radically different analyses of previous years. In one passage it did hint at a self-criticism of what were now seen as sectarian and inflexible positions in relation to the bourgeois opposition:

The Communist Party was always and in all circumstances the most determined champion of anti-salazarist unity. However, in this new situation (of Cold War division beginning in 1949) the Communist Party was unable, while standing firmly on positions of principle, to demonstrate the necessary patience and flexibility towards the other anti-salazarist forces ...

The initial successes of the MND led the Communist Party to forget about Unity with other democratic forces and to see in that Movement the complete expression of democratic unity ...[37]

The Party should have understood (according to this new analysis) that Salazarism could not indefinitely retain the support of small and medium capitalists oppressed by its regime of big financiers and monopolists, and hence that situations favourable to opposition unity would increase in the long run, despite temporary divisions and lapses.

What the new Party leadership did not and could not demonstrate, however, was that there had been any fundamental change in the regime's determination to preserve its monopoly of power. Moreover, the repeated affirmations that 'all classes' were increasingly united in opposition to the 'Salazarist clique' were just that: bold affirmations unsupported by any very solid evidence. Certainly the Salazar regime in the mid-1950's faced widespread discontent, as it had done for some time, but it is by no means clear that it had been reduced to an isolated 'clique' divorced from the entire nation. This was an analysis incorporating a large dose of wishful thinking – never a sound basis for political action.

Interestingly, it seems that one of the factors encouraging the PCP in this direction was a rare instance of close contact with the neighbouring Spanish party. Normally the two Iberian Communist Parties, like their compatriots in almost all walks of life, maintained a healthy distance from each other; but in the mid-fifties there were closer contacts. Thus in April 1956 there appeared an important 'Joint Declaration' of the two parties, expressing their repudiation of the Franco – Salazar Iberian Pact and of American domination of the peninsula. The declaration also condemned fascism as 'a government of civil war' and proclaimed that:

The Communist Parties of Portugal and Spain consider that at the present time a change from he fascist régime to a democratic regime is possible in the two countries without the need for a civil war, by peaceful means, if in order to achieve this the broadest possible political and social forces, of left and right, come to an agreement.[38]

Indeed, it seems possible that in this case there was some influence of the Spanish party on the Portuguese; in this period the Spanish party was pursuing the tactic of a 'Peaceful General Strike' (*Huelga Nacional Pacífica*), and the PCP would soon begin to campaign for a 'Peaceful National Protest for the Resignation of Salazar and Santos Costa' (*Jornada Nacional Pacífica pela Demissão de Salazar e Santos Costa*). When Cunhal later criticised the 'right-wing deviation' in the PCP's line, he made an oblique – and implicitly critical – reference to the influence of an unnamed 'fraternal party'.[39] The Political Report to the Party's V Congress in 1957 (presented by Fogaça) also recognised the new ties to the PCE.[40]

The V Congress, held clandestinely in September 1957 some-where near the coast north-west of Lisbon,[47] saw the reformist line completely in the ascendant. The Political Report began with a reference to the XX Congress of the Soviet Communist Party and the thesis of the peaceful transition to socialism, and then argued that in Portugal also, peaceful transition (although for the time being, only to democracy) was possible. All sectors of the population except a small monopolist clique were alienated from the régime. Intellectuals, facing censorship and denied employment opportunities unless they conformed to official ideology, were overwhelmingly with the opposition. Small and medium industrialists were more and more resentful of monopolistic privileges and of burdens imposed by the *grémios* and other agencies of the corporate state. Youth, women, the great majority of the Catholic population, all were longing for a change. 'That which separates us is nothing compared to that which unites us', in other words opposition to Salazarism.[42]

This very optimistic analysis was qualified by the recognition that the government was prepared to resort to 'all forms of struggle' to defeat the opposition, and that it could count on 'a vast and powerful state apparatus' which only a truly massive popular movement could overcome. The Report pointed out with some justice that precisely because of the strength of the State machine, no single opposition party or organisation could achieve victory; only a united movement of the whole people could do that. It was because the Communist Party had failed to understand this after 1949 that it had fallen into sectarian positions and abandoned the struggle for unity with other sectors of the opposition.[43] The document also pointed out the continuing weakness of the Party's work among the peasantry; although progress had been made, it was almost exclusively among the rural labourers of the Alentejo.[44]

Fogaça's Report, then, did make valid criticisms of the Party's previous line and practice. But it still failed lamentably to demonstrate its central thesis, namely that the Salazar régime was so isolated and divided that a peaceful transition to democracy was a serious possibility in the near future. The picture it painted of overwhelming mass opposition, with the detailed enumeration of different classes and groups in struggle, carried little conviction when it was common knowledge that strikes and mass protests had been greater and more intense ten or twelve years earlier. The government had also demonstrated repeatedly its willingness to use force rather than permit any significant sharing of power. In other words, the Political Report was strategically sterile, although tactically it did open up new possibilities of alliance with the bourgeois opposition.

The one significant tactical proposal in Fogaça's Report, developed further in a statement delivered to the Congress by 'Manuel' (Guilherme da Costa Carvalho), was that the PCP should once again participate in election campaigns along with other opposition forces, and that the candidates they nominated should go right through to the polls (i.e. not withdrawing in protest as before). This did represent a major change, since the PCP had always insisted before that opposition candidates must withdraw unless adequate guarantees were given of a free and fair vote. The leadership's justification of this change was first, that the Party's previous position had been sectarian; secondly, that objective conditions were now much more favourable to a large-scale opposition mobilisation in an election campaign (because of the 'growing disintegration of the Salazarist regime'); thirdly, that a truly massive movement of all opposition and dissident sectors without exception could force the government to give way and organise the elections with at least 'a minimum of honesty'; and finally, that the election of even a few opposition deputies would have an enormous impact and would accelerate the disintegration of the regime.[45] Again, it is hard to avoid the conclusion that these arguments embodied a large dose of wishful thinking; the 'objective conditions' favourable to opposition mobilisation were derived, as we have seen, from very scant evidence; there was little to suggest that the government would desist from electoral fraud simply because of mass pressure; and consequently the election of even one or two opposition deputies was likely to remain a mirage.

Costa Carvalho's special statement 'On the Forthcoming Parliamentary Elections', however, did advance a more persuasive argument in favour of electoral participation. The twelve-year period since 1945, he said, should be divided into two phases: the first, from 1945 to 1949, was a phase of rising revolutionary struggle in which 'the forces of opposition to the régime were becoming strong and combative, while Salazarism was labouring under great difficulties'; the second, after the end of Norton's presidential campaign, was one of revolutionary retreat, of increased repression, of division among the democratic forces and the ebb-tide of the mass movement. The tactics appropriate to the first phase could not be applied to the second; whereas in 1945 and even in Norton's campaign abstention constituted a victory for the opposition, demonstrating the people's rejection of a fraudulent electoral manoeuvre designed to disguise the regime's true character, from 1949 onwards, with the opposition on the defensive and the government trying to whittle away even the limited political rights which existed, it was necessary to make use of every legal opportunity for action, however inadequate.[46] This was a serious tactical argument which many on the left might well accept; the only problem was that it scarcely seemed consistent with the thesis of a vast and growing mass movement against the régime. If electoral participation was a defensive tactic of a weakened opposition, it could hardly be expected to lead to the voluntary capitulation of Salazar's government.

The V Congress also produced a Programme for the PCP – the first such document officially adopted by the Party in all its years of activity. It was not the same as the Draft Programme put forward by the previous leadership under José Gregório in 1954, which would have been quite out of keeping with the new

conciliatory line. Instead, the new document reiterated the case
for a 'peaceful solution of the Portuguese political problem',
avoiding any mention of insurrection or of 'popular democracy' as
a political goal.[47] If the PCP had persisted with such a platform, it
would have become 'Eurocommunist' *avant la lettre*; that this did
not happen was due to the renewed leadership of Alvaro Cunhal
from 1960 onwards and to the objective situation of Portugal as
the most underdeveloped country in Western Europe, engaged in
a savage colonial war beginning in 1961.

4 Working-class and popular struggles, 1949–62

We have already seen that the early fifties were years of retreat
and of defensive struggles for the Portuguese working class. This
was also a period of gradual economic recovery and reorganisation, leading if not to prosperity at least to an easing of hardship
for some sectors of the population, and accentuating divisions
among the working class as old industries declined and new ones
emerged. While direct foreign investment was still kept at arm's
length, the government negotiated its first large-scale credit (for
$455 m.) with the Economic Co-operation Administration in
1951.[48] Even if the impact of such plans was limited, Portugal
benefited from the general expansion of international trade, with
the result that the gross domestic product grew at an average rate
of 4–5% p.a. during the decade 1950–60, reaching 5–7% p.a. in
1957–61.[49] This expansion was reflected in speculative building
in the Avenidas Novas district of Lisbon and in a small-scale
consumer boom among the new bourgeois strata.

This gradual and limited improvement in the economic
climate, however, was of no benefit at all to the rural masses,
whose conditions remained almost medieval. The grain requisitioning and speculation of the war years were over, leading to a
cessation of the bread riots among the peasantry of the Centre
and North, but they continued to suffer from lack of credit,
primitive agricultural methods, and exploitation by middlemen
aggravated by the régime's policy of alienating the common lands
– the effects of which were graphically exposed by Aquilino
Ribeiro in his novel *Quando os Lobos Uivam* ('When the Wolves
Howl'), published – and banned by the censor – in 1958.[50]
Nevertheless, isolation, disunity and the conservative influence

of the Catholic Church ensured that protests by peasant small-holders would remain sporadic and localised. It was the agricultural proletariat of the South which revealed continued and growing militancy, becoming a permanent thorn in the side of the regime.

Unrest in the Alentejo and Ribatejo had become chronic since the early forties; scarcely a year passed without more or less widespread struggles over employment, wages, hours and conditions of work in the wheat fields and cork and olive groves of southern Portugal. The pattern of conflict was conditioned by the peculiar and primitive system of labour recruitment prevailing in the region, the *praça de jorna*, whereby the workers would gather in the town square early in the morning to be contracted for the day or the week by the landlords' agents. It was here that rates of pay, hours of work and the number of labourers to be hired would be determined, and it was here that strike action – in the form of a collective refusal to accept the employers' offer – could occur. Some observers argued understandably that the *praça de jorna* was a retrograde institution reminiscent of a slave market, but the workers – and the PCP – defended it as their most effective bargaining tool.[51]

As early as 1945 the PCP had established itself as the pre-dominant political force among the agricultural labourers, and to some extent its fortunes were reflected in the ups and downs of the workers' movement. Thus the years 1947–49 witnessed intense struggles in the Alentejo, reaching a peak in 1949, but this was followed by two years of relative calm, coinciding with the Party's great organisational crisis of 1949–51.[52] In 1952 the struggles resumed with considerable vigour, with the emphasis on wage demands; the movement began with strikes in Pias and Vale do Vargo (near the Spanish border in the Lower Alentejo) demanding a daily wage of thirty escudos (as against the landlords' offer of seventeen). The struggles were organised by workers' 'Unity Committees' and 'Wage Committees' in each locality, formed in response to local conditions but with PCP activists in the lead. The strike spread to several other towns in the Beja and Evora districts, and was largely successful – in Pias and Vale de Vargo the thirty-escudo target was reached, and elsewhere a more modest but still substantial target was obtained.[53]

These wage struggles naturally occurred principally at the

beginning of the harvest in May, or at any rate during the harvest season (May–July); some conflicts occurred later in the year, during the olive-gathering season. In 1953 there were again extensive strikes in May, mainly in the Lower Alentejo; the PCP newspaper *O Camponês* ('The Peasant') launched the target of a daily wage of fifty escudos (already the theoretical target in previous years, but now within sight of realisation). Several thousand labourers struck for periods ranging from a few days to a week or more, generally winning significant concessions (agricultural labourers' strikes rarely lasted more than a week, given the urgency of the harvest). Once again, Vale do Vargo set the pace, winning the fifty-escudo target after a strike lasting from 10 to 16 May. Big gains were also made in many other communities: fifty escudos in Cuba, Ferreira do Alentejo and Portel, and thirty-five to forty-five escudos in most other Alentejo towns. This was despite frequent intervention by the GNR and the PIDE, with pitched battles between police and workers and many arrests.[54]

The dramatic but brief wage struggles in May–June should not overshadow other less spectacular but equally significant conflicts: demands for employment in the winter, in the form of mass meetings outside the *Casa do Povo*, town hall or police station, or demonstrations and hunger marches; wage demands during the weeding season (March–April); and conflicts relating to the olive-gathering, mainly involving women. There was in fact an annual cycle of unrest, with major or minor peaks in different months, which was repeated year after year with monotonous regularity. The importance of this in the national context can scarcely be overstated; in the words of José Pacheco Pereira:

In Salazarist Portugal, where social struggles were cast forth into the limbo or the hell of clandestinity, there was a province which in the full view of everyone did not behave in a very 'corporative' fashion ... The Government itself admitted openly that the Alentejo had problems of subversion, and, more significantly, admitted that there was some justification for this. The regular repetition of conflicts during the harvest, the weeding season, the olive-gathering, preventing the reduction of wages or making them rise, and also the pressures to demand employment in winter, had put all the traditional means of social control to the test – from the police to charity – and had exhausted them. If matters continued in the same way, they would finally explode; and the progressive institutionalisation of violence was a sign of this.[55]

Pacheco Pereira goes on to point out how petty crime had become endemic in the region, with the tacit acceptance of the authorities; robbery of crops and livestock and poaching in the landlords' private hunting-grounds were common practices, and indeed unemloyed workers would openly threaten such practices if they were denied work. Violent confrontations between armed GNR and workers using stones, clubs and agricultural implements were a regular occurrence, leading to injuries and occasional deaths.

The first death to occur as a result of repression in the Alentejo in our period (there had been others in previous decades, notably in 1910–12) was that of Germano Vidigal, leader of the Construction Workers' Union in Montemor-o-Novo. A Communist, Vidigal was arrested by the GNR in 1945 following an agricultural. labourers' strike in the region; he died in PIDE custody on 28 May of that year.[56] Two years later, on 21 June 1947, José Patuleia died at PIDE headquarters as a result of torture; he was a rural worker from Vila Viçosa in the Upper Alentejo. In Alpiarça in the Ribatejo the GNR opened fire on striking labourers on 4 July 1949, killing Alfredo Dias de Lima.[57] Another serious incident occurred in Montemor-o-Novo ten years later; on 24 June 1958 the censorship deleted the following report from *O Século*:

MONTEMOR-O-NOVO, June 23 – The rural labourers who had finished working in the harvest went to the Town Hall (*Paços do Concelho*) to ask the mayor for welfare benefits and a wage increase. The GNR tried to disperse them, but since they were unable to do so, they requested reinforcements from the Evora battalion, which sent several guards to the place.

There was an exchange of fire in which Mr José Adelino dos Santos, a 46-year-old bachelor and a native of Escoural, lost his life, and the workers Alexandrino Inácio Veríssimo, 41 and single, and José Augusto Veiga, 17, also a bachelor, both natives of this town, were wounded and taken to hospital.[58]

No more infomation is available, and it is not clear whether the dead man was a labourer or a member of the GNR; but this clash was typical of the sporadic violence which prevailed.

The most famous victim of police action in the region was Catarina Eufémia, the young woman of Baleizão near Beja who was shot by Lt Carrajola of the GNR on 19 May 1954. The fact that she was a woman and also pregnant at the time seems to account for the publicity her case has received; she was also a member of the local PCP committee, and there are some indications that Carrajola may have been 'out to get her' because of her role in a local strike. The accounts of her death have been so romanticised that the exact circumstances are difficult to judge; that she was shot by Carrajola is clear, although whether it was a case of premeditated murder – as some have argued – is open to dispute. What matters most is that she (and her unborn child) were innocent victims to add to the growing list of proletarian martyrs from the Alentejo (and from the ranks of the PCP); she rapidly became a symbol of the régime's brutality and of popular resistance.[59] The dynamic of class conflict on the vast labour-intensive latifundia was such that the Communist Party's message could hardly fail to strike home; conditions were so bad and the labour system so obviously exploitative that revolutionary class consciousness arose (for once) virtually spontaneously. Unlike Lisbon or the North, the Alentejo had almost no middle class to act as a buffer between the workers and the wealthy proprietors or their agents.

Even when there were no deaths and no shots fired, the repressive measures employed against the Alentejo labourers were varied and severe. In May 1945, in the strike which led to the arrest of Germano Vidigal in Montemor-o-Novo, the police and GNR rounded up 1,500 men and women in the local bullring in an attempt to break the strike.[60] Workers from other regions were regularly brought in to lower wages and break strikes, and one of the major concerns of the *commissões de praça* was to prevent work being given to outsiders, or to persuade the outsiders not to accept a lower wage than the local workers. This was the principal issue in the Baleizão strike that led to Catarina Eufémia's death: the labourers were trying to prevent a *rancho* (work-team) from the neighbouring village of Penedo Gordo from accepting the landlord's terms and taking their work.[61] The local authorities also collaborated with the landlords by creating artificial unemployment just before harvest-time, closing down public works such as road-maintenance and ditch-cleaning in order to flood the local labour market.[62] Even when the workers succeeded in imposing a wage increase or an improvement in conditions, this was no guarantee that the agreement would be honoured, and as can be imagined, new disputes could easily flare up in the fields.

Although these were years of relative quiescence among urban workers, the Alentejo labourers were not the only sector engaged in struggle. In 1950 there was a successful strike of Lisbon wine-coopers; in 1952 in Setúbal 600 women at a fish-canning plant went on strike; and there was a series of militant struggles in the textile industry, one of the country's largest manufacturing sectors and an important contributor to exports.[63] Some of these disputes were over wages, but several were against redundancies or against the national 'productivity campaign' launched by the government in the mid-fifties. It was this latter issue which led to one of the most serious strikes of this period, involving 1,600 textile workers from several factories in Oporto in May 1954; the police arrested thirty workers, but they were released after vigorous protests by their comrades. During this strike workers in the woollen mills of Covilhã in the Serra da Estrela (150 miles away) came out in sympathy, also onfronting police repression – a very unusual and difficult action to organise under the fascist regime. Another major struggle was that of the fishermen in several ports in May 1955, involving as many as 15,000 men.[64]

From 1957 onwards the rhythm of conflict intensified once again; a new wave of working-class offensives had begun, lasting through the early sixties. The fishermen of Matosinhos (near Oporto) went on strike in August 1957 to demand their right to a weekly rest-day; less than two years later, from March to May 1959, they were out for seventy days in support of a wage claim.[65] In April 1958 there was an agricultural labourers' strike in Tortozendo, Covilhã, Lamego and Pampilhosa da Serra, in the mountainous Serra da Estrela of central Portugal; their demands were for better wages and an eight-hour day. Thirteen of the strikers were arrested as 'ringleaders' and brought to trial nearly a year later, accused of incitement to strike and 'subversive activities'.[66] No doubt the authorities were alarmed at the potential significance of this strike as indicating the spread of agrarian unrest well away from the usual regions of the Alentejo and Ribatejo.

Further disputes over wage issues, not necessarily involving work stoppages, occurred in March 1959 among bakery workers in Lisbon and Oporto, railwaymen and miners at Aljustrel in the

Alentejo. The miners of Aljustrel displayed exceptional militancy; after a brief dispute in March 1959, in April 1960 they were locked in a bitter struggle against dismissals. Following violent police intervention, 150 workers occupied the mine for thirty-three hours while their relatives occupied the union office; in response, the police arrested 130 miners and interned them in the Peniche prison-fortress. Yet in 1962 there were renewed protests in Aljustrel; this time the police opened fire on the demonstrators, killing two and wounding many others.[67]

5 The PCP in crisis, 1958–59, and Cunhal's 'rectification' of 1960–61

The resurgence of proletarian militancy inevitably put the PCP's reformist leadership to the test. In some respects conditions did seem to favour the new strategy: the beginnings of East-West 'détente' might encourage a certain liberalisation of the Iberian dictatorships, while domestically there were signs, for the first time in eight years, that important sectors of the bourgeois opposition were willing to collaborate with the Communists. A very promising sign was the celebration in the central coastal town of Aveiro of the First Republican Congress of the Democratic Opposition, on 6 October 1957. Organised on the initiative of Mário Sacramento, a respected local intellectual with a national reputation as a neo-realist writer, it brought together representatives of most opposition currents to engage in public debates on social, economic and political problems. The very fact of its authorisation came as a surprise – and may well have been a factor in the dismissal of the local Civil Governor a year later.[68]

Efforts to restore unity were also made in relation to the parliamentary elections of November 1957; prolonged discussions took place on a local basis between Communists and representatives of other groups such as the *Directório Democrato-Social*, but in the end opposition lists were presented in only three districts (Aveiro, Oporto and Braga), and even in these districts the DDS withdrew its support at the last minute.[69] Undaunted, the PCP leadership set about finding a compromise candidate for the Presidential election of June 1958; their unitary zeal went so far as to lead them into an alliance with the right wing of the bourgeois opposition – monarchists and conservative Republi-

cans – in supporting the candidacy of Engineer Cunha Leal, a
political maverick with a very dubious record. When this failed
(Cunha Leal withdrew, allegedly for health reasons) the PCP
chose a more progressive figure, Dr Arlindo Vicente; but
Vicente's appeal was limited, and he was soon swept aside by the
Delgado whirlwind. The campaign of General Humberto Delgado, an ex-fascist whose democratic conversion revolutionised
the political scene, was so important that it is examined in detail
in Chapter VI; its significance here lies in the way in which it
exposed the inadequacies of the PCP's 'peaceful solution' line,
creating a totally unexpected revolutionary confrontation for
which the Party was quite unprepared.

It was in the wake of the Delgado upheaval that the Party
launched its 'Peaceful National Protest for the Resignation of
Salazar and Santos Costa' – a tactic which had been in
preparation for some time under the evident influence of the
Spanish Party. But such a tactic, inadequate at the best of times,
was totally irrelevant in the insurrectionary climate created by
Delgado's campaign. Formally proclaimed in May 1959, the
Jornada Nacional Pacífica was quietly abandoned in August,
having made no noticeable impact on the national scene.[70] This
was in a sense the swan-song of the reformist leadership, and
paved the way for its repudiation with the return of Cunhal and
others to active politics in 1960.

The spectacular escape from Peniche on 3 January 1960 of
Alvaro Cunhal and nine other Communist cadres was of in-
calculable importance to the Party. Although Cunhal was not
the only capable strategist in the Central Committee, his pre-
eminence was unquestionable; and it was his trenchant critique
of the 'peaceful solution' line which carried the day. The escape, a
product of meticulous planning and careful observation of the
weaknesses in the prison vigilance system, was worthy of the best
Hollywood traditions. One of the escapees, Francisco Miguel, had
collected bedsheets and tied them together; other prisoners had
obtained a wet towel and anaesthetic with which to overpower
the guard who was escorting them back to their cells after dinner
that Sunday evening. With the complicity of a sympathetic
guard they were than able to climb down from the inner fortress
and scale the outer wall, proceeding rapidly to two getaway cars
waiting at pre-arranged locations. By the time the alarm was

given they were well on their way to safety in clandestine 'Party houses' around the country.[71]

It seems that for the PCP this was a case of one success leading to another, since less than two years later, on 4 December 1961, another group of Communist prisoners escaped, this time from Caxias and in even more spectacular fashion. In an exploit which immediately became justly famous, seven men burst out of the fortress in an armoured Mercedes presented to Salazar by Hitler, breaking down the outer door of the main entrance by the sheer force of the car, and trusting – correctly, as it turned out – that the German armour would be solid enough to protect them from the machine-gun fire of the astounded prison-guards.[72] In Lisbon the comrades rapidly separated and made their way to safe 'Party houses'; the escape had been coordinated with the clandestine apparatus outside the gaol, and once again the Party machine had proven its organising capacity.

The reaction against the conciliatory line began as soon as the Peniche escapees returned to active politics. In February 1960 the Political Commission of the Central Committee criticised the organisational laxity which it said had grown during the previous three to four years; the attack on the 'excessive centralism' of the 1949–55 period had led to a 'disqualification' (*desautorização*) of the Central Committee's Secretariat and to a false egalitarianism among cadres, with excessive and dangerous rotation of personnel in leading positions.[73] This was described as 'The anarcho-liberal tendency in the organisation of the work of leadership' in a document of that title issued by the Central Committee in December 1960. This document also criticised the belief in a more or less automatic 'decomposition of the regime' which had been the basis for the 'peaceful solution' line, and the consequent acceptance of 'the hegemony of the liberal bourgeoisie and the conservative forces'.[74] Then in the March 1961 Central Committee meeting the major critique of the previous line was adopted – 'The Right-Wing Deviation in the Portuguese Communist Party in the Years 1956–59'.

This document, undoubtedly the work of Cunhal, declared that the definition of a peaceful road, 'in the terms in which it was formulated', represented 'a right-wing deviation, an opportunist deviation'.[75] The conception of the peaceful solution, not just as a desirable possibility but as *the road* for the overthrow of the regime, had led the Party to suffer a series of political setbacks. Partly under the influence of the XX Congress of the Soviet Communist Party – which had adopted the thesis of the peaceful transition to socialism in certain countries – the PCP leaders had erroneously applied this analysis to the democratic revolution against the fascist régime, a régime 'characterised precisely by the strength of its military and police apparatus'. Not only this, but the exact character of the 'peaceful solution' was never defined, so that it merely served to encourage the fashionable political illusions of the moment.[76] The Party's failure to provide leadership in the frankly insurrectional climate prevailing during and after the 1958 Presidential election campaign was criticised, and âlso its uncritical support for a possible military coup at that time.[77] Finally, Cunhal's critique condemned the 'Peaceful National Protest for the Resignation of Salazar and Santos Costa', in which 'the influence of the line of a fraternal party had weighed more than the study of Portuguese reality'.[78] The line for the overthrow of fascism must continue to be that of the 'national uprising' (*levantamento nacional*), and the proletariat's principal allies must be, not the medium or petty bourgeoisie as implied by the 'peaceful solution', but the peasantry and the peoples of the colonies.

The reformist line of these years, however, was not simply an ideological error; it had grave practical consequences for the Party also, in Cunhal's view. It encouraged lax security and over-confidence, exposing the clandestine apparatus to police detection once again; thus from 1957 to December 1962 a total of 86 Party functionaries had been arrested and 29 'Party houses' assaulted by the police.[79] Naturally, such disasters had an impact beyond the Party's underground core; from 1957 to 1959 the total membership had fallen by a third. There was obviously a danger of another collapse on the scale of the 1949–51 débâcle. The return of the experienced 'Peniche group' to the leadership in 1960, and the rectification of the Party's line, had stopped the rot; by the end of 1962 the membership had doubled again.[80] This resurgence was also related to the upsurge of popular protests in 1961–62 and the Party's recovery of a leading role in these movements, which will be discussed below; but even in this improved context, losses still occurred. Thus at the end of 1961, only shortly after the great Caxias escape, the police captured a group of leading cadres including part of the Secretariat: Joaquim Pires Jorge, Octávio Pato, Carlos Costa, Américo de Sousa and others. Then in the spring of 1962, during the great popular demonstrations in Lisbon and Oporto, further comrades were arrested, including António Dias Lourenço and José Magro.[81] It was towards the end of 1962 that Cunhal left Portugal to take up residence in the Soviet bloc, not returning until 1974; presumably this decision was related to the growing insecurity of clandestine existence. Although understandable in view of the Secretary-General's importance and his recent emergence from eleven harsh years in gaol (with his health seriously weakened), the symbolic significance of this move cannot be denied; it is hard to avoid the conclusion that after 1962 the prospect of the PCP leading a popular revolution in Portugal had for practical purposes come to an end.

The influence on the PCP of the crisis in the international Communist movement may well have been decisive at this point. According to some, the Soviet Union and those parties closest to it showed reservations about Cunhal's critique of the 'right-wing deviation', and the Spanish party was offended by the criticism of the 'Peaceful National Strike'.[82] The Albanian-Soviet and Sino-Soviet splits had inevitable repercussions in the Portuguese party; although the marxist-leninist schism did not come to a head until December 1963 or January 1964, with the departure/expulsion from the Party of Francisco Martins Rodrigues, the differences had been crystallising since the summer of 1962 in the form of conflicting analyses of the popular upheavals of that year. But before discussing these developments it is necessary to analyse the popular struggles of 1960–62 and the overall national situation at this critical juncture.

6 The revolutionary upsurge of 1960–62: the end of the PCP's 'heroic era'?

The entire five-year period from 1958 to 1962 was one of severe crisis for the Salazar regime. It began with the Delgado election campaign in May–June 1958, and continued with the 'Cathedral conspiracy' (*revolta da Sé*) in March 1959, the escapes from custody of the PCP leaders in January 1960 and December 1961 and of Henrique Galvao in January 1959, the hijacking of the cruise liner Santa Maria in January 1961 and the outbreak of colonial revolt in Angola the following month, the coup attempt of Botelho Moniz in April of the same year, the hijacking of a TAP plane in November 1961 and the loss of Goa in December; and finally 1962 began with the Beja revolt on 1 January and continued with massive student and worker protests as the culmination of the popular disturbances of the previous two years. Never since the Second World War and its immediate aftermath had the régime been in such deep trouble – and never again would it find itself in such a situation until the final denouement of 1973–74.

In retrospect, the crisis of these years was both the final act of a drama which had been unfolding since the early forties, and the beginning of a new type of opposition politics. The popular protests of 1958, 1961 and 1962 were the last of the great working-class offensives which had occurred periodically since 1942, but they also displayed new characteristics through the links with military populism (Delgado, Galvão and the Beja revolt) and the student movement. The emergence of a militant Catholic left also dates from this period, illustrated by the Sé conspiracy and the prominence of Catholic activists in Delgado's campaign. International developments on the revolutionary left also had an impact: in addition to the marxist-leninist schism in the Communist movement there was the example of the Cuban and Algerian revolutions, both of which had a far from negligible influence on the Portuguese resistance. After 1962 there would be a prolonged hiatus in opposition activity, in part related to the outbreak of the colonial wars and the economic expansion of the sixties; but it also reflected the exhaustion of established patterns of opposition politics and the rise of a vigorous 'New Left', marxist-leninist, Guevarist and radical Catholic, which in Portugal had more influence than almost anywhere in Europe.

With regard to the history of the PCP, the popular upsurge of 1960–62 is of crucial importance. It was the first major mass offensive in which the Party had been involved since the Norton de Matos campaign of 1949 (if we except the Delgado campaign, which was notable precisely for the Party's failure to take a leading role). It was also the first such movement since the rectification of the *desvio de direita*, and hence a clear test of Cunhal's restored leadership and of the line of 'national uprising'.

If the PCP did not now show a capacity to lead the anti-fascist movement to a new level of revolutionary struggle, then its political hegemony within the movement must be in doubt.

The student body, which since the thirties had been largely quiescent and under the control of the regime, began to show signs of activity from 1956 onwards. In that year a new law regulating student associations was issued by the government; it was so restrictive of students' rights that there were unanimous protests from student representatives, to such an extent that the Decree was sent to the National Assembly for amendment, and then suspended pending new legislation. However, as late as January 1962 no such legislation was forthcoming, and the students' associations operated in a legal vacuum.[83] In March 1958, on the occasion of the traditional 'Students' Day', there was an open meeting of Lisbon University students in the Students' Union building of the Instituto Superior Técnico, to discuss the 'better coordination of student organisations' and the desirability of holding a national students' conference.[84] In July 1959 there was a joint meeting in Lisbon of students' and workers' representatives, under Catholic auspices. Shortly before this there had been student demonstrations in Castelo Branco, a quiet provincial town where this would seem most unlikely.[85] Then in November 1960 the Coimbra students protested against a rise in the price of cinema tickets, and in December the Oporto medical students went on strike.[86] In January 1961 – very significantly, in view of the outbreak of revolt in Angola the following month – there was conflict in the *Casa dos Estudantes do Império*, an Institute for students from the colonies; the authorities refused to recognise the elected leaders of the students' association.[87] In March the Lisbon students extended the celebrations of the 'Students' Day' to four days (16–19 March) with a public 'Allegorical Procession' of a satirical character, despite being denied official permission to do so.[88] Then in May in Coimbra, on the occasion of student elections, the candidates of the official Portuguese Youth (Mocidade) were boycotted.[89] There were further student disturbances in Lisbon later in the year.

In March 1962 the long-awaited National Students' Conference finally took place in Coimbra. But the delegates faced many forms of petty harassment by the authorities and all news of the

event was censored from the newspapers.[90] When the Students'
Day celebrations in Lisbon occurred a few weeks later, large-scale
police intervention was the response; an intervention which was
particularly controversial because of the traditional autonomy of
the University.

From the point of view of the regime, the student movement
presented unfamiliar and perplexing problems. Here was a
movement which was not Communist-dominated; although the
official press indulged in the usual red-baiting propaganda,
everyone knew that the students were not led or organised by the
PCP. These were the sons and daughters of the bourgeoisie and
petty bourgeoisie, sectors which in the main had traditionally
supported the regime. While they had specific demands concerning academic freedom, the right to control their own organisations, for better scholarships and benefits, and so on, the movement was characterised by typical student spontaneity and
anarchy and was therefore unpredictable and difficult to negotiate with. From the point of view of the PCP also, the students
were somewhat problematic; although the Party certainly supported the students' protests and most of their demands, it was
acutely aware that here was a movement in which it was not
hegemonic and which might take unforeseeable directions. Quite
a few student activists did join the PCP, and many were
influenced by its prestige; but neither discipline nor ideological
orthodoxy had much appeal to them, and it was precisely the
students who would provide the basis for many of the new
organisations which would challenge the Party from the Left in
future years.

The prohibition of the Students' Day celebrations was justified
by the Ministry of Education in classic obscurantist terms; official
communiqués declared that 'elements of openly subversive
action' had tried to divert 'University, high school and even
primary school students' from their academic work, and that 'The
intervention of the forces of order became imperative because of
information regarding plans to disturb academic life and even
public order ....'[91] But everyone knew that the real reasons
were quite different: it was the increasingly satirical nature of the
student festivities, their increasingly open criticism of government policies, and the prospect of the regime losing control of the
Universities which aroused official fears.

A very significant aspect of the movement was the unity (even if temporary) of professors and students. The government's heavy-handed reaction provoked protests from the academic authorities and finally the resignation of the Rector of Lisbon University, Marcelo Caetano – one of the architects of the *Estado Novo*. On 28 March 1962 the press published a statement from the Lisbon University Senate condemning the police invasion of the University City four days previously, and defending the principle that 'police agents can only enter the academic precincts in the event that the academic authorities request or authorise' such action; it also expressed full confidence in the Rector and in the 'independence' and 'spirit of discipline' of the students.[92]

The student movement and its repression were not confined to Lisbon, and in fact events in Lisbon at this time aroused a movement of solidarity in the other two University cities. In the Oporto Faculty of Sciences what was described as the first general student assembly held in that University occurred on April 2 to discuss a motion of solidarity with Lisbon.[93] In Coimbra a meeting of over 2,000 students on 26 March voted to hold a 'day of mourning' (*luto académico*) in protest against the repression in Lisbon.[94] The *luto académico*, in effect a strike with symbolic gestures of protest, was maintained indefinitely in Lisbon, subject to the authorities' making certain concessions: full authorisation of Students' Day, release of all arrested students and the lifting of all academic penalties imposed in the course of the dispute. On 7 April a mass meeting of students decided to march to the Ministry of Education where their leaders would once again attempt to establish a dialogue, but once again the police intervened and there were more violent clashes and arrests.[95] The government would not accept any conditions for ending the *luto académico*, and it announced its intention of suspending the elected committees of all Students' Associations and banning any student organisations which functioned 'outside the law'.[96] This threat was put into effect a week later – on April 19 the Ministry decreed the supension of the governing bodies of almost all the Lisbon Students' Associations.[97]

The bitter conflict, which was rapidly acquiring much wider political implications, reached a climax in May. At the end of April there was a serious attempt to restore order; the University Senate resolved on 27 April to urge the students to accept the 'immediate and definite normalisation of academic life' and to request from the government a willingness to show understanding in resolving the problem. This conciliatory gesture did not succeed: another student assembly held on 5 May found that no progress had been made in the resolution of grievances. This time the students resolved to occupy the cafeteria, and many of them began a hunger strike. There was continued agitation in Coimbra also, and on 7 May the government suspended the leadership of the Students' Association of that University (*Associação Académica de Coimbra*), thus provoking further protests there.[98] This renewal of conflict cannot be isolated from the general political context: 1 May had seen the biggest and most combative workers' demonstrations for years in Lisbon, followed by further demonstrations and riots on the 8th, and the first week in May also witnessed a massive strike of agricultural workers in the Alentejo.

Very significantly, this new phase in the struggle also saw a breach in the common front of students and professors. On 10 May the Lisbon University Senate, having discussed the situation created by the cafeteria sit-in and having listened to a student delegate (the young Medeiros Ferreira, later to be Foreign Secretary in Mário Soares's Socialist government), nevertheless voted unanimously to give the students a deadline of one hour in which to evacuate the building. When the students refused, the Senate gave authority over the building to the government, thus for the first time in effect inviting police intervention.[99] This led to the worst repression yet; a special unit (*companhia móvel*) of the PSP moved into the University City accompanied by further police with sub-machine guns and a large PIDE contingent. They arrested all those occupying the cafeteria – 'about 1,000 students of both sexes, with relatives and some professors' according to a partially censored report – and also eighty-six students, 'including seven girls', who were occupying the Reading Room and who had been on hunger strike for forty-eight hours.[100] Several students continued their hunger strike in gaol, and some became long-term political prisoners. In Coimbra also the police seized the offices of the *Associação Académica* and made many arrests.[101] The massive repression produced further protests from some professors and Faculty Councils, and agitation continued into June; but for the time being the movement had reached the point of exhaustion. It would flare up again in the late sixties, when the

Universities would become a fertile recruiting ground for the revolutionary left.

Politicisation was a logical consequence of the experience of struggle and repression, leading many students to enter the PCP; according to Alvaro Cunhal, 'among the students there was formed a vast Party organisation, with one of the highest figures of Communist students ever registered in the Party's history ....'[102] However, Cunhal recognised that there were problems for the Party in the orientation of the student movement; if the Students' Associations themselves, not content with fighting for their own democratic rights, tried to lead openly political struggles against the regime, then obviously they would be banned.

We consider it to be a grave error, resulting from ultra-leftist conceptions, to have acted in some cases as if (student) associations were anti-fascist political organisations. Despite the political radicalisation of the student masses that such actions reveal, it cannot but be considered an incorrect orientation, which led to serious harm.[103]

In one sense this criticism was quite valid; if students' (or for that matter, workers' or peasants') organisations brought upon themselves massive political repression, it would only reduce the limited scope for legal opposition activity. But this reasoning ignored the fact that it was often the spontaneous escalation of partial economic or social struggles which, under a dictatorial regime, would lead to open confrontation, and potentially to revolution; one could not *a priori* limit the elected or constitutional leadership of mass organisations to a purely legal, moderate role.

What was true of the students was also true, *a fortiori*, of the working class. The rising tide of strikes and sectoral conflicts since 1957 now took a more political direction (as indeed it had already done, briefly, in May–June 1958). In November 1961, following another round of parliamentary 'elections', there were spontaneous protest demonstrations in Almada, Lisbon, Alpiarça, Coimbra, Couço, Covilhã, Grândola and other towns. Highly political slogans – 'Out with Salazar! Down with fascism! Bring back the troops! – were combined with very militant action: in Almada the workers rescued some of their arrested comrades from the hands of the police, and in Alpiarça they mounted pickets at night to prevent arrests. In Almada on 11 and 14

November thousands of workers battled with police, and one worker, the Communist Cândido Capilé, was killed.[104] Alvaro Cunhal recognised that this militancy represented a new stage of mass struggle against the regime; until November 1961, he said, the great mass political struggles almost always developed by taking advantage of the opportunities for legal action opened up by the election campaigns, but it was now clear that 'the conditions were created to pass on to the open political struggle of the masses outside these periods.'[105]

This spirit of combativity continued and developed steadily during the next six months. There were strikes and other forms of labour unrest in the Lisbon transport system (*Carris*), the telephone company, the Parry and Son shipyard, the CUF works at Barreiro, the postal and insurance workers.[106] In Oporto the regular commemorations of the Republican uprising of 31 January 1891 took the form of mass demonstrations leading to pitched battles with the police: tens of thousands of people occupied the streets for seven hours, shouting slogans against fascism, for a political amnesty, and against the sending of troops to Angola. They confronted baton charges, high pressure water hoses and the use of firearms by the police; although as usual shots were officially fired 'into the air' as a warning, at least one young worker received a bullet wound. At least eighteen people received hosptial treatment afterwards, most of them workers – an indication of the class composition of the demonstration, very different from that of the usual 31 January commemorations which were dominated by the Republican notables of the bourgeois opposition.[107] This pattern was repeated just over a month later on 8 March, International Womens' Day, also in Oporto. Once again a large crowd gathered in the ironically-named *Praça da Liberdade*, singing the national anthem and chanting slogans such as 'Peace, Yes; War, No!' and 'Portugal, Yes; Salazar, No!' They were responding to leaflets which, on behalf of Portuguese women, demanded the return of sons, husbands or brothers serving in the colonies. Although the censored press tried to deny it, speaking of groups of men and 'a few' women, the fact was that many working women partici-pated, indicating that they also were becoming more political.[108] Once again the police intervened in force, making numerous arrests and wounding dozens of people. Students were also involved; a week later some 200 students from Oporto University staged a silent march in protest at the continued detention of some of their colleagues arrested on the 8th.[109]

Although these demonstrations were in part spontaneous, the leading role of the PCP was apparent to all. It was the Party's decision to promote mass participation in such symbolic democratic events as 31 January and 8 March which converted them into acts of working-class protest. In the same way the Party decided to celebrate 1 May, International Workers' Day, on a scale not seen in Portugal for many years. This time the biggest crowds were in Lisbon, where different sources speak of anywhere from 50,000 to 100,000 demonstrators confronting the 'forces of order'. Once again there were slogans against the colonial war, against popular hardship and hunger in Portugal, and for democracy. Demonstrators poured into Lisbon from the working-class suburbs and from the South Bank of the Tagus, gathering in the great *Praça do Comércio*, the monumental square by the waterfront. By 6.30 p.m. a large crowd had gathered around the hated Ministry of Corporations building (the Ministry responsible for the fascist organisation of labour and industry) on the eastern side of the square. It was at this point that the police tried to disperse the crowd, and conflict began. There were several arrests of 'known agitators', but the workers resisted and rescued some of those seized by the police; one PSP agent suffered a deep knife-wound in the neck. As usual, the police fired warning shots into the air from sub-machine guns, but as was noted by a reporter from *O Século* (in a passage which the censor naturally did not allow to pass), at a certain point the rounds were no longer fired into the air, 'as can be deduced from the number of wounded'. The conflict soon developed into a running battle throughout the streets of the *Baixa*, with rioters throwing paving-stones and ripping out traffic signs to use as weapons. Eventually a large force of mounted GNR intervened, and even a unit of regular infantry with armoured cars; one or two rioters also used firearms. After midnight order was restored, with hundreds of arrests and scores of casualties; one worker, Estevão Giro, was killed by a police bullet.[110]

May Day also saw protests in other towns: in Oporto, Almada, Barreiro and many towns in the Alentejo and Ribatejo there were demonstrations involving thousands of people and battles with the police. Then on 8 May there were renewed struggles: in Lisbon thousands of workers, students and others filled the streets of the *Baixa* once again, confronting large numbers of police who had been posted in anticipation of trouble. The number of demonstrators was smaller this time, but the riots still continued for two to three hours from the Avenida da Liberdade to the Praça do Comércio, forcing the shops to close early and causing panic among the upper-class clientele of fashionable stores and cafés in the area.[111] In Oporto the PCP had also called for protests on the 8th, but apparently the police apparatus in the city centre was so overwhelming that nothing happened; bus and tram service into the area was suspended, and people in the commercial district, 'especially foreign tourists', were taken aback by the police presence.[112] Finally, on 28 May – anniversary of the 1926 coup – further protests occurred, although on a smaller scale, in Lisbon, Oporto, Faro (where three people were arrested), and Setúbal, where there was a serious riot.[113]

Protests in May 1962 were not confined to urban workers and students; it was also in that month that the struggle of the Alentejo farm labourers reached a peak. The late fifties had seen a big increase in mechanisation of the harvest, reducing demand for labour and threatening to lower wages. The centre of the workers' concerns therefore changed from wage increases to hours of work; in order to maximise employment, the key demand was for the eight-hour day.[114] This was accompanied by a defensive demand for a minimum daily wage (thirty escudos for men and twenty for women) rather than pressing for further increases. The concern to guarantee employment also led to new forms of struggle: rather than waiting to be hired in the *praça de jorna*, gangs of workers would sometimes go directly to the fields and start work, demanding payment afterwards – thus trying to predetermine the size of the labour force.

Strikes in the Alentejo generally began in May because of the harvest, but in 1962 the PCP made a deliberate effort to co-ordinate them in the first few days of the month in order to coincide with the urban workers' protests. It succeeded, at least to the extent that the first actions occurred on May 2 in Alcácer do Sal, Grândola, Sines, Ermidas, Odemira and other localities of the Alentejo Litoral; from there the movement spread rapidly to the interior in the second week of May – the districts of Evora and

Beja, and parts of the Ribatejo and Portalegre district.[115] The form of action was direct and aggressive: in most cases the workers did not negotiate with the foremen, but simply presented themselves for work at a later hour than usual, and set their own schedule of eight hours (typically, from 8 a.m. to 5 p.m. with an hour's break for lunch). In some cases such as Alcácer do Sal, the landlords gave way after the first day; in other cases they resisted and a real work stoppage developed, lasting several days. In several towns in the Setúbal district the strike lasted as long as three weeks. As usual, the GNR were often brought in with the consequent violent confrontations to which the region was accustomed; but the extent and coordination of the strike throughout the region made it more difficult for the owners to resist.[116] It should not be forgotten that in several towns the strike had been immediately preceded by the May Day demonstrations, often involving open clashes with the police as in Lisbon.

The wave of popular struggles and protests in 1961–62 was impressive by any standards, especially coming in the wake of the conflicts which had been developing since 1957: students, industrial and white-collar workers, farm labourers, fishermen, the miners of Aljustrel – all were involved in a crescendo of revolt culminating in May 1962. When set in the context of other blows against the regime in these years – the actions of Galvao and Delgado, the Cathedral conspiracy, the loss of Goa and the outbreak of war in Angola, the Beja uprising of 1 January 1962, and so on – they give a picture of an all-encompassing crisis, a classic revolutionary situation. Not since 1945–47, perhaps not even then, had the edifice of the *Estado Novo* revealed so many cracks. It is therefore legitimate to ask if a more determined and aggressive offensive by the opposition might not have brought the entire structure to the ground. Such an impression was certainly widespread at the time. Alvaro Cunhal recognised as much by devoting extensive passages in *Rumo à Vitória* – his and the Party's major strategic document of the sixties, written in 1964 – to refuting such ideas:

Some comrades express serious doubts that the popular mass struggle can reach a higher level than that which it already attained in the magnificent popular demonstrations of 1 and 8 May 1962. 'Beyond this (they say) only armed struggle' ... It is not to be expected, nor to be demanded, that after demonstrations such as those of 1 and 8 May 1962 there should follow further peaceful struggles at an even higher level on the local scale ...[117]

But, said Cunhal, the struggle in the rest of the country was at 'an incomparably inferior level' compared to Lisbon, and it was necessary to multiply mass struggles in other regions and other social strata in order to achieve a truly revolutionary movement. Yet the weakness of this reasoning was revealed by Cunhal himself when in another passage he emphasised popular protests in other localities: the Oporto demonstrations of 31 January and 8 March, the 1 May demonstrations in Almada, Barreiro, Oporto and other towns, the Alentejo and Ribatejo strikes, the Coimbra student protests, and so on.[118] The fact was that short of an armed mass insurrection, a more intense and generalised wave of national discontent was indeed hard to imagine. This does not mean that a revolutionary insurrection would necessarily have succeeded in Portugal in 1962, but the preconditions in terms of mass discontent and combativity, not to mention the situation of crisis for the regime in the military and colonial spheres, could scarcely have been more advanced. A great opportunity was lost; Salazarism was given a breathing-space, and the resistance fell into disarray. Both Portugal and the peoples of Angola, Guiné and Mozambique were condemned to thirteen years of savage warfare, and the character of the Portuguese revolution was profoundly altered.

Notes to Chapter IV

1   Fernando Gouveia, *Memórias de um Inspector da PIDE: 1. A Organização clandestina do PCP*, Lisboa, 1979, Roger Delraux; p. 272.

2   *Ibid.*, pp. 277–9.

3   *Ibid.*, pp. 280–2.

4   Ramiro da Costa, *Elementos para a História do Movimento Operário em Portugal, 2° Volume, 1930–1975*, Lisboa, 1975, Assírio e Alvim, p. 99.

5   *Ibid.*, 2° Vol., p. 87.

6   Gouveia, p. 342; *Conversando com Octávio Pato*, Lisboa, 1976, Ediçao da SIP do PCP, p. 9.

7   Da Costa, *Elementos*, 2° Vol., p. 99; Francisco Martins Rodrigues, *Elementos para a História do Movimento Operário e do Partido Comunista em Portugal*, Lisboa, n.d., Edições Militão Ribeiro, p. 42; *Conversando com Octávio Pato*, p. 9.

8   Gouveia, pp. 277–8. He simply says that neighbours suspected that there was something odd about the residents of the two houses (in

Macinhata do Vouga and Luso), and told the GNR. This is of course possible, but given other suspicious circumstances (evidence pointing to informers or provocateurs), it cannot be taken at face value.

9 Francisco Martins Rodrigues, *Elementos*, p. 42; Da Costa, *Elementos*, 2° Vol., pp. 83−4 (n. 22) and 99−100; *Conversando com Octávio Pato*, p. 9.

10 Author's interview with Octávio Pato, Lisbon, 25 February 1977.

11 Da Costa, *Elementos*, 2° Vol., pp. 83−4 (n. 22).

12 Mário Soares, *Portugal Amordaçado: depoimento sobre os anos do fascismo*, Lisboa, 1974, Arcádia, pp. 172−3; Gouveia, pp. 318−24; Martins Rodrigues, *Elementos*, p. 42 (who simply says, rather ingenuously, that Domingues 'appeared dead soon afterwards').

13 *A Voz* (Lisbon), 31 March 1949.

14 Ramiro da Costa, *Elementos*, 2° Vol., p. 87.

15 Cunhal trial records (in 3° Juízo Criminal de Lisboa, Processo No. 14499 de 1949, 1° Volume, fls. 20−1 & 31).

16 *Ibid.* (Apenso (1956), 1° Volume, fls. 30).

17 *Ibid.* (10° Volume, fls. 662).

18 *Ibid.* (12° Volume, fls. 1113−14).

19 *Biografia do Camarada Alvaro Cunhal*, Edições 'Avante!', 1954 (in Cunhal trial records, Apenso (1956), 1° Volume, fls. 31).

20 *Ibid.*; and Apenso (1956), 1° Volume, fl. 12.

21 Da Costa, *Elementos*, 2° Vol., p. 99.

22 *Ibid.*, 2° Vol. pp. 83−4, 100 & 114−15; Martins Rodrigues, *Elementos*, pp. 41, 43−4 & 52.

23 *Conversando com Octávio Pato*, p. 9.

24 Militão Ribeiro's report to the Central Committee, quoted in Da Costa, *Elementos*, 2° Vol., p. 83.

25 *Debate dentro do Partido em defesa dos principios do Marxismo − Leninismo (Auto-crítica do camarada Ramiro) e algumas observações do Secretariado do CC do PCP*, Editorial 'Avante!', 1951, pp. 11−13; consulted in *Avante!* archive.

26 *Ibid.*, pp. 13−15.

27 *Ibid.*, pp. 2−6.

28 Soares, *Portugal Amordaçado*, pp. 177−87; and author's interview with Mário Soares, Lisbon, 29 June 1978.

29 Author's interview with Mário Soares, Lisbon, 29 June 1978.

30 Manuel Garcia & Lourdes Maurício, *O Caso Delgado: autópsia da 'Operação Outuno'*, Lisboa, 1977, Edições Jornal Expresso, p. 182.

31 *Ibid.*; and *Auto de Perguntas de Fernando António Piteira Santos* (in Cunhal trial records, 8° Volume, fls. 512−19).

32 *Avante!*, VI Série No. 168, Junho de 1952, quoted in Garcia & Maurício, *O Caso Delgado*, p. 184.

33 Da Costa, *Elementos*, 2° Vol., pp. 100−1; Martins Rodrigues, *Elementos*, pp. 43−5.

34 'Amílcar' (Sérgio Vilarigues), *O Caminho para uma Ampla Frente Nacional Anti-Salazarista* (Informe Político à VIa. Reunião Ampliada do Comité Central do Partido Comunista Português; Edições '*Avante!*'); consulted in *Avante!* archive.

35 Comité Central do Partido Comunista Português, *A Situação Política Actual e a Posição do Partido Comunista Português*, Outubro de 1956, Edições *'Avante!'*, p. 1; consulted in *Avante!* archive.
36 *Ibid.*, p. 21.
37 *Ibid.*, p. 3.
38 *Declaração Conjunta do Partido Comunista de Espanha e do Partido Comunista Português*, Abril de 1956 (1 p.); consulted in the PCE archive, Madrid.
39 *O Desvio de Direita no Partido Comunista Português nos Anos 1956– 1959 (elementos de estudo)*, Março de 1961, Edições *'Avante!'*, pp. 15–17; clandestine document consulted in the *Avante!* archive.
40 V Congresso do Partido Comunista Português, *A Unidade das Forças Anti-Salazaristas, Factor Decisivo para a Libertação Nacional* (Informe Político do Comité Central), Informante: camarada Ramiro (Outubro de 1957, Edições *'Avante!'*), p. 42. In PDR – Processo, 3° Volume, fls. 255.
41 Gouveia, p. 399.
42 V Congresso do Partido Comunista Português, *A Unidade das Forças Anti-Salazaristas*, pp. 17–18, 23–4, 27–9 & 33.
43 *Ibid.*, p. 34.
44 *Ibid.*, p. 27.
45 *Ibid.*, p. 37.
46 V Congresso do Partido Comunista Português, *Sobre as Próximas Eleições para Deputados* (Intervenção pelo camarada Manuel), Outubro de 1957, Edições *'Avante!'*, p. 1. In PDR – Processo, 3° Volume, fls. 254.
47 *Programa do Partido Comunista Português, Aprovado no V Congresso*, Outubro de 1957, Editorial *'Avante!'*, pp. 2–3 & 13–20; consulted in *Avante!* archive.
48 Francisco Rafael *et al.*, *Portugal: Capitalismo e Estado Novo: Algumas Contribuições para o seu Estudo*, Porto, 1976, Afrontamento, p. 53; António de Figueiredo, *Portugal: Fifty Years of Dictatorship*, Middlesex, 1975, Penguin, pp. 169–70.
49 Figueiredo, pp. 171–2.
50 Aquilino Ribeiro, *Quando os Lobos Uivam*, Amadora, 1974, Bertrand.
51 José Pacheco Pereira, *Conflitos Sociais nos Campos do Sul de Portugal*, Lisboa, 1982, Europa-América, pp. 134–5.
52 Alvaro Cunhal, *Relatório da Actividade do Comité Central ao VI Congresso do PCP* (Lisboa, 1975, Edições *'Avante!'*), p. 119; Pacheco Pereira (*Conflitos Sociais*, pp. 142–3) disputes this argument in general, but admits its validity for the years 1949–52.
53 Da Costa, *Elementos*, 2° Vol., pp. 106–7.
54 *Ibid.*, p. 107.
55 Pacheco Pereira, *Conflitos Sociais*, p. 143.
56 José Dias Coelho, *A Resistência em Portugal*, Porto, 1974, Editorial Inova, p. 50. Da Costa, *Elementos* (2° Vol., p. 86) gives the date of Vidigal's death as 9 June 1945; since he died in custody, news of his death was probably only released after several days, and the exact date may never be known.

57 *O Camponês (Orgão de Unidade Nacional Anti-Fascista para os Camponeses do Sul), Série 1 – No. 4, Julho de 1947; Carlos da Fonseca, História do Movimento Operário e das Ideias Socialistas em Portugal, I: Cronologia,* Lisboa, n.d., Europa-América, p. 200; Da Costa, *Elementos,* 2° Vol., p. 87.

58 *O Século* archive, report deleted by the censor, 24 June 1958.

59 José Miguel Tarquini, *A Morte no Monte: Catarina Eufémia,* Lisboa, 1974, Empresa Tipográfica Casa Portuguesa, gives a highly romanticised version of the event. See also Da Costa, *Elementos,* 2° Vol., pp. 107–8, and Dias Coelho, *A Resistência em Portugal,* pp. 18–23.

60 *Avante!* VI Série No. 79, 2a. Quinzena de Junho de 1945.

61 Da Costa, *Elementos,* 2° Vol., p. 107; Tarquini, *A Morte no Monte,* pp. 125 & 134–7; Dias Coelho, *loc. cit..*

62 Pacheco Pereira, *Conflitos Sociais,* p. 145.

63 V Congresso do Partido Comunista Português, *A Unidade das Forças Anti-Salazaristas,* pp. 23–4.

64 Carlos da Fonseca, *História,* pp. 204–6.

65 Carlos da Fonseca, *História, pp. 206 & 208;* Da Costa, *Elementos,* 2° Vol., p. 138.

66 *O Século* archive, partially censored report of 4 March 1959.

67 Cunhal, *Relatório ... ao VI Congresso,* pp. 16 & 109; Carlos da Fonseca, *História,* pp. 208 & 211; Da Costa, *Elementos,* 2° Vol., p. 138.

68 Alvaro Seiça Neves, 'Alocução de Abertura do Congresso', in II Congresso Republicano de Aveiro, *Teses e Documentos: Textos Integrais,* Lisboa, 1969, Seara Nova, Vol. I, pp. 9–10.

69 Informe da Commissão Política ao Comité Central do Partido Comunista Português: *Sobre a Actividade do Partido nas Campanhas Eleitorais para Deputados à Assembleia Nacional e para a Presidência da República,* Lisboa, Agosto de 1958, Edições 'Avante!'; Relator: Gomes; pp. 5–6; consulted in the *Avante!* archive.

70 Da Costa, *Elementos,* 2° Vol., p. 130.

71 Francisco Miguel, *Uma Vida na Revolução,* Lisboa, 1977, 'A Opinião', pp. 131–7.

72 Richard Robinson, *Contemporary Portugal: A History,* London, 1979, George Allen & Unwin, p. 8; Francisco Miguel, *Uma Vida na Revolução,* pp. 144–50; Martins Rodrigues, *Elementos,* p. 71.

73 *O Militante,* III Série No. 108, Janeiro de 1961.

74 *Ibid.;* and Da Costa, *Elementos,* 2° Vol., p. 150.

75 *O Desvio de Direita ...,* p. 1.

76 *Ibid.,* pp. 1–2.

77 *Ibid.,* pp. 2–6.

78 *Ibid.,* pp. 15–17.

79 *VI Congresso do PCP: Relatório sobre Problemas de Organização* (Relator: Joaquim Gomes), Editorial 'Avante!' 1965, pp. 4–5.

80 Cunhal, *Relatório ... ao VI Congresso,* p. 184.

81 *Ibid.,* p. 163; *VI Congresso do PCP: Relatório sobre Problemas de Organização,* pp. 4–5; Martins Rodrigues, *Elementos,* p. 71.

82 Da Costa, Elementos, 2° Vol., p. 154.

83 *Comunicado das Associações de Estudantes,* January 1962; consulted by courtesy of Dr Francisco Sousa Tavares.

84   *O Século* archive, partially censored article of 20 March 1958.
85   Carlos da Fonseca, *Historia*, p. 208.
86   *Ibid.*, p. 209.
87   *Ibid.*.
88   *Ibid.*; and correspondence between the Commission of the Lisbon Students' Associations and the Ministry of Education, consulted by courtesy of Dr Francisco da Sousa Tavares.
89   Carlos da Fonseca, *Historia*, p. 210.
90   *O Século* archive, articles censored from the issues of 4 & 10 March 1962.
91   See the Ministry's *Notas Oficiosas* in *O Século*, 25 & 27 March 1962.
92   *O Século*, 28 March 1962; *Diário de Notícias*, 28 March 1962.
93   *O Século* archive, report deleted by the censor, 3 April 1962.
94   *Comunicado No. 3 das Associações de Estudantes de Lisboa*, 29 March 1962; consulted by courtesy of Dr Francisco da Sousa Tavares.
95   Comunicado No. 10 das Associações de Estudantes de Lisboa, 8 April 1962; consulted by courtesy of Dr Francisco da Sousa Tavares.
96   *Diário de Notícias*, 11 & 13 April 1962.
97   *O Século* archive, article censored from the issue of 20 April 1962.
98   *O Século*, 8 May 1962.
99   *Ibid.*, 11 May 1962.
100   *O Seculo* archive, partially censored article from the issue of 12 May 1962.
101   Carlos da Fonseca, *História*, p. 212.
102   Cunhal, *Relatório . . . ao VI Congresso*, p. 128.
103   *Ibid.*, p. 127.
104   Cunhal, *Rumo à Vitória: As Tarefas do Partido na Revolução Democrática e Nacional*, Lisboa, 1975, Edições 'A Opinião', pp. 210–11 & 233; Martins Rodrigues, *Elementos*, p. 67; Da Costa, *Elementos*, 2° Vol., p. 158; Carlos da Fonseca, *História*, p. 210.
105   Cunhal, *Rumo à Vitória*, p. 211.
106   Carlos da Fonseca, *História*, p. 211; Cunhal, *Relatorio . . . ao VI Congresso*, p. 163.
107   *O Século* archive, partially censored article from the issue of 1 February 1962; Cunhal, *Rumo à Vitória*, p. 212; Carlos da Fonseca, *História*, p. 211.
108   *O Século* archive, partially censored article from the issue of 9 March 1962; Cunhal, *Rumo à Vitória*, p. 212; Da Costa, *Elementos*, 2° Vol., p. 158.
109   *O Século* archive, article deleted by the censor from the issue of 17 March 1962.
110   *O Século* archive, partially censored article from the issue of 3 May 1962; Cunhal, *Rumo à Vitória*, p. 212; Ramiro da Costa, *Elementos*, 2° Vol., pp. 158–9; Martins Rodrigues, *Elementos*, p. 69.
111   *O Século* archive, partially censored articles from the issues of 9 & 16 May 1962.
112   *Ibid.*, partially censored article from the issue of 9 May 1962.

113 *Ibid.*, articles deleted by the censor from the issue of 29 May 1962; Da Costa, *Elementos*, 2° Vol., pp. 158–9; Cunhal, *Rumo à Vitória*, p. 213.
114 Pacheco Pereira, *Conflitos Sociais*, pp. 147–51.
115 *Ibid.*, pp. 152–5.
116 Cunhal, *Rumo à Vitória*, pp. 193–4.
117 *Ibid.*, p. 170.
118 *Ibid.*, pp. 211–13.

5

The emergence of military populism: Galvão and Delgado

Houve em Lisboa as *archotadas* quando Saldanha caiu, e d'esse tumulto plebeu e republicano ganhou o general a fama de demagogo, sem o ser. Do povo queria só as acclamações, dos soldados o amor, dos reis a adulação. Entre o throno, a tropa e a rua, o seu génio reclamava o logar de árbitro: não o de usurpador, nem o de tribuno o consul. Os que lhe chamavam D. João VII e os que o accusavam de republicano, enganavam-se ambos. Elle queria um reinado de facto à sombra de um throno antigo, para combinar as suas vaidades ingénuas com os sentimentos sympáthicos e com as exigências do seu temperamento irrequieto.

There were incendiary attacks in Lisbon when Saldanha fell, and from that plebeian and republican riot the General gained the reputation of a demagogue, which he was not. From the people he wanted only their applause, from the soldiers their affection, from the royalty their adulation. Between the throne, the troops and the street, his genius demanded the position of referee: not that of usurper, nor that of tribune or consul. Those who called him King John VII and those who accused him of republicanism were equally mistaken. He wanted a *de facto* dominion in the shadow of an ancient throne, in order to combine his ingenuous vanity with his sympathetic sentiments and the demands of his restless temperament.

Oliveira Martins, *Portugal Contemporâneo* (1881)

1 The background: military republicanism and the populist tradition

The association of the Portuguese military with republicanism, going back to the origins of the Republican movement (and even before that with liberalism), was continued after 1926 with the prominence of military men in the opposition and the pattern of *reviralhismo*, of the constant military conspiracies and coup attempts against the *Estado Novo*. It was undoubtedly a crucial factor in Salazar's decision not to restore the monarchy, despite his association with monarchist circles and the pressure – vigorous in the early thirties and again in the early fifties – for a restoration. Military republicanism had strong populist overtones, of the men in uniform as 'sons of the people', plebeian tribunes standing on guard against aristocracy, clericalism and reaction – a tradition which could easily combine with another recurrent phenomenon, that of the charismatic leader, the 'man on horseback', to create a potent political force. Here the old myth of *sebastianismo*, of the vanished leader who would return to save the nation, could also be evoked in the popular imagination – and there were numerous precedents, on both Left and Right. The concept of the 'honour of the army'[1] and of the armed forces as a moral reserve of the nation provided further ideological underpinnings for an identification of the martial profession with the popular cause.

A phenomenon such as populism or Bonapartism does not recur over a long historical period unless there is a condition of social stasis maintaining a similar balance of class forces for an unusual length of time, or alternatively, if certain conditions produce recurrent crises of political representation despite social change. But it is arguable that these conditions did obtain to a significant degree in Portugal from the late 19th to the mid-20th century: a very gradual and limited process of industrialisation and urbanisation was combined with repeated political stalemates between Liberals and Conservatives, Monarchists and Republicans, bourgeoisie and proletariat. Moreover, in any crisis the ideological tradition of military populism, reinforced with each such experience, was available to rationalise the ambitions of would-be candidates for the praetorian role. The regime itself had after all originated in a military coup, and while Salazar's most notable achievement was to civilianise it, the threat of a *putsch*, from either Left or Right, was constant. It is not accidental that Salazar maintained a military man as President (even if only as figurehead) throughout, and that three of the five presidential candidates presented by the opposition in the official 'elections' were officers – the exceptions (Ruy Luis Gomes and Arlindo Vicente) being those most closely identified with the Left.

During the early stages of the régime, military opposition

expressed itself for the most part simply as a component of the republican resistance, through the PRP, the Freemasons and related organisations emanating from the First Republic. This pattern was still predominant during the Second World War, symbolised by the nomination of the venerable General Norton de Matos to head the MUNAF. It can be seen also in the personnel associated with the various coup attempts in the forties: Admiral Mendes Cabeçadas, Colonel Tamagnini Barbosa, Colonel Lelo Portela, and so on. But it was in the late forties that there appeared the first signs of a new trend, potentially more disturbing to the régime: the desertion of right-wing officers, previously stalwart supporters of the *Estado Novo*, who had even been vigorous proponents of fascist ideology. The first clear case of this was Captain Henrique Galvão, technical director of the Colonial Exhibition in Oporto in 1934 and an outspoken propagandist of the Portuguese 'colonial mission'. Galvão was in many ways typical of the officers who had participated in the 28th of May, and who believed, in the words of Douglas Wheeler, 'that the Portuguese Army was not only the most important institution in society but was a vital instrument of national revival', or as expressed by the *Revista Militar*, 'The army (is) the highest essence of the national soul.'[2] Such views were difficult to square with those of the Democratic Opposition, but hostility to Salazarism would make some strange bedfellows.

2 Henrique Galvão: the outraged honour of a conservative idealist

Henrique Carlos Mata Galvão was born in Barreiro in 1895; he attended high school in Lisbon, and then the Polytechnic and Military Academy, before going to France for a course at the Ecole Supérieur d'Education Physique. As a young man he was one of the 'cadets of Sidónio', an active participant in the revolution which brought Colonel Sidónio Pais to power in December 1917, instituting a regime which many see as the forerunner of the *Estado Novo*.[3] A supporter of the 28th May coup, Galvão advanced rapidly as a servant of the new regime; he served a term as District Governor of Huila (Angola), and then, following his responsibility in the 1934 Colonial Exhibition, in 1935 he was appointed Chairman of the Board of the National

Radio (*Emissora Nacional*) and simultaneously Senior Inspector of Colonial Administration.[4] According to Humberto Delgado, Galvão was not promoted beyond the rank of captain 'since in his age-group the upper ranks were filled with infantry subalterns', and this is why he opted for civilian posts.[5] But regardless of his military situation. it seems clear that he had political ambitions; he became a deputy in the National Assembly, and lost no opportunity to voice his vigorous and sometimes controversial views. Speaking of the parade which closed the Oporto Exhibi-tion, Galvão stressed that its 'brilliance and grandeur' must correspond to 'its high objectives of colonial propaganda'.[6] On another occasion he referred to the Exhibition as being 'neither the beginning nor the end of a task', but rather a phase in its development 'in the true interests of the country'.[7] In October 1935 we find him giving a lecture to the prestigious Portuguese Geographical Society in which he made a classic apology for colonialism.[8]

The young propagandist soon received further opportunities to influence colonial policy in the desired direction. In April 1937 he was sent on a six-month mission to Angola to study the problem of white settlement in that 'province', and a year later he went on a tour of inspection to Portuguese India and Macau.[9] Throughout this time he continued his activities as publicist and polemicist, which were not limited to lectures and interviews; he also had literary ambitions, and by 1936 had already published 21 books. His prolific literary output was remarkably varied, ranging from technical works (an 'Economic Report on Angola' and a study of 'Packaging in Colonial Trade') to travel memoirs ('In the Land of the Blacks' and 'Lands of witchcraft'), history and theatre. But the colonial theme was present throughout, as in his three-act play 'The Golden Veil' presented in the National Theatre on 29 July 1936 and described as a 'colonial fantasy'.[10] Galvão's colonialist obsession and his romanticism about European activi-ties in the tropics were undiminished eight years later; in a work published in 1944, 'Kuriká, a story of wild beasts', our author's imagination ran wild in a study of 'animal psychology' with political overtones. In the questionable opinion of the reviewer in the official *Diário de Notícias*, this 'fantasy on real themes' revealed 'a profound understanding of the mysteries of the backlands . . .'.[11]

Throughout the thirties and forties, and indeed later, Galvao's ideological position remained perfectly clear; and he did not limit his expressions of opinion to colonial issues. On 22 August 1936, for example, he gave a talk on *Rádio Club Português* in the series 'Cinco minutos anti-comunistas' in which he warned that 'the Marxist enemy is springing up now everywhere, and it is absolutely necessary to organise our defence against the red danger':

There are people who for convenience or from political passion do not believe, or pretend not to believe in the danger which threatens them ... They are also enemies, although of a different kind. In Spain there were cases like these: those who behaved like this were slaughtered. There are also the opportunists – as for them, in Spain they were shot ...[12]

Clearly Galvão was not one for half-measures; and he proclaimed his views boldly, even aggressively. He was also a man who acted on his beliefs, indeed who was eager to put them into practice; in a panegyric published in 1936, a journalist described him in these terms:

Henrique Galvão is the perfect model of a man of action. Dynamism and a sense of reality. Proudly he declares in this interview, insisting upon it repeatedly, that he is a colonialist ...[13]

Such outspokenness served the young officer well so long as he remained faithful to the fascist régime, but when he began to voice criticisms it would swiftly get him into trouble. And paradoxically, it was precisely his colonialism – or to be more precise, his idealistic conscience combined with his colonialism – which would bring about his downfall.

Galvão's crucial act of dissidence, leading to his break with the *Estado Novo*, was his famous report ('aviso-previo') on forced labour in Angola, presented to the National Assembly in March 1949.[14] This was the end-product of years of frustration, as the conservative but idealistic colonialist campaigned vainly for reforms designed to promote economic development and social integration in the colonies. In fact Galvão had already given an indication of his disillusion with the regime; a few months earlier, in late 1948, he appeared in court as a defence witness for his friend Col Carlos Selvagem, one of the accused in the trial of those involved in the coup attempt of 10 April 1947. At the time, according to Mário Soares, Galvão declared: 'I have just signed my own sentence. Salazar will not forgive me any more' – suggesting that he had already decided to go into opposition.[15] Also in the Presidential election of 1949, in which Norton de Matos ran for the opposition, Galvão's position was ambiguous. In a radio message to his Angolan constituents, he said that both sides were obscure amalgams of different ideologies; the only difference was that the opposition included the Communists, and therefore 'it is advisable to vote for the situation, despite its errors and deficiencies, in order to combat the Communist danger . . .'.[16]

Once the deputy for Angola had shown his disenchantment with the 'Situation', he was of course rapidly relieved of his position in Parliament. Never one to hesitate, he swiftly moved to develop contacts with other dissidents and some sectors of the opposition – primarily the more conservative oppositionists such as Cunha Leal. Galvão became one of the prime movers of Admiral Quintão Meireles' campaign for the Presidency in 1951 – a logical move, since Meireles was a dissident like himself, although lacking Galvão's boldness and determination. It seems probable that Galvão was responsible for injecting a more polemical tone into some of Meireles' rather bland electoral communiqués.[17] Some of Galvão's statements at this time do suggest a significant change in outlook; thus in an article written in September 1951 and dealing with the theme of 'Order' – one of the regime's favourite shibboleths – he showed a surprising openness to liberal ideas of tolerance and compromise:

In fact I am much more wary of those who want to establish order yet cannot agree as to the means, than of those who show less concern with order and more with trying to understand and consider the natural movement of human movements and conflicts . . .[18]

Such a conception, almost dialectical, implies a fundamental objection to the authoritarian philosophy of the corporate State; and Galvão's subsequent utterances suggest that his position, even if not always consistent, was that of a right-wing liberal.

When Meireles' campaign ended, and in fact even before, Galvão was engaged in conspiratorial preparations involving both military men and Republican politicians in a 'National Civic Organisation'. But the coup, planned for January 1952, failed as usual, and on 6 January Galvão was arrested along with other conspirators.[19] In December 1952 a military court sentenced him to three years in gaol, but on appeal the sentence was quashed; however, the re-trial, which was held in March 1953 in the Santa Clara Military Court, maintained the gaol sentence plus the loss of political and civil rights for fifteen years.[20] While awaiting the re-trial, Galvão tried to escape from the Trafaria Military Fortress where he was detained; but reinforced vigilance thwarted his plans.[21] The prisoner also protested that his officer's pay had been stopped, contrary to regulations, and threatened a hunger-strike; this had the desired effect since that same afternoon the Overseas Ministry ordered that this salary be paid as legally required. The next day it was reported that Galvão was receiving medical treatment for 'congestion' which had brought on 'paralysis of his left side'; a few days later he was said to be recovering from 'a nervous accident of a functional character'.[22] It seems likely that this strange ailment was a product of Galvão's indomitable personality, some kind of temporary nervous breakdown; such incidents would recur several times during his long incarceration, 'presaging that other breakdown which would later kill him, driven to insanity, in São Paulo'.[23]

During his years in gaol Galvão was in permanent rebellion, entering into endless disputes with the guards and the authorities, writing, agitating and even conspiring. In the words of Vasco da Gama Fernandes, he was like a wild beast in a cage, incapable of accepting his situation. With the tolerance of sympathetic guards, he began to publish a clandestine newspaper, *Moreano*, in which he denounced official corruption. It was as a result of the particularly virulent contents of one issue of this pamphlet (which may have been a police provocation) that Galvão found himself in the bizarre situation of being tried for libel while still in gaol. When this trial was finally concluded (in March 1958), he was condemned to a further sixteen years in gaol plus loss of political rights for twenty years.[24] But in the meantime the incorrigible prisoner had caused further trouble: transferred because of poor health to the Santa Maria Hospital, it was reported that he had, 'on the night of 4 November 1955, thrown a chair, with aggressive intent, at Sr Armando Cristofaretti da Costa Lima, an agent of the International Police who was guarding him in that hospitalary establishment ...'. The chair

missed the PIDE agent but broke a window, and for this the
culprit was condemned to pay damages and sentenced to a
further 25 days (!) in gaol.[25] On another occasion, annoyed
because he was only allowed the use of a typewriter during
certain hours, Galvão assaulted one of his guards; and when the
time came for him to make a judicial statement about the
incident, he refused to sign it until the honorific 'Excelentíssimo'
was removed from the police agent's name.[26] What is perhaps
most remarkable is that, by the force of his personality, he got his
way in such petty disputes.

Galvão's remarkable career entered a new phase with his
escape from the Santa Maria Hospital on 16 January 1959; giving
the lie to the two guards posted to watch him, he took refuge
in a friend's house in Lisbon, and on 17 February entered the
Argentine Embassy to request political asylum. In May 1959 the
Portuguese Government finally gave him a safe-conduct to leave
the country, and he travelled to Buenos Aires and later Caracas,
where he would conspire among the exile opposition, linking up
for a while with his fellow-dissident, Humberto Delgado.[27]

Once he had moved into opposition, Galvão dedicated all his
rhetorical fury to attacks on the regime and especially on Salazar;
but the essential content of his discourse changed very little. In
his 'Open Letter to Dr Salazar' published in Brazil in the sixties,
he accuses the dictator of having destroyed the dignity and
manliness of the Portuguese people: '. . . Your Excellency has
intimidated and beaten into submission eight million Portuguese
whom you have turned into the wretched morons who wander
around to the tune of Fado, Fátima and Football . . .'[28] Delgado
also, in his election campaign, would accuse Salazar of having
destroyed the virility of the Portuguese people.[29] Galvão defended his participation in the 28th of May and in the dictatorship
with the argument that the original purpose of the regime – the
moral reconstruction of the country – had been distorted by
Salazar; it was a dictatorship 'which circumstances had made
temporarily necessary for the re-establishment of a serious basis
of government, politics and administration . . . The question of
the type of regime was not an issue'.[30] Nevertheless, Galvao in
opposition persisted in his violent anti-communism, the only
difference being that now he accused Salazar of being responsible
for the spread of Communist ideas:

In this country, which is essentially anti-communist, and where
Communism could not gather even a thousand sincere supporters, Your
Excellency set about manufacturing artificial Communists in order to be
albe to prate constantly to the world that in Portugal there was only one
political alternative: either Salazar or Communism ...[31]

Indeed, Galvão's anti-communism was so deep-rooted that
unlike Delgado, he never accepted the necessity of any kind of
alliance or collaboration with the PCP in the resistance; and he
made anti-communism a fundamental feature of the shadowy
organisation he set up in exile, the 'Anti-Totalitarian Front of
Free Portuguese Abroad'.

Also fundamental to Galvão's outlook was his colonialism –
a position which he maintained to the end, even when he was
repudiated by virtually the entire exile opposition on this account. Thus he criticised Salazar for having introduced (in his
Colonial Statute) the designation 'colonies' instead of 'overseas
provinces' to refer to the Portuguese territories in Africa and Asia;
if it were not for this, Portugal would have a better legal defence
at the United Nations, and would be in the process of becoming
an Euro-African Federal Republic, instead of facing the imminent
danger of losing everything.[32] In other words, the neo-colonial
dream, which other sectors of the opposition abandoned when
faced with the reality of the world-wide collapse of colonialism,
still dominated Galvao's thinking.

In the final analysis, in order to really understand the mentality
of this highly individualistic officer, one has to seek the roots of
his ideology in the Iberian mystique of military honour or
hidalguía. Perhaps the best expression of his ideology is in an
article he wrote in 1944, entitled 'The Man and the Crowd':

The crowd and the Man separated from the crowd – above or below it
– do not speak the same language, nor do they revolve about the same
axis ...
Those Men who are separated from the crowd – leaders, artists,
thinkers, scientists, etc., and also the great misanthropists – are
Individuals, autonomous organisms, virtually independent ...
Now, since the Man and the crowd do not understand each other and
their understanding is a fundamental condition of the health and
strength of the peoples, it is necessary that, between the One and the
other, there should move some element of mutual understanding, a
faithful interpreter of the crowd to the Man and of the Man to the crowd
...

If the interpreters are mediocre, inadequate ... then the Man will always misjudge the crowd, just as the crowd will always misjudge the Man ...[33]

In other words, in addition to the cult of the Leader – always with a capital 'L' – the key to any social and political system, for Galvão, is an enlightened and morally superior élite; presumably, in most cases, a military élite. This is the classic apology for the political dominance of the military; and in another form, it would be revealed once again in the Armed Forces Movement in 1974–75. Although Galvão was a maverick of markedly right-wing views, he was a characteristic representative of the military populist trend which would continue in Delgado and surface in a more leftist guise in the MFA.

3 Delgado's origins and ideological tendencies

The second flamboyant military dissident from the *Estado Novo*, Humberto da Silva Delgado, was born in Torres Novas on 15 May 1906, the son of a Republican army officer and a 'profoundly devout, rather superstitious' mother.[34] The only boy among four children, he claimed to have absorbed from his mother 'instincts of kindness and protectiveness towards the weak', and from his father, 'to eschew the practice of religion' and also 'a transcending love of justice and hatred of oppression'.[35] As a young man he was influenced by the pamphleteer Homem Cristo, in whom he admired the traits of 'detestation of meaningless words, contempt for rhymes or slogans which affront one's intelligence, abhorrence of the search for a scapegoat'.[36] Delgado opted early for a military career, and by 1925 had reached the rank of Second Lieutenant in the Artillery. It was at this stage that he began to demonstrate the qualities of bravery, impatience and irascibility which were to be so prominent in his later career; on 2 February 1926 Delgado was injured trying to disarm a rebellious sergeant at the Artillery Training School where he was posted, and later the same year, having entered the Air Force, he was lucky to survive a plane crash after insisting on flying in appalling conditions.[37] Also at this time, having failed to obtain what he regarded as adequate redress through official channels for the aforementioned assault by the sergeant, Delgado went personally to seek him out at another unit and gave him a beating in order to salvage his besmirched honour – an incident which he subsequently recounted with relish![38]

Given these authoritarian traits, it was scarcely surprising that the young Delgado was an active participant in the military uprising which broke out on 28 May 1926 with the aim of 'restoring order' and 'saving the nation' from the corruption and incompetence of the politicians. Although participation in the 28th of May does not in itself demonstrate fascist leanings, Delgado's subsequent evolution left no room for doubt regarding his sympathies at this time. He rose rapidly in the military, and also came to occupy political offices in the 'New State'; thus in 1936 he was nominated Assistant Commissar of the *Mocidade Portuguesa* (the fascist youth organisation) and Military Adjutant to the General Command of the Portuguese Legion.[39] Although the Delgado of 1958 tried to play down the significance of these appointments, arguing that they were 'purely military', it is clear that not only were they in fact highly political but also that the Delgado of 1936 was a convinced, even a vigorous, supporter of the regime. During the 1930s, and until at least 1942, the young Air Force officer made numerous public statements, in the press, on the radio and in speeches, exhibiting strong and explicit identification with the ideology of the 'New State'.

Delgado's first venture in this direction was the publication in 1933 of a book, perhaps better described as an extended political tract with the colourful title 'Da pulhice do "Homo Sapiens" (Da Monarquia de vigaristas, pela Republica de bandidos à Ditadura de papa)'[40] – which roughly translates as 'On the decay of "Homo Sapiens" (From the Monarchy of swindlers, via the Republic of bandits to the weak-kneed Dictatorship)'. As the title would suggest, if the work implied any criticism of the regime, it was for not being repressive enough; and its criticisms of Republican politicians can only be described as scurrilous. The book displayed a total contempt for parliamentary institutions, well expressed in passages such as the following:

The sovereign people represented in its most sovereign parliament spat, talked and shouted in the great saliva factory which was S. Bento
. . .
. . . What a sad spectacle! I thought the parliament was an assembly of grown men and I found instead a gang of adolescents making wisecracks

to each other in the midst of an indecent commotion more suited to a bullring or a tavern ...[41]

Such a description of proceedings in the parliament of the First Republic may have been partially justified, but Delgado went further than this, making an outspoken apology for dictatorship and authoritarian methods in society as a whole. He revealed the typical fascist predilection for 'practical deeds' as against 'empty words':

There is greater benefit for the country and for humanity in a sturdy General out in a colony, clearing the bush, opening roads, bringing discipline and civilisation to the natives, than in all the speeches which the deputies for the same colony recite to a somnolent audience ...[42]

In the same terms, Delgado was explicit in his praise of Salazar, whose constructive work 'can be *felt* (Delgado's emphasis) in the smallest things' and which fully justified the Dictatorship.[43] Not only this, but in the conclusion of the book he ruled out any prospect of a future return to parliamentary democracy, condemning in advance precisely the political solution which he himself was to propose and defend some twenty-five years later:

I oppose and will combat tomorrow, quite willingly, any tendency towards an understanding with the political parties, *even if this proposal comes from an honourable man, and even if that honourable man deserves my greatest respect and even friendship* ...
Do you believe (that the parties would be better when they returned)? What ingenuity!
They would return with more refined gluttony and thievery ...[44]

It was scarcely possible to be more categorical than this, and from this time onwards the young officer began to acquire a reputation as a partisan of a stronger, more openly fascist regime. He began to write newspaper articles on themes relating to aviation, but with heavily political overtones, and also gave occasional talks on the radio which were pure Salazarist propaganda.[45] He also ventured into the field of drama, writing two radio plays characterised chiefly by muscular patriotism and anti-intellectualism.[46] There is consequently little reason to doubt the later claims of apologists for the regime who, attacking the new democratic Delgado from 1958 onwards, described him as one of the most extreme fascists in 1938 or 1940.[47]

Until the early 1940s, then, Delgado was advancing steadily

within the system, being appointed successively a member of the Military Mission to the Colonies in 1938–39, Portuguese Air Force representative in the secret negotiations with Britain regarding the Azores bases in 1941–43, *professor catedrático* of the Military Academy, and in 1944, Director-General of the Secretariat of Civil Aviation.[48] Yet in the following decade he was to put all of this at risk, rejecting his previous ideological convictions to move into opposition and acceptance of ideas and alliances which he had previously scorned, adopting a political posture which was to ruin his career and drive him to exile and ultimately death. Through this dramatic transformation, Delgado showed an honesty and integrity (and also at times temerity and arrogance) which were quite exceptional. To all those, ranging from old Republicans to Communists, who – adhering understandably to the principle that the leopard does not change his spots – greeted his change of heart with scepticism, Delgado replied with characteristic impatience, but also with a firmness and a consistency in action which ended by convincing even the most sceptical. The inveterate fascist had indeed learnt from experience, and once convinced of the superiority of liberal principles, he plunged into the anti-Salazarist struggle with the same boldness and lack of regard for his own (and other people's) safety which he had displayed in everything he did.

Delgado's change of heart is normally, and no doubt correctly, attributed primarily to his extensive contact with democratic societies from the early 1940s onwards: after his experience of negotiations with the British in 1941–43, he resided for three years in Montreal as Portuguese delegate to the International Civil Aviation Organisation (1947–50), and then from 1952–57 in Washington as head of the Portuguese mission to NATO.[49] However, these experiences would scarcely have had such a profound impact if there had not been some element in his ideological formation which predisposed him to acceptance, and it is therefore necessary to examine more closely his earlier development and outlook.

The initial attraction of authoritarian politics for a man of Delgado's background and circumstances is not at all surprising: raised in a military family, trained as a military man in a society with a strong authoritarian tradition, and in a period when recently-created republican institutions were in evident crisis, it was natural that he should be attracted by such ideas. But the key elements in his personality and outlook were compatible with other ideologies (within certain limits, for sure); they need not lead automatically to fascism. Thus two of Delgado's most consistent themes were the military virtues of honour and discipline; values which are typical of the ideologies of authoritarian regimes, but which can in certain circumstances turn against them. Once corruption and nepotism set in, an excessive preoccupation with honour could easily become a liability for the regime; and as for 'discipline', with Delgado it seems to have been almost a synonym for efficiency – and this could also lead to disenchantment with the 'New State' once its archaism and rigidity could be contrasted with the dynamism of post-war Europe and North America. In Delgado's vitriolic propaganda piece of 1933, *Da Pulhice do 'Homo Sapiens'*, there are occasional passages which are much more moderate in tone, suggesting a more open mentality:

In Portugal – how ridiculous this is! – all the Republicans compete with each other to see who is more republican, as if British politicians, for instance, who are monarchists, were not all much more liberal, democratic and *honourable, which is the main thing* (Delgado's emphasis) than almost all of these fourth-rate republicans ...[50]

Also very significant is the Anglophilia which emerges here – and which thus clearly antedates Delgado's contact with the British during the Azores negotiations in 1941–43. This is a constant theme in Delgado's writings and speeches, reflecting the deeply-rooted Portuguese tradition of alliance with and dependence on Britain. Despite his profoundly authoritarian formation, and genuine admiration for fascist heroes like Mussolini, Delgado did not share the intense Anglophobia so typical of the Iberian extreme right. As with many military men, what attracted him to fascism was above all its image of discipline and efficiency; but since these characteristics could also be found in the Anglo-Saxon world, it was not difficult for Delgado (and others like him) to transfer his allegiance once the defeat of the Axis had shown that predictions of 'the decline of the West' were somewhat premature.

Unlike Salazar (or Franco), whose reluctant acceptance of Anglo-Saxon hegemony was not accompanied by any adoption of liberalism, Delgado did genuinely change his allegiance. The seeds of his liberalism were evidently present from the beginning, although initially submerged beneath a heavy overlay of military authoritarianism. It is not possible here to undertake a thorough analysis of the roots of this difference, but one important distinction is that among those agents of Iberian fascism who proved incapable of evolving in a democratic direction – like Salazar – the spirit of clerical obscurantism and class privilege was much stronger. Delgado, even in his most fascist period, was an open man, willing to accept anyone who showed ability and industry, and with little time for the Church. Even in his apologetic statements in defence of the regime, his main preoccupation was with honour, efficiency and progress rather than with tradition and religion. When praising Salazar's 'self-sacrifice' and dedication to the 'salvation of the Fatherland', Delgado in a radio broadcast of 1938 described the dictator as labouring 'pertinaciously, like a Saxon' – betraying once again his Anglophilia.[51]

For Humberto Delgado, the key values guiding his political career were neither those of the corporate State nor those of liberal democracy, but the quixotic and individualistic code of honour, integrity, manliness and independence. Mário Soares described him as 'a hot-headed man, in some respects ridiculously vain, with a strong authoritarian bent and full of his own importance', but went on to add that 'Humberto Delgado had qualities of moral integrity, of courage, of personal confidence and even of affection, which were quite extraordinary ...'.[52] Precisely because of his frankness and lack of circumspection, Delgado's journalistic essays are very revealing. In 1943 he wrote in the *Diário de Notícias* that '... courage, whether in peace or in war, in the trench or on the speaker's platform, under fire or in the struggle of ideas, is the finest quality of Man!'[53] In another article of the same period, he stressed the importance of boldness or daring as leadership qualities:

... those spirits which are by nature gentle and mild will never be great leaders of multitudes, even if they also possess other virtues, such as the capacity for work and intelligence. They will always lack that which is missing from food without salt, from preserves without vitamins, from grape juice without fermentation, from the woman without femininity ...[54]

Despite this exaltation of stereotypically masculine qualities, Delgado was not opposed to the social and political advancement of women. Here also, although his attitude was no more than moderately liberal, he diverged from the clerical-conservative ideology of the regime, which bound women not merely to the home but to the confessional. Favourably impressed by what he had seen of the wartime mobilisation of women in Britain, Delgado drew from this a critique not merely of social attitudes towards women in Portugal but also, once again, of 'Latin' cultural patterns in general:

A truly titanic effort of Woman, this alone deserves the respect of all those who, forgetting questions of circumstance, race or petty hatreds, appreciate any indication of superior spiritual forces which overcome the despicable 'ego'.
Without attempting to draw too many conclusions from the monument I have just erected to Nordic women, it seems to me that something of value can be derived from their example as a lesson for the 'weeping peoples' ('povos-choroes'), in whom tears and self-pity too frequently take the place of tenacity and the healthy love of life.[55]

This somewhat idealised portrayal of 'Nordic' or 'Anglo-Saxon' virtues undoubtedly spoke to the aspirations of large sections of the Portuguese middle classes; although it was also clear that Delgado had not ceased to be thoroughly Portuguese, indeed that he shared some of the very 'Latin' characteristics which he criticised so scathingly. But consistency is scarcely a necessity for success in politics; and in any case, at a deeper level there was a certain consistency in Delgado's posture: a consistency of personality and style which spoke to many Portuguese of all social classes. To many, therefore, it would not appear as a contradiction when Delgado in his Election Manifesto of 1958 spoke of 'a People of noble and ancient traditions, whose moral and civic stature springs from strong roots in the depths of History', and who were always 'austere, united and firm with regard to the essential values – Fatherland, Family and Religion . . .'[56] What Delgado offered was a Portuguese version of Anglo-Saxon liberalism guaranteed by the individual courage and honour of a charismatic leader; a leader whose vision was international and modern but whose roots and character were thoroughly Portuguese. It was to prove an explosive combination; but in order to understand its impact, it is first necessary to consider the state of the opposition in the mid-fifties.

4   The crisis of the Opposition in the mid-fifties and the search for a Presidential candidate

In the mid-1950s, the situation of the democratic forces in Portugal was not, on the face of things, encouraging. The popular enthusiasm of the post-1945 campaigns had dissipated; the anti-fascist unity of that period had been lost; and the regime had gained new international recognition, being admitted to NATO in 1949 and to the United Nations in 1955.[57] It was in this period that some of the most outspoken apologies for Salazarism were published in Britain, France and the United States;[58] and the regime's growing 'respectability' was given the ultimate seal of approval by the State visit of Queen Elizabeth II and the Duke of Edinburgh in February 1957.[59] Having consolidated its ties with the neighbouring Spanish dictatorship (Franco's visit to Portugal, September 1949; Salazar's meeting with Franco in Ciudad Rodrigo, April 1952; President Craveiro Lopes' visit to Spain in 1953),[60] Portugal's 'organic democracy' seemed more secure than at any time since the apogee of fascist power in Europe early in the Second World War.

Within the opposition, the division fomented by the Cold War climate of ideological rigidity prevented any united action. A new grouping which emerged after 1950 was the *Directório Democrato-Social* (DDS) led by Mário de Azevedo Gomes and Jaime Cortesão; its influence derived mainly from the intellectual prestige and integrity of its leaders, since its practical activity was limited to critical analyses of the regime and occasional public declarations.[61] The DDS, interestingly, became the main force insisting on the necessity of abstention in the fascist 'elections', whereas the Communist Party, with its line of 'peaceful transition' from 1956 onwards, favoured participation, even in the face of blatant official fraud – a complete reversal of the situation a few years earlier. The divisions revealed at the Republican Congress of Aveiro in October 1957 were continued in the legislative elections of the same month, in which opposition candidates were presented in only three districts: Aveiro, Oporto and Braga.

Early in 1958 the Communist Party, in a gesture of unity, joined with the most conservative sectors of the opposition in proposing Engineer Cunha Leal as candidate for the presidential elections. This could be seen as a positive move towards unity, were it not for the very chequered career of Cunha Leal (a former Prime Minister from the First Republic, he had flirted with the dictatorship in the early years, and on various occasions had become involved in personal disputes with other leading Republicans such as Teixeira Gomes and Norton de Matos).[62] As it was, the DDS was openly opposed to this candidacy, and so were many independent leftists, who regarded it as a concession which would give control of the entire campaign to the most right-wing section of the opposition.[63] Nevertheless, a banquet in honour of Cunha Leal on 11 January 1958 brought together nearly 700 guests;[64] and the Communist Party's internal bulletin, *O Militante*, argued that he was 'a democratic citizen, prepared to struggle and to combat the Salazar government . . . and also prepared to combat the monopolies which are known to have close connections with foreign imperialism'.[65]

Those who were not happy with Cunha Leal lost no time in organising to search for an alternative. The DDS pronounced itself in favour of one of its own more prominent mentors, Jaime Cortesão – an intellectual of great prestige who had just returned from a long period of exile.[66] Another large Republican feast, in Oporto on 30 January, brought together some 300 guests including the group of independent candidates from the previous year's legislative elections, emphasising the need for a Presidential candidate who would go all the way (not withdrawing in protest at the last minute, as had been the practice hitherto).[67] Several of the guests of honour at this banquet would subsequently play a leading role in Delgado's campaign – although his name was not yet publicly mentioned. But the division in the opposition camp was now plain for all to see, for simultaneously with this banquet there was a rally in the Oporto Coliseum which voiced strong support for Cunha Leal.[68]

It is worth asking why the Communist Party, in Particular, gave such strong backing to the candidacy of Cunha Leal, in view of his opportunist record and his known conservative leanings. The PCP had evidently extracted a series of progressive programmatic pledges from the would-be candidate, and at first sight this seems like an excellent example of a genuine attempt to achieve broadly-based anti-fascist unity, supporting a candidate acceptable to the more conservative sectors of the opposition. But here the Communists were giving exaggerated importance to written agreements and public statements, and not enough to the real political dynamic which these statements served to obscure. Whatever his electoral programme, to the Portuguese people Cunha Leal would mean a repetition of what the opposition had been offering for years: a liberal gesture, a reaffirmation of Republican principles, and another demonstration of political impotence. No one would sacrifice life or limb, or even security of employment, for a discredited old man of doubtful integrity.

In fact, the weaknesses of Cunha Leal's candidacy were apparent from the beginning to many on both the right and left of the opposition. Some sympathised with the DDS when it proposed Jaime Cortesao or António Sérgio as possible alternatives. But an intellectual, however distinguished and whatever his record of political integrity, would have limited mass appeal. The real alternative (and this was increasingly clear to all concerned) was Delgado, precisely because he was a dissident from the regime and a man of action; the question was, first, whether he was politically reliable, and secondly, whether he was acceptable to all sectors of the opposition. Many, including the Communists, were convinced (understandably so, in view of his record) that he was not reliable, and they insisted for months that whoever the opposition's candidate might be, it would not be Humberto Delgado. Thus in mid-April Cunha Leal finally let it be known that he would not run (supposedly because of illness, but quite possibly also because of the reservations about his candidacy among important sections of the opposition). But when Cunha Leal's withdrawal was announced by Dr Cámara Reis at a meeting in the *Seara Nova* offices on 18 April, those present declared publicly that 'the candidacy of General Humberto Delgado will not be the candidacy of the democratic opposition'.[69] Not only were Delgado's recently-acquired democratic convictions viewed with suspicion, but some believed that his entire candidacy was nothing more than a divisionist manoeuvre inspired by the government. In the view of the PCP, he was 'a trusted friend of the government and of American imperialism' whose candidacy 'will serve to deepen the divisions which may still exist among the Opposition forces . . .'[70]

These fears were not confined to the Communist Party, and it is not surprising that Delgado was received with caution by many members of the opposition. Manuel Sertório, a young lawyer who was to become one of Delgado's closest associates, refused to work with the General when he was first approached on the subject (early in 1958) because he believed it was necessary to build a broad front of anti-fascist unity, which Delgado's candidacy (initially, at least) could not represent.[71]

In these circumstances, when Cunha Leal withdrew, the reaction of the Communist Party and the left wing of the opposition in general was to promote a candidate closer to their own political positions: the Lisbon lawyer, Dr Arlindo Vicente. This was a decided step backwards, for although Dr Vicente was a capable man whose integrity and democratic convictions were not in doubt, he was too closely associated with the PCP to be acceptable to all sectors of the opposition.[72] In spite of this, Dr Vicente's candidacy was publicly proclaimed on 20 April, with the support of many of those who had backed Cunha Leal.[73] In the following weeks, the organisation of both Vicente's and Delgado's campaigns advanced rapidly, and the split in the opposition ranks seemed irreversible; once again, Cold War divisions were proving more powerful than anti-fascist unity. It was the suspicion that Delgado's candidacy was simply another device for isolating the Communists which had to be overcome; but this could not really be done until Delgado himself had shown, by his bold and open-minded conduct during the opening weeks of the campaign, that this was far from being his intention.

Apart from political principle or ideology, what was at stake was the issue of personal leadership and charisma as against structure and programme: in fact, the problem of populism. Arlindo Vicente made this plain in an interview he gave to *República* on 9 May:

'I am a man like all other men' – began Dr Arlindo Vicente – 'nominated by my fellows to represent them.'
'We do not need, nor is is part of our vision, nor do we accept – in fact we reject – a man to lead the masses, a *caudilho* or a chief who will impose a system . . .'

'I do not have any responsibility for what happened in the past, or in the twisted course of the Dictatorship ...'[74]

In fact, of course, Dr Vicente was absolutely right in suspecting that Delgado was a potential *caudilho* capable of leading the masses by his personal magnetism; but what neither he nor probably anyone else realised at the time was that a personalistic campaign of this type was perhaps the only way, in the circumstances of 1958, for the opposition to break out of the stalemate into which it had been driven by the regime's rigidity and its own tactical impoverishment.

Until the closing months of 1957, Delgado's links with the antifascist movement were tenuous at best. It was known that for several years he had been taking his distance from certain aspects of the regime, expressing liberal sentiments derived from his experience in Canada and the United States. A hint of what was to come was his gesture of solidarity with Henrique Galvão, whom he visited in gaol in Peniche while on leave from his post in Washington in the autumn of 1956. Later, in his *Memoirs*, Delgado claimed that already at this stage he was engaged in a military conspiracy against the regime, a conspiracy which did not get off the ground because the government extended his term of duty in Washington.[75] It was only in the autumn of 1957 that he returned to Lisbon to become Director-General of Civil Aviation (possibly an attempt by Salazar to buy him off), and was able to make further contacts.

It seems that the idea of proposing Delgado as a candidate for the Presidency originated with Henrique Galvão, who suggested it to him on 25 October 1957 during another of the General's visits to Peniche. Since Delgado was agreeable, Galvão contacted António Sérgio who became the prime mover in organising civilian support for Delgado.[76] Sérgio was already thinking along similar lines, favouring the scheme of proposing a military dissident from the regime as a tactic for dividing the government's forces; so he immediately began to promote the idea among the opposition. The idea was communicated to the group of former candidates from Oporto, and it was they who took the first collective initiative to propose Delgado. The architect Artur Andrade was sent by this group to contact Delgado early in January 1958; and active preparations now began to organise the campaign.[77] It is significant that the 'classic' opposition was scarcely involved at all in these first moves; even Sérgio, though long connected with opposition circles, had a reputation for independence. Another outstanding intellectual, Jaime Cortesão, himself proposed by the DDS as a possible candidate, argued that Delgado would be better in the circumstances.[78]

It is apparent from this brief account that Delgado's candidacy did not emerge entirely by chance. There was a trend, although a limited one, of military dissidence from the regime; and Delgado was merely the most prominent dissident officer. Also, some civilian opposition circles were already looking for a General in active service as a tactic to divide the regime. On 19 April, Delgado's candidacy was officially registered at the Supreme Court; and around the same time, a manifesto was issued, signed by many well-known oppositionists, explaining the reasons for the General's stand and their support for him:

> Identified with the tendency of most Portuguese, the signatories ... are preparing to present (together with many other citizens) an independent candidate in the next Presidential elections.
> And why an INDEPENDENT CANDIDATE?
> Because only a Portuguese citizen, who is removed from groups or factions and who can in reality assume responsibility before the entire Nation as an impartial judge in the present political conjuncture ... can lead the country's dramatic political problem to a national solution.
> This Portuguese Citizen is General Humberto Delgado, a citizen identified with the present Constitution and with the precepts of the Universal Declaration of Human Rights approved by the United Nations. He alone at this moment is in a position to break out of the 'dead end' in which we live, opening up new directions to National Life and dispelling the suspicions and doubts and fears of every kind which are common and frequent among us.[79]

This document is remarkable for its appropriation of the rhetoric of 'national unity' and 'salvation' so beloved of the regime itself; the combination of such values with the democratic and progressive principles defended by the opposition was certainly a major reason for the remarkable popular appeal of Delgado's candidacy, and is very typically populist.[80] But this does not seem to have been the primary consideration of those who promoted the candidacy initially; rather, they were interested in the potential which Delgado appeared to offer for provoking division in the fascist camp.

Delgado's initial supporters made it clear that they did not want a man who might appear to have rallied to the opposition after being disgraced and stripped of rank and position, but a General in active service who would nevertheless risk prestige and status to achieve reform: an approach which would certainly have greater impact on other malcontents in the Salazarist ranks. Some of the Oporto group who launched Delgado's candidacy told him they thought he should present himself as one who recognised the need for changes in the system without destroying it entirely, but not as an outright opponent; and it was Delgado himself who refused this, insisting that his break with the regime was complete and that he would not be content with minor modifications. This was the origin of the energetic public position taken by the General in his Manifesto and in his opening press conference, with the famous promise to dismiss Salazar ('Obviamente, demito-o!') – even as late as this (14 May) his campaign organisers had asked him not to make such a categorical statement, but Delgado himself insisted on taking a clear stand.[81] His sincerity and determination, then, have to be recognised: from the beginning he refused to compromise or 'hedge his bets', and this was undoubtedly a major reason for his dramatic popular impact.

It was precisely Delgado's boldness, his military training, his sense of honour – even vanity – which gave his campaign its distinctive character; many of the same characteristics which had earned him a successful career in the fascist regime, would enable him to transform the perspectives of the Portuguese opposition. These were characteristics which he shared with that other famous dissident, Henrique Galvão, whose influence on Delgado's campaign should not be underestimated. Delgado's correspondence with Galvão, while the former was in Washington and the latter languishing in Peniche, is fascinating for the light it throws on the military and personalistic mentality of the two men. Galvão, in a letter of 28 December 1952, reveals in all its intensity the sense of outraged honour and quixotic determination which drove him to persist in his solitary struggle:

... As they have left me with nothing but my life, I will risk it too. And without hatred (I swear this to you on my honour) I am going towards that to which they are forcing me: to revolt. Not to conspiracy in the classic style, with meetings, plans, betrayals, etc.; I am going alone. If anyone wants to come with me, let him do so of his own accord, because I won't enlist anyone. I shall be merely the pioneer of a 'national anti-totalitarian Resistance'. As you can see I am not very well equipped for victories – But I still have my life which I am going to risk.

I am telling you this because I know that if you were suddenly thrown thus into the same situation, or a similar one, you also would not accept it calmly, you also would fight . . .[82]

Obviously Galvão recognised in Delgado a kindred spirit – and he was not mistaken. Despite important differences – Galvão was cold and cerebral; Delgado mercurial and emotional, and politically they would diverge in later years as Delgado moved further to the left – they were both outspoken and uncompromising men of action, obsessed with the military values of honour and discipline. Delgado might not be the ideal democrat – although his change of views as a result of his years of contact with liberal societies seems to have been genuine – but by style and temperament he was ideally suited to the task of transforming and rejuvenating the opposition after more than thirty years of dictatorship and thirteen years of futile 'electioneering'.

Notes to Chapter V

1 Douglas L. Wheeler, 'The Military and the Portuguese Dictatorship, 1926–1974: 'The Honor of the Army'', in Lawrence S. Graham & Harry M. Makler (eds.), *Contemporary Portugal: The Revolution and its Antecedents*, Austin & London, 1979, University of Texas Press, pp. 191–219, provides a good summary of military opposition to the *Estado Novo*.

2 Douglas L. Wheeler, *Republican Portugal: A Political History, 1910–1926*, Madison, 1978, University of Wisconsin Press, pp. 182–3. The second quotation is from the *Revista Militar* of 1905.

3 'Nota biográfica' on Galvão in *O Século*, 26 June 1970.

4 *O Século*, 12 May, 14 July and 27 November 1935, & 16 April 1936; Humberto Delgado, *The Memoirs of General Delgado*, London, 1964, Cassell, pp. 167–8.

5 Humberto Delgado, *Memoirs*, pp. 167–8.

6 *O Século*, 12 August 1934.

7 *Ibid.*, 10 January 1935.

8 *Ibid.*, 29 October 1935.

9 *Diário de Lisboa*, 23 April 1937; *Diário de Notícias*, 25 April 1937; *O Século*, 31 October 1937, 27 September & 9 December 1938.

10 *O Século*, 30 July 1936; *Diário de Lisboa*, 18 December 1936.

11 *Diário de Notícias*, 17 May 1944.

12 *O Século*, 23 August 1936.

13 *Diário de Lisboa*, 18 December 1936.

14 *Diário de Manhã* and *O Século*, 27 March 1949.

15 Mário Soares, *Portugal Amordacado: depoimento sobre os anos do fascismo*, Lisboa, 1974, Arcádia, pp. 202−3.

16 *Diário de Notícias*, 13 February 1949.

17 Soares, *Portugal Amordaçado*, pp. 202−3; Vasco da Gama Fernandes, *Depoimento Inacabado (Memórias)*, Lisboa, 1974, Europa-América, p. 93.

18 *Jornal de Notícias*, 30 September 1951.

19 Richard Robinson, *Contemporary Portugal: A History*, London, 1979, George Allen & Unwin, p. 72; *A Voz*, 30 October 1952; António de Figueiredo, *Portugal: Fifty Years of Dictatorship*, London, 1975, Penguin Books, p. 199.

20 *O Século*, 18 December 1952, 31 March & 1 April 1953.

21 *O Século* archive, article deleted by the censor, 6 February 1953.

22 *O Século*, 7 & 12 February 1953.

23 Vasco da Gama Fernandes, *Depoimento*, p. 96.

24 *Ibid.*, pp. 102−103; *O Século*, 10 March 1955 & 18 March 1958.

25 *O Século*, 27 July 1957.

26 Vasco da Gama Fernandes, *Depoimento*, pp. 104−5.

27 Alvaro Lins, *Missao em Portugal*, Lisboa, 1974, Centro do Livro Brasileiro, pp. 254−6 & 268−9; Humberto Delgado, *Memoirs*, pp. 167−8 & 177; *Diário de Notícias*, 17 January & 19 February 1959; *O Século*, 18 February 1959 & 13 May 1960.

28 Henrique Galvão, *Carta Aberta ao Dr. Salazar*, Lisboa, 1975, Arcádia, pp. 10−11.

29 Interview with Humberto Delgado in the *Diário Ilustrado*, 10 May 1958.

30 Galvão, *Carta Aberta*, p. 19.

31 *Ibid.*, p. 32.

32 See for example Galvão, *Carta Aberta*, pp. 58−9 & 65.

33 *Diário de Notícias*, 13 June 1944.

34 *Proclamação do General Humberto Delgado Candidato à Presidência da República*, Maio de 1958, Editada pelos Serviços de Candidatura do Porto, p. 1; consulted by courtesy of Sr. Oliveira Valença; and Humberto Delgado, *Memoirs*, p. 3.

35 Humberto Delgado, *Memoirs*, p. 5.

36 *Ibid.*, p. 10.

37 *Ibid.*, pp. 33−4.

38 *Ibid.*, pp. 44−5.

39 *Proclamação do General Humberto Delgado* . . . , p. 2.

40 Humberto Delgado, Tenente Aviador, *Da pulhice do 'Homo Sapiens' (Da Monarquia de vigaristas, pela República de bandidos à Ditadura de papa)*, Lisboa, 1933, Casa Ventura Abrantes.

41 *Ibid.*, pp. 102−3.

42 *Ibid.*, p. 129.

43 *Ibid.*, pp. 191−2.

44 *Ibid.*, pp. 244−5 (emphasis in original).

45 E.g. the talk given by Delgado on the *Emissora Nacional* on 17 February 1938, quoted in the pamphlet *Humberto Delgado: Antes ... e Depois*, published in 1961 as official propaganda against Delgado. Although this was a somewhat scurrilous exploitation of Delgado's past by the regime, its substance could scarcely be denied.

46 *28 de Maio* (Peça em 3 actos radiodifundida em 28 de Maio de 1939 pelo Rádio Club Português – Parede – Portugal). 1ª Edição, 1939 – Casa Portuguesa, Lisboa. Also, *A Marcha para as Indias* (Peça histórica em 2 actos, emitida pela Emissora Nacional no dia 8 de Julho de 1940, 443º aniversário da primeira partida de Vasco da Gama para a India). Edição da Revista 'Defesa Nacional'. 2ª Edição, Lisboa, 1954.

47 Thus a Spanish right-winger, Jesús Suevos, writing in *Arriba* of 29 January 1961 (and quoted in *Humberto Delgado: Antes ... e Depois*, pp. 8–9), claimed that the Delgado he had met in January 1938 at a fascist banquet in Estoril had volunteered the opinion that the Portuguese régime was 'not very fascist' and 'that he thought it necessary to 'stiffen up' in the Portuguese Legion and, above all, the Youth Movement ... I was left with the impression, then, that he was the individual with the most pronounced fascist and authoritarian tendencies of all those I met in Portugal.'

48 *Proclamação do General Humberto Delgado* ..., p. 2.

49 *Ibid.*, pp. 2–3.

50 Humberto Delgado, *Da pulhice do 'Homo Sapiens'*, pp. 242–3.

51 Delgado's talk broadcast on the *Emissora Nacional* on 17 February 1938, quoted in *Humberto Delgado: Antes ... e Depois*, p. 13.

52 Soares, *Portugal Amordaçado*, pp. 211–12.

53 Humberto Delgado, article entitled 'O Medo' ('Fear'), in the *Diário de Notícias* of 29 August 1943.

54 Humberto Delgado, article entitled 'Chefias Militares' ('Military Commands'), in the *Diário de Notícias* of 6 September 1943.

55 Humberto Delgado, article entitled 'Mulheres de Armas' ('Women under Arms'), in the *Diário de Notícias* of 23 November 1943. See also Delgado's articles on education, in the *Diário de Notícias* of 20 May and 17 June 1944.

56 *Proclamação do General Humberto Delgado* ..., p. 20.

57 Hugh Kay, *Salazar and Modern Portugal*, London, 1970, Eyre & Spottiswoode, pp. 182–3.

58 For example, Christine Garnier, *Vacances avec Salazar*, Paris, 1952, Grasset; Richard Pattee, *Portugal and the Portuguese World*, Milwaukee, USA, 1957, Bruce Publishing Co.

59 Hugh Kay, *Salazar*, p. 335.

60 *Ibid.*, pp. 182–3.

61 Mário Soares, *Portugal Amordaçado*, pp. 195–7.

62 Informe da Commissão Política ao Comité Central do Partido Comunista Português, *Sobre a Actividade do Partido nas Campanhas Eleitorais para Deputados à Assembleia Nacional e para a Presidência da República* (Lisboa, Agosto de 1958, Edições 'Avante!'; relator: Gomes),

p. 7 (consulted in the *Avante!* archive); also Soares, *Portugal Amordaçado*, p. 106; and author's interview with Manuel Sertório, Lisbon, 22 March 1977.

63   Soares, *Portugal Amordaçado*, pp. 217–25; and author's interview with Manuel Sertório, Lisbon, 22 March 1977. See also the correspondence about Cunha Leal's candidacy in *O Jornal* of 19 February 1982 (article by Clara Pinto Correia), 5 March 1982 (article by Manuel Sertório), 12 March 1982 (letter from Rear-Admiral Ramos Rocha) & 2 April 1982 (letter from Manuel Sertório).

64   *O Século* archive, partially censored article of 12 January 1958.

65   'O momento político nacional e as tarefas dos comunistas', by 'Lídia', in *O Militante*, III Série, No. 95, March 1958.

66   Soares, *Portugal Amordaçado*, pp. 217–25.

67   *O Século*, 31 January 1958.

68   *Ibid.*.

69   *O Século* archive, partially censored article of 19 April 1958.

70   Article by 'Lídia' in *O Militante*, III Série, No. 95, March 1958.

71   Author's interview with Manuel Sertório, Lisbon, 22 March 1977.

72   *Ibid.*, and author's interview with Alcina Bastos, Lisbon, 15 June 1978.

73   *O Século*, 21 April 1958; *República*, 17 & 21 April 1958.

74   *República*, 9 May 1958.

75   Humberto Delgado, *Memoirs*, pp. 84–5.

76   *Ibid.*, pp. 88–90.

77   Author's interviews with the architect Artur Andrade, Oporto, 29 June 1977, and with Fernando Piteira Santos, Lisbon, 13 January 1977.

78   Soares, *Portugal Amordaçado*, pp. 217–25.

79   *Eleições para a Presidência da República: Candidatura Independente do General Humberto Delgado* (circular dos serviços da candidatura, em organização), Lisbon, April 1958; document consulted by courtesy of Maria Humberta Delgado Lourenço.

80   In this respect, Delgado's discourse corresponds very well to the analytic model proposed by Ernesto Laclau in his *Politics and Ideology in Marxist Theory*, London, 1977, New Left Books. I disagree with Laclau's analysis of the foundations of populism (see D. L. Raby, *Populism: A Marxist Analysis*, McGill Studies in International Development No. 32, Centre for Developing-Area Studies, McGill University, Montreal, 1983), but accept his argument that a very characteristic trait of populism is its appropriation of extremely diverse and even contradictory ideological elements.

81   Author's interviews with Artur Andrade, Oporto, 29 June 1977, and with Dr. Olívio França, Oporto, 6 June 1978.

82   Quoted in Vítor Dimas, *Humberto Delgado: o Homem e Três Epocas*, Lisboa, 1977, Edições Jornal Expresso), p. 168.

6
The populist whirlwind: Delgado's campaign and its aftermath

... que importava a cenografia, a frivolidade, a misturada com comparsas inautênticos, se Vasco sabia, se Osório sabia, se todos sabiam ou pressentiam que, por muito que tivessem deixado de acreditar nos outros e em si próprios, essa era uma descrença de enclausurados, à espera que um nada o desmentisse?

... what did it matter about the play-acting, the frivolity, the mingling with imposters, if Vasco knew, if Osório knew, if they all knew or understood that however much they had ceased to believe in others and in themselves, this was the despair of the imprisoned, waiting only for the slightest thing to contradict it?

Fernando Namora, Os Clandestinos (1972)

1 The 'fearless general' takes the field

Delgado's campaign was indeed an explosion; almost from the first day, when at a press conference in Lisbon he stated bluntly that if elected, he would dismiss Salazar, he became the object of enormous popular demonstrations of enthusiasm without precedent in the entire history of the *Estado Novo*. It was a spontaneous plebiscite, the most spectacular proof imaginable of the regime's failure to win real popular support for corporatism. The government dared not cancel or postpone the elections, or invalidate Delgado's candidacy on some technical pretext, since the reaction to such a decision would almost certainly be worse than the consequences of allowing the campaign to continue. But at the same time it was clear that the more Delgado was allowed to speak, the more places in which he was allowed to appear, the greater would be the damage to the social stability so carefully preserved by the regime: the system of popular submission, apoliticism and collective inhibition, cultivated for decades, was visibly disintegrating with every day that passed.

The campaign was launched in effect with the publication on 8 May 1958 in the *República* newspaper of Delgado's Election Manifesto.[1] This was followed by interviews with the press and public declarations from his supporters, and the historic press conference of 10 May in the *Chave d'Ouro* café in Lisbon. It was in this first public act of the campaign that Delgado was asked by the correspondent of *Agence France-Presse*, 'If you are elected President of the Republic, what will you do with the Prime Minister?' – and the reply, without hesitation, was 'Obviously, I shall dismiss him!' – a simple but unprecedented statement of the disposition to break with Salazar, which produced an immediate sensation.[2] The same correspondent then asked the candidate's opinion regarding the manner in which the *União Nacional* had chosen its candidate (Admiral Tomás), to which he replied with equal candour:

Although many people discussed the possible candidate of the National Union, I confess that the question was never of any interest to me. I knew that whoever was chosen would have to represent the present political situation and the intention of maintaining it without change ...[3]

It was this tone of superiority, bordering on comtempt for the leading representatives of the regime which distinguished Delgado's campaign from the beginning and which helped to create a political movement of great subversive potential. The 'independent' character of Delgado's candidacy was stressed by the General himself and by Professor Vieira de Almeida who introduced him in the press conference:

The support which (the candidate) seeks and expects is that of independent men like himself; of those who although – or even because – they recognise the limitations, the contingent nature of human actions, refuse to absolutise a doctrine and refuse even more categorically to abdicate their right to think ...[4]

The liberalism of Delgado's campaign was qualified by a certain paternalism, expressed for example in these reservations about party politics. Thus Delgado also declared at this press conference that if elected he would set up a transitional military government, 'capable of ensuring order and tranquility', because 'until the political level of our people has been improved there will be a need for a strong government which has authority', although an authority limited by law and morality.[5] But if this attitude of Delgado's aroused misgivings in the minds of some democrats (and specifically among the supporters of Dr Arlindo Vicente), to many it seemed a moderate and reasonable position which did not detract from the merit of his candidacy.

Certainly, the regime had no illusions about the potential threat represented by Delgado, especially now that he had broken the tacit rules of the electoral charade by daring to openly deny the divine right of Dr Oliveira Salazar to preside over the nation's destiny. Already his campaign was subject to the usual petty harassments and provocations reserved for the opposition during the electoral periods of the *Estado Novo*. In the press conference Delgado denounced the continued practice of press censorship (the government had generously promised to suspend censorship during the campaign period), drawing attention to phrases which had been deleted from his interview of the previous day (the offending passages referred to the torture of political prisoners and to official pressure on military officers to pay homage to Salazar).[6] Not surprisingly, this denunciation itself was cut by the censors from the reports of the press conference in the following day's papers. Two days later, Delgado demanded police protection after unidentified individuals had provoked disturbances outside his home and his campaign headquarters and smeared the walls with tar.[7] But this sort of thing was routine; far worse was to come later in the campaign.

If the tone of Delgado's campaign was set by the *Chave d'Ouro* press conference, its mass character was established by his extraordinary reception in Oporto on 14 May. The northern capital, with its long standing republican tradition and intense rivalry with Lisbon, had played an important part (through the group of ex-parliamentary candidates of the previous year) in the genesis of his candidacy, and it was logical that it should be chosen for Delgado's first open-air meeting. But the popular reception when he arrived at the São Bento station exceeded all expectations: an enormous multitude estimated at 200,000 people – half the total population of the city – crowded into the narrow streets and filled the neighbouring square, the *Praça da Liberdade*. Delgado was carried shoulder-high to the open car which awaited him, and the car then edged its way with difficulty through the crowd to his campaign office. Once there, he appeared on the balcony to be greeted by prolonged applause and 'Vivas!' for Delgado, for Portugal and for Liberty, and declared with emotion:

People of Oporto! The answer (to the régime) is here in this demonstration. You are the truth. We want an end to tyranny. We do not want to be slaves. Long live the Republic. Long live Liberty. Long live Oporto.[8]

In an atmosphere of delirious enthusiasm, the veteran republican Colonel Helder Ribeiro described Delgado's career, affirming that 'Today, as yesterday, General Humberto Delgado continues to be the same vigorous, resolute man who never failed the Fatherland and Liberty'[9] – a somewhat idealised picture of the candidate's political record, but one which was understandable in the enthusiasm of the moment. The extraordinary scenes continued as the General moved on to his hotel and from there to the Oporto Coliseum, where a formal election rally had been organised. It was here that Dr Carlos Cal Brandão, picking up a phrase from Delgado's Lisbon press conference, described the General as 'the fearless man' – 'o homem sem medo' – which was to become his motto from now on; and Delgado himself picked up the theme, declaring: 'I hope to emerge victorious from this campaign, because fear has vanished.' Here Delgado also attacked the regime on its own terrain, appropriating such themes as honour, morality and patriotism, and comparing the Portuguese people to the slave of 'Uncle Tom's Cabin':

If we all began to think like that poor slave, but with the difference that instead of wanting to reach Canada, we want to reach the Terreiro do Paço (the seat of government in Lisbon), there would be no more tyranny among us.
Are you ready, gentlemen, to think and act like the slave Tom? To live in Liberty?
Then we will once again be Portuguese and not strangers in our own country, which is ours at least as much as it is theirs.
It's time for you (the régime) to leave!
We are tired of you! We have had enough!
Get out! Resign![10]

Such violent rhetoric could only be construed by Salazar as a direct challenge, and from this point onwards the election campaign became transformed into an ever more open battle for power. If Delgado was not immediately arrested, it was only because the regime feared the consequences in terms of both popular unrest and possible military support for the dissident General. As for Delgado, he seems to have hoped for precisely this – military sympathy which he could organise into a more or less bloodless *coup* – or that massive popular discontent would lead to such internal division and demoralisation in the regime that it would finally concede electoral victory and constitutional change. Not that he had any illusions about the implacable hostility and persecution he could expect from the authorities, which was already apparent in many petty but well-calculated forms of harassment. Delgado referred to this also in his speech at the Coliseum:

Those who come together here have overcome fear. Many people have ceased to be afraid. That's why they (the authorities) do not rest in their desire for revenge against the General who was brave enough to do the worst: to become a dissident, placing himself openly on the side of the liberals and of those who suffer. They seek therefore to get rid of me by dishonest means, even to the extent of spreading a strange rumour about my personal security. What are we coming to![11]

Delgado was well aware of the treatment he could expect from the regime, especially if his bid for power were to fail. Where he miscalculated was not in regards to Salazar's malice, but rather in terms of the dictator's tenacity and the solidity of his power base in the military and the police. Characteristically, Delgado the military individualist regarded the struggle in excessively personal and moralistic terms, underestimating the resistance of structures and interests.

Despite this, it was also in Oporto that Delgado for the first time referred clearly and explicitly to the social question and to the need for a redistribution of wealth. He did so with typically radical rhetoric, although without any specific programme:

Economic salvation is the road to socio-economic justice, of which Corporatism is the total negation. Corporatism is the socio-economic status-quo in which the rich are always richer, the poor always poorer and the middle classes always in crisis.
The powerful groups are, of necessity, those who control our destiny. For a certain time they needed dictators; now they can do without them, since they themselves are in direct control. Today the country belongs to them. Is this the land of Santa Maria or the land of Monopoly and

Company Limited? Portugal is no longer Portugal. It is Plutocracialândia.
Lisbon is not Lisbon. It is Plutocraciaville.[12]

It was well known that the Portuguese standard of living was,
as Delgado pointed out, one of the lowest in Europe, 'even in the
category of an underdeveloped country', and that economic
power was massively concentrated in the hands of a few monopolistic groups. It was of course these conditions which led
to the well-known (although unquantified) strength of the
Communist Party, and to the growing disaffection of a middle
class for whom Salazar's claims to economic wizardry had long
since ceased to carry any credibility. There was little logic in
Delgado's rhetoric, for if as he said the 'powerful groups' which
had once needed dictators could now do without them, then it
was quite possible to conceive of a democratic transition favoured
by these very monopolies which he attacked (precisely the path
which Spain would take two decades later). However, this
possibility did not occur to most of Delgado's public, because in
1958 the big Portuguese monopolies showed no inclination to
favour such a transition, and in any case the popular movement
demanded economic, and not merely political, transformation.
The Portuguese people were not – for the moment at least –
demanding socialism, but there was a generalised desire for an
end to economic privilege and inequality.

The regime's sensitivity to any discussion of the social question
was such that it tried to suppress any suggestion that there might
be a class, as opposed to a purely liberal-democratic, basis of support for the opposition. Thus in the newspaper reports of the
General's activities, although many indications of popular
enthusiasm were allowed to pass uncensored, any specific
mention of the working class was deleted. Those who relied on
the press for information were not allowed to know that on
Delgado's arrival in Oporto, a group of railway workers climbed
into the coach to greet him, or that on the second day of his visit,
in São Martinho do Campo, a group of 'workers of both sexes'
had 'abandoned their labours' in order to greet the General.[13]
The regime had a very well-developed class consciousness; it
tolerated (with reluctance) a limited expression of opposition, but
the slightest hint of working-class disaffection was to be systematically eliminated. By the same logic, anyone who mentioned
the social question was automatically a Communist.

Delgado's return to Lisbon on 16 May signalled clearly the end
of any tolerance on the part of the authorities; from now on,
although the election campaign was allowed to continue because
of fear of even more serious unrest, every available means of
open or covert harassment would be used to disrupt the General's
campaign. There was to be no repetition of the delirious popular
reception in Oporto. The huge crowd which had gathered about
the Santa Apolónia station was held at bay by hundreds of police
while Delgado was whisked away through the back streets and
delivered to his home out of the sight of the multitudes. When
the regular police (PSP) proved incapable of restraining the
crowd, hundreds of mounted guards of the GNR moved in with
clubs swinging, provoking a situation of panic and mass disturbances which spread to the Terreiro do Paço and throughout the
Lisbon *Baixa*. Later reports – deleted, of course, by the censorship
– indicated that shots were fired and that several civilians were
killed. The atmosphere of open confrontation is dramatically
conveyed by the original, uncensored, report in *O Século* (the
passages in brackets were deleted by the censors):

The intervention of the mounted police gave rise to various expressions (of discontent by the crowd), as a result of which some people were
hurt and some arrests were also made. (More than once and despite the
hostility of the GNR, the crowd started to sing *A Portuguesa* and to shout
'vivas' for the Republic and for the independent candidate) . . .
(The moment of arrival of the independent candidate was one of
extraordinary enthusiasm, as his followers carried him shoulder-high to
his car. Ladies threw flowers to him and his name, together with that of
Portugal and the Republic, was constantly acclaimed. Smiling, he waved
to the people, thanking them for their demonstration of support.) . . .
The car in which General Humberto Delgado was riding, accompanied
by his family, departed finally along the Avenida Infante Dom Henrique
(towards Moscavide), flanked by police cars and motorcycles. (Although
it had been expected that his route would be Santa Apolónia – Terreiro
do Paço – Rossio, thousands of people cheered General Humberto
Delgado throughout the length of the unexpected detour. As soon as he
left Santa Apolónia, the horns of the cars parked along the Avenue
became deafening, together with the 'vivas' and endless chants of
General Humberto Delgado's name.) Many demonstrators broke
through the cordons of the GNR and PSP (hoping to follow the
independent candidate's car . . .) but they were prevented from doing
so, and beside the Cais dos Soldados there occurred a number of arrests
(of people from the crowd, who protested even more vigorously against
the police action) . . .
(After passing the Airport roundabout, it seems that because of some

confusion, while the police vehicles continued along Avenida Brasil, General Humberto Delgado's car turned on to the Avenida Aeroporto in the direction of Areeiro, followed by the other cars of his Committee. As he continued, the bystanders chanted his name whenever they recognised him) . . . [14]

The same account described the violent confrontation in the Baixa in some detail, including a couple of very revealing incidents:

(At his campaign headquarters we also learned that General Humberto Delgado was in contact by telephone from his home with the Head of State. The group of journalists who were waiting there were also approached by a young man, Hermínio Duarte Borges Menano, an employee of the Lambretta company whose address is Avenida de Roma, 43, 2o., who said that he had been invited to make a statement at 10 p.m. in the campaign office 'because near Santa Apolónia he had seen a policeman shoot a man in the head'.)

(A young man who said he was a reporter for the 'New York Times' also started to talk with the journalists, in a mixture of good English, bad French and bad Portuguese. He began to enquire what information the other journalists had, but at one point a representative of our esteemed colleague the *Diário Ilustrado* noticed that the 'foreigner' was taking his notes in good and fluent Portuguese. As soon as he realised this, the 'soi-disant' reporter started to run down the Avenue, and was not seen again . . .)

Harassment and provocation was not limited to journalists or ordinary citizens, but was practised directly against the candidate himself. When Delgado arrived at his home after the unintended detour via the airport, a GNR officer with gun in hand forced him to enter the house alone in order to prevent any public contact; and later the same day, when the General tried to leave home, his way was blocked by three individuals whom he denounced as PIDE agents. [15] For several hours he was virtually under house arrest, until the following day when the atmosphere had calmed down slightly and he was allowed to renew public activities.

However, the authorities' attempt to control news of the extent of the disturbances – and of the repression – was not very successful; the next day they were obliged to issue an official communiqué denying that there had been 100 deaths and many more wounded, as had been stated to the international news agencies by Delgado's campaign headquarters. [16] This casualty figure may in fact have been exaggerated; it is unlikely that the true figure will ever be known. But what did rapidly become general knowledge, both in Portugal and abroad, was that on May 16 Lisbon had witnessed its largest public protest, and most indisciminate police repression, in the 32 years of the dictatorship.

Delgado's next major appearance was also in Lisbon, two days later, when he gave a speech in the Gymnasium of the Camões High School. Once again, the authorities did everything possible to disrupt the proceedings, provoking violent incidents which degenerated into another pitched battle as the police chased opposition supporters – and simple bystanders – through the streets of the middle-class *Avenidas Novas* district. Press reports, which the censorship allowed to pass, indicated that the police used truncheons and sabres, and then firearms, to disperse stone-throwing crowds which had gathered in the Praça de Saldanha and nearby streets. The GNR intervened again, entering the fashionable Monte Carlo café and ordering the clientele to leave, provoking further disturbances which reduced the café to ruins. As the disturbances continued, armoured cars were driven up to intimidate the rioters, and the conflict finally died down around 2 a.m.[17] The press was not allowed to print specific details of the large number of casualties, nor to mention that PIDE agents had intervened using automatic weapons against unarmed civilians;[18] but the next day the Ministry of the Interior was forced to admit – given the widespread public denunciations of the repression – that the police had used firearms, 'but shooting into the air', and that some people ('only four') had gunshot wounds.[19] Delgado himself was obliged by the PIDE to wait after the meeting had finished and was then taken home, against his wishes, in a police car.[20] The authorities, in the same communiqué from the Ministry of the Inteiror, accused the opposition of wanting to disrupt the elections and create 'an insurrectional climate', but the truth was probably rather the reverse, as argued by Delgado's campaign committee: that the Government was fomenting a climate of social agitation in order to find a pretext to suspend the elections or arrest the General.[21]

The immediate effect of such brutal repression was, on the contrary, to increase popular support for Delgado. On 18 May *República* announced the decision of a key group of Oporto democrats -Prof. Ruy Luis Gomes, Engineer Virgínia Moura, and the Architect Lobo Vital – to support the 'Independent Candidate'.[22] Two days later Cunha Leal, the ex-candidate of an important sector of the opposition, declared himself for the General.[23] Prominent representatives of all ideological tendencies were rallying behind Delgado: on 25 May it was the turn of a group of Socialists and Social-Democrats to publish a manifesto explaining their positions and their reasons for backing the General,[24] and on 30 May the well-known monarchist (and ex-Integralist) Dr Luis de Almeida Braga announced his support.[25] Opposition unity, which for years had been an elusive chimera, was being forged day by day on the anvil of Delgado's example and under the hammer of police repression. Portugal's greatest 'novelist, Aquilino Ribeiro, summed up the general feeling in an interview for the *Diário de Lisboa*:

... My candidate and that of the great majority of Republicans is General Humberto Delgado. We owe it to him that the Nation had been galvanised into life. It was thanks to his panache and determination that, fortunately, it became apparent that beneath the calm surface there were troubled waters ... The General has left fear behind him, as used to be said of Saldanha ...[26]

This growing spirit of unity among political and intellectual representatives of all groups and ideologies not completely identified with the 'Situation' was by all accounts even more apparent among the mass of the people. But there was still one major obstacle to the consummation of unity in practice, namely the continued existence of another opposition candidacy, that of Dr Arlindo Vicente. Dr Vicente's campaign, backed by the Left and above all by the Communist Party, should not be under-estimated. His election rallies did attract a large and enthusiastic audience, particularly in working-class districts of Lisbon and the South where the clandestine Communist Party had a solid and well-organised following.[27] However, it did not and could not by its nature achieve the dimensions or the degree of popular euphoria of Delgado's campaign; Vicente was not Delgado, and the orientation of his campaign was too closely identified with a specific political tendency. The problem was analysed with characteristic clarity by the young left-wing lawyer Manuel Sertório, hitherto active in Dr Vicente's campaign, in an open letter published in *República* on May 23:

... Politics should not be practised in Machiavellian fashion; but neither can it be approached under the influence of sentimental attitudes which prevent the true understanding of what is possible ...

An Opposition incomparably greater and more majestic than the traditional democratic Opposition has emerged on the national scene.

This opposition is represented at present by the candidacy of General Delgado. The principles of his manifesto and the guidelines of his campaign correspond to the immediate interests of the opposition's struggle. A national consensus, undeniably representative, had been created around his candidacy ...

Sertório then referred to Dr Arlindo Vicente's candidacy, addressing the argument that it should be retained in order to preserve the continuity of an important sector of the Opposition:

The most recent events demand the immediate formation of an organ of National Salvation, of a *single headquarters*, to watch the course of events hour by hour. And the electoral side of this single command-centre has to be a single opposition candidacy, that which will deal the greatest blow against the *Estado Novo*: that of General Delgado ...

Above all, the frustration of October 1945 must not be repeated ...

Sertório concluded by calling for the immediate withdrawal of Dr Vicente's candidacy in favour of Delgado; the formation of a united Opposition headquarters with representatives of both campaign committees and of the *Directório Democrato-Social*; and the organisation of all Opposition forces to continue the struggle for democracy by all means possible.[28] Sertório's appeal was not only a convincing analysis of the actual situation but also an effective answer to the arguments of the Communist Party, that the working class forces should not collaborate with certain bourgeois forces in the Delgado camp.

This appeal was not in vain, for a week later Dr Vicente announced his withdrawal and, in the so-called 'Cacilhas Pact', called on his followers to support Delgado.[29] This decision was the logical response to the growing chorus of voices from within Vicente's own ranks – of which Sertório's was only one – for unity with the 'National Independent Candidate'. But more than anything else, it was a response to popular pressure – to the tidal wave of mass mobilisation behind the 'fearless General'. The two candidates signed a Joint Proclamation to the Portuguese People indicating that the 'Independent Opposition' (Delgado) and the 'Democratic Opposition' (Vicente), recognising the need for unity

of action at the polls, had agreed to work together for the election
of General Humberto Delgado; and the General committed
himself to a minimum programme of five points to be applied if
he were elected:

a) To create conditions for the immediate application of Article 8 of the
   Constitution (which theoretically guaranteed freedom of speech and
   assembly);
b) Implementation of an effective electoral law;
c) To hold free elections within one year of the formation of his
   Government;
d) Liberation of all political and social (sic) prisoners;
e) Immediate measures favouring the democratisation of the country.[30]

Needless to say, the regime did everything in its power, first to
prevent and then to sabotage this unification of the Opposition.
Dr Vicente has since revealed that the police attempted to prevent
him from meeting Delgado to negotiate the unity of the
campaigns;[31] and on the eve of the elections, an anonymous
leaflet was distributed suggesting that Dr Vicente was the only
candidate deserving the confidence of true democrats – a patently
divisionist manoeuvre on the part of the regime.[32]

The atmosphere in the final ten days of the campaign was one
of increasing tension and expectation on both sides. Opposition
activities were systematically disrupted by the PIDE and the
regular police forces; the censorship redoubled its vigilance, and
hundreds of activists were arrested. It was widely expected that
General Delgado would be arrested at any moment, or that the
Government would seize on some pretext to disqualify him or
cancel the elections. When Delgado visited Braga on 27 May, he
found that Santos Costa, the Minister of Defence, had arranged a
parade of the Portuguese Legion for the same day, effectively
occupying the city and preventing the candidate from having any
contact with the people; and a few days later, when he made
plans to visit the city again, he was prohibited from doing so by
the military authorities on the basis of specious allegations that
his supporters there had committed 'disorders'.[33] In fact, on June
1 many people had gathered outside Delgado's campaign office in
Braga, expecting him to arrive, and when his visit was delayed
the PSP and GNR moved in and dispersed the crowd by force,
injuring at least 11 people and provoking a riot. The Civil
Governor, blaming the trouble on 'Communist agitators', banned

any further meeting – with the predictable result of provoking further riots the next day.[34] Wherever Delgado went, he was surrounded by PIDE officers, a fact against which he protested repeatedly, but in vain. Towards the end of the campaign, many of his leading supporters were arrested, including the President of his National Campaign Committee, the respected Professor Vieira de Almeida, the Architect Artur Andrade, and the entire committees of Chaves, Braga, Guimarães and other towns.[35]

By election day (June 8) it was obvious that the Government was determined to go through with the usual farce, 'manufacturing' a majority by any means available. The regime resorted to every conceivable device of fraud and intimidation. One of the most effective was the seizure by plain-clothed PIDE agents or Legionnaires of thousands of Opposition ballot-lists; in a press conference on June 9 Delgado charged that on the eve of the elections, over 150,000 ballots were seized by force from taxis hired by his campaign organisers.[36] But by far the most damning evidence of the methods used by the regime was a secret document with instructions from the National Union to local polling officers on how to control the vote. A copy of this was obtained and circulated by the Opposition, and it makes fascinating reading:

1. – Not to allow any invigilation (by representatives of the Opposition).
2. – To consider as spoiled the maximum number possible of Opposition ballots.
3. – Beside the ballot-boxes some 15 to 20 plain-clothes Legionnaires will be stationed in order to provoke disturbances at the appropriate time, as a pretext for arresting all Opposition sympathisers who may be present; the Presiding Officers will then close the polls, taking advantage of the situation to stuff the ballot-boxes with all our ballots which the election officers will have ready.
4. – For every elector who does not vote, a ballot will be placed in the box, on the understanding that the Government has saved them the trouble (of voting in person).
5. – It does not matter if in the ballot-boxes there appear a thousand or more ballots than the number of voters on the electoral roll.
6. – We have to win in order to carry out a thorough purge afterwards.[37]

The cynical contempt for democratic rights and legality revealed in this document should surprise no one familiar with the methods of the *Estado Novo*; it conforms to a pattern described in similar documents 'leaked' in previous election campaigns.[38] However, what is significant is that on this occasion no one was deceived; the foreign press, often indifferent or even frankly apologetic with regard to the suppression of civil rights in Portugal, ridiculed the Government's claims and voiced pointed criticisms of the electoral fraud.[39] The official results gave Admiral Tomás 758,998 votes, and Delgado 236,528;[40] for anyone who had witnessed the campaign, this was patently absurd. Although polling was reported to have been very heavy (and indeed the official results did indicate a much larger vote than in previous elections), in Lisbon only 105,978 votes were reported (in a city of nearly one million population) and in Oporto, 27,107 (out of a population of 400,000).[41] In a few rural districts, and among the small white electorate of Angola and Mozambique, majorities favourable to the Opposition were actually reported; this in itself was a novelty. But in general, and especially in the major centres, the official results obviously bore no relation to the real sentiments of the electorate. As Delgado himself proclaimed, the natural conclusion to draw was that the votes attributed to Admiral Tomás were his, and vice versa.[42]

Protests against the electoral fraud began almost immediately. Delgado's initial reaction in his press conference on 9 June was followed by a formal letter to President Craveiro Lopes.[43] The protest was immediately dismissed on the basis of legal technicalities and Delgado made it clear that he did not expect to obtain satisfaction by legal means.[44] Of greater potential significance were the General's plans for a military revolt, which had begun a couple of weeks before the elections. Delgado himself later claimed that a revolt had been planned for the night of 2/3 June, but some of those involved were discovered – one of them, a Captain Romba, was arrested on 29 May – and others refused to go forward at the last minute.[45] Delgado had begun the campaign wearing full military uniform, which – apart from its symbolic value – entitled him to give commands to the police and troops responsible for maintaining order at election meetings; but after his overwhelming reception in Oporto, the Minister of Defence (Santos Costa) forbade him from appearing in uniform. During the rest of the campaign Delgado travelled with his General's uniform in a suitcase, ready to assume command at any moment should the expected revolt materialise.[46] He assumed – and in this he may well have been right – that it would be sufficient for one or two units to come out in his favour for the regime to fall, such was the atmosphere of public unrest.[47] There was some evidence of the existence of widespread discontent among the military, or at least an unwillingness on the part of most of the Armed Forces to use their weapons in defence of the regime.

Signs of military discontent with the political situation were not lacking. Anonymous leaflets were circulated by military sympathisers of Delgado, appealing to the sense of honour of their comrades at arms and repudiating the political use of the Armed Forces by the Government:

TO THE COMMANDERS OF THE ARMED FORCES
A group of officers of the Army, Navy and Air Force, who, like the great majority of their comrades, place the Fatherland above all other human values . . ., wish to direct this ardent appeal to their Commanders before it is too late:
(We appeal to you) not to use the Armed Forces in tasks of public order, unless there is a real and demonstrated threat which exceeds the capacities of the Police and GNR.
That you do not permit the use of the Armed Forces in provocative or offensive exhibitions of force.
That you do not order the use of firearms against Portuguese citizens, except in extreme emergency, and if such an order has to be given, that it should always be given via the proper chain of command and in writing . . .[48]

This appeal conceded that the Armed Forces might have to intervene to prevent subversion by 'Communist elements' – there were after all ideological boundaries which could not be ignored – but it warned against the abuse of this pretext to justify repression of all manifestations of the popular will. Finally, and most significantly, it declared that 'the defence of a given regime must not be confused with the defence of the Public Order', and that 'tomorrow (your Officers) may be judged by the adversaries of today'. The message could scarcely be more explicit, and it is not surprising that the authorities were concerned. On some occasions also, soldiers in uniform mingled with the crowds who welcomed the Independent Candidate; in Covilhã 600 troops were reported to have demonstrated in his favour.[49]

Faced with a potential military threat, the Government took swift measures. Soon after Delgado's first visit to Oporto, Santos Costa convened a meeting of the Chiefs of the General Staff, and transferred command of the police and the GNR to his own Ministry (Defence) rather than that of the Interior. A statement was then issued indicating that the military Chiefs had agreed upon 'security measures' necessary for 'the maitenance of public peace and order'.[50] Another meeting of the General Staff was reported on 6 June, just two days before the elections.[51] According to some reports, such was the panic in the fascist ranks that several leading supporters of the regime had virtually gone into hiding in the provinces, or had their bags packed ready to leave the country; and Santos Costa was said to have attacked them at the General Staff meeting as 'cowards' who 'hasten now to abandon their normal places of residence, fleeing from the fulfilment of their duty', and who 'ought to be ashamed of the sorry spectacle they are presenting'. The crisis was such that Salazar appealed blatantly to the self-interest of his colleagues: 'in these difficult times, none of the perquisites which we enjoy are safe if we ourselves do not strive to contribute to their security'.[52]

In this climate of desperation, it was to be expected that the regime would strike hard at the Opposition leadership as soon as it felt capable of doing so. Thus only three days after the elections there came the first direct reprisal against Delgado: a succinct communiqué of 11 June announced that the Minister of Defence had dismissed General Humberto da Silva Delgado from his post as Director-General of Civil Aviation.[53] A week later, despite his senior rank in the Air Force, he was banned from flying[54] – clearly the authorities feared the use he might make of his influence in the Air Force. Subsequently, he was offered lucrative missions abroad (which he refused): the classic combination of stick and carrot. Delgado, for his part did not remain inactive: on 17 July, as is well known, he wrote a long letter to four leading Generals – Botelho Moniz, Lopes da Silva, Costa Macedo and Beleza Ferraz – calling on them (as he later said in his Memoirs) to 'do something'.[55] The response, not surprisingly, was uniformly negative – none of these commanders had given any serious indication of dissent from the regime – and Delgado was thus reduced to the classic strategy of numerous previous military conspirators against the *Estado Novo*: contacts with small groups or junior or middle-ranking officers, too isolated and lacking sufficient influence in the military institution as a whole, and subject to almost insuperable risks of discovery or betrayal.[56]

Delgado was probably correct in assuming that there was a widespread malaise among the rank-and-file of the Armed Forces; but he failed to appreciate the difficulty of breaking the established chain of command in order to bring out one or two units in open rebellion. His letter to the four Generals revealed the limitations of Delgado's political understanding: a rhetorical appeal to honour and justice, full of personal asides ridiculing leading figures of the regime, it would have been more suitable to an election rally than as an attempt to subvert high-ranking military commanders (who in any case, as Delgado should have known, were not willing to be subverted).

The regime's cynical disregard of the popular will was greeted with numerous protests throughout Portugal. Apart from letters and declarations to the press – generally censored, as was to be expected – many people wore black ties or black armbands as a symbolic protest (a device used by the opposition on previous occasions). Delgado's followers appealed to the population to boycott any business or service directly connected to the regime, such as the leading newspapers, the national lottery, shops and stores run by the Government or by individual functionaries of the National Union, the PIDE or the Legion, and the State petrol companies SACOR and SONAP. It was also suggested that people should ostentatiously leave buses or trains whenever soldiers or police in uniform entered them.[57] But such protests were only gestures, and might expose those who practised them to harassment and reprisals. More significant, and potentially much more effective, were the strikes which began to break out a few days after the elections in industrial centres such as the South Bank of the Tagus, Oporto, Marinha Grande, and Lisbon itself.

Despite the efforts of the censorship to suppress such news, there is general agreement that there were extensive protest strikes in the two or three weeks following the Presidential elections of 1958; and that they were largely spontaneous, occurring (initially at least) without the support of the PCP and even against its policy. Hence when contemporary PCP documents estimate that more than 60,000 workers engaged in intermittent strikes and other forms of protest between 12 June and 9 July,[58] there is more than usual reason to accept their estimates. Beginning on 12 June, thousands of workers in the cork industry, in construction, in the shipbuilding firm Parry &

Son and in the Naval Arsenal of Alfeite – all on the South Bank of
the Tagus – walked out in protest; they were followed from the
16th onwards by thousands more in the industrial belt of the
Ribatejo, in construction, engineering, ceramics and agriculture;
in the Oporto region, by fishermen, workers in canning factories
and textile mills, engineering plants and breweries; by agricultural labourers throughout the Alentejo, fishermen in the
Algarve, and so on.[59] In most cases the political character of the
strikes was clear: in many cases the workers shouted slogans or
carried placards proclaiming 'Free all political prisoners!',
'Abolish the censorship!', ''Down with fascism!' and 'Free
elections!'. In several places there occurred the predictable
confrontations with the PSP and the GNR, although in Almada –
remarkably enough – the local GNR commander took the side of
the people against a provocative incident fomented by the PIDE.
Hundreds of arrests were made, and at least one demonstrator
was killed, the agricultural labourer José Adelino dos Santos of
Montemor-o-Novo in the Alentejo.[60] Very significantly, there
were tradesmen who closed their shops in sympathy with the
strikers, and quite a number of managers and factory owners
who showed support or at least did not oppose the work
stoppages. From the point of view of the regime, this attitude was
intolerable, and – very unusually – a number of industrialists
were arrested and interrogated by the PIDE. The Government
ordered the closing of many factories where strikes had occurred
and the dismissal of the workers involved; production could only
resume with the hiring of a new, obedient labour force, or with
those workers whose reliability had been certified by the PIDE.
However, faced in many cases with the continued opposition of
both workers and management, the Government was forced to
give way and allow most plants to reopen with the existing
labour force.[61]

Very little of this unrest was allowed to appear in the press, and
in fact the censorship became more rigorous as soon as the
elections were over. Small items of information continued to
appear for months afterwards; thus in April 1959 *O Século*
reported the trial of thirteen workers from the Efa-Acec factory,
accused of having instigated a strike in June of the previous year.
One of the managers who was called as a witness made a very
interesting statement, saying that it was a purely political strike

and not for any work-related demand; it did not seem to him that there was any organisation involved (i.e. the PCP), and he was sure the workers would have returned the next day if they had not been prevented by 'higher authority' (i.e. the government, which wanted to take punitive measures).[62] It was later reported that there were 120 defence witnesses in the trial, which in itself is an indication of the mass support for the strike.[63] The authorities evidently decided that the trial was not serving their interests, since very little further news about it was allowed to reach the press.

Inevitably, in the absence of political leadership, the strike wave died down, to be followed by an atmosphere of tense calm and then gradual disillusionment as the regime intensified its repression and recovered control of the situation. But there is little doubt that for a period of a few weeks before and after the elections of 8 June 1958, the Salazarist regime was in greater danger than at any other time in its long history, and a coordinated general strike accompanied by a limited but well-planned military action would almost certainly have brought it down.

Delgado's extraordinary impact undoubtedly owed a great deal to his style, which was quintessentially populist: the forceful rhetoric, the impromptu and opinionated outbursts, the quest for direct contact with the people and the urgent desire for action. As I have argued elsewhere,[64] the movement which grew up in response to his leadership was also populist in its structure and dynamics. If by populism is understood a heterogeneous, loosely-structured mass movement, uniting sectors of diverse class origin around a charismatic leader on the basis of an anti-establishment or anti-oligarchic discourse, then the Delgado phenomenon undoubtedly fits the model. Presenting himself as 'independent' and 'above party', he directed his appeal to the entire nation. 'The moralisation of public life', or the end of corruption – another classic populist refrain – was one of the key points in his electoral programme.

When Delgado appeared on the scene, the main organised forces of the political opposition were in crisis, the bourgeois sectors barely recovering from the effects of cold-war anti-communism, and the PCP embarking on its ill-fated line of the 'peaceful solution'. There was, then, a very genuine crisis of political representation among the anti-Salazarist forces. Delgado's great virtue was that, despite his adroit use of the rhetoric of 'unity' and 'reconciliation', he had no illusions about negotiations with the regime; he was prepared to use force, and as a General in active service he inspired many people with the belief that he could stage an effective military action were others had failed. But it was not only a question of his military rank; he also represented – and this is where his rhetoric and style were so important – the belief in the need for active struggle against the regime, and (although inadequately) the need for mass politics. His boldness, his impatience, and his refusal to contemplate defeat all spoke directly to the climate of popular frustration and disorientation arising from the existence of newly mobilised social strata, the general weakness of political organisation, and the strategic failure of the anti-fascist opposition. The conjunction of Delgado's personal magnetism with the specific conditions of Portuguese society in the late fifties and early sixties is well brought out in a recent work by Manuel Sertório:

> It is true that, in the period of his candidacy for the Presidency of the Republic and immediately afterwards, Delgado, as a General in active service, was in an ideal situation to create the illusion of being able to bring about the rapid overthrow of the fascist regime by the sheer force of his action. And it is also true that later, in exile ... the name of Humberto Delgado enjoyed once again the specific conditions to acquire, as indeed happened, a *mythological* dimension ...
>
> It is clear, however, that these phenomena would have been insufficient to allow Humberto Delgado to play the role that he did in Portuguese society. They had to be inserted, as was in fact the case, in a highly favourable set of circumstances, which included the real convergence under fascism of different class interests, the weakness of the Portuguese proletariat as a social class *for itself*, the virtual non-existence of organised political parties, the *ideology* of anti-fascism (which concealed the antagonistic contradictions, even under the fascist regime, of the class interests at stake), and the extreme weakness of proletarian theory in our country ...[65]

Although in my view Sertório exaggerates the weakness of the Portuguese proletariat as a class-conscious force, this is a convincing analysis of the general situation in which the Delgado phenomenon occurred. It was in many ways an ideal conjuncture for the emergence of a populist coalition: and unpopular and anachronistic regime, slow to adapt to the new demands of

capital;[66] a large, subordinate mass of heterogeneous class composition; growing but ill-focussed popular discontent; and an
ideological and organisational crisis within the working class.
The problem was how to translate the populist whirlwind into
effective action to overthrow the regime, and this Delgado, with
the forces at his disposal, proved incapable of doing.

2 The consequences of Delgado's campaign

The impact of the 'Delgado explosion' was traumatic, not only for
the regime but for the opposition. The politics of the traditional
Republican opposition were completely discredited; what
Delgado called the 'paper opposition' (*oposição de papéis*), with its
chronic legalism, its moderation, its attachment to old republic
shibboleths, was shown to be completely irrelevant. The preoccupation with careful public statements, with agreements
among small groups of intellectuals and professionals, with
'playing the game', was replaced by mass politics and bold, direct
action. It is no accident that the next few years witnessed a series
of attempts to organise an armed uprising distinct from the
traditional *reviralhista coup* (notably the 'Cathedral plot' of March
1959 and the Beja revolt of New Year's Day 1961). These actions
were the first concrete manifestations of new political currents
which would mature in the sixties: a militant Catholic Left, and a
series of organisations dedicated to immediate armed action – the
LUAR (*Liga de Unidade e Acção Revolucionária*) of Palma Inácio, the
Marxist-Leninist *Frente de Acção Popular* and the *Brigadas Revolucionárias* (subject to Guevarist and Trotskyite influences).
Although these new organisations can be related to international
trends during the sixties, their prominence in Portugal can be
traced back to the political climate created by the 1958 campaign.

But Delgado's campaign also placed severe strains on the
credibility of the PCP. It was not so much the Party' early distrust
of Delgado's candidacy – a distrust which was entirely understandable in view of his background – but its initial preference for
such a questionable candidacy as that of Cunha Leal, and its
slowness to respond to the explosion of mass enthusiasm during
the campaign. Many observers could not help remarking that
what occurred in May – June 1958 approximated quite closely to
the line previously advanced by the PCP, of the 'national anti-

fascist insurrection'; certainly it was difficult to imagine how the popular mood could ever be more favourable to an insurrectionary strategy than it was at this time. In any event, the Party was unable to restrain many of its militants from participating in the spontaneous protest strikes which occurred in several localities after the election. It was clear that the PCP had completely misjudged the situation, and this raised fundamental questions about its political line. Thus in two documents published cladestinely shortly after the event,[67] the Party gave the impression that the wave of protest strikes in many towns of the *Margem Sul*, the Ribatejo and the Oporto region was organised on its initiative:

> Following the call of the Communist Party, the working class declared itself on strike in support of the demands put forward by the Party, which proposed the following as a condition for the pacification of the Portuguese family:
> – *A government without Salazar and Santos Costa!*
> – *The abolition of censorship!*
> – *Immediate liberation of all political prisoners!*
> – *The holding of new elections for the Presidency of the Republic!*
> Thus, by declaring themselves on strike in support of these slogans, the labouring masses gave a correct interpretation to the immediate demands of the whole nation after the 8th of June ...[68]

Unfortunately for the PCP, not only was this not the case (the strikes began spontaneously and the Party did not back them until at least a week later, by which time the initial momentum had been lost), but these slogans in themselves did not adequately express the mood of many workers at the time. The slogan 'a government without Salazar and Santos Costa' reflected the Party's 'peaceful solution' line, and implied that they key issue was the removal of these two individuals from the Government, rather than the overthrow of the fascist regime. But many reports, including some PCP documents,[69] indicate that the spirit of the striking workers was frankly insurrectionary; their spontaneous slogans were simply 'Down with fascism!' and 'Down with Salazarism!'. It seems clear that more and more workers were coming to the conclusion, as stated by Manuel Serra (one of the key figures of the 'Cathedral plot'), that 'only by force of arms would it be possible to overthrow fascism'.[70]

It has to be recognised that the PCP did subsequently self-criticise on this question, abandoning the line of the 'peaceful transition' and accepting some of the above criticisms. In Cunhal's 1961 attack on the 'Right-Wing Deviation', he went so far as to state that in 1958 'We lived through a pre-insurrectional situation without realising it'; and that if the Party had disseminated among the masses the idea that the crucial question was not the elections as such, but the overthrow of the regime, 'perhaps the crisis of 1958 would have had a different direction and a different outcome'. The document continues:

... The Party was in large measure overtaken by the initiatives, fighting spirit and determination of the popular masses. For the crucial moment (June 9) – and such moments, in which the fighting spirit of the masses reaches its peak and the enemy's difficulties also reach a peak, occur very rarely – for that moment nothing was foreseen, nothing was prepared, nothing was organised, nothing was done.

The same document also recognises that the strike movement of those days was in fact largely spontaneous:

The Secretariat's Manifesto (of the Central Committee) dated the 9th only in passing mentions the word 'strike' as one of several forms of struggle ... Also, in the political strikes, the Party to a large extent followed *in the wake of the spontaneous movement*. The calls to strike beginning on June 16 (Regional Committee of the North), the 18th (Political Commission) and the 25th (Lisbon Region) came after the first strikes, which took place from the 12th to the 16th in several factories and enterprises of Almada, Cova da Piedade, Cacilhas, Alverca, etc. ... It was only after many strikes had broken out spontaneously or through local initiatives of Party members that the Party leadership finally took the initiative at the national level ...[71]

There can be no doubt that this constitutes a very significant and salutary recognition of the reality of the 1958 situation; and this document was the key statement in the rectification of the Party's line which would culminate in Cunhal's *Rumo à Vitória* of 1964. But it is questionable whether the Party's self-criticism really went to the roots of the problem. It was consistent with the Party line in 1958 that the leadership should try to avoid armed conflict, but not that they should fail to organise for a political strike. Indeed, one of the tactical propositions associated with the 'peaceful transition' line was precisely that of a 'peaceful general strike for the resignation of Salazar and Santos Costa', an idea borrowed, as we have seen, from the Spanish Party. The failure to

prepare for such a strike in 1958, given the very favourable situation for such action, suggests the absence of any real strategy
to overthrow the regime, whether by peaceful means or violent.
Moreover, while Cunhal's criticism of the 'Right-Wing Deviation'
condemned this failure, it also criticized the Party's subsequent
support for Delgado's *Movimento Militar Independente* and its initial
support for the 'Cathedral conspiracy' of March 1959. These were
condemned by Cunhal as being typical petty-bourgeois *putschist*
conspiracies ('com as características tradicionais dos movimentos
reviralhistas'),[72] but as we shall see, this is a somewhat questionable interpretation of the March affair. Furthermore, the
Party's failure to provide anything resembling an insurrectional
lead during the mass strikes and protests of 1962 is the clearest
confirmation that the 'rectification' had failed to resolve the
PCP's strategic impasse.

With regard to General Delgado himself, his conspiratorial
efforts in June–July 1958 were indeed lamentably ineffective.
They were followed by his attempt to institutionalise military
dissidence in the *Movimento Militar Independente*, which in Mário
Soares' words 'did not have much political viability, given that
from the beginning it appeared to be poorly defined in its
objectives'.[73] It was never clearly established whether the
movement was meant to be legal or clandestine, and whether
it was to have a strictly military or mass membership. That
Delgado still enjoyed prestige among his fellow-officers is
apparent from an incident which occurred several months later,
in November 1958. A public invitation to the British Labour Party
leader Aneurin Bevan to visit Portugal was issued by Delgado
along with Jaime Cortesão, Mário de Azevedo Gomes, António
Sérgio and Vieira de Almeida; the four civilian signatories were
arrested, but Delgado was not, apparently because the Minister of
Defence (Botelho Moniz) warned Salazar that he could not be
sure of the reaction of many high-level officers if Delgado were
arrested.[74] But soon after this, disciplinary action against Delgado
was initiated by the Under-Secretary of State for the Air Force,
leading up to his dismissal on 7 January 1959.[75] In the meantime,
the General was involved in plans for another *coup* attempt,
which was to have occurred on 18 December 1958 – but once
again, the key officers withdrew at the last minute.[76] Significantly, though, new and younger elements were involved in the

conspiracy, such as Manuel Serra, a young merchant navy officer and ex-Catholic Youth Leader; Serra was typical of many who entered politics through the Delgado movement. Also significant, but in a negative sense, was the presence in Delgado's entourage of suspect individuals who may well have been PIDE agents; thus the General mentions as his chief civilian liaison in Oporto at this time a Dr Rodrigo de Abreu, whom a number of oppositionists have since mentioned as highly suspect. It was a series of PIDE provocations which led to Delgado's hasty decision (some would say over-hasty) to seek asylum in the Brazilian Embassy on 12 January 1959; following an intimidating gathering of Legionnaires outside his house, and intensive vigilance by the PIDE, Delgado was apparently persuaded by Rodrigo de Abreu and Plácido Barbosa that his life was in danger. Several of those who were close collaborators of the General at this time are convinced that this was a ruse by the regime in order to get him out of the country, and that the authorities would never have dared to lay hands on him had he remained in Portugal.[77]

But Delgado's asylum did not put an end to the plans and conspiracies inspired by his example. A movement of great significance, the so-called *conspiração da Sé* or Cathedral plot, occurred while Delgado was still in the Brazilian Embassy awaiting Government authorisation to leave the country. The movement, which was to have taken place on 11–12 March 1959, was discovered at the last minute by the PIDE, as so often happened. But in the words of Mário Soares, 'it was a revolutionary attempt which had nothing to do with the old 'putschist' movements of former times . . . . Neither by its basic inspiration nor by the people who participated in it, in responsible positions . . . .'.[78] One of the key organisers was Manuel Serra, and along with him there were many young activists whose formation had been in the *Juventude Operária Católica* (Catholic Workers' Youth) and *Juventude Universitária Católica* (Catholic Student Youth). There were a number of monarchists, both civilian and military, and socialists of various tendencies – but few of the old Republicans or the opposition 'establishment' in general. The PCP was in contact with the movement, but in the end refused to support what it saw as another *putschist* adventure; some Communist militants did, however, participate as individuals. The movement was a continuation of the abortive December conspiracy, and several of the conspirators had in fact been engaged in clandestine meetings with Delgado since July or August 1958; according to Manuel Serra, a number of meetings took place in the office of the *Revista Náutica*, a magazine which he had founded along with fellow merchant navy officers. As the preparations matured, a military directorate was formed in Lisbon, headed by Major Pastor Fernandes of the *Academia Militar*; another key figure was Captain Almeida Santos, an ex-leader of the *Mocidade*; also prominent were Captain Vasco da Costa Santos, Cavalry Major Luis Cesariny Calafate and Infantry Major Luis Sá Viana de Alvarenga. What most of them had in common was their youth and their Catholic background; some, like Delgado, had been active supporters of the regime, but in most cases their adherence to fascist ideology had been no greater than that of any army officer trained under the *Estado Novo*. Some, such as Major Alvarenga (who after 25 April came to preside over one of the Tribunals responsible for judging ex-PIDE agents) were consistent democrats, within the limits imposed by their military status at the time. What is most significant about them, then, is that they represented a new generation of active revolutionaries.[79]

Although Delgado could not be actively involved after January, his influence was apparent in many ways. The conspirators signed a Programme indicating their political goals on 11 February 1959, and did so in the name of the *Movimento Militar Independente* – Delgado's movement. The Programme was limited to the overthrow of the 'regime of force and personal dictator-ship', the restitution of all basic freedoms, abolition of the political police and other repressive institutions, and the esta-blishment of a freely-elected constitutional government within 18 months of the seizure of power. This document was signed in the office of one of the leading civilians involved, Dr Francisco Sousa Tavares – a Catholic lawyer who would later join the Socialist Party (although he has moved further to the right in recent years). Another prominent civilian participant who survived to play a political role after 1974 was Ing. Gonçalo Ribeiro Teles, a monarchist who is now General Secretary of the *Partido Popular Monárquico*.[80] Those who set the tone of the movement, however, were the 'young Turks' like Manuel Serra, Pastor Fernandes, Costa Santos (later to be active on the left wing of the MFA) and Almeida Santos. It is interesting to note that the movement also included Captain Varela Gomes (who would be a leading protagonist of the Beja revolt nearly three years later, and another future MFA left-winger) and, initially, Captain Vasco Gonçalves – the only member of the future MFA Coordinating Committee to be politically active at this time. Gonçalves, who was, then as now, close to the PCP (if not a Party member), led a group of officers whose participation was to occur under his orders; it seems highly probable that this was part of the PCP's military network, since Gonçalves announced his group's withdrawal from the movement a few days before 12 March, immediately after the PCP had done the same – a double blow which may well have been fatal to the entire plan.[81] Gonçalves maintains (as does the PCP) that they decided to withdraw because it became apparent that the movement was just another *putsch*, with 'identical methods of preparation' to previous *coup* attempts, 'without precautions' and without mass support.[82] The conspirators, of course, were hoping that mass support would be generated by their action, as indeed it would be on 25 April 1974 by a *coup* from which Vasco Gonçalves did not withdraw ...

The movement of March 11–12 was indeed planned as a military *coup*; but it was to have been a military *coup* with considerable civilian participation, and the key moves in the seizure of power were planned with unusual care and extensive preparation. Manuel Serra was to be in charge of some 300 armed civilians in about fifty small units, who would be responsible for seizing or surrounding many leading officials of the regime and taking over the main radio stations and means of communication, while rebel military units neutralised key military installations. The main civilian unit was to operate out of the crypt of Lisbon Cathedral, where their weapons were stored – this thanks to Father Perestrelo de Vasconcelos, chaplain to the merchant navy (once again, the Manuel Serra connection!). On the crucial night, virtually all the conspirators were at their appointed posts and ready to act – some had already begun to move – when the senior officers involved (officers of the General Staff) called for the plan to be postponed. Despite the protestations of Serra and others, this was done, with the inevitable fatal results: the following day the group of conspirators in the Cathedral were arrested (some 30 in number), and during the next few days the authorities detected and arrested several of the military conspirators.[83] But, significantly, the majority of those involved were never detected by the PIDE, demonstrating the relative success of the organisers in protecting an extensive conspiratorial network. The failure of the authorities was made plain for all to see in the trial, which did not begin until May 1960; the prosecution lacked evidence to support serious charges against many of the accused, who therefore received comparatively light sentences. Little information of interest emerged from the trial, except for a few circumstantial details such as the allegation (very probably correct!) that Manuel Serra had urged the armed civilians in the Cathedral 'to follow the example of Fidel Castro',[84] that Colonel Vilhena (the only old Republican to participate openly) confessed to having contributed 3,000 escudos and the use of his automobiles for the movement,[85] and that Manuel Serra and Major Calafate were sentenced in their absence,[86] both having managed to escape. Serra, like Galvão before him, escaped from the Santa Maria hospital, and sought refuge (significantly) in the Cuban Embassy; later he moved to the Brazilian Embassy, receiving asylum in that country where he joined Delgado once again.[87]

3   From the cathedral to the barracks: the *Juntas Patrióticas*, Botelho Moniz and Beja

Although the March 1959 affair was followed by a two-year lull in insurrectionary attempts, this was certainly not true of the opposition activity or popular resistance in general. The upsurge in strike and other forms of labour unrest has been documented in Chapter IV, and while it may not have been directly connected to the Delgado campaign, it is indicative of a new climate of contestation to which the General had contributed more than any other individual or group. Legal and illegal opposition activities also displayed renewed vigour, and here Delgado's influence – direct or indirect – was frequently apparent. Beginning in the spring of 1959 there was a movement to establish *Juntas Patrióticas* – an interesting designation which harks back to earlier liberation movements in Iberia and Latin America. These were conceived as broadly-based committees embracing all ideological trends within the opposition, and were

in principle clandestine. Initially a *Junta Patriótica Central* was
created in Lisbon with a very restricted membership, but it was
gradually expanded and consolidated; two or three months later,
similar *Juntas* were set up in Coimbra and Oporto, and they began
to produce a clandestine bulletin. This inspired the formation in
some areas of *Juntas de base*, rank-and-file committees dedicated
to the same goals. The *Junta Central* consisted of representatives of
Delgado's former campaign committee and of Dr Arlindo
Vicente's campaign committee; of the Freemasons; and of
various left-wing groups, but not initially of the PCP, which was
only invited to join a few months later.[88]

In some ways the formation of the *Juntas Patrióticas* resembles
that of the MUD or the MUNAF – particularly the latter, since
they were clandestine. Although their exact rôle and strategy
were somewhat nebulous, the eventual goal was clearly insurrection. Their propaganda evidently aimed to create a mass
following, although perhaps not a mass membership; and the
relatively subordinate role of the Communist Party differentiated
them from earlier movements. Nevertheless, the *Junta Central*
was the first organisational expression of opposition unity, embracing all important sectors of the anti-fascist movement from
the liberal monarchists to the PCP, since the Norton de Matos
campaign ten years earlier. For this reason the PIDE was
particularly anxious to destroy it, and sought actively to identify
its members and find a pretext to arrest them. Such a pretext was
provided by the publication of the 'Programme for the Democratisation of the Republic', a classic document in the mould of
traditional opposition statements.

The idea of drafting the Programme for the Democratisation
of the Republic was floated in the autumn of 1959 by Jaime
Cortesão, but it was not until a year later that a large group of
republican and socialist intellectuals began to meet systematically
to elaborate the document. Dated 31 January 1961, it was in fact
only made public on 11 May of that year, at a press conference
presided over by Mário de Azevedo Gomes.[89] It is an extensive
document expounding all the well-worn liberal criticisms of
the regime, and proposing detailed programmatic objectives in
economic policy, agriculture, health, education and other fields.
But it suffers from the characteristic deficiencies criticised by the
PCP in similar documents a decade and a half previously: the ab-

sence of any tactical or strategic plan for overthrowing the regime, the diversion of opposition energies from active political struggle, and excessive timidity in some of its policy statements, (for example, on the colonial issue, where it favours democratic reforms within the framework of a Portuguese Federal Republic).[90] Precisely for these reasons it was rejected by the PCP, and also – a key point – by the exiled General Delgado. The General's former campaign secretary, Artur Andrade, made this clear when interrogated by the police in connection with the Programme:

Indeed, the General sent him his observations on the 'programme', which, however, were not made public, since the respondent was quite sure that they would not be well received by the majority of the signatories, especially since the terms in which these 'observations' had been formulated were not in keeping with the spirit of the 'programme' and would be considered too combative ...[91]

The Programme was clearly out of keeping with the new revolutionary sectors which had emerged in the post-1958 atmosphere. When all allowances are made for the political contingencies which influenced the authors, the document remains striking for its lack of new thinking. Thus it maintains the opposition's uncritical and frankly romanticised view of the First Republic:

Indeed, despite the noise of the propaganda machine installed and set into motion with the aim of wiping out the memory of those years of ardent hope and freely accepted sacrifice, it is necessary to conclude and to affirm that the balance-sheet of those 16 short years of the Republic of 1910 is frankly positive, so that it can be said that the key to all the problems of the time was outlined correctly, and the foundations of the far-reaching work (of reform) which was urgently needed were truly laid at that time.[92]

This assessment of a period in which factional politics, narrow anticlericalism and financial disorder had done so much to pave the way for Salazarism was not a promising basis for political renovation.

The immediate consequence of the Programme's publication was the arrest and interrogation of most of the signatories by the PIDE. This contributed to the effective demise of the *Junta Patriótica Central*, several of whose members were also involved in the Programme. Opinions differ on the duration and significance of the *Junta Central*, but certainly by 1962 it had to all intents and purposes ceased to exist. Thus in the words of Alvaro Cunhal:

... for a few years the broad-front movement had as its highest expression the *Junta Patriótica Central*. With a very irregular mode of operation, this was more a coordinating than a directive body. In no way did it assume the effective leadership of the democratic movement, and *after a certain point* it practically ceased to meet.[93]

From the context, it seems clear that Cunhal is referring to some time in 1961 or early 1962 as the date when the *Junta Central* 'practically ceased to meet'. There is some doubt as to whether the organisation ever functioned very effectively,[94] but it does appear that the *Junta Central* or its subordinate *Juntas* contributed to the conspiratorial preparations during 1961, leading up to the Beja revolt. Fernando Piteira Santos, who was arrested in the summer of 1961 in connection with the Programme for the Democratisation of the Republic, states that when he was released from Caxias in November, members of the *Junta Central* contacted him and informed him of preparations for 'more significant actions against the regime'.[95] Another member of the *Junta Central*, Nikias Skapinakis, maintains that it was Beja and the consequent police repression which effectively put an end to the *Juntas*.[96]

The story of the *Juntas Patrióticas* is indicative also of the growing impact in Portugal of the exile opposition. Delgado, Galvão, Manuel Serra, Calafate, Sertório and others maintained a febrile activity of propaganda, fund-raising and intrigue in Brazil, Argentina, Venezuela, Morocco and various European countries, lobbying in international forums against the Salazar regime, attacking its interests overseas, and making clandestine visits to Portugal. If they were not always well-co-ordinated – their efforts were often amateurish and they suffered from the chronic dissension and factionalism which plagues all exile communities from the Spanish Republicans to the Chileans of the 1970's – they made up for this in panache and determination. They had different channels of contact in Portugal, but the *Juntas*, or some of their leading members, were the principal contacts for Delgado and his associates (such as Serra and Sertório). As is also typical of such situations, some of the domestic opposition activists tend to minimise the significance of the exiles, pointing out that resistance continued in Portugal regardless of the exploits of those who had left,[97] but evidence suggests that the direct and indirect influence of the exiles in these years was considerable.

The first spectacular action of the exile opposition was the *Santa Maria* affair, amply reported in the world press at the time and described in detail in Delgado's *Memoirs*. The seizure of the Portuguese cruise liner off the coast of Venezuela on 22 January 1961 and its thirteen-day odyssey in the South Atlantic before surrendering to Brazilian authorities in Recife certainly did more to bring the Portuguese resistance to international attention than anything that had happened for many years past.[98] Its practical impact in Portugal is much more debatable, but it undoubtedly contributed to maintaining the spirit of militant and direct action which had developed since the 1958 elections. The collaboration with Spaniards in the DRIL (Iberian Revolutionary Directorate of Liberation) and the plan to sail to Africa (Fernando Pó, São Tomé and Angola) in order to link up with a rebel movement there, were significant innovations in the tactics of the resistance; and the proclamation of Delgado as legitimate Head of State served to remind the world of the fraudulent character of the Portuguese elections. The bold leadership of Henrique Galvão appeared to indicate a promising unity in action among the military exiles. But the commandos' poor organisation and their failure to reach Africa pointed to continuing weaknesses of the type which had always characterised military actions against the *Estado Novo*. Nevertheless, the action was one of the more successful of the many *coups* and conspiracies against the regime, and despite Delgado's subsequent disclaimers,[99] his actions at the time of Beja and subsequently down to his death in 1965 showed that he also had not abandoned his penchant for the dramatic gesture.

Another significant aspect of the *Santa Maria* affair, to judge by a report in the official Portuguese press (which, despite its evident propagandistic intent, there is no reason to discount entirely), is the link of its organisers to the Cuban revolutionaries and to Colonel Alberto Bayo, the Spanish Republican exile who had helped Fidel Castro's band with military training in Mexico.[100] Expecially in the early period of gestation of the *Santa Maria* project (spring-summer 1960), when the Cuban Revolution had not yet taken on a pronounced pro-Soviet character, such a connection with the international Ibero-American revolutionary fraternity was a natural development. It also confirms the influence on the more militant elements of the Portuguese resistance of the Cuban example – an influence which was to be reinforced in the next few years by that of the Algerian Revolution. This influence would be apparent once again at Beja, and would continue in the exile *Frente Patriótico de Libertação Nacional* (linking Delgado with the PCP and other opposition forces from 1962 to 1964).

The other crucial new factor impinging on the political scene in 1961, and which would eventually transform it totally, was the beginning of the colonial wars (to be examined in the next chapter). With the outbreak of revolt in Angola in February, both the regime's and the opposition's priorities would have to change – although it would take time for these changes to work themselves through. Beja and the great wave of popular protest of March–June 1962, although influenced by the colonial question, represented in a sense the last great revolutionary upsurge in which domestic concerns were paramount; but before this, the *annus mirabilis* of 1961 witnessed other events of great significance.

It was in April 1961 that there occurred a serious *coup* attempt from within the regime, led by the Defence Minister, General Júlio Botelho Moniz. While not linked with Delgado or with the opposition, there can be little doubt that Botelho Moniz was influenced in his thinking by the impact of Delgado's election campaign and subsequent events, coming to regard the removal of Salazar as both possible and necessary. The other, immediate stimulus for his action was the Angolan revolt, which sent shockwaves through the entire military establishment and posed the need for an urgent re-evaluation of colonial policy (impossible while Salazar remained). The Air Force chief General Albuquerque de Freitas was apparently also a central figure, arguing that Portugal must not fight a losing battle against 'savages' and that the country's isolation must be ended. The plan was to pass a motion of non-confidence in Salazar at a meeting of the Defence Council on 8 April, but the Prime Minister (probably forewarned) did not attend; over the next few days, the plotters' attempts to win over President Tomás failed, and on the 13th, when they were finally about to take action without Tomás, Salazar dismissed Botelho Moniz and rallied sufficient military support to persuade the dissidents to back down.[101] Although a coup from within the system rather than an attempt to change the regime, the April 1961 plot is generally regarded as one of the most dangerous moments for Salazar throughout his long career, and it provided further evidence of the regime's vulnerability in these years.

The vitality of the exile opposition and the urgency of the colonial question were both brought to the fore once again towards the end of the year. On 10 November 1961 came Henrique Galvão's pioneer venture into the field of aircraft hijacking, with the seizure of a TAP airliner on a regular flight from Casablanca to Lisbon in order to drop propaganda leaflets over the capital and other towns (Barreiro, Beja and Faro) before seeking refuge in Tangier. Although Galvão did not participate personally for health reasons, he declared to journalists in Tangier that he had been preparing the hijacking for seven weeks; the six men who actually carried out the plan were led by Hermínio da Palma Inácio, one of the air force mechanics who had sabotaged planes at the Sintra airfield during the April 1947 *coup* attempt.[102] The action was condemned by Delgado, who was also staying in Morocco at the time, but Galvão later claimed that Delgado had master-minded the entire operation.[103] This was simply part of the ongoing bickering between the two exiled *condottieri*, and certainly did not improve the public image of the exile opposition; in fact it seems likely that Delgado was not involved, or had withdrawn after some initial involvement, and his annoyance was probably due to fear that the hijacking would disrupt his plans for participation in Beja six weeks later. Once again, for all its adventurism, the action had a dramatic impact both in Portugal and abroad.

The colonial question was thrown into sharp relief again by India's invasion of the Portuguese enclaves of Goa, Damão and Diu in December 1961. The problem had been coming to a head for years, and it was clear that the territories were militarily indefensible; only a referendum combined with a vigorous diplomatic campaign might have saved them for Portugal. But Salazar's blind refusal to negotiate was fatal, and when India invaded on 17 December with 30,000 troops, tanks, aircraft and naval units, the position of the small Portuguese force under Governor-General Vassalo e Silva was hopeless.[104] The im-

mediate effect was to underline the vulnerability of Portugal's
colonial empire; later, the court-martial of Vassalo e Silva and
other officers would fuel a powerful military resentment against
their use as scapegoats, which would grow steadily during the
African wars.

The final blow of a traumatic year for the regime (in fact,
ushering in the New Year of 1962), the Beja uprising was to
be the last military revolt in Portugal for a decade. This was
fundamentally due to the exhaustion, after July 1962, of the
great wave of revolutionary struggle during the previous five
years, and to the development of the African wars as a dominant
and permanent feature of the political scene. Beja itself was the
culmination of the insurgent activities associated with Delgado,
the *Juntas Patrióticas* and the new opposition groups arising since
1958. Even if the *Junta Central* as such was scarcely functioning,
its members and associates were preparing a revolutionary
movement for months before. Meanwhile in June–July 1961
Delgado sent agents to Europe and Morocco 'to maintain contacts
and to put into action my plan for the revolution in Portugal'.[105]
The most important of these agents was Manuel Serra, who
entered Portugal clandestinely and played a key role in preparing
the conspiracy. Fernando Piteira Santos, a member of the *Junta
Central*, says that shortly after his release from gaol in November
he entered into contact with Manuel Serra and established
contact between Serra and certain civilian and military groups
which were ready to support a revolutionary plan. Captain Varela
Gomes, another member of the *Junta Central* at that time, who
had just stood as an opposition candidate in the November
elections and had participated in the popular protests following
the electoral fraud, joined the conspiracy a few weeks later and
became its military chief of operations.[106]

As always happened, the revolutionary plan changed several
times during preparations. Originally the Alentejo was to have
been a secondary field of operations, but the withdrawal or
unreliability of some conspirators in the Centre and North led to
the decision to concentrate on Beja. The scheme was for a joint
civilian-military uprising which would rapidly take control of
most of the Alentejo and Algarve, and broadcast revolutionary
proclamations by radio to the rest of the country while Delgado
entered from Morocco to take charge of the movement. This was

supposed to spark off a popular insurrection and the collapse of the régime, since most military units were not expected to resist. If the movement had ever reached this point, this expectation might well have been fulfilled; the problem, as always, was that the plan misfired in the early stages. As in March 1959, the clandestine preparations had gone remarkably well, without detection by the police – partly, according to Manuel Serra, because of the involvement in key positions of Catholic Youth activists who were not under surveillance by the PIDE. Delgado, who had problems of liaison in Morocco, did not manage to enter Portugal until December 30, and was out of touch with the conspirators; he went to a boarding house in Lisbon and began phoning friends and contacts! Amazingly, he was not discovered, and was able to link up with the revolutionaries and reach Beja in the early hours of New Year's Day, when the action was already under way. Varela Gomes and a few other insurgent officers entered the barracks of the Third Infantry Regiment in Beja as planned, and a unit of about thirty armed civilians led by Manuel Serra scaled the walls. Several of the regiment's officers surrendered to Varela Gomes without resistance, but the commander, Major Calapez, realized that something was amiss because Serra's rifle went off accidentally when the civilians were climbing the walls; Calapez resisted, firing on Varela Gomes who was quite badly wounded. The Major then fled, alerting the local GNR and the Lisbon authorities.[107] After this the game was up; forces from Evora, originally supposed to join the revolt, surrounded the barracks and over-powered the insurgents, who lost two or three dead and several wounded. Varela Gomes was in critical condition for a week, undergoing three operations in the Beja hospital before being taken to Lisbon for interrogation.[108]

The revolt was the most serious armed action against the regime in many years in terms of clarity of objectives and disposition to fight. Here there were no major last-minute withdrawals and no supine surrender at the first sign of resistance by loyal troops. The movement failed because of inadequate coordination and because of the insurgents' underestimation of their opponents: they did not expect serious resistance from pro-regime units. This was a mistake of anti-Salazarist rebels all the way down to 1974; even on 25 April the regime did not surrender until it was clear that the movement had spread to several military units and MFA tanks were in control of the streets.

Following this new failure, Delgado escaped (miraculously) to Oporto, and then on January 11th crossed the border into Spain, returning via Morocco to Brazil. Serra, Varela Gomes and others languished in gaol for years, and the opposition's clandestine networks (except that of the PCP which was not directly involved) were seriously disrupted. If Beja had occurred five or six months later, coinciding with the mass strikes and riots of May–June, the outcome might have been very different. Once again, the anti-fascist resistance failed because of the lack of coordination between the strategies of the PCP and of the non-communist revolutionaries. There was no doubt that, as Alvaro Cunhal later admitted, Beja was different from earlier *putschist* conspiracies; the extensive civilian participation, including several Communist militants who participated despite contrary instructions from the Partly, was one indication of this. A combination of the PCP's clandestine efficiency and capacity for mass mobilisation with the panache and determination of the new military and civilian insurgents would certainly have liberated Portugal twelve to fifteen years before April 25, in 1959 or 1962 – thus sparing both the Portuguese and African peoples thirteen years of bitter colonial warfare. But the story of those crucial years is an object lesson in the deficiencies of both the Communist Party and military populism – not to mention the classic 'Democratic Opposition' of republicans, socialists and liberals, whose sterility in terms of active resistance could not have been more abundantly demonstrated.

Notes to Chapter VI

1 *República*, 8 May 1958. The same document is also available in *O Século* of 9 May 1958, and in a fuller, uncensored version which was distributed publicly at the time: *Proclamação do General Humberto Delgado Candidato à Presidência da República* (Editada pelos Serviços de Candidatura do Porto); consulted by courtesy of Sr. Oliveira Valença.

2 *República*, 10 May 1958.

3 *Ibid.*

4 *Diário de Lisboa*, 10 May 1958.

5 *Ibid.*

6 *O Século*, 11 May 1958, passage cut by censorship; consulted in the *O Século* archive.

7 *República*, 13 May 1958.

8 *República*, 15 May 1958.

9 *Ibid.*

10 This and previous quotations are from *República*, 15 May 1958. It is interesting that many passages from this speech were censored from *O Século*, but not from *República*; presumably the government assumed that the latter newspaper would only be read by committed supporters of the opposition, and was as it were 'preaching to the converted'.

11 *O Século*, 15 May 1958, passage cut by the censorship; consulted in the *O Século* archive.

12 *Ibid.*; this entire passage was cut by the censor. The 'social question' was a very delicate one for the regime.

13 *Ibid.*; 15 & 16 May 1958.

14 *O Século* archive, censored material from 17 May 1958.

15 *O General Humberto Delgado Dirige-se ao Sr. Presidente da República* (Lisboa, 19 May 1958), p. 5; consulted by courtesy of Maria Humberta Delgado Lourenço.

16 *O Século*, 18 May 1958.

17 *O Século*, 19 May 1958.

18 *Ibid.*, censored material from 19 May 1958.

19 *Nota oficiosa do Ministério do Interior*, in *Diário Ilustrado*, 19 May 1958.

20 *O General Humberto Delgado Dirige-se ao Sr. Presidente da República* (*op. cit.*), p. 5.

21 *O Século*, 18 May 1958, censored material: communiqué from Delgado's campaign committee.

22 *República*, 18 May 1958.

23 Declarations of Engineer Cunha Leal in an interview with Major Botelho Moniz on *Radio Clube Português*, 20 May; reported in *República* and *Diário de Lisboa*, 21 May 1958.

24 *República*, 25 May 1958: 'Definição dum pensamento socialista: ao povo português'.

25 *Diário de Lisboa*, 30 May 1958 and *República*, 1 June 1958.

26 *Diário de Lisboa*, 2 June 1958.

27 See for example the reports of Dr. Vicente's campaign in *República*, 17, 21, 23, 24, 25, 27, & 29 May 1958, and in *O Século*, 20 & 21 May.

28 'Formação imediata de um organismo de salvação nacional', pelo Dr Manuel Sertório, in *República*, 23 May 1958.

29 *República*, 30 May 1958.

30 *República* and *O Século*, 31 May 1958. See also Dr Vicente's statement in the *Diário de Lisboa*, 31 May 1958.

31 Declarations of Dr Arlindo Vicente in an interview published in the *Diário de Notícias*, 5 March 1977.

32 This was denounced in a statement submitted to the press by Dr Vicente on 8 June, but deleted by the censors. *O Século* archive, censored material from 8 June 1958.

33 *República*, 3 June 1958; and Humberto Delgado, *The Memoirs of*

General Delgado (London, 1964, Cassell), pp. 112–13.

34 *Diário de Notícias*, 2 & 3 June 1958; *O Século*, 2 June 1958.

35 *The Memoirs of General Delgado* (*op. cit.*), p. 114; *O Século*, 10 June 1958: report of Delgado's press conference of 9 June, with passages cut by the censor.

36 *O Século*, 10 June 1958, including censored material. The Opposition was required by the electoral law to print its own ballot-lists and deliver them to the polling-stations, hence the effectiveness of this particular method of harassment.

37 '*Copiar e Circular – Instruções dadas na União Nacional às Presidências das Mesas de Voto.*' Undated document, consulted by courtesy of Maria Humberta Delgado Lourenco.

38 For example, '*O Que são as ELEIçÕES do ESTADO NOVO! . . . Circular confidencial, dirigida pelos Governadores Civis aos Presidentes das Câmaras Municipais, obedecendo a mesma a instruções recebidas do Ministro do Interior*'. Leaflet circulated by Delgado's campaign committee, also published in *O Comêrcio do Porto*, 13 May 1958. The statement reproduces a Circular of December 1948 in which provincial Civil Governors instructed local mayors on how to rig the elections. Consulted by courtesy of Maria Humberta Delgado Lourenço.

39 The best-known and potentially most influential criticism was in the *New York Times*, which Delgado quoted: *New York Times*, 6 June 1958.

40 Hugh Kay, *Salazar and Modern Portugal* (London, 1970, Eyre & Spottiswoode), pp. 347–50; Kay, an apologist for the regime, suggests that in a fair election, 'Delgado would have secured a higher percentage of the poll, but not victory.' (!)

41 *Ibid.*

42 *O Século* archive, censored material from 9 June 1958.

43 *O Século* archive, censored material from 22 June 1958; *The Memoirs of General Delgado* (*op. cit.*), pp. 117–30.

44 Delgado's attitude was made clear in his press conference of 9 June, when he declared that the Portuguese Government 'always steals the elections' and that he doubted the value of a legal challenge: *O Século* archive, censored material from 9 June 1958. Craveiro Lopes' reply is in Delgado's *Memoirs* (*loc. cit.*)

45 *The Memoirs of General Delgado* (*op. cit.*), pp. x & 147.

46 Author's interview with the Architect Artur Andrade, Oporto, 29 June 1977.

47 *Ibid.* Many participants in Delgado's election campaign have since expressed the same opinion.

48 '*Aos Chefes das Forças Armadas*'; anonymous leaflet dated Lisbon, May 1958; consulted by courtesy of Maria Humberta Delgado Lourenço.

49 *Sobre a Actividade do Partido nas Campanhas Eleitorais para Deputados à Assembleia Nacional e para a Presidência da República* (Informe da Commissão Política ao Comité Central do Partido Comunista Português); Relator: Gomes (Edições 'Avante!', Agosto de 1958), p. 19.

50 Author's interview with the architect Artur Andrade, Oporto, 29 June 1977; *República*, 20 May 1958.

51 *República*, 6 June 1958.
52 *Sobre a Actividade do Partido nas Campanhas Eleitorais* ... (*op. cit.*), pp. 10–11.
53 *República*, 11 June 1958.
54 *The Memoirs of General Delgado* (*op. cit.*), p. 146.
55 Delgado's letter is published in full in Alvaro Lins, *Missão em Portugal* (Lisboa, 1974, Centro do Livro Brasileiro), pp. 238–48; also in Delgado's *Memoirs*, pp. 131–41, with the date given as 27 July.
56 On the record of military dissent, see Douglas Wheeler, 'The Military and the Portuguese Dictatorship, 1926–1974: 'The Honor of the Army'', in Lawrence S. Graham and Harry M. Makler (eds.), *Contemporary Portugal: The Revolution and Its Antecedents* (Austin and London, 1979, The University of Texas Press), pp. 191–219.
57 *'Aos Portugueses Honestos. Aos Liberais de Portugal'* (unpublished clandestine leaflet, typescript); consulted by courtesy of Maria Humberta Delgado Lourenço.
58 *Sobre a Actividade do Partido nas Campanhas Eleitorais* ... (*op. cit.*), p. 12; *Sobre as Greves Políticas* (Informe da Commissão Política ao Comité Central do Partido Comunista Português), Relator: Freitas (Edições 'Avante!', Agosto de 1958), p. 1.
59 *Sobre as Greves Políticas* ... (*op. cit.*), pp. 2–4.
60 *Ibid.*, p. 3; *O Século* archive, censored material from 24 June 1958.
61 *Sobre as Greves Políticas* ... (*op. cit.*), pp. 2–4 & 6–7.
62 *O Século* archive, censored material from 29 April 1959.
63 *Ibid.*, censored material from 5 May 1959.
64 D. L. Raby, 'Populism and the Portuguese Left: From Delgado to Otelo', in Lawrence S. Graham and Douglas L. Wheeler (eds.), *In Search of Modern Portugal: The Revolution and Its Consequences* (Madison, Wis., 1982, University of Wisconsin Press), pp. 61–80.
65 Manuel Sertório, *Humberto Delgado: 70 Cartas Inéditas – A luta contra o Fascismo no exílio* (Lisboa, 1978, Praça do Livro), pp. 13–14; emphasis in original.
66 This factor, which cannot be analysed in detail here, was fundamental; by the 1950s the *Estado Novo* was not only repressive and unpopular, it was also revealing its incapacity to reconcile the needs of small and medium capital with the increased domination of the monopoly sector. See Francisco Rafael, Jorge B. Preto *et al.*, *Portugal: Capitalismo e Estado Novo* (Porto, 1976, Afrontamento).
67 *Sobre a Actividade do Partido nas Campanhas Eleitorais* ... (*op. cit.*); *Sobre as Greves Políticas* (*op. cit.*).
68 *Sobre as Greves Políticas* (*op. cit.*), p. 1.
69 *Ibid.*, pp. 2–3.
70 Author's interview with Manuel Serra, Lisbon, 10 March 1977.
71 *O Desvio de Direita no Partido Comunista Português nos Anos 1956–1959 (Elementos de Estudo)* (clandestine document of March 1961), p. 9; emphasis in original. Consulted in the Avante! archive.
72 *Ibid.*, pp. 10–13.
73 Mário Soares, *op. cit.*, pp. 252–3.

74 Alvaro Lins, *op. cit.*, 72–3.
75 *The Memoirs of General Delgado* (*op. cit.*), pp. 155–62.
76 *Ibid.*, pp. x & 162.
77 I owe this information to Fernando Piteira Santos (interview with the author, Lisbon, 20 January 1977), to the architect Artur Andrade (interview with the author, Oporto, 29 June 1977), and to Alcina Bastos (interview with the author, Lisbon, 15 June 1978).
78 Mário Soares, *op. cit.*, pp. 262–6.
79 Avelino Rodrigues, Cesário Borga e Mário Cardoso, *O Movimento dos Capitães e o 25 de Abril: 229 Dias para Derrubar o Fascismo* (Lisboa, 1974, Morães), pp. 163–6; Mário Soares, *loc. cit*; and author's interviews with Fernando Piteira Santos (Lisbon, 28 February 1977) and with Manuel Serra (Lisbon, 10 March 1977).
80 Avelino Rodrigues, Cesário Borga e Mário Cardoso, *op. cit.*, pp. 168–9; and author's interview with Fernando Piteira Santos, Lisbon, 28 February 1977.
81 Avelino Rodrigues, Cesário Borga e Mário Cardoso, *op. cit.*, pp. 163–6 & 171–3.
82 Author's interview with Vasco Gonçalves, Lisbon, 24 March 1977.
83 Avelino Rodrigues, Cesário Borga e Mário Cardoso, *op. cit.*, pp. 163–166 and 174–177; author's interview with Manuel Serra, Lisbon, 10 March 1977.
84 *O Século*, 12 July 1960.
85 *Ibid.*, 15 June 1960.
86 *Diário de Notícias*, 17, 18, 21 & 22 December 1960; *O Século*, 22 December 1960.
87 Mário Soares, *op. cit.*, pp. 318–19.
88 Author's interview with Fernando Piteira Santos, Lisbon, 28 February 1977; and with Nikias Skapinakis, Lisbon, 4 May 1977.
89 Mário Soares, *op. cit.*, pp. 282–6; and Tribunal do 1o. Juízo Criminal de Lisboa, Processo 16, 016–C de 1961 (Ministério Público contra Acácio Gouveia e outros), 1o. vol., fls. 35 (text of Azevedo Gomes's speech dated 11 May 1961).
90 *Programa para a Democratização da República*, in Serafim Ferreira e Arsénio Mota (eds.), *Para um Dossier da 'Oposição Democrática'* (Tomar, 1969, Nova Realidade), pp. 169–247.
91 Tribunal do 1o. Juízo Criminal de Lisboa, Processo 16, 016–C de 1961, 3o. Vol., fls. 288–293 (auto de perguntas de Artur de Andrade, 20 June 1961).
92 *Programa para a Democratização da República*, in Serafim Ferreira e Arsénio Mota, *op. cit.*, p. 173.
93 Alvaro Cunhal, *Rumo à Vitória* (Lisbon, 1975, Edições 'A Opinião'), p. 150; emphasis in original.
94 Author's interview with Manuel Sertório, Lisbon, April 1977. Sertório is categorical in affirming that in his view, the *Junta Central* never really began to function on a regular basis. However, as he admits, he was in exile at the time.

95   Author's interview with Fernando Piteira Santos, Lisbon, 28 February 1977.

96   Author's interview with Nikias Skapinakis, Lisbon, 4 May 1977.

97   Piteira Santos, for instance, casts doubt on the influence of Delgado on events in Portugal, and maintains that there was no connection between the *Juntas Patrióticas* in Portugal and the *Juntas Patrióticas* created in exile. (Interviews with the author, Lisbon, 20 January and 28 February 1977.)

98   *The Memoirs of General Delgado* (*op. cit.*), pp. 186–99.

99   In October 1961, after Delgado had publicly broken with Galvão, he expressed the following opinion: 'If it is true that I assumed full responsibility for the 'Santa Maria' operation, it was only to provide cover for the Opposition. I recognise that that spectacular action did not achieve its goal. As a military man, I disapprove of such a crazy enterprise.' (Delgado's declarations in Rabat, cited in an AFP cable of 30 August 1961; in *O Século* archive.)

100   'A Verdade sobre o caso do 'Santa Maria'', in *Diário de Notícias*, 5 July 1961.

101   Richard Robinson, *Contemporary Portugal: A History* (London, 1979, George Allen & Unwin), p. 77; Hugh Kay, *op. cit.*, pp. 388–99.

102   *O Século*, 11 November 1961 & 13 October 1963; also article cut by the censor from *O Século*, 12 November 1961 (in *O Século* archive).

103   *Diário de Notícias*, 11 November 1961; *O Século*, 15 & 19 November 1961.

104   Richard Robinson, *op. cit.*, p. 104.

105   *The Memoirs of General Delgado* (*op. cit.*), pp. 210–11.

106   Author's interview with Fernando Piteira Santos, 28 February 1977; Mário Soares, *op. cit.*, pp. 318–22; Alvaro Cunhal, *Rumo à Vitória* (*op. cit.*), p. 211.

107   Mário Soares, *op. cit.*, pp. 323–8; *The Memoirs of General Delgado* (op. cit.), pp. 214–17; author's interview with Manuel Serra, Lisbon, 10 March 1977.

108   *O Século* archive, report deleted by the censorship, 10 January 1962.

7

Through war to liberation, 1962-74

Grândola, vila morena
Terra da fraternidade
O povo é quem mais ordena
Dentro de ti, ó cidade.

Grândola, dusky town
Land of brotherhood
It is the people who give the orders
Within your walls, O city!

José Afonso (1971)

1 The colonial wars and the transformation of Portugal

On 3 February 1961, supporters of the MPLA (Popular Movement for the Liberation of Angola) attacked the prison in Luanda,
the Angolan capital, where several of their comrades were held;
they were repulsed with considerable bloodshed. On 15 March
and for several days thereafter, supporters of the rival UPA
(Union of the Populations of Angola) of Holden Roberto, carried
out massacres of white settlers and pro-Portuguese Africans in
the Bakongo tribal regions of northern Angola. These actions
triggered much greater retaliatory pogroms against Africans by
settlers and Portuguese troops, leaving a total of perhaps 30,000
dead. With these events, the colonial war in Angola had begun,
and it was to be followed by revolt in Guiné (beginning in
January 1963) and in Mozambique (in August 1964).[1] Although
largely contained militarily by the Portuguese for several years,
these insurgencies rapidly transformed the situation both in the
colonies and in Portugal itself.

The most immediate political result of the Angolan revolt was the attempted coup of General Botelho Moniz, in April 1961. With the failure of this move, any prospect of a political solution to the colonial question was removed for years, and the reaction in the ranks of the regime – and perhaps among wider sections of middle-class opinion – was to rally behind Salazar's intransigent defence of 'pluricontinental Portugal'. Even some sectors of the opposition (notably the old Republicans) still had problems with the colonial question, and were unwilling to contemplate anything more advanced than a chimerical 'Federation' of Portugal and its colonies – a solution which (had it ever been attempted) would have been totally unacceptable to the African liberation movements.

The policy of intransigence implied two things: a vastly expanded military presence in Africa, and a dynamic policy of development of the 'Overseas Provinces' on an unprecedented scale. Within a few years the strength of Portuguese regular forces in the colonies (including African recruits) had risen from about 30,000 to around 200,000. Surface and air communications were rapidly expanded for both military and economic purposes; hydro-electric power was promoted, with the Cunene river scheme in Angola and the huge Cabora Bassa project in Mozambique; educational facilities were expanded by as much as 300% in a decade, so that by 1970 in Angola over half the children of primary-school age were enrolled; health services were greatly improved, and so on.[2] But none of this would have been possible with the scant resources of Portugal's underdeveloped economy and Salazar's traditional penny-pinching financial nostrums: the new situation demanded nothing short of a revolution in economic policy.

The new trend was already prefigured by Portugal's entry into the European Free Trade Association in 1960. A crucial measure was Decree-Law 46312 of April 1965, which greatly facilitated the entry of foreign capital;[3] but already in the previous three to four years various measures had heralded the end of Salazarist autarchy. NATO countries supplied military aid, officially unconnected with the African situation, but clearly assisting the Portuguese war effort; a good example is the 1963 agreement with West Germany under which Portugal provided a training base for the German Air Force at Beja, in return for loans, arms, technical training and specialised medical treatment in Germany for Portuguese war casualties. Similarly, France obtained a base at Flores in the Azores, and supplied planes, frigates and submarines for the Portuguese air force and navy.[4] The USA and Britain, while voicing public reservations about Portuguese colonial policy, also gave substantial military and economic support to the Salazar regime.

The economic transformation of these years was dramatic, perhaps even more so than the military. The economist Mário Murteira points out that from 1950 to the mid-seventies, the Portuguese economy underwent the most rapid growth in its history, 'and the process was in almost regular acceleration until the general economic crisis of capitalism began in 1974'.[5] The entry of long-term foreign capital into the country was almost ten times greater in seven years (1961–67) than the total for nearly two decades previously (1943–60).[6] In the early sixties this took the form mainly of public credit, with the emphasis in later years being more on private foreign investment. Industrial expansion was particularly rapid, and by the early seventies manufactured goods accounted for more than 60% of exports (where in 1950 primary products had accounted for 70%). Balance of payments surpluses made possible accumulation of reserves equivalent to almost two years of imports by the end of 1973.[7]

The above summary seems very positive, but it conceals major structural weaknesses which were getting worse. The balance of payments surplus was made possible only by tourism, emigrants' remittances, transfers from the colonies and incoming investment – factors which offset a large balance of trade deficit which quadrupled from 1964 to 1973. Agriculture remained stagnant and archaic, leading to increased dependence on food imports and a massive exodus of the rural population. Emigration increased dramatically, mainly to France and other more advanced European countries; the annual flow of emigrants to EEC countries rose from 6,567 in 1960 to 156,610 in 1970, with the result that total population actually declined in the late sixties.[8] Internal migration to the Lisbon – Setúbal and Oporto – Braga urban areas also increased. In response to official stimuli, emigration to the colonies grew as well, but not on the scale intended; most estimates put the white population of Angola at between 300,000 and 350,000 in the early seventies (up from

175,000 in 1960) and that of Mozambique at maybe 250,000 (up from 85,000).[9] Investment in the colonies, both Portuguese and foreign, was substantial, but in terms of trade the country's growing integration with Europe was again apparent: the percentage of exports going to the colonies fell from 26% in 1960 to 14% in 1970, whereas that to the EEC and EFTA rose from 43% to 62% in the same period.[10] Portugal's dependence on advanced countries was growing faster than its ability to exploit its own colonies.

The uncontrolled growth of emigration to Europe (and also from the Atlantic islands to the USA and Canada) was clearly a sign of crisis. While it brought benefits in the from of emigrants' remittances and lower unemployment, a drain of human potential on this scale was a classic symptom of underdevelopment. The rural population was no longer prepared to accept third-world conditions, and the expanding industries of the two main metropolitan regions could not absorb the surplus. Portugal was at last achieving a significant level of industrialisation, but as a low-wage, peripheral economy with no indigenous technological base. In 1963 industrial wages in Portugal were approximately one-fifth of those in the UK and one-seventh of those in Sweden[11] – a differential which has not changed significantly since then. The Salazarist solution of closer metropolitan – colonial integration – of a strong Euro-African lusophone community, perhaps including a special arrangement with Brazil – was clearly a non-starter in the conditions of the second half of the twentieth century. The only alternative – although one which was also fraught with problems, and was unacceptable to Salazar and the hard-liners – was closer European integration.

For the urban middle class the boom of the sixties brought greater prosperity and commercial or professional opportunities in both the metropolis and the colonies. But it also brought rising expectations through closer contact with Europe – tourism, television and other cultural influences increased both economic aspirations and frustration with official obscurantism. Censorship and Victorian moralism were increasingly resented on cultural as well as political grounds. Hence, although the colonial wars brought a lull in opposition activities for several years, they did not lead to a massive surge of support for the régime. Identification with the cause of a 'pluricontinental fatherland' was not strong enough to provide a solid mass base for reactionary policies; as would become apparent in response to the abortive liberalisation of Marcelo Caetano (who replaced the ailing Salazar as Prime Minister in 1968), the yearning for liberation, social justice and modernity was stronger than any colonialist nostalgia. Even in the trauma of a chaotic decolonisation and the arrival of more than 700,000 dispossessed colonial settlers (*retornados*) in 1975–76, the ultra-right was unable to capitalise politically on wounded patriotism.

2   The PCP and the Marxist – Leninists

After the mass struggles and insurgent movements of 1958–62, there followed a period of about six years of relative quiescence both in the mass movement and in organised opposition activity. The Communist Party, despite the dramatic escapes from Peniche and Caxias, had lost quite a number of cadres arrested during the protests and demonstrations of the preceding years, and with Alvaro Cunhal's departure from the country the Party entered a phase of retreat and consolidation. In May 1963 eleven prominent cadres were arrested, including the engineer Fernando Blanqui Teixeira who was acting as secretary-general in Cunhal's absence; and in August of the same year another group of nine Party officials was arrested while meeting in a house near Oporto. Reportedly a PIDE Inspector was killed while making these arrests, indicating resistance on the part of the Communists; but this was small comfort for the PCP, which could ill afford so many losses.[12] It was also precisely at this time that the international schism in the Communist movement, associated with the Sino-Soviet dispute, came to a head.

In the August 1963 meeting of the Central Committee, one of its outstanding younger members, Francisco Martins Rodrigues, presented a highly critical document entitled 'Peaceful struggle and armed struggle in our movement'. Extending Alvaro Cunhal's critique of the 'right-wing deviation' of 1956–59, he argued for the immediate creation of 'combat units' as 'the application of Marxism – Leninism to national conditions and the decisive precondition for us to lead the masses to insurrection'.[13] In Rodrigues' view, the Party's interpretation of the 'national uprising' was essentially bourgeois, because it relied on progressive officers to mount a military coup, and conceived of the masses as having no more than a supportive rôle. This erroneous conception was reflected in the Party's passivity, leading it to lose contact with the vanguard of the working class and to become bureaucratised, facilitating police infiltration and betrayals. The incorrect line on the question of armed struggle was linked to erroneous positions on the question of anti-fascist unity and on the line of the international Communist movement.[14]

According to the Marxist – Leninists, Rodrigues was prevented from presenting his views to most Party activists and even to the full membership of the Central Committee; he left the Party in December 1963 and was declared expelled in January 1964. According to Cunhal, he was expelled not for expressing divergent views but because 'he deserted the Party, abandoning his duties, refusing to obey any instructions from the leadership, taking Party possessions and money and engaging in divisionist activity . . .' The Marxist–Leninists maintain that the 'Party possessions' consisted of the clothes he was wearing and the cash necessary from immediate survival.[15] As always, an ideological split of this kind brought hostility and recriminations; each side accused the other of betrayal, immorality and complicity with the police. The main result was to obscure the serious political issues at stake and to weaken the anti-fascist resistance.

Immediately after his departure/expulsion, Martins Rodrigues formed (with like-minded militants) an organisation dedicated to armed struggle, the FAP (Patriotic Action Front). This was followed in April 1964 by the CMLP (Portuguese Marxist-Leninist Committee), intended as the nucleus of the new, authentic Communist Party. The split did reflect serious unease among younger Party activists and some veteran cadres about the PCP's failure to take effective revolutionary action, but it did not gain the adherence of the bulk of the Party machine or of its working-class supporters. The CMLP began the arduous task of developing its own clandestine structure and publishing a theoretical journal, *Revolução Popular*, but in 1965 its leaders and many of its cadres were arrested, and it disintegrated. Two CMLP leaders, João Pulido Valente and Rui d'Epinay, were arrested following publication of their names and their clandestine situation in the PCP organ *Avante!*; this was bitterly condemned by the Marxist – Leninists as tantamount to denouncing them to the police, and interestingly, Cunhal did self-criticise for the PCP on this score.[16]

After the failure of the FAP and CMLP, a multiplicity of tiny Marxist–Leninist groups began to spring up, mainly among middle-class youth and in *émigré* circles in France and elsewhere. They were almost all romantic, dogmatic and sectarian, and had little significance until the early seventies, when some of them achieved greater maturity and limited implantation in working-class sectors around Lisbon and on the south bank of the Tagus. A prominent Marxist–Leninist writer, Ramiro da Costa, makes a severe judgement of their record:

Contaminated by petty-bourgeois adventurism, which to a large extent prevailed in the FAP, drawing support more from the petty bourgeoisie than the working class, failing to understand the change in the objective situation, showing contempt for mass organisations and in particular the trade unions, ... the Marxist–Leninist schism fell into ultra-left vanguardism and was unable to reorganise the advanced sector of the working class ...[17]

This criticism could be applied to almost all the multiplicity of Marxist–Leninist groups which arose in Western countries following the Sino-Soviet split; it would scarcely be necessary to devote attention to them here were it not for the fact that the PCP clearly saw them as a threat to its revolutionary prestige, and also that in the revolutionary upsurge of 1974–75 they would acquire much greater prominence.

The main practical achievement of the Marxist – Leninists was to put the PCP on the defensive against attacks from its left. Although specific events like the Delgado campaign and Beja had exposed the Party's vulnerability in this respect, it was not since the decline of the anarchist movement in the thirties that the PCP had faced consistent left-wing competition. The question dominated the Central Committee's debates in 1963–65, including the VI Party Congress in September 1965. The Party's response to its critics was elaborated in a major policy document written by the exiled Cunhal and approved at a Central Committee meeting in April 1964: *Rumo à Vitória* ('Towards Victory') was to remain the basis of the Party line for the next ten years.

In this key document, and in his report to the VI Party Congress, Cunhal reiterated the need for armed revolution against fascism – 'The Portuguese people have long been convinced that to overthrow the fascist dictatorship and instal democracy, it will be necessary to resort to force'[18] – and he insisted that the structures of dictatorship would have to be thoroughly destroyed – 'The revolution cannot pose as its objective to take charge of the fascist state machine and use it in its present form, modifying it slightly and replacing some of the personnel ... The first task of the revolutionary forces is to destroy the fascist state and replace it with a democratic state ...'[19] But unlike his left-wing critics, Cunhal gave no indication of concrete plans to initiate armed resistance. He ridiculed Martins Rodrigues ('an ex-comrade with pretensions to a professorship in Leninism') and Manuel Sertório ('an individual of Tròtskyite tendencies isolated in the Americas') for suggesting that conditions in Portugal were ripe for revolution.[20] Here Cunhal certainly had a point, given the conditions prevailing in the mid-sixties; but what he failed to address adequately was the question of revolutionary preparations for the next upsurge of popular revolt, which would surely come in a few years as it had done before. It was this which led to impatience among many both inside and outside the PCP, and Cunhal recognised that 'Some of our friends become perplexed or discouraged by 'so many preconditions' which the Communist Party insists on before unleashing the insurrection. 'This way we shall never get there', they say. Yes, we shall get there, we reply ...'[21] – and he discussed at length the question of systematic infiltration of the Armed Forces.

Extremist, adventurist and even infantile many of Cunhal's critics may have been, but they had hit on a crucial question to which the Party had no answer. If after defending an insurrectionary line for decades it still had not initiated armed revolt, then either the line was unrealistic or the Party had failed to put its self-proclaimed principles into practice. Faced with such persistent criticisms the Party did now make some preparations for taking up arms, and carried out acts of military and economic sabotage in the early seventies; but these actions were still quite limited in scope.

3 The exiles: factional strife and Guevarism

Initially it was not the Marxist–Leninists but General Delgado and his exile associates who drew the PCP into plans for armed rebellion. The FPLN, bringing together *émigrés* of several different political tendencies, was undeniably influenced by the Cuban and Algerian examples and by ˙the liberation movements in Portugal's own colonies, and the one thing which temporarily united its diverse components was a commitment to military action of one kind of another. In the end it disintegrated in factional strife without having organised effective action, but its very existence is significant; it implies that the colonial wars, following on the intense domestic struggles of 1958–62, were beginning to push Portuguese politics into a more openly polarised, Latin American pattern.

The FPLN's origins can be traced to exile initiatives in both Brazil and Europe. In Brazil, where long-standing Portuguese opposition groups existed without taking any effective action, the arrival of new exiles stimulated activity. Around April–May 1961 a liaison committee was created, led by Manuel Sertório, Manuel Tito de Morais (socialist) and a PCP representative; they undertook to contact exiles in other countries with the aim of a possible meeting of representatives from all the *émigré* communities, and later with delegates from Portugal.[22] In Europe and North Africa, preparations were stimulated by the exile of several members of the Junta Patriótica Central after the Beja attack. In Paris in mid-1962, a European Conference for Amnesty in Portugal was held. As pressure for united action among the exile communities grew, the PCP decided to take the initiative, and it was largely as a result of Communist Party organising efforts that the First Conference of the FPLN was held in Rome in December 1962. A Portuguese émigré who worked for the FAO in Rome, Mário Ruivo, who was close to the PCP but not a member, was responsible for many of the preparations. The participants were Alvaro Cunhal for the PCP, Piteira Santos and Lopes Cardoso (both recently-exiled members of the Junta Central), Manuel Sertório (both in his own right and as a representative of General Delgado), Mario Ruivo, Manuel Tito de Morais (socialist) and Francisco Ramos da Costa (ex-PCP, now socialist).[23]

A major issue at the Rome Conference was whether the leadership of the anti-fascist movement should be based inside Portugal or abroad. Given the recent exile of many leading figures including Delgado, and the decision of the PCP for the first time in more than two decades to locate several of its Central Committee members abroad, it seemed logical to establish the leading body outside the country. But since the Junta Central still nominally existed in Portugal, the permanent executive set up to run the FPLN was called a *Commissão Delegada* – an Acting Committee. It consisted of Piteira Santos, Tito de Morais, Manuel Sertório, Rui Cabeçadas (a left-wing Socialist) and a PCP representative; and an invitation was sent to General Delgado to join them.[24] As a Committee, it was representative of the most active tendencies in the opposition, and was small enough to operate effectively.

The second bone of contention at the First Conference was the location of the exile headquarters; the PCP favoured Rome, while most other delegates favoured Algiers (where contacts had already been established with the new revolutionary government of Ben Bella). The choice of Algiers was politically significant; it implied a commitment to armed action, whereas Rome would tend to imply more traditional methods of peaceful struggle and propaganda, with armed resistance relegated to an uncertain future.

In Algiers the authorities granted facilities to the FPLN, providing asylum and sometimes employment to a small but growing Portuguese *émigré* community, and access to radio transmission; the *Voz da Liberdade* (Voice of Liberty) began regular broadcasts to Portugal in 1963. The Front began to issue regular press releases and to send statements to international bodies and governments in Europe and Africa. It tried to develop a direct presence in Portugal through the Juntas de Acção Patriótica, but with only limited success – according to some, because the PCP did not give it wholehearted support,[25] and according to the PCP, because the opposition inside the country, 'with the exception of the Communist Party', did little or nothing to develop it.[26] What the FPLN acquired in Portugal was prestige, rather than actual membership – a prestige which was greatly increased by the knowledge that it enjoyed the support of both the PCP and General Delgado.

Delgado had been unable to attend the First Conference for lack of a valid travel document, but shortly afterwards he obtained a Brazilian passport, and early in May 1963 a crucial meeting took place in Prague between the General and Alvaro Cunhal. The meeting was secret at the time, but limited information was released a month later, confirming that the two parties had agreed to collaborate within the FPLN.[27] A confidential memo reveals the unresolved problems that remained: Delgado wanted to enter Portugal clandestinely as soon as possible and to make lightning public appearances in order to inspire the people to rebel; the PCP thought this impractical and dangerous. Delgado wanted to set up a Provisional Government in Exile; Cunhal preferred to strengthen the FPLN's Acting Committee. Delgado wanted to undertake immediate armed actions, such as bombings; Cunhal was not prepared to risk the PCP's clandestine apparatus in such actions, which he regarded as adventurist. But they agreed to create an 'external leading organism' of the resistance, of which they would both be members and which would have a limited membership, and to establish a headquarters 'closer to Portugal'.[28]

In December 1963 the FPLN's Second Conference took place, this time in Prague. The participants were Delgado, Cunhal, Ruy Luis Gomes (the mathematics professor who had led the MND in the fifties), Manuel Sertório, Mário Ruivo, Tito de Morais, Piteira Santos and a Communist youth delegate from inside Portugal. The tone of the meeting was set right away by Delgado, who immediately took charge and declared 'Agenda. – Item One: Election of the Vice-President!' – taking it for granted that he himself was President. Although Alvaro Cunhal was reportedly not amused by this unilateral action, the meeting accepted Delgado's leadership.[29] Once again, Delgado pushed for the establishment of a Government in Exile, but other delegates felt that such a body, in order to have credibility, must have resources and prestige which the Front could not at that time provide. They compromised by calling it the *Junta Revolucionária Portuguesa*, and it replaced the Acting Committee in Algiers (although its membership was the same, with the addition of Delgado and the replacement of Pedro Soares by Pedro Ramos de Almeida as PCP delegate). Delgado's weakness was that in Portugal, despite his undoubted popularity, he had hardly any organised support; this is why he emphasized exile activity to such an extent.[30]

With the successful conclusion of the Second Conference and the active involvement of Delgado, the FPLN was acquiring real international signficance, and was capable of inflicting serious harm on Portuguese government interests. Events were temporarily delayed by Delgado's ill-health – he underwent surgery in

Prague shortly after the Conference and stayed there for some
months to recuperate. But in late June 1964 – probably on 27 or
28 June – he arrived in Algiers to take charge of the *Junta
Revolucionária*. He was received virtually as a Head of State, and
had a personal interview with Ben Bella; and he immediately
requested material aid to equip an exile force which would make
a clandestine landing somewhere on the Portuguese coast.[31] In
Algiers there were half-a-dozen Portuguese military deserters
from the war in Guiné, but Delgado had apparently been led to
believe that they were much more numerous, and planned to
use them as the nucleus of a force of 500 men. He was bitterly
disillusioned to discover the modest reality, and worse still, the
profound reservations of all other members of the Junta with
regard to his adventurous plans. The PCP remained committed
to its cautious long-term strategy of gathering strength for an
eventual mass insurrection, which in practice seemed as far off
as ever. The other members of the Junta were open to more
concrete plans of action, but wanted more realistic preparations
and political consensus as to ways and means.

These political differences were serious enough, but in Algiers
they became inextricably intertwined with factional intrigues and
personal jealousies. In the words of Mario Soares:

The ideological, political and even personal conflicts became much worse
and the polemics rose to a pitch of rare acrimony. He (Delgado) was now
in open opposition to all the members of the *Junta Revolucionària* – in
most cases for reasons which originated in futile questions and were of a
temperamental nature. His antagonism to the Communist Party was
now total. Of a bold temperament and personally very courageous,
Delgado wanted to go into action immediately. Unashamed partisan of a
surprise attack or a bold coup, he neither understood nor accepted the
delays of a long-term political effort ...[32]

Matters came to a head over preparations for the Third Conference, to be held in Algiers a couple of months later. Manuel
Sertório, who had returned to Brazil after the Prague Conference, arrived in Algiers in the second week of August 1964
to find the atmosphere 'completely deteriorated'. Although he
was Delgado's closest associate on the Junta and had travelled
from Brazil on a ticket paid for by the General, he soon found it
impossible to accept Delgado's arbitrary decisions. As President of
the Junta, Delgado immediately appointed Sertório Vice-Presi-

dent – a position which the latter did not accept since it would further antagonise the other members.[33] For the Third Conference Delgado wanted to introduce as delegates some of his personal associates who were regarded as totally untrustworthy by established opposition leaders – for example, Mário de Carvalho, Delgado's 'personal representative' in Rome, who was widely suspected to be a PIDE agent, and Henrique Cerqueira, an adventurer based in Morocco whose loyalty was also suspect.[34]

The small Portuguese exile community in Algiers – at most 100 people, women and children included – was a cocktail of all the most explosive elements in the politics of the 1960's. As well as the Communists, several varieties of socialists, representatives of the more traditional sectors of the opposition, Delgado and his maverick associates, and members of the African liberation movements, there were Trotskyites and marxist-leninists of the CMLP/FAP. The latter exaggerated their own strength, apparently telling Delgado that the bulk of the PCP was with them against Cunhal; and it is possible that he believed them. It was around this time that he began talking of 'Operation Orange', a scheme to negotiate with the Chinese through their embassies in Algiers and Paris, in order to seize Macau and set up a 'Free Government' there.[35] Such projects aroused no sympathy at all among experienced members of the opposition, who tried to instil a greater sense of realism.

Early in August 1964 Alvaro Cunhal had arrived in Algiers, and stayed for a fortnight, negotiating personally with the General whom he evidently recognised as the key figure in the FPLN; but the political differences were too great, and the PCP finally joined the rest of the *Junta Revolucionária* in unanimous opposition to its unpredictable President.[36] The day before the Third Conference was due to start, in late September, Delgado left, followed by one or two friends including Dr Emídio Guerreiro, a Republican exile based in Paris; and it was in the French capital that he issued a proclamation in the name of his own 'FPLN', using the same initials but substituting the word 'Portuguese' for 'Patriotic'! The proclamation said that a Conference of the FPLN had just been held 'somewhere on the frontier' (presumably, the Portuguese frontier) – but it is generally agreed that this was pure invention by Delgado.[37] What actually happened was a meeting of a handful of people in Emídio Guerreiro's residence in Paris, where

Delgado took the fatal decision to go to the Spanish town of
Badajoz – this time indeed, 'on the Portuguese frontier' – where
he had been led to believe he could meet dissident military
officers. It was near Badajoz in February 1965 that the General
and his Brazilian secretary were murdered by PIDE agents, in a
tragic but predictable ending to a heroic career.[38]

It would be quite wrong to suggest that only Delgado was to
blame for the fiasco in Algiers. It is clear that the PCP was
prepared to do very little, if anything to prepare for armed actions
within a reasonable time-span. Other members of the Junta have
been the object of numerous accusations of nepotism, corruption and abuse of power. Many of these allegations, by former
associates of Delgado or ex-militants of ephemeral Marxist –
Leninist organisations, can be dismissed as scurrilous rumour or
gross exaggeration; this is the case with some authors who accuse
Piteira Santos, Tito De Morais, Rui Cabeçadas and others of a
nefarious conspiracy with the PCP to destroy Delgado.[39] What
does seem to be true is that some FPLN leaders such as Piteira
Santos and Tito de Morais were over-zealous in trying to exclude
police agents and in guarding their hard-won access to the
Algerian authorities, thereby alienating many Portuguese *émigrés*
in Algiers who were subjected to inquisitorial inverstigations and
arbitrary decisions regarding employment, housing and other
routine matters.[40]

The FPLN did not disappear with Delgado's departure. The
Third Conference was held without him, and appears to have
consolidated the Front as a representative organisation of the
resistance, both internal and external. Participants included a
military officer representing the Junta Central in Portugal; one
student representative from Coimbra, and two from Lisbon;
several delegates from Italy, France, and Morocco; as well as the
existing members of the *Junta Revolucionária*. The Front received
messages of support from exiles in Brazil and elsewhere, and
continued to develop its international relations with delegations
to Italy, France, Switzerland, Bulgaria, East Germany and
elsewhere.[41] But in terms of concrete plans for action, little was
achieved for some years. In 1965 Tito de Morais and Ramos da
Costa left the Front in order to dedicate themselves to rebuilding
a socialist organisation (the *Acção Socialista Portuguesa*, ASP) which
would give birth to the present-day Socialist Party. In 1970 the

PCP left or was expelled from the Front by elements favouring direct action; and in 1973 the organisation was completely taken over by leaders of a Trotskyite/Guevarist tendency who founded the PRP (Revolutionary Party of the Proletariat), taking control also of the already existing Revolutionary Brigades (armed underground contingents founded in 1971).[42] These activists were already taking direct action, planting bombs in Portugal at military installations connected with the colonial wars. They almost certainly influenced the PCP to do likewise, setting up its own Armed Revolutionary Action (ARA) which also attacked military installations and communications in Portugal. But by this time the FPLN had long ceased to be in any way representative of the bulk of the opposition.

4 The Democratic Opposition: Socialists and Catholics

The turmoil of 1958–62 and the outbreak of the colonial wars also produced important changes in the ranks of the *Oposição Democrática*. The classic Republicans were becoming less prominent, new tendencies were at work among the dispersed and factionalised socialists, and Catholic opposition groups were becoming more active and innovative. As previously indicated, Catholic students and worker associations independent of the régime had been evolving rapidly since the mid-fifties, and had received powerful stimulus from the Bishop of Oporto's famous critical letter to Salazar in July 1958,[43] followed by the prelate's exile – a very embarrassing situation for a régime which identified itself so closely with traditional Catholic values. Catholic activists in Portugal rejected the idea of founding a Christian Democratic party, and so their movement was somewhat dispersed; some like Manuel Serra, involved in the Cathedral plot and Beja, became committed to militant revolutionary activity, while others followed more moderate and legalistic channels and ended up in close alliance with secular liberals and socialists.

Attempts to unite and renovate the fragmented and ineffective socialist movement began to bear fruit in the early sixties. In 1962 an organisation called *Resistência Republicana e Socialista* (RRS) was created by Tito de Morais, Ramos da Costa and Mário Soares;[44] as already noted, two of its leaders participated in the

FPLN for a while. In July 1963 a broadly-based group (they claimed about 1,000 initial supporters) formed the *Acção Democrato-Social* (ADS), which on 3 August of that year delivered a formal request for legal recognition to Salazar's office[45] – as usual, a futile gesture. ADS was led by old Republicans such as Cunha Leal and Mendes Cabeçadas as well as others who could more properly be described as socialists; it was a positive move towards unity of these sectors of the opposition, but little more.

In 1965 a small group of exiles in Switzerland and Italy, in association with others inside Portugal, founded a more explicitly socialist organisation, the ASP (*Acção Socialista Portuguesa*); several of its leaders had previously been involved in the RRS. It was the ASP which would develop contacts with the Socialist International, leading to the official founding of the present Socialist Party at a Congress in West Germany in 1973.[46] Mário Soares was increasingly prominent in the opposition's organisational efforts from the mid-sixties onwards, and also acquired prestige because of his role as lawyer for the Delgado family after the General's murder in 1965. It was Soares who took up the case in the Spanish courts, and campaigned untiringly on the issue in Portugal; he was the first person in the country (as opposed to the exiles and foreign commentators) to openly accuse the PIDE of responsibility. Also in late 1967, when several leading establishment figures including members of the government were linked in press reports to a prostitution racket involving young girls, Soares was thought to have leaked the information to foreign correspondents.[47] He paid for his audacity with deportation to the colonies; in December 1967, twenty years after the last victims had been transported to Tarrafal, he was deported to the African island colony of São Tomé. This created such a scandal – since it was thought that deportation as a punishment had been abandoned – that Soares' prestige was greatly increased when he was released a year later (in November 1968, after Marcelo Caetano had taken over as Prime Minister).[48]

An important indication of change in Catholic circles was the appearance early in 1963 of a new monthly magazine, *O Tempo e o Modo*, which was comparable to *Seara Nova* as a vehicle of expression for the progressive intelligentsia. The majority of its editorial board and contributors were Catholic intellectuals, although there was participation also by non-Catholic socialists and liberals. Its editor for the first six years was a prominent Catholic liberal, António Alçada Baptista, who had entered politics as an opposition candidate in the 1961 elections with a call for national reconciliation, 'for a Portugal of all the Portuguese, more human, more just and more Christian';[49] but there were other contributors of more radical views, including some who later assumed a marxist-leninist position, and who took over the magazine in 1969.[50] Also in 1963 there was an important conference of Catholic economists, discussing such sensitive issues as nationalisation of basic industries and agrarian reform; and in 1965 many of these intellectuals formed a cultural co-operative called Pragma, which served as an important focus for progressive Catholic activity, holding public meetings, publishing policy analyses and offering educational courses.[51]

This ferment of Catholic activity converged to some extent with the new developments in socialist and social-democratic circles; they worked together in election campaigns and other public activities. Thus the year 1965 witnessed both presidential elections (in July) and parliamentary elections (in November). The presidential elections were even more devoid of meaning than before, since they were now indirect; an electoral college of guaranteed loyalty to the régime automatically re-elected Admiral Tomás, and the opposition did not even bother to put up a candidate. But the ADS did protest to Salazar, declaring that he had turned Portugal into 'a nation of sleepwalkers';[52] and a prominent Catholic economist who was identified with the regime through membership in the Corporative Chamber, Francisco Pereira de Moura, created a stir by criticising Tomás's reelection.[53] Two months earlier (in May) a new Catholic Movement of Democratic Action had published a manifesto on 'Christianity and National Politics', and this was followed on 25 October by a more detailed political statement, known as the 'Manifesto of the 101' from the number of its signatories.[54]

This statement marked the definitive shift of a large sector of Catholic opinion into the opposition camp, working with the socialists of ADS in the parliamentary election campaign; the forty opposition candidates withdrew in protest before polling day (as usual), but they had demonstrated that the democratic movement had acquired new breadth and unity. Both the parliamentary candidates and the '101' spoke out clearly in favour of colonial self-determination, echoing an ADS statement of 1964 which was the first unequivocal stand on this question by the *Oposição Democrática*:

We uphold the view that the overseas problem cannot have the military solution which is being implemented . . .
We maintain that what is needed without delay, is the political solution based on the *principle of self-determination*, effected by democratic means. This solution imposes itself on our conscience as free men, who consider themselves men of their time and who regard decolonisation and respect for colonised peoples as an irreversible phenomenon . . .[55]
(Emphasis in original)

Such political clarity represented undeniable progress for sectors of the opposition characterised a few years earlier by chronic timidity and vacillation on the colonial issue. The new-found unity of liberals, Socialists and Catholics was also a positive development, which was bound to preoccupy the regime. But the opposition's activities at this time, though apparently greeted with broad public sympathy, were unable to generate the mass response of previous campaigns – the huge demonstrations, protests and strikes which had sometimes threatened the regime's foundations. This was no doubt because most people no longer expected change through regular political activity – only through direct action, as espoused by the FPLN and the Marxist–Leninists, or through an internal crisis of the regime.

The position taken by the Church hierarchy remained cautious and moderate; there was no Portuguese equivalent of Dom Helder Câmara, the Archbishop of Recife who became such a thorn in the side of the Brazilian military regime. Neither was there anything quite as explicit and organised as the 'Christians for Socialism' movement which emerged in Chile and one or two other Latin American countries in the early seventies. But the Second Vatican Council encouraged new trends within the Church, and the very fact that some Catholic leaders were distancing themselves from the régime and speaking out for social justice and colonial self-determination had a powerful impact on lay activists, especially among the younger generation. Thus by 1970 some of the most militant opposition to the colonial wars was coming from Catholic groups, who circulated clandestine information about the African liberation movements or reports of atrocities committed by Portuguese troops.[56]

As a public manifestation of dissent, in 1968 Catholic activists began celebrating New Year's Day as a 'Day of Peace' in protest against the colonial wars, and each year from then onwards they would hold vigils beginning on 30 or 31 December in a Lisbon church. At the end of December 1972 such a Vigil began in the Rato chapel, but all the participants were arrested, and many of them who had civil service jobs were dismissed (including Francisco Pereira de Moura, the ex-member of the Corporative Chamber who had now moved well to the Left).[57] It was Catholics involved in these types of activity who joined left-wing parties such as the MDP (*Movimento Democrático Popular*), the MES (*Movimento da Esquerda Socialista*) and even the Marxist–Leninist UDP (*União Democrática Popular*) after liberation in 1974.

5 Caetano's false liberalisation: the beginning of the end

On 6 September 1968 Salazar fell from his deck-chair in São João do Estoril and suffered a clot on the brain. After surgery he appeared to recover well, but ten days later he had a stroke, and although he again recovered somewhat, it was clear that he could no longer run the country. The effective removal of the man who had governed Portugal for forty years appears to have caused near-paralysis and then intense infighting in the upper ranks of the régime, but the crisis was resolved on 26 September with the appointment by President Tomás of Marcelo Caetano as Acting Prime Minister.[58]

Although seventeen years younger than Salazar, Caetano had been associated with the *Estado Novo* from its foundation, having enjoyed a meteoric rise in right-wing political circles as a young man. He had personally drafted many of the basic laws of the corporative state, and remained philosophically committed to an organicist view of society. But during the fifties and sixties he had gained a reputation as something of a liberal, particularly after his resignation as Rector of Lisbon University in protest against the invasion of the campus by police in 1962. This reputation was reinforced by his personal qualities as a family man with an affable manner and wide contacts with the outside world, in marked contrast to Salazar. It was therefore natural that his succession should lead to expectations of reform – expectations which at first appeared to be justified.

Speaking of 'renewal within continuity', Caetano relaxed press censorship, allowed the return to the country of Mário Soares and then of the Bishop of Oporto, and introduced a series of liberalising measures. A progressive Catholic, José Guilherme de Melo e Castro, was appointed head of the National Union, which in 1969 was reorganised as the ANP (National Popular Action). The dreaded PIDE was renamed the DGS (General Directorate of Security) and lost some of its arbitrary powers. A new electoral law was introduced, extending the franchise to all literate adults.[59] All of this created a new atmosphere in which it appeared possible that the régime was really going to change from within.

The first real test of Caetano's reformist intent – or of his capacity to deliver on promises of change – came in November 1969 when parliamentary elections were due. In preparation for the elections the opposition held a great Republican Congress, the second of its kind, at Aveiro from 15 to 17 May 1969. As in the first Congress held in 1957, it served as a forum for presenting policy documents of all kinds, and as another demonstration of opposition strength (there were 900 guests at a Congress dinner).[60] But it also showed that the opposition's classic weaknesses had not yet been overcome – Congress debates were long on theory and short on practice, in the sense of strategy and tactics for political change. Moreover, another fatal weakness – glossed over at the Aveiro Congress but clear for all to see in the real world outside – was the opposition's internal division along left/right lines. The old Republicans, concentrated now in the ADS under Cunha Leal, decided not to present candidates; the Socialists and Communists, supported by many progressive Catholics, began working together in CDEs (Democratic Electoral Committees), but the tensions were too great and led to division in three of the most important districts (Lisbon, Oporto and Braga). In these three centres the Socialists, in alliance with moderate Catholics and liberals, formed their own CEUDs (Electoral Committees of Democratic Unity), while the CDEs represented Communists, left Catholics and some of the 'new left' tendencies which had been gaining strength during the sixties. Elsewhere unity was maintained under the CDE label – thus in Santarém two Socialists (Francisco Lino Neto and Maria Barroso, Mário Soares' wife) shared the CDE list with one Communist and one independent leftist.[61]

In the event, not only was the opposition's showing weakened by disunity, but Caetano's liberalisation was exposed as little more than window-dressing. Censorship, although less severe, was still maintained, opposition representatives were still denied access to the media and to the electoral registers, they were not allowed to participate as scrutineers, and so on. The results were much the same as always: the CDE was 'awarded' 10.5% of the vote, the CEUD 1.6%, and the remaining 88% went to the official party.[62] The only change of any significance was that the regime had allowed a few reformist-minded candidates to be elected on the official ticket. In the absence of any real opposition in Parliament, these UN/ANP reformists did attempt to push for further liberal legislation; most of them, such as Francisco de Sá Carneiro and Francisco Pinto Balsemão, would become prominent in the centre-right PPD (Popular Democratic Party) after 1974.

For a year or so after the elections, it was still possible to believe that there might be some substance to Caetano's reforms. In January 1970 he reorganised the cabinet, bringing in several young technocrats with liberal reputations, among them an outstanding scientist, Veiga Simão (Education), three reform-minded economists (João Salgueiro, Rogério Martins and Xavier Pintado), and the first woman appointed to a Portuguese government (Maria Teresa Lobo, Under-Secretary for Health and Welfare). But key positions remained in the hands of hardliners, notably the Minister of the Interior, António Gonçalves Rapazote; and Admiral Tomás began to assert his presidential powers to an unusual degree, in favour of the 'ultras' within the regime. In 1972 Tomás had himself re-elected for another seven-year term by the rubber-stamp electoral college.

It is not entirely clear whether Caetano was prevented by the 'ultras' from carrying out further reforms, or whether he willingly chose to take no more than cosmetic measures; there is much evidence to suggest that he remained at heart an authoritarian corporativist.[63] In the crucial area of military and colonial policy there was no change, and in domestic affairs it seemed more and more, in the words of a popular phrase, that he had 'signalled left but turned right'. By 1972 members of the 'reform wing' of the ANP, now grouped together with many non-regime intellectuals in SEDES (Study Group for Social and Economic Development), were becoming disillusioned; thus

early in 1973 Sá Carneiro resigned his seat in the National
Assembly.

While these political manoeuvres were occurring within the
régime and among its domesticated critics, there was a resurgence of active resistance in militant opposition circles and some
popular sectors. The student movement, quiescent since 1962,
emerged again late in 1968. To some extent student activity
responded to similar unrest that year in France and throughout the world, but it also addressed specific Portuguese issues.
Trouble began early in November at the Technical University of
Lisbon and spread to the Lisbon Faculty of Law a couple of
months later, leading to the closure of this Faculty by the
authorities in February· 1969.[64] But more serious disturbances
came in Coimbra in spring–summer 1969.

For several months, far-reaching debates on educational
reform had been taking place in the Coimbra student 'republics',
the University's traditional associative bodies. Such debates
inevitably took on broader political overtones, and the movement came to a head on 17 April when President Tomás made an
official visit to the ancient University in order to inaugurate the
new Maths Department building. During the official ceremony
the President of the Students' Association rose to demand the
right to speak, but was refused by President Tomás; the ceremony
rapidly degenerated into chaos, and the authorities departed in
the midst of 'manifestations of profound disrespect' for the
nation's chief executive. From that day onwards, in the words
of the Minister of Education, 'the University of Coimbra was
invaded by a wave of anarchy which rendered impossible the
holding of classes ...'[65] On 6 May all classes were suspended,
and in July–August exams had to be postponed because of
continuing unrest. There were repeated mass meetings of
students, debating everything from the educational process and
the reactionary nature of the examination system to the colonial
wars and the transition to socialism; the movement developed a
constantly rotating leadership and guerrilla tactics which made
repression more difficult. Coimbra was occupied several times by
the police (GNR) and troops, until order was restored in
October.[66]

The politicisation of the student movement was now irreversible; many student activists were now involved in anti-war

agitation and in Marxist–Leninist or other revolutionary groups, and for this reason repression was more severe. Early in 1971 unrest flared up again. For months previously discontent had been growing over governmental projects for educational reform, followed by non-recognition of elected student representatives. In mid-January mass meetings and student strikes were subjected to violent police repression in Coimbra and in the Law and Commerce Faculties of Lisbon University. The Lisbon Technical University (*Instituto Superior Técnico)*) was closed by the academic authorities. In February there were further clashes and dozens of arrests in Lisbon and Coimbra, and on 20 April at the University of Oporto also; student leaders claimed that their imprisoned comrades had been subjected to 'savage tortures' by the PIDE/DGS. The students proclaimed that they were 'on the side of the majority, which is opposed to this anti-popular and anti-democratic government'.[67] A year later, in May 1972, serious clashes began again in all three University cities, continuing for two to three months; the pattern was repeated in spring 1973. The tone of the conflict is clear from a statement of the Lisbon Students' Associations:

The government says about everything that happens in the University, that it is the work of agitators paid by foreigners. BUT WHO IS THE GOVERNMENT PAID BY? Who makes abundant profits from exploitation and from the colonial war? – IT IS NOT THE STUDENTS, NEITHER IS IT THE PORTUGUESE PEOPLE![68] (Capitals in original).

The students then proclaimed that if expelled from University, they would continue the struggle in the streets, with the people, 'against exploitation, war and oppression'.

Unrest was by no means confined to the students. The labour movement also returned to the offensive in these years, encouraged by labour shortages resulting from the industrial boom, military service and emigration. Caetano's initial liberalisation also affected labour legislation: a Decree-Law of June 1969 loosened government control over elections in the *sindicatos nacionais* and over arbitration procedures. The result was a series of PCP victories in key unions (textile and metallurgical workers, journalists, bank employees and others), considerably greater than the presence the Party had already achieved by working inside the official unions. This paved the way for the formation in

242 Fascism and resistance in Portugal

October 1970 of an independent inter-union committee, the *Intersindical* – in effect, an opposition union federation. Within a few months there were about forty unions, representing hundreds of thousands of workers, affiliated to this body.[69]

As in other fields, partial liberalisation of labour relations was soon followed by retreat. The régime was alarmed by a wave of strikes in 1969 among fishermen in Setúbal, at the Naval Arsenal, at a cement plant in the Ribatejo, and at a score of factories in the Lisbon area and on the south bank of the Tagus. The strike wave continued in 1970, again throughout the Lisbon area and the south bank, but also among dockers in Leixões (Oporto), fishermen in the Algarve, Peniche and Matosinhos (Oporto), textile workers in Covilhã, and elsewhere. In July 1970, in reaction to this, the government resumed its power to suspend elected union leaders and to appoint the presidents of arbitration boards.[70] These powers were used several times during the next two years to dismiss democratic union leaderships and close union offices; protest demonstrations and further strikes occurred anyway, but the régime had made clear its desire to turn the clock back.

Active resistance to the régime also revived in these years on a third front, that of armed struggle. After Beja in 1962 nothing happened on this front for some years except for the unsuccessful and even farcical efforts of the FPLN and Delgado. But in 1967 another romantic revolutionary, Hermínio da Palma Inácio (who had been involved in the sabotage of military aircraft during the April 1947 coup attempt and in the TAP airline hijacking organised by Galvão in 1961) founded an organisation called LUAR (League of Revolutionary Unity and Action). It acquired almost instant fame by a very successful bank robbery, seizing some thirty million escudos from the Bank of Portugal in Figueira da Foz. Its subsequent actions were mainly abroad, including assaults on Portuguese consulates in Rotterdam and Luxembourg (1971) and on an armoured van belonging to a Portuguese bank in Paris (1972).[71] LUAR was ill-defined ideologically; Palma Inácio had personal ties to Mário Soares who had been his defence lawyer, but this did not imply any organisational link to the Socialist Party or its precursors.[72]

More closely linked to the organised opposition (or to some sectors of it) were the Revolutionary Brigades, founded by the rump of the FPLN in Algiers following the expulsion (or departure) of the PCP in 1971. Among those involved were Piteira Santos and Manuel Alegre, an exiled poet who would later join the Socialist Party and become a minister in one of Mário Soares' post-1974 governments. In 1973 these two were ousted during a further split in the Algiers group, and a faction led by Carlos Carneiro Antunes founded a new party, the PRP (Revolutionary Party of the Proletariat) influenced by Cuban and Trotskyite tendencies. But both before and after this last split, the Revolutionary Brigades were able to undertake effective action inside Portugal. From November 1971 onwards they carried out a series of well-executed acts of sabotage against military installations – for example, destruction of a gun battery at Santo António da Charneca on the south bank of the Tagus, on 12 November 1971; destruction of 15 Berliet lorries intended for the colonial forces, in Lisbon, 11 July 1972; a theft of maps from the Army's cartographic office in December 1972, for the benefit of the African liberation movements; destruction of the Army Recruitment Centre in Oporto, 6 April 1973; and so on. They did not lack a sense of humour; in July 1972, when President Tomás was 're-elected' for the last time, they released two pigs dressed in Admiral's uniforms in the streets of Lisbon![73]

Beginning in 1970, the PCP also resorted to armed action through a military front known as ARA (Armed Revolutionary Action). Its début was the sabotage of the warship 'Cunene', due to sail for Africa, on 26 October 1970; this was followed by destruction of helicopters at the Tancos Air Base on 8 March 1971; of telegraph and telephone lines and electricity pylons, on various occasions; by the bombing of the NATO Comiberlant (Iberian Atlantic Command) HQ in Oeiras, west of Lisbon, on 27 October 1971; and other similar actions.[74] Several marxist–leninist groups planned acts of sabotage and bombings also, but mostly lacked the resources to carry them out.

None of these actions, by the ARA, the Revolutionary Brigades, the LUAR or anyone else, would bring down the régime. But they did have a negative impact – material and more especially moral – on the war effort in Africa, and they aroused public opinion in Portugal by providing evidence that armed resistance against fascism was now, at long last, a fact. Legal opposition activities continued – thus from 4 to 8 April 1973 a Third Republican

Congress was held at Aveiro[75] – but by now disillusionment
with Caetano's reforms was universal. Parliamentary elections
were due again in November 1973, but this time none of the
opposition wanted to participate in an obvious farce. Conditions
were ripe for another major upsurge of struggle against the
régime, as in 1945, 1958 or 1962 – except that no-one appeared
to have an effective revolutionary strategy, and the mass of the
population, aware of this crucial deficiency, could see no point
in further fruitless battles with a well-armed and entrenched
system. It was in this situation that the military once again
became the decisive factor – but not quite in the way generally
anticipated.

6 The Movement of the Captains and the 'Revolution of Flowers'

The *Estado Novo*, renamed the *Estado Social* by Caetano, was
finally overthrown on 25 April 1974 by an almost bloodless
military coup. After nearly forty-eight years, having survived
innumerable crises, coup attempts, strikes and mass protests, the
extraordinarily durable edifice erected by Antonio de Oliveira
Salazar collapsed when challenged by a recently-formed association of junior officers with almost no political experience. The
key to this remarkable event undoubtedly lay in the colonial
wars, in war-weariness among officers and men and resentment
against what was seen as political manipulation by the authorities back home. But there were other factors involved also; the
MFA (*Movimento das Forças Armadas* or Armed Forces Movement)
was not totally divorced for the domestic situation in Portugal.

The influence of the African conflicts was clear and obvious.
Not only did the MFA begin among officers recently returned
from a tour of duty (or from two or three tours of duty) in the
colonies, but the burden of the wars on Portugal's economic and
human resources was becoming unsustainable. Defence expendi-
ture reached 45.9% of the budget in 1971, and the official count
of Portuguese servicemen killed in Africa by May 1974 was 7,674,
with 27,919 seriously wounded. It is estimated that well over
100,000 young men emigrated to avoid conscription between
1961 and 1974. The war burden in terms of men in uniform and
casualties per head of population was greater than that of the
USA in Vietnam.[76]

Such a burden might be acceptable so long as there was some prospect of victory (or of an early solution to the conflict). But as the wars entered their second decade, a solution seemed further away than ever. In Angola the situation seemed relatively good for the Portuguese, with the liberation movements chronically divided and with boom conditions sustained by foreign investment and white immigration. But Guiné was virtually a lost cause, with the PAIGC (African Party for the Independence of Guiné and Cape Verde) controlling most of the territory by the late sixties; on 24 September 1973 it officially proclaimed the country's independence, and was recognised by about sixty countries within three weeks. In Mozambique, as in Angola, foreign investment and a large settler population helped strengthen the Portuguese position, but after 1971 the military situation deteriorated rapidly. FRELIMO, already strong in the northern provinces, opened a second front in the central region, threatening the giant Cabora Bassa hydroelectric project. Massacres committed by Portuguese troops at Wiriyamu and other villages in this region in December 1972 caused an international scandal, with the expulsion of Catholic priests who had denounced the affair. Then in January 1974 the patience of the settler population broke, with angry demonstrators stoning the troops for failing to provide adequate protection.[77] Soon afterwards Jorge Jardim, a local capitalist, aired a scheme for Mozambican independence under a compromise arrangement providing guarantees for settler interests; the situation was becoming untenable.

The actual genesis of the MFA has been described in detail by many authors.[78] The initial spark was the notorious Decree-Law 353/73 of 13 July 1973, which tried to resolve the officer shortage caused by the wars by offering conscript officers permanent commissions after a one-year crash-course in the Military Academy (as opposed to the regular four years). This aroused the ire of regular officers who felt that they would be overtaken in their careers by conscripts with inferior training. In response to their protests, the government tried to rectify matters with another Decree-Law (no. 409/73 of 20 August 1973) which only made matters worse, since it protected the seniority of higher-ranking regular officers but not that of captains and subalterns – precisely those who bore the brunt of action in the field. Hence the initial organisation of a 'Captains' Movement'

based on purely professional grievances, with a first clandestine
meeting of 136 junior officers in a field near Evora on 9
September 1973.

It became clear very quickly that these narrow professional
concerns were only the tip of the iceberg. Not that most of
the officers involved had a prior political agenda – with a few
exceptions, they had no initial plan of action. But their resentment against the politicians who placed ever-increasing demands on them for meagre rewards, and against senior officers
with comfortable desk jobs in Lisbon or the colonial capitals,
led them to draw rapid political conclusions once they began
collective discussions outside the regular chain of command.
Already in June tensions of a political character had become
apparent when the 'ultras' staged an Overseas Veterans' Congress
in Oporto to rally support for an intransigent colonial policy; this
was repudiated in a telegram signed by some 400 officers, who
denied that the Congress represented the true feelings of the
Armed Forces. Among the 400 were several future MFA leaders
such as Lt-Col Firmino Miguel, Major Ramalho Eanes and Capt.
Vasco Lourenço.[79]

In the months that followed, messages of support for the
Movement arrived from officers in service in Angola, Guiné and
Mozambique, and in the face of official stonewalling, further
meetings were held. In October the Movement's 'Co-ordinating
Committee', which was to be its crucial executive organ during
and after the liberating coup, was elected; among its members
were Captains Vasco Lourenço and Dinis de Almeida, and Major
Otelo Saraiva de Carvalho (just returned from service in Guiné).
On 1 December in Obidos (fifty miles north of Lisbon), eighty
delegates representing hundreds of officers from units all over the
country discussed plans for a *coup d'état* and a political programme.[80] Although many preparations had still to be made, the
Movement had come a long way in three months.

What is most striking about the whole process is the paralysis
of the regime in the face of this challenge. It is clear that the
authorities had some idea of what was going one; the Minister of
Defence knew within a week of the Obidos meeting most of what
had been discussed, but his only action was to transfer one officer
to Guiné and another to the Azores. In the following months, as
the conspiracy matured, there is little doubt that the government

was informed of at least some of the Movement's key personnel and plans. The only explanation for official inaction is political division; contradictions over political solutions, particularly regarding the colonies, had become almost insuperable. Already is September the Chief of the General Staff, General Costa Gomes, had expressed sympathy for the Captains' professional grievances; it later became clear that he was politically sympathetic also. General António de Spínola, the energetic and reformist Governor of Guiné until August 1973, was also regarded as potentially sympathetic; appointed Deputy Chief of the General Staff on 15 January 1974, he soon acquired notoriety with the publication on 23 February of his book *Portugal and the Future*.[81] A confused and contradictory volume, it advocated the old idea of a 'Luso-African Federation'; its importance lay in the public support, by one of the highest commanders in the Armed Forces, for a political solution to the colonial wars.

That events were rapidly coming to a head is evident from the fact that simultaneous and antagonistic conspiracies were maturing in parallel. The 'ultras' were looking for a hard-line coup, to be led by the ex-commander in Mozambique, General Kaúlza de Arriaga; in December he actually contacted the Captains' Movement, hoping to win them over to his side (and a few of them were probably close to being won over). After Spínola's book was published Caetano actually offered to hand over power to him and Costa Gomes; when they refused, the Prime Minister seems to have decided after all on a hard-line approach. On 8 March, six MFA leaders were arrested or transferred. Caetano then demanded a public pledge of loyalty from all top military commanders; Costa Gomes and Spínola refused, and were promptly dismissed. The new Chief of the General Staff was an 'ultra', General Joaquim da Luz Cunha, ex-commander in Angola. More MFA officers were now arrested or transferred, and it was this which precipitated a premature and ill-prepared coup attempt by some of the Movement's officers on 16 March: the Caldas da Rainha coup, so named from the town where one military unit rebelled and marched on Lisbon. They were halted by loyal troops, and surrendered without firing a shot. It looked ominously like the same sad story all over again.

It was at this point that the deterioration of the regime's position really became clear. Despite the hard-line crackdown of

previous weeks, the government was reluctant to impose severe
penalties on most of those arrested for fear of a military backlash.
Most of the MFA's leaders were still at liberty, and decided now
to act before it was too late. The Movement's political programme
was drafted early in April by Major Ernesto Melo Antunes – one
of the few members with prior political experience, having been
an opposition candidate in the 1969 elections. It was revised by
other members of the Coordinating Committee and by General
Spínola, who refused to accept the notion of self-determination
for the colonies; Spínola's conservatism on the colonial question
would cause an open rift between him and the Coordinating
Committee a few months after liberation, but for the time being
most of them felt it necessary to have him as an ally.

The coup, planned for the early hours of 25 April, was meti-
culously organised by Otelo Saraiva de Carvalho, the disarmingly
frank and engaging Major who would become enormously
popular (and controversial) during the next eighteen months.
Born of a settler family in Mozambique, the 39-year-old Otelo
had no political experience, but had strong popular and democratic sympathies derived from his family background. It was
Otelo who chose the song 'Grândola, vila morena', quoted at
the head of this chapter, as the signal for the coup to begin;
played on the Catholic station Rádio Renascença at 0.30 hours by
a sympathetic disc jockey, these verses with the symbolic message
'It is the people who give the orders!' would become the anthem
of the Portuguese revolution. Otelo, the man most closely
associated with the liberation of 25 April, would move far to the
left during the tumultuous events that followed, but would prove
unable to control the revolutionary process which he helped to
unleash.

Few of the officers involved in the MFA had contact with the
opposition which had struggled for so long against the Salazar
regime. Melo Antunes had been an opposition parliamentary
candidate; Col Vasco Gonçalves had been linked to military
conspiracies going back to the 1950s, and was close to the PCP;
Captain Varela Gomes had been seriously injured in the Beja
revolt of 1962; and there were a handful of others with opposition backgrounds. But the Movement as a whole emerged
directly from the military crisis caused by the colonial wars. This,
however, does not mean that there was no connection at all with

the long anti-fascist struggle in Portugal. MFA leaders such as Otelo and Dinis de Almeida have recounted how as young men they were impressed by important events such as the Delgado campaign and Beja. More immediately, in 1973 while the Movement was organising, they were influenced by opposition activities during the parliamentary election campaign. The MFA did establish limited contacts with civilian opposition circles in the months before the coup, but decided to keep such contacts to a minimum for reasons of security. After 25 April, they assumed automatically that power should be shared with civilian representatives of the former opposition, and eventually handed over to them almost completely through elections.

It was precisely in this respect that the internal contradictions of the MFA, and its political naiveté, became apparent, as some of its members allowed themselves to be manipulated by the PCP, others by the Socialist Party and the right-wing reaction – and some, like Otelo, by the multiple fractions of the revolutionary left. The MFA tried to be 'above party' and to appeal directly to the people – the old populist dream, like that of General Delgado; but it ended up being torn apart by the parties – and by the pent-up antagonisms of a society which had been deprived of open political expression for half a century. Those antagonisms had long been channelled through the activities of the opposition, and especially through movements of active resistance to the régime: strikes, demonstrations, bread riots, attempted uprisings. These movements of resistance now continued after liberation, as oppressed classes and marginalised groups strove to turn a liberal coup into a social revolution. The opposition did not make the coup, but it had done much to create the crisis of regime which the MFA exploited; and its component parts had a profound influence on the intense struggles to determine the future of Portugal which dominated the next eighteen months.

Notes to Chapter VII

1   R. A. H. Robinson, *Contemporary Portugal: A History*, London, 1979, George Allen & Unwin, pp. 109–10, 117 & 120; António de Figueiredo, *Portugal: Fifty Years of Dictatorship*, Harmondsworth, Middlesex, 1975, Penguin Books, pp. 209–10.
2   Robinson, *Contemporary Portugal*, pp. 110–11, 117–18 & 121; Figueiredo, *Fifty Years*, pp. 214–15; Tom Gallagher, *Portugal: A Twentieth-*

Century Interpretation, Manchester, 1983, Manchester University Press, P. 175.

3   Gallagher, *Portugal*, p. 156.
4   Figueiredo, *Fifty Years*, pp. 212–13.
5   Mário Murteira, 'The Present Economic Situation: Its Origins and Prospects', in Lawrence S. Graham and Harry M. Makler (eds.), *Contemporary Portugal: The Revolution and its Antecedents*, Austin & London, 1979, University of Texas Press, p. 332.
6   Figures from L. Salgado Matos, quoted in Francisco Rafael *et al.*, *Portugal: Capitalismo e Estado Novo (Algumas Contribuições para o seu Estudo)*, Porto, 1976, Afrontamento, p. 60.
7   Murteira, 'The Present . . .', pp. 332–4.
8   Murteira, 'The Present . . .', p. 334; Guy Clausse, 'Portuguese Emigration to the EEC and the Utilization of Emigrants' Remittances', in Thomas C. Bruneau, Victor M. P. da Rosa & Alex Macleod (eds.), *Portugal in Development: Emigration, Industrialization, the European Community*, Ottawa, 1984, University of Ottawa Press, pp. 146–7.
9   Robinson, *Contemporary Portugal*, pp. 106, 115; Gervase Clarence-Smith, *The Third Portuguese Empire, 1825–1975: A Study in Economic Imperialism*, Manchester, 1985, M. U. P., p. 213.
10   Francisco Rafael *et al.*, *Portugal: Capitalismo e Estado Novo*, p. 111.
11   *Ibid.*, p. 69.
12   *New York Times*, 5 August 1963; Francisco Martins Rodrigues, *Elementos para a História do Movimento Operário e do Partido Comunista em Portugal*, Lisboa, n.d., Edições Militão Ribeiro, p. 74.
13   Ramiro da Costa, *Elementos para a História do Movimento Operário em Portugal*, Lisboa, 1979, Assírio e Alvim, vol. II pp. 160–2.
14   Ramiro da Costa, *Elementos*, vol. II pp. 161–3.
15   Alvaro Cunhal, *Relatório da Actividade do Comité Central ao VI Congresso do Partido Comunista Porguguês*, Lisboa, 1975, Edições 'Avante!', p. 194; Ramiro da Costa, *Elementos*, vol. II p. 163.
16   J. A. Silva Marques, *Relatos da Clandestinidade: O PCP visto por dentro*, Lisboa, 1976, Edições Jornal Expresso, p. 186; Alvaro Cunhal, *Relatório*, p. 196.
17   Ramiro da Costa, *Elementos*, vol. II p. 164.
18   Alvaro Cunhal, *Rumo à Vitória: As Tarefas do Partido na Revolução Democrática e Nacional*, Lisboa, 1975, Edições 'A Opinião', p. 165.
19   Alvaro Cunhal, *Relatório*, p. 80.
20   Cunhal, *Rumo à Vitória*, p. 169.
21   Cunhal, *Rumo à Vitória*, p. 180.
22   Author's interview with Manuel Sertório, Lisbon, 22 March 1977.
23   Author's interviews with Fernando Piteira Santos, Lisbon, 28 February 1977, and with Manuel Sertório, Lisbon, April 1977.
24   Author's interview with Manuel Sertório, Lisbon, April 1977.
25   Author's interview with Fernando Piteira Santos, Lisbon, 28 February 1977.
26   Cunhal, *Rumo à Vitória*, pp. 150–2.

27 Interview with Alvaro Cunhal broadcast by Rádio Portugal Livre, June 1963 (clandestine document, 6 pp., consulted by courtesy of Manuel Sertório).

28 'Documento Reservado' signed by Humberto Delgado and Alvaro Cunhal, Prague, 5 May 1963; and covering note (also 'Reservado') signed by Delgado, Rio de Janeiro, 14 May 1963. Consulted by courtesy of Manuel Sertório.

29 Author's interview with Manuel Sertório, Lisbon, April 1977.

30 Author's interviews with Manuel Sertório, Lisbon, April 1977, and with Fernando Piteira Santos, Lisbon, 28 February 1977.

31 Patricia McGowan, *O Bando de Argel: responsabilidades na descolonização*, Lisboa, 1979, Intervenção, pp. 91–4; and author's interview with Manuel Sertório, Lisbon, April 1977.

32 Mário Soares, *Portugal Amordaçado: depoimento sobre os anos do fascismo*, Lisboa, 1974, Arcádia, pp. 332–4.

33 Author's interview with Manuel Sertório, Lisbon, April 1977.

34 Author's interview with Fernando Piteira Santos, Lisbon, 28 February 1977. Documentation which has come to light since 1974 shows that Mário de Carvalho was indeed a PIDE agent and played a crucial role in arranging the fatal expedition to Badajoz which led to Delgado's murder. See Manuel Garcia & Lourdes Maurício, *O Caso Delgado: autópsia da 'Operação Outuno'*, Lisboa, 1977, Edições Jornal Expresso, pp. 528 *et seqq.*.

35 Robinson, *Contemporary Portugal*, p. 78; and author's interview with Fernando Piteira Santos, Lisbon, 28 February 1977.

36 Author's interview with Manuel Sertório, Lisbon, April 1977.

37 Soares, *Portugal Amordaçado*, pp. 332–4; and author's interviews with Fernando Piteira Santos, 28 February 1977, and Manuel Sertório, April 1977.

38 On Delgado's murder, there is an extensive literature, much of it sensationalist and full of contradictory accusations. See Garcia & Maurício, *O Caso Delgado*, for one of the more sober and better documented accounts.

39 Such scurrilous accusations, based on very tendentious use of evidence, are made in Henrique Cerqueira, *Acuso! O Crime* (2 vols.), Lisboa, 1976–77, Intervenção, and Patricia McGowan, *O Bando de Argel*.

40 Author's interview with Manuel Sertório, April 1977.

41 Author's interview with Fernando Piteira Santos, 28 February 1977; 'Os Democratas Portugueses do Brasil saúdam a Junta Revolucionária Portuguesa'. communiqué dated São Paulo, 4 November 1964 (in Sertório papers); and other documents consulted by courtesy of Manuel Sertório.

42 Author's interviews with Manuel Sertório and Fernando Piteira Santos.

43 The text of the letter is in Padre José da Felicidade Alves (ed.), *Católicos e Política: De Humberto Delgado a Marcello Caetano*, Lisboa, 1970, published by the editor, pp. 31–64.

44 *Diário de Notícias*, 29 March 1984; article entitled 'Da guerra do carimbo à ASP' by Manuel Sertório.

45 *Mensagem entregue na Presidência do Conselho no Sabado, 3 de Agosto de 1963, às 11 horas*; mimeographed document (2 pp.) consulted by courtesy of Alcina Bastos. See also Robinson, *Contemporary Portugal*, p. 79.

46 Robinson, *Contemporary Portugal*, p. 168; and author's interview with Mário Soares, Lisbon, 29 June 1978.

47 Gallagher, *Portugal: A Twentieth-Century Interpretation*, p. 160; Figueiredo, *Portugal: Fifty Years of Dictatorship*, p. 224.

48 Figueiredo, *Portugal: Fifty Years of Dictatorship*, pp. 223–4; and author's interview with Mário Soares.

49 *Manifesto ao povo do Distrito de Castelo Branco*, signed by António Alçada Baptista, Armindo Gonçalves Ramos, João Alexandre Sá Lima & Vasco Luis Rodrigues da Conceição e Silva, Lisboa, 1961, Latinográfica, p. 5.

50 *O Tempo e o Modo*, no. 73 (Novembro 1969) and No. 74 (Dezembro 1969).

51 Author's interview with Mário Murteira, Lisbon, 23 March 1977.

52 Hugh Kay, *Salazar and Modern Portugal*, London, 1970, Eyre & Spottiswoode, p. 390.

53 Robinson, *Contemporary Portugal*, pp. 79–80; and author's interview with Francisco Lino Neto, Lisbon, 7 July 1977.

54 Pe. José da Felicidade Alves (ed.), *Católicos e Política*, pp. 137–60 & 175–208.

55 Letter from the leaders of ADS to the Prime Minister, 13 April 1964; quoted in Oposição Democrática, *Campanha Eleitoral de 1965: Documentos de Interesse para a Pátria* (Lisbon, n.d.; consulted by courtesy of Dr Francisco Sousa Tavares), pp. 7–8.

56 A good example of this would be the GEDOC (Group of Study and Documentation) in 1969–70; also the CIDAC (Interdiocesan Community for Clerical Dialogue and Action, but also – unofficially – the Centre for Anti-Colonial Information and Documentation).

57 *Diário de Lisboa*, 23 February 1973; and author's inteview with Frei Bento Domingues, Benfica, 21 April 1977.

58 Gallagher, *Portugal: A Twentieth-Century Interpretation*, pp. 160–1; Figueiredo, *Portugal: Fifty Years of Dictatorship*, p. 218. In fact, Salazar survived until July 1970, apparently unaware that he had been relieved of his official responsibilities.

59 Gallagher, *Portugal: A Twentieth-Century Interpretation*, pp. 166–8; Robinson, *Contemporary Portugal*, p. 168.

60 II Congresso Republicano de Aveiro, *Teses e Documentos (Textos Integrais)*, Lisboa, 1969, Seara Nova; 2 vols.; and Hugh Kay, *Salazar and Modern Portugal*, pp. 420–1.

61 Robinson, *Contemporary Portugal*, p. 169; and author's interviews with Mário Soares (Lisbon, 29 June 1978) and José Magalhães Godinho (Lisbon, 26 February 1977).

62 José Magalhães Godinho, 'A fraca memória (?) de Marcelo Caetano'; series of articles in *O Jornal* (Lisbon), 11, 18 & 25 July & 1 August 1980; and Gallagher, *Portugal*, p. 167.

63 Robinson, *Contemporary Portugal*, pp. 169–71; Gallagher, *Portugal*, pp. 168–71; Magalhães Godinho, 'A fraca memória (?) de Marcelo Caetano'.

64 *O Século*, 12 December 1968; *Diário de Notícias*, 15 February 1969.

65 Televised speech of the Minister of Education, 30 April 1969, quoted in *O Século*, 1 May 1969.

66 *O Século*, 7 May, 1 July, 7 & 8 August 1969; *Diário de Lisboa*, 16 April 1977 (article entitled 'Coimbra, 17 de Abril de 1969: A luta dos estudantes apontava no sentido do Socialismo').

67 18 January 1971, 'Lisboa e Coimbra em luta', manifesto of the General Council of the Coimbra Students' Association; 21 January 1971, leaflet distributed by the Students' Association of the Instituto Superior Técnico; 22 January 1971, motion approved at a general assembly of teaching assistants of the Instituto Superior de Ciências Economicas e Financeiras; 26 May 1971, 'Comunicado aos estudantes e à população' from the Lisbon Students' Associations. Documents consulted by courtesy of Dr Jorge Sampaio.

68 Pamphlet issued by the Lisbon Students' Associations, 24 May 1972, entitled 'Dos estudantes à população'. Information on the 1972–73 student movement was obtained from several documents consulted by courtesy of Jorge Sampaio, and from newspaper reports.

69 Ramiro da Costa, *Elementos*, II, pp. 317–18; Robinson, *Contemporary Portugal*, pp. 173–4.

70 Ramiro da Costa, *Elementos*, II, pp. 318–20.

71 Robinson, *Contemporary Portugal*, p. 80; *A Capital* (Lisbon), 26 September 1972 (official note from the DGS announcing 20 arrests of individuals suspected of involvement in terrorist acts).

72 Author's interview with Mário Soares.

73 Ramiro da Costa, *Elementos*, II, p. 212; author's interview with Manuel Sertório, Lisbon, 19 April 1977.

74 *A Capital*, 26 September 1972.

75 3°. Congresso da Oposição Democrática de Aveiro, *Teses*, Lisboa, 1974, Seara Nova; 7 vols..

76 Robinson, *Contemporary Portugal*, pp. 126 & 184; Gallagher, *Portugal*, pp. 182–3; Ramiro da Costa, *Elementos*, II, p. 213.

77 Otelo Saraiva de Carvalho, *Alvorada em Abril*, Lisboa, 1977, Bertrand, pp. 142–3, 189–90, 202–3; Robinson, *Contemporary Portugal*, pp. 179–82.

78 See Otelo Saraiva de Carvalho, *Alvorada*; Avelino Rodrigues, Cesário Borga e Mário Cardoso, *O Movimento dos Capitães e o 25 de Abril: 229 dias para derrubar o fascismo*, Lisboa, 1974, Morães; Dinis de Almeida, *Orígens e evolução do Movimento de Capitães*, Lisboa, 1977, Edições Sociais; Robinson, *Contemporary Portugal*, pp. 184–91; Gallagher, *Portugal*, pp. 185–8.

79 Rodrigues, Borga e Cardoso, *O Movimento*, pp. 309–10.

80 Rodrigues, Borga e Cardoso, *O Movimento*, pp. 330–4.

81 António de Spínola, *Portugal e o Futuro: Análise da conjuntura nacional*, Lisboa, 1974, Arcádia.

8

Resistance and liberation: the limits of change

... era necessário que a sociedade, atacada pela Internacional, se refugiasse na força dos seus princípios conservadores e religiosos, cercando-os bem de baionetas! ... Sujeitos, palitando os dentes, decretavam a vingança. Vadios pareciam furiosos 'contra o operário que quer viver como príncipe'. Falava-se com devoção na propriedade, no capital!

Do outro lado eram moços verbosos, localistas excitados, que declamavam contra o velho mundo, a velha ideia, ameaçando-os de alto, propondo-se a derrui-los em artigos tremendos.

E assim uma burguesía entorpecida esperava deter, com alguns policias, uma evolução social: e uma mocidade, envernizada de literatura, decidia destruir num folhetim uma sociedade de dezoito séculos.

... it was necessary that society, under attack by the International, should take refuge in the strength of its conservative and religious principles, surrounding them carefully with bayonets! ... Individuals proclaimed revenge as they picked their teeth. Vagrants waxed furious 'against the worker who wants to live like a prince'. People talked devoutly of property, of capital!

On the other hand there were loquacious young men, excited and parochial, who declaimed against the old world and against old ideas, threatening them from on high, proposing in furious articles to overthrow them.

And thus a sluggish bourgeoisie wanted to hold back a process of social evolution with a few policemen; and a group of young men, with a thin veneer of literary culture, decided to destroy a society with eighteen centuries of history by means of a pamphlet.

Eça de Queiroz, *O Crime do Padre Amaro* (1874)

Although the liberation of 25 April 1974 was the work of the MFA, the popular explosion which followed owed much to the patient political work of the PCP for decades past, to the ideas spread and the example set by men like Delgado, Galvao, and Manuel Serra, and to the rise of the revolutionary left since the early sixties. The concepts of popular liberation and revolution had gained wide currency, and the people had high expectations of any post-fascist régime – expectations which went far beyond the mere restoration of political liberty (although that, of course, was fundamental).

The PCP continued to be a major force in the resistance right up to 1974, even if it no longer enjoyed the hegemony it had achieved in the forties. Its continuing strength in Portugal today, where it remains the dominant force in the labour movement and the best-organised party on the left, with around 18% of the electorate, is testimony to its persistent and tenacious underground activity, unrivalled by any other party or organisation. For the mass of the Portuguese working class – at least, the hard-core industrial proletariat and the agricultural labourers of the Alentejo – the PCP *was* the resistance, and continues to be their party by definition (even if its grip has weakened slightly in recent years). The impressive roll-call of Party members who died in gaol or in action against the forces of repression, the 400 years in gaol accumulated by Central Committee members, the stoic example of those like Cunhal, 'Chico' Miguel, Dias Lourenço, José Magro and others who refused to give way under torture and prolonged maltreatment – these things created a mystique and a moral force which no other political tendency could hope to match. The marxist-leninists, who tried and in a few cases did succeed in emulating this record of heroism during the sixties and early seventies, were like pigmies competing against a giant: they greatly over-estimated their capacity to win over any substantial section of the working class in the short or medium term. Only massive internal crisis, such as that experienced by the Spanish CP in recent years, would undermine an institution like the PCP in the short term.

This said, it is necessary once again to make a critical examination of the Party's history and evaluate its errors, failures and limitations. The Party did not, after all, make or lead a revolution in Portugal, despite being the dominant force in the resistance for more than three decades; the 'national anti-fascist insurrection' remained a myth, a political slogan to inspire popular struggles, but not a concrete project capable of realisation in a specific conjuncture. For if that conjuncture never occurred, one has to ask under what circumstances it might conceivably have occurred. The Party's hesitation to adopt bolder forms of action in 1945, 1958 and 1962 could not but cause despondency among the more combative workers, and ultimately left it in a political impasse, rejecting reformism and *putschism* but failing to provide the revolutionary alternative which in theory it claimed to represent. We have seen that Cunhal in his criticism of the *Desvio de Direita* recognised the Party's crucial failure to provide a lead in the political strikes of June–July 1958, and that later, in *Rumo à Vitória*, he partially admitted that the Party had erred in its condemnation of the Beja uprising; and also that in the 1962 demonstrations, the Party could have done more to organise tactical squads for 'armed self-defence'. But these self-criticisms fail to address the question of why, even after rectification of the *Desvio de Direita*, the Party failed to prepare for these situations of open combat and confrontation. One answer, that of the marxist-leninists, is to say that the Party was already 'revisionist' and was not genuinely committed to revolution. Diametrically opposed to this is the view of some socialist and liberal critics, that there was never anything approaching a revolutionary situation in Portugal, and that the Party instinctively recognised this, although it continued to pay lip-service to the idea of insurrection for tactical reasons. But this criticism can be seen as self-serving, a rationalisation of its authors' own aversion to revolutionary action; and one can certainly make a strong case for the existence of a revolutionary situation in 1958 or 1962.

The marxist-leninist criticism is superficially more convincing, but it overlooks the complexities of mass political organisation and the difficulties of combining peaceful, confrontational and openly insurrectional methods of struggle. The issue of armed struggle versus the peaceful road, raised to the level of abstract principle by Chinese and Albanian polemics against the Soviet line, is in a way a false debate. Methods and tactics of political action must depend on a wide variety of considerations – class structure, national culture and traditions, the political conjuncture – and to what extent a particular form of struggle and a specific configuration of forces will imply violence, open or partially contained, cannot always be predicted in advance. What is crucial is clarity of political objectives and disposition to hold to a specific line of demarcation; in other words, in the present context, a question of strategic revolutionary commitment, which might or might not lead to armed conflict in varying degrees. A related problem is that of political organisation and adaptability; the capacity to respond to a rapidly changing political conjuncture. In the case of the PCP, this capacity was clearly lacking in May–June 1958 and May–June 1962; and this lack was in turn related to the classic problem of the structure and organisation of Communist parties. The highly centralised and bureaucratised structure of 'democratic centralism', in which centralism prevailed over democracy, prevented a dynamic interplay between the leadership and the rank-and-file or between the Party and the non-Party masses. Moreover, the determination of policy by the Central Committee (subject only to the restraint of occasional Congresses, largely controlled by the Central Committee in any case) and the principle of adhering to a given political line until it had been repeatedly tested in practice, tended to sacrifice flexibility to consistency.

Thus in 1958, if the Central Committee had been more sensitive to the changing popular mood and less intent on maintaining a predetermined tactical stand, it would have realised within days of the start of the election campaign (following Delgado's overwhelming reception in Oporto, for example) that the time had come to prepare for decisive action: that a general strike immediately following the inevitable electoral fraud, combined with other forms of mass action to force a change of regime, was the only logical way forward. How peaceful or violent such action would be was obviously difficult to predict, and would not depend exclusively on the PCP. This is a totally different question from that of the political reliability of Delgado, or the class character of the opposition groups which had promoted his candidacy, or the political position of dissident officers who might in such a crisis launch a coup in support of Delgado. All of these questions (which greatly preoccupied the Central Committee at the time) would have been very relevant to a consideration of tactics in a post-revolutionary (or post-Salazarist) conjuncture; but the key issue *at that moment* was the development and exploitation of a profound political crisis and a manifest popular will for a change of regime. The ultimate reason for the Party's failure to respond to this (and to other critical conjunctures) lies not in simple capitulation to the bourgeoisie ('revisionist betrayal') but in a stereotyped, and ultimately metaphysical, conception of political organisation and struggle. This, of course, is a problem which is not confined to the PCP but is characteristic of Communist parties in general – with occasional exceptions.

Another major failing of the PCP, more specific than the above (but equally serious), was its well-known inability to penetrate the peasantry of central and northern Portugal. If anything, as we have seen, there is evidence to suggest that the Party made more progress in rural areas of the North in the early to mid-forties than it ever did later – its early network in the region having been largely destroyed by police repression. Peasant isolation and individualism, suspicion of all outsiders, the influence of the conservative clergy and of the local *caciques* – all these factors impeded Communist penetration of the peasant population. What is not clear is whether such obstacles were in themselves insuperable or whether in slightly different circumstances, with a slightly different approach, the PCP could have overcome them. The 'peasant question' has been a major problem for many Communist parties; and those which have succeeded in gaining a large peasant following (as in China, Vietnam, Yugoslavia and Albania) have generally done so on the basis of national resistance to a foreign invader. Where this factor is not present, Communist experience has been similar to that in Portugal: in France, Spain or Chile, Communist parties have had little rural strength except among landless labourers.

Communist failure in this regard was probably due both to the structural characteristics of the peasantry and to the inappropriate nature of the Party's propaganda and methods of work, developed in an urban setting. The success of a populist leader like Delgado in peasant areas is striking; his bold, direct style, his moralistic message and simple rhetoric appealed much more effectively to the peasant mentality. But this was of limited value, since it did not resolve the problem of organisation: Delgado's appeal suffered from the typical weaknesses of populism. His impact as charismatic leader could be immensely valuable in a short-term confrontation with the regime, but in terms of revolutionary organisation his contribution was nil. Once in exile, his significance was essentially in the inspiration he provided for a new generation of revolutionary militants in Portugal. In the absence of an effective new political party, his influence was limited to keeping alive a revolutionary popular tradition.

Broad anti-fascist unity on a long-term basis is only possible where there is minimal agreement on a common strategy which can be implemented with some degree of success: either mass insurrection, or a combination of mass insurrection and military conspiracy, or mass pressure on the regime through strikes, protests and demonstrations. If a given strategy fails, or if the latent contradictions between different strategies come to the fore, then unity can be no more than an empty shell. This was the fate of the MUNAF and MUD after 1946, although they continued to exist for a few more years. The PCP's strategy of working-class organisation and mobilisation with a perspective of mass insurrection, could not ultimately be reconciled with the Republican officers' coup or the legalistic electoral strategy of most of the bourgeois opposition. The attempt to square the circle bore witness to good-will on both sides, but its breakdown under Cold War pressures was inevitable. During the Second World War there was some possibility of overcoming the latent differences, but within a year or two of the war's end the domestic and international situation was much less favourable.

The significance of Delgado, in temporarily achieving popular unity in practice by submerging ideological and partisan differences in a wave of mass euphoria, should not be dismissed or minimised. Populism can often express latent mass revolutionary sentiments with dramatic clarity, although offering no solution. Delgado's impact in 1958 demonstrated beyond doubt that there was mass opposition to the Salazar regime embracing vast sectors of the population, with pent-up frustrations and resentments built up over the years. This massive popular revolutionary energy would burst forth again in 1974, once more stimulated by military populism; and once again, although in a post-liberation context, the latent contradictions of such a movement would be laid bare. The MFA was a typically populist movement, with its leadership of petty-bourgeois junior officers, its vague and contradictory ideology, its appeal to 'the people' in the abstract, and its attempt to bypass political parties and construct a revolutionary democracy based on 'popular power' and charismatic leadership. The populist personal appeal of MFA officers such as

Vasco Gonçalves, Vasco Lourenço, Rosa Coutinho, and above all Otelo Saraiva de Carvalho, was remarkable. The Movement's major problem was precisely this multiplicity of rival leaders with differing ideological projects. The continuity with earlier manifestations of military populism, notably Delgado, is clear; although some MFA leaders, especially Otelo, moved much further to the Left than Delgado ever did, their populist style remained strikingly similar. The ideological and operational differences between the MFA and the PCP proved fatal to the Portuguese revolution in 1974–75, just as the differences between Delgado and the PCP had proven fatal to the revolutionary movement in 1958–62.

Despite great variations, the history of resistance movements in other countries tends to confirm the conclusions to be drawn from the Portuguese case. The early years of the Franco regime in Spain were very different: much of the left was destroyed in the Civil War or driven into exile, and the mass executions of the first two years following Franco's victory eliminated most of the militants who remained. In particular, the total destruction of the Republican military explains the almost complete absence of military dissidence and liberal coup attempts in Spain, in contrast to Portugal.[1] Both Communists and anarchists strove to maintain armed guerrilla groups in mountainous regions – the *maquis* – and did so until the late 1940s, when lack of progress and the consolidation of the regime led them to abandon the attempt. The repression in Spain was so great that it led to the collapse of the Communist Party's clandestine network in the late forties, and for a while the Spanish CP, like other Spanish parties, was predominantly an exile organisation. In the sixties the Communists were able to re-establish an effective clandestine apparatus, but the Party's top leadership was always in exile, unlike the Portuguese CP. This appears to have been one cause of the serious rifts which have rent the Spanish CP since the death of Franco.

The extent of repression in Spain and the absence of pseudo-liberal devices such as controlled 'elections' meant that legal or semi-legal manifestations of the opposition were fewer and much more difficult to organise, at least until the mid-sixties. When repression did begin to ease, new patterns began to emerge. The Socialist Party was stronger in Spain, having done more than the

Portuguese Socialists to maintain a trade union presence. The Communist Party had been following a peaceful line of 'national reconciliation' for years, and its General Secretary, Santiago Carrillo, became a pioneer of 'Eurocommunism' in the early seventies; this was a crucial factor in facilitating the gradual liberalisation of Spanish politics under King Juan Carlos and Adolfo Suárez.[2] The Portuguese upheaval of 1974–75 undoubtedly contributed to the Spanish regime's decision to liberalise at this time; Franco's death was an essential preliminary, no more. But the structures of dictatorship – army, police, corporate institutions – remained intact to a much greater extent than in Portugal, and the restoration of the monarchy served as a symbolic and institutional guarantee against radical 'excesses'. The changes which have occurred in Spain since 1975 are more the delayed results of capitalist modernisation than of political opposition: relaxation of censorship, legalisation of divorce and abortion, secularisation of society in general. While the Spanish resistance can claim many more martyrs than the Portuguese, its political achievements are more limited.

The case which perhaps reveals the greatest similarity to that of Portugal is Chile under Pinochet. Here, as in Spain, the initial repression was much greater than in Portugal; but the Chilean CP was able to maintain a constant clandestine organisation, emerging after several years as clearly the strongest party in the resistance. The Socialists, as in Portugal, underwent a process of fragmentation, and although some of the different socialist parties and groups have re-established an effective underground presence in Chile, the historic importance of the Socialist Party seems to have suffered a serious decline. As in Portugal, any socialist organisation which emerges in a future democratic Chile is likely to be significantly different from its historic predecessor.

There is no sign thus far in Chile of a liberal or dissident military, and for the same reason as in Spain: all progressive officers were systematically eliminated before or during the coup. But the pattern of civilian opposition does bear comparison to the Portuguese case: the Christian Democrats, initially complicit in the coup but subsequently forced into opposition, have come to dominate a coalition of bourgeois parties, the *Alianza Democrática*, which advocates change through peaceful and legal pressure on the regime. Although the *Alianza Domocrática* has collaborated with the Communist-led MDP (*Movimiento Democrático Popular*) in a few protest actions, it refuses any formal alliance with the Communists, and there are indications that it would be content with a 'limited democracy' excluding the marxist parties from participation.[3] Its overtures to the regime have so far been met only with increased repression, and it is in danger of being driven into the same situation of political sterility which afflicted the Portuguese *Oposição Democrática*. On the other hand, the Chilean Communist Party, having been the principal advocate and architect of the 'peaceful road to socialism' which ended in disaster in 1973, has since 1980 adopted a strategy of armed struggle – and has organised an underground armed apparatus, the *Frente Patriótico Manuel Rodríguez*, which has begun to act in collaboration with other parties favouring armed resistance (the MIR and the pro-Almeyda Socialists).[4] Recent Chilean experience demonstrates, as in Portugal, the extreme difficulty of trying to win a 'democratic space' of legal or tolerated political expression under a firmly entrenched fascist regime. During the mass protests of 1983–84 trade unions and popular organisations began to operate more openly, and an outspoken opposition press developed; but this was followed by a massive wave of repression towards the end of 1984 in which many trade unionists and popular leaders were arrested and most of the opposition press was closed down. As in Portugal, so long as the military and police apparatus remains loyal to the régime and the United States shows no serious displeasure with Pinochet, the prospects for substantial change are poor.

Other comparable examples confirm the importance of change originating within the regime or through external pressure, at least as a complement to domestic resistance. The recent Argentine dictatorship (1976–83) abandoned power because the military were profoundly divided and discredited as a result of their economic and political failures, and above all because of their humiliation in the Falklands/Malvinas war. Domestic opposition was both limited in scope and profoundly divided: the armed revolutionary activity of the ERP and Montoneros[5] was swiftly crushed, and the Peronist movement was split between right-wing elements which collaborated with the military and progressive sectors which tried to organise working-class resistance through strikes and protest rallies. Strike activity did achieve a substantial impact early in 1982, and may have contributed to General Galtieri's decision to launch his military adventure; to this extent, working-class resistance was a factor in the regime's collapse. The greatest moral blow against the Argentine regime was dealt by the Mothers of the Plaza de Mayo, courageously protesting against the fate of the 'disappeared'; but how far their example contributed to the downfall of the regime is impossible to judge. As with the PIDE/DGS in Portugal, the torturers and executioners are always the last elements of a regime to abandon power, fearing reprisals; and since in the Argentine case complicity in torture and brutality appears to have reached into the highest ranks of the military, it became a powerful motive for hanging on to power at all costs. In this sense, Mrs. Thatcher's quixotic post-colonial stubbornness was probably crucial in Argentina's swift return to democracy.

A case of special sentimental relevance to Portugal is Brazil, where the military have recently withdrawn after more then twenty years in control of the nation's affairs. As in previous phases of Brazilian history, there are some interesting similarities with Portuguese experience, despite the vast differences in size and ethnic composition between the two Lusophone countries. As in Portugal, direct repression under the Brazilian dictatorship was limited and selective; though torture and 'disappearances' were certainly practised, in terms of scale there was no comparison with Chile or Argentina. Thus the last military President, General Figueiredo, offended by a comparison with Pinochet, is said to have retorted that 'one cannot compare a surgeon with a butcher'. The objection is valid – within limits; but the fact remains that, as in Portugal, the surgeon's knife was very painful for those subjected to it, and the entire body politic has suffered from the effects of the prolonged anesthesia inflicted upon it. The convalescence also appears to be a slow one, and the patient's long-term health is still in doubt; moreover, many observers question whether the operation was really necessary in the first place.

Opposition in Brazil was initially deeply divided, with populist, liberal, Communist and Marxist–Leninist tendencies all adopting different tactics. Brazil was one of the few Western countries in which the Marxist–Leninist tendency was relatively strong, the Communist Party split into the marxist-leninist *Partido*

Comunista do Brasil and the pro-Moscow *Partido Comunista Brasileiro*. The marxist leninists did organise armed resistance, maintaining for a few years a guerrilla movement in the Araguaia River region; there was also a small (and unconnected) urban guerrilla movement, led by Carlos Marighela in São Paulo.[6] But armed struggle was unsuccessful; the urban guerrillas never won significant popular support, and although the Araguaia movement did gain some local peasant sympathy, it died out after a few years. As against this, the *Partido Comunista Brasileiro* engaged in semi-clandestine peaceful agitation in trade unions and popular organisations. The populist, socialist and liberal sectors maintained a variety of legal and semi-legal activities, and became increasingly bold and open as the regime began to liberalise in the mid-seventies. The regime's organisation of controlled elections, with a tolerated opposition, evoked some of the same responses as in Portugal, with the underground resistance (mainly the PC do B) refusing to participate; but unlike the Portuguese experience, it was swiftly apparent that the Brazilian elections were designed to allow genuine (if at first severely circumscribed) opposition participation. Hence the rapid and massive 'entrism' into the 'official' opposition party, the MDB (*Movimento Democrático Brasileiro*), which soon came to encompass a vast range of tendencies from right-wing liberals to the PCB. The abolition of press censorship and the legalisation of more parties in 1983 made it clear that the liberalisation process was genuine, although still subject to military control; and the victory in March 1985 of the civilian Presidential candidate, Tancredo Neves (replaced following his unimely death by his running-mate José Sarney), apparently marked the genuine return of liberal democracy to Brazil. But the military evidently retains a tacit veto on the extent of change under the new democratic régime, and in this sense Brazil is an excellent illustration of the limitations of liberalisation 'from above'.

Both organised opposition and popular unrest undoubtedly contributed to the Brazilian liberalisation, but the decisive factor was the decision of the military to undertake a phased withdrawal from government. Labour unrest – the major strikes in São Paulo associated with the rise of the independent union leader 'Lula' – and food riots in the principal cities helped to convince the Generals that a strategic retreat was desirable, precisely to avoid a Chilean situation of confrontation. Once again, the remarkable flexibility of both civilian and military politicians in Brazil has averted an open rupture; but the cost will no doubt be paid by the Brazilian people, with fundamental reform being further postponed. Here again is the classic dilemma of resistance and opposition movements: liberalisation by compromise is possible under favourable circumstances, but only on terms favourable to the international neo-capitalist order.

Our last international comparison concerns a small country whose affairs are intimately connected with the previous two: Uruguay. The assumption of power by the Uruguayan military in 1973 was particularly traumatic for a country with a democratic tradition unparalleled in Latin America; and the experience of resistance was also therefore an unprecedented one for most of the country's political forces. One has to say 'most', since there was one political tendency with clandestine experience under the last years of the parliamentary regime, namely the Tupamaros. To some extent the Tupamaros contributed – within an already deteriorating political situation – to the crisis in which the military assumed power. In any case, once the military regime was installed, the strategy of armed resistance represented by the Tupamaros proved to be a failure, as in Argentina: military repression was overwhelmingly efficient. Opposition was expressed instead by peaceful means, through the traditional parties (*Blancos* and *Colorados*) and the left-wing *Frente Amplio* (dominated by the Communist Party). The opposition made little apparent progress for several years, but in 1980 broad and effective popular mobilisation was achieved on the occasion of the regime's constitutional referendum (designed to institutionalise military tutelage over a carefully controlled and probably deceptive 'liberalisation'). The popular forces achieved a stunning success with victory for the 'No' vote in the referendum, effectively stymying the regime's plans. This remarkable victory, almost certainly an international first in terms of opposition success in controlled elections under a repressive regime, was apparently possible only because the military had failed to appreciate the impartiality of the civil service and judiciary. This reverse for the regime, followed during the next few years by further mass demonstrations and strikes, culminated in free elections and a complete return to parliamentary democracy early in 1985.

The Uruguayan liberalisation was thus a clear victory for the democratic resistance; but at the same time it was undeniably influenced by external factors, namely the Argentinian and Brazilian processes which had a powerful impact on the Uruguayan military. Nevertheless, the initial impact of the Argentinian process may well have been negative, since it reinforced the Uruguayan rulers' fear of reprisals for crimes committed by the repressive forces; a fear which was only overcome by the opposition's undertaking not to seek justice against their former oppressors. Here again, liberalisation by consent was possible, but only at the price of leaving the repressive institutions intact. The military genie had been put back in the bottle, but it has not been fully exorcised.

The Portuguese experience, confirmed in many respects by those of Italy, Spain, Chile and Brazil, and to a lesser extent Argentina and Uruguay, suggests that the task of anti-fascist resistance movements is distressingly similar to that of Sisyphus, condemned in perpetuity to pushing a rock up a mountainside, only to see it roll down again. In the long run this is not the case, since fascist regimes do ultimately collapse or abandon power, but the process is never simple and direct, and rarely takes the form of open and dramatic triumph for the resistance. External pressures, dissidence within the regime or controlled liberalisation from above – designed precisely to neutralise the more militant sectors of the resistance – frequently deprive opposition forces of political initiative or mediate the impact of their struggle.

It is possible to point to other examples which appear to contradict this: examples of open revolutionary victory over dictatorial regimes, the most recent being the Nicaraguan revolution. But the socio-economic context of such revolutionary victories is very different: the examples we have concentrated on in this discussion are much more comparable to Portugal in terms of levels of industrialisation, urbanisation and institutional density. Moreover, the Somoza regime (and similarly the Batista dictatorship in Cuba, or the current Salvadorean regime) differed in important respects from the regimes we have been discussing. The institutionalised military regimes of Brazil and the Southern Cone in recent decades are, as I argued in Chapter I, functionally similar to classic fascism – even in the absence of fascist parties and mass organisations. Coming to power in semi-industrialised countries with a high degree of urbanisation, in situations of severe social and political crisis, they take measures to neutralise or destroy working-class political parties, trade unions and any form of independent popular organisation; they seek to rally mass support for a reactionary political project; and they impose policies designed to restructure the economy in the interests of monopoly capital. They are therefore much more complex and more resistant to revolutionary overthrow than simple oligarchic or *caudillo*-type regimes.

Under fascist or institutionalised military regimes, resistance tends to adopt clearly identifiable patterns. Without being schematic, it is possible to draw several general conclusions:

(i) Except in circumstances of war or foreign invasion, attempts to develop mass armed struggle rarely succeed. Repression is too well organised and the popular forces lack the means to develop effective military action. But armed struggle may be relevant in combination with other factors.

(ii) Legal and semi-legal opposition may operate with varying degrees of openness depending on the extent and character of repression, but in the absence of other factors favourable to change (external pressures or changes within the regime) it faces a strategic impasse, often leading to political sterility.

(iii) Military conspiracies (*putschism*) will proliferate where, as in Portugal, the regime has not first been able to conduct a thorough purge of liberal elements in the armed forces. But for such conspiracies to succeed, external pressures and/or internal resistance must have developed to a very high level.

(iv) Mass resistance through class struggle – organisation in unions, clubs, and neighbourhood associations, strikes, rallies and food riots, land invasions and factory occupations – will develop spontaneously, and can be extensively and successfully stimulated and directed by a clandestine political organisation (typically a Communist Party). It may contribute powerfully to weakening a regime and to hastening the search for political alternatives, but is rarely sufficient by itself to bring about a political rupture.

(v) Opposition political unity is never easy to achieve, and founders on basic ideological and strategic divisions. But in critical conjunctures, as at times of great popular mobilisation, unity in practice may develop, either through a convergence of rival opposition forces or through populist leadership.

(vi) Populist leadership may sometimes express popular discontent and resistance more effectively than any organised political tendency; but it is incapable of offering a true political solution.

In Portugal the development of the resistance was quite impressive, given generally unfavourable conditions. The solid support for the regime from Western powers, the selective character of repression, the reliance on traditional instruments of social control such as the Catholic Church and local notables, all combined to give Salazarism a stability which urban proletarian militancy and Republican conspiracies could not undermine. If Portugal had been only Lisbon and the South, the story would have been different; the predominance of peasant smallholdings in the Centre and North, and the consequent influence of clerical-conservative ideology, was crucial. Within these limitations, the PCP's development of a permanent clandestine network and a mass working-class organisation was remarkable. The persistence of intellectual protest and public contestation by the Democratic Opposition was testimony to the regime's vulnerability among its natural petty-bourgeois constituency. The great strike waves and mass demonstrations of November–December 1942, July–August 1943, May 1944, May and October– November 1945, April 1947 and so on were proof of the breadth and depth of popular discontent; discontent which would manifest itself again in the Norton de Matos campaign and, overwhelmingly, in 1958 in response to Delgado. If one lesson can be drawn from the most crucial moments – November 1945, June 1958 and May 1962 – it is that hesitation is fatal: if the régime were given the slightest respite, it would recover the initiative and reassert control. Only a resolutely revolutionary leadership could have brought about a different outcome; and such leadership did not exist. The PCP came close to fulfilling this role, but failed at the decisive moments. This hesitation on the part of the Communists, combined with the historic weakness of the Portuguese Socialists, opened the door to populist tendencies; but the charisma and *élan* of the populist hero Delgado were not sufficient to oust the regime in the absence of a planned strategy. The liberation of Portugal had to wait many years, and finally came from an unexpected quarter. The long-frustrated resistance had to watch as a group of young military upstarts stole the limelight, and the ambiguities of revolutionary populism came to dominate the political scene again. Even in victory, the opposition was upstaged by other forces; but this should not be allowed to obscure its historic contribution.

Today in Portugal, as in other societies just emerging from prolonged subjection to repressive régimes, the readjustment to liberty is disconcerting, especially for those who have borne the greatest burden of resistance. In the words of Vasco in Fernando Namora's novel *Os Clandestinos*:

Even today I can feel that unease. Even today I feel as if the whole city is watching me, as if there are hidden eyes inside me and outside of me, that I have to hide what I am and what I am not; even today I do not know when words and gestures are really mine.[7]

Notes to Chapter VIII

1 See Raymond Carr and Juan Pablo Fusi, *Spain: Dictatorship to Democracy*, London, 1979, George Allen & Unwin, pp. 22–4.

2 *Ibid.*, pp. 222–7.

3 Carmelo Furci, *The Chilean Communist Party and the Road to Socialism*, London, 1984, Zed Books, pp. 163–4.

4 *Ibid.*, pp. 165–8.

5 ERP: *Ejército Revolucionario del Pueblo* (Revolutionary Army of the People), of Trotskyite tendencies. *Montoneros*: leftwing Peronists favouring guerrilla struggle.

6 See João Quartim, *Dictatorship and Armed Struggle in Brazil*, New York & London, 1971, Monthly Review Press, pp. 167–91; and Georges-André Fiechter, *Le régime modernisateur du Brésil, 1964–1972*, Leiden, 1972, A. W. Sijthoff, pp. 167–72.

7 Fernando Namora, *Os Clandestinos*, Lisboa, 1981, Betrand, p. 196.

Sources and bibliography

Archival sources

Avante! archive, Lisbon. PCP material including extensive (although incomplete) series of *Avante!* and *O Militante*, and numerous clandestine pamphlets.

Biblioteca Nacional, Lisbon. Pamphlets, newspapers, secondary works.

Hemeroteca Municipal, Lisbon. Contemporary newspapers and magazines.

O Século archive, Lisbon. Complete runs of *O Século* newspaper, including galley proofs of articles cut by the censor, and other documents.

Tribunal da Boa Hora, Lisbon. Some of the political trial records have very abundant documentation (detailed references are given in the footnotes).

In addition, much valuable documentation was obtained from various private collections; these are acknowledged in the Preface, and specific references are given in footnotes. Limited use was also made of the British Library and the Public Record Office, London.

Newspapers and Magazines

Avante! (clandestine, fortnightly or monthly). *1941–74.*
Diário de Lisboa, Lisbon. Selected issues consulted.
Diário da Manhã, Lisbon. Selected issues.
Diário de Notícias, Lisbon. 1941–74.
O Militante (clandestine, usually published monthly). 1941–74.
República, Lisbon, 1941–74.
Seara Nova, Lisbon (weekly, sometimes less frequent). 1941–74.

O Século, Lisbon. 1941–74.
O Tempo e o Modo, Lisbon (monthly). 1963–74.
A Voz, Lisbon. Selected issues.
The Times, London. Selected issues.
New York Times. Selected issues.

Interviews

All interviews were open-ended and based on questionnaires which varied for each participant. Interviews were conducted in Lisbon unless stated otherwise. Tapes and/or transcripts of interviews are in the author's possession and may be consulted on request.
Manuel Alegre, 5 June 1978.
Luis Dias Amado, 27 May 1978.
Artur Andrade, Oporto, 29 June 1977.
Ernesto Melo Antunes, 5 July 1977.
Alcina Bastos, 15 June 1978.
Nuno de Bragança, 3 June 1978.
António Lopes Cardoso, 6 July 1977.
Otelo Saraiva de Carvalho, Oeiras, 25 May 1977.
Armando de Castro, Oporto, 29 June 1977.
Colonel Correia, 5 February 1977.
António Rosa Coutinho, 15 June 1977; 17 June 1977.
Alvaro Cunhal, 26 June 1978.
Frei Bento Domingues, Benfica, 21 April 1977.
Olivio França, Oporto, 6 June 1978; 20 June 1978.
José Magalhães Godinho, 22 January 1977; 26 February 1977.
Ruy Luis Gomes & José Morgado, Oporto, 30 June 1977.
Vasco Gonçalves, 24 March 1977.
António Dias Lourenço, 29 April 1977.
José Magro, 16 June 1978.
Francisco Pereira de Moura, 23 June 1978.
Virgínia Moura, Rio Tinto, 30 June 1977.
Mário Murteira, 23 March 1977.
Francisco Lino Neto, 7 July 1977.
Octávio Pato, 25 February 1977; 4 March 1977.
Edmundo Pedro, 9 June 1978.
Joaquim Ribeiro, Oporto, 20 June 1978.
Emídio Santana, 1 March 1977.

Fernando Piteira Santos, 9 December 1976; 13 January 1977; 20
January 1977; 28 February 1977.
Manuel Serra, 10 March 1977.
Joél Serrão, 12 May 1977.
Manuel Sertório, 22 March 1977; 14 April 1977; 19 April 1977.
Artur Santos Silva, Oporto, 28 June 1977.
Nikias Skapinakis, 4 May 1977.
Mário Soares, 29 June 1978.
Colonel Vilhena, 31 January 1977.
Francisco Salgado Zenha, 6 June 1978.

Secondary works

1 *Theoretical and comparative*
Carr, Raymond & Juan Pablo Fusi, *Spain: Dictatorship to Democracy*,
    London, 1979.
Dimitroff, Georgi, *The United Front*, San Francisco, 1975.
Fiechter, Georges-André, *Le régime modernisateur du Brésil, 1964–
    1972*, Leiden, 1972.
Furci, Carmelo, *The Chilean Communist Party and the Road to
    Socialism*, London, 1984.
Hoare, Quintin, and Geoffrey Nowell Smith (eds.), *Selections from
    the Prison Notebooks of Antonio Gramsci*, London, 1971.
Laclau, Ernesto, *Politics and Ideology in Marxist Theory*, London,
    1977.
Laqueur, Walter (ed.), *Fascism: A Reader's Guide*, Berkeley, 1976.
Mayer, Arno J., *Dynamics of Counterrevolution in Europe, 1870–
    1956: An Analytic Framework*, New York, 1971.
Poulantzas, Nicos, *Fascism and Dictatorship*, London, 1974.
Quartim, João, *Dictatorship and Armed Struggle in Brazil*, London,
    1971.
Raby, D. L., *Populism: A Marxist Analysis*, Montreal, 1983.
Sinclair, Peter R., 'Fascism and crisis in capitalist society', *New
    German Critique* IX, Fall 1976, pp. 102–7.
Woolf, S. J. (ed.), *European Fascism*, London, 1968.

2 *Portugal and the Salazar régime*
Bruneau, Thomas C., Victor M. P. da Rosa and Alex Macleod
    (eds.), *Portugal in Development*, Ottawa, 1984.

Cabral, Amílcar, *Revolution in Guinea*, London, 1969.

Caetano, Marcello, *Depoimento*, Rio de Janeiro/São Paulo, 1974.

Campinos, Jorge, *A Ditadura Militar, 1926–1933*, Lisbon, 1975.

Ideología Política do Estado Salazarista, Lisbon, 1975.

Clarence-Smith, Gervase, *The Third Portuguese Empire, 1825–1975*, Manchester, 1985.

Commissão do Livro Negro Sobre o Fascismo, *Eleições no Regime Fascista*, Lisbon, 1979.

Cruz, Coronel Antonino e Vitoriano Rosa, *As Mentiras de Marcello Caetano*, Lisbon, 1974.

O Fascismo em Portugal: Actas do Colóquio realizado na Faculdade de Letras de Lisboa em Março de 1980, Lisbon, 1982.

Figueiredo, António de, *Portugal: Fifty Years of Dictatorship*, Middlesex, 1975.

Fryer, Peter & Patricia McGowan Pinheiro, *Oldest Ally: A Portrait of Salazar's Portugal*, London, 1961.

Gallagher, Tom, *Portugal: A Twentieth-Century Interpretation*, Manchester, 1983.

Garnier, Christine, *Vacances avec Salazar*, Paris, 1952.

Graham, Lawrence S. & Harry M. Makler (eds.), *Contemporary Portugal*, Austin & London, 1979.

Kay, Hugh, *Salazar and Modern Portugal*, London, 1970.

Lucena, Manuel de, *A evolução do sistema corporativo português* (2 vols.), Lisbon, 1976.

Madureira, Arnaldo, *O 28 de Maio* (2 vols.), Lisbon, 1978 & 1982.

Makler, Harry Mark, *A 'Elite' Industrial Portuguesa*, Lisbon, 1969.

Manuel, Alexandre, Rogério Carapinha e Dias Neves, *PIDE: A História da Repressão*, Fundão, 1974.

Medeiros, Fernando, *A Sociedade e a Economia Portuguesas nas Orígens do Salazarismo*, Lisbon, 1978.

Mónica, Maria Filomena, *Educação e Sociedade no Portugal de Salazar*, Lisbon, 1978.

Murteira, Mário, *Política Económica numa Sociedade em Transição*, Lisbon, 1977.

Pattee, Richard, *Portugal and the Portuguese World*, Milwaukee, 1957.

Rafael, Francisco, *et al.*, *Portugal: Capitalismo e Estado Novo*, Oporto, 1976.

Robinson, R. A. H., *Contemporary Portugal: A History*, London, 1979.

Telo, António José, *Decadência e Queda da I República Portuguesa*,

Vol. I, Lisbon, 1980.

Vasco, Nuno, *Vigiados e perseguidos*, Lisbon, 1977.

Wheeler, Douglas L., *Republican Portugal*, Madison, Wis., 1978.

Wiarda, Howard J., *Corporatism and Development: The Portuguese Experience*, Amherst, Mass., 1977.

3 *The opposition: general*

Aquino, Acácio Tomás de, *O Segredo das Prisões Atlânticas*, Lisbon, 1978.

Alves, Padre José da Felicidade (ed.), *Católicos e Politica*, Lisbon, 1970.

Barros, Henrique de e Fernando Ferreira da Costa, *António Sérgio: uma nobre utopia*, Lisbon, 1983.

Braga da Cruz, Manuel, *Monárquicos e Republicanos no Estado Novo*, Lisbon, 1986.

Ibid., 'A Oposição Eleitoral ao Salazarismo', in *António Sérgio: Número especial da Revista de História das Ideias*, V, 1983; Coimbra.

Coelho, José Dias, *A Resistência em Portugal*, Oporto, 1974.

II Congresso Republicano de Aveiro, *Teses e Documentos* (2 vols.), Lisbon, 1969.

III Congresso da Oposição Democrática de Aveiro, *Teses* (7 vols.), Lisbon, 1974.

Duarte, Diogo, Emílio Rui Vilar e Manuel Bidarra de Almeida, *Portugal 73: Ano político*, Oporto, 1973.

Fernandes, Vasco da Gama, *Depoimento Inacabado*, Lisbon, 1974.

Ferreira, Gabriela, *et al.*, *Boletim Anti-Colonial, 1 a 9*, Oporto, 1975.

Ferreira, Serafim, e Arsénio Mota (eds.), *Para um Dossier da 'Oposição Democrática'*, Tomar, 1969.

Godinho, José Magalhães, *Carta Aberta ao Presidente do Conselho*, Lisbon, 1973.

—— *Causas que foram Casos*, Lisbon, 1974.

—— *Falar Claro*, Lisbon, 1969.

Lins, Alvaro, *Missão em Portugal*, Lisbon, 1974.

Magalhães-Vilhena, Vasco de, *António Sérgio: O Idealismo Crítico e a Crise da Ideologia Burguesa*, Lisbon, 1975.

Marques, A. H. de Oliveira, *Dicionário de Maçonaria Portuguesa*, vol. I, Lisbon, 1986.

Matos, A. Campos, *Diálogo com António Sérgio*, Lisbon, 1983.

McGowan, Patricia, *O Bando de Argel*, Lisbon, 1979.

Moura, Virgínia (ed.), *Eleições de 1969*, Oporto, 1971.

Namorado, Rui, *Movimento Estudantil e Política Educacional*, Águeda, 1972.

Nobre de Melo, Rose Nery, *Mulheres portuguesas na resistência*, Lisbon 1975.

Norton de Matos, José Mendes Ribeiro, *Os Dois Primeiros Meses da minha Candidatura à Presidência da República*, Lisbon, 1948.

Oliveira, Cândido de, *Tarrafal: o pântano da morte*, Lisbon, 1974.

Oposição Democrática, *Campanha Eleitoral de 1965*, Lisbon, n.d..

Rego, Raúl, *Horizontes Fechados*, Oporto, 1970.

Ribeiro, Joaquim, *No Tarrafal, prisioneiro*, Lisbon, 1976.

Rodrigues, Edgar, *Breve História do Pensamento e das Lutas Sociais em Portugal*, Lisbon, 1977.

Rodriguez, Edgar, *O Retrato da Ditadura Portuguesa*, Rio de Janeiro, n.d.

Rodrigues, Manuel Francisco, *Tarrafal: aldeia da morte*, Oporto, 1974.

Santana, Emídio, *História de um Atentado*, Lisbon, 1976.

Silva, José, *Memórias de um Operário* (2 vols.), Oporto, 1971.

Soares, Mário, *Portugal Amordaçado*, Lisbon, 1974.

Soares, Pedro, *Tarrafal: Campo da Morte Lenta*, Lisbon, 1977.

Soeiro, Humberto (ed.), *Intervenção Política: Democratas de Braga, 1949–1970*, Oporto, 1973.

Zenha, Francisco Salgado, *et al.*, *O Caso da Capela do Rato no Supremo Tribunal Administrativo*, Oporto, 1973.

4   The Communist Party and the labour movement

Anon., *Os Comunistas, 1: Bento Gonçalves*, Lisbon, 1976.

'Campos' (Francisco Martins Rodrigues), *Luta Pacífica e Luta Armada no Nosso Movimento*, Lisbon, 1974.

Colectivo das Edições 'Avante!', *O PCP e a Luta Sindical*, Lisbon, 1975.

Comité Marxista–Leninista Português, *Revolução Popular: órgão do Comité Marxista–Leninista Português. Edição completa, 1964–65 (fac-simile)*. Lisbon, n.d..

Cunhal, Alvaro, *Relatório da Actividade do Comité Central ao VI Congresso do PCP*, Lisbon, 1975.

—— *Pela Revolução Democrática e Nacional*, Lisbon, 1975.

—— *A Revolução Portuguesa: O Passado e o Futuro*, Lisbon, 1976.

—— *Rumo à Vitória*, Lisbon, 1975.

Da Costa, Ramiro, *Elementos para a História do Movimento Operário em Portugal, 1820–1975* (2 vols.), Lisbon, 1979.

Ferreira, Francisco, *26 Anos na União Soviética*, Lisbon, 1975.

Fonseca, Carlos da, *História do Movimento Operário e das Ideias Socialistas em Portugal* (2 vols.), Lisbon, n.d.

Gonçalves, Bento, *Palavras Necessárias*, Oporto, 1974.

Gouveia, Fernando, *Memórias de um Inspector da PIDE: 1. A Organização Clandestina do PCP*, Lisbon, 1979.

Magro, José, *Cartas da Prisão (1) Vida prisional*, Lisbon, 1975.

Manta, L. H. Afonso (ed.), *O 18 de Janeiro de 1934*, Lisbon, 1975.

Ibid.; *A Frente Popular Antifascista em Portugal*, Lisbon, 1976.

Marques. J. A. Silva, *Relatos da Clandestinidade*, Lisbon, 1976.

Miguel, Francisco, *Uma Vida na Revolução*, Lisbon, 1977.

Norton, António, *Depoimentos Gravados: A vida nas minas de S. Pedro da Cova contada pelos próprios mineiros*, Lisbon, 1975.

Pereira, José Pacheco, *Conflitos Sociais nos Campos do Sul de Portugal*, Lisbon, 1982.

Rodrigues, Francisco Martins, *Elementos para a Historia do Movimento Operário e do Partido Comunista em Portugal*, Lisbon, n.d.

Tarquini, José Miguel, *A Morte no Monte: Catarina Eufémia*, Lisbon, 1974.

5   *The military, Delgado, the MFA*

Almeida, Dinis de, *Orígens e evolução do Movimento de Capitães*, Lisbon, 1977.

Banazol, Tenente-Coronel Luís Ataíde, *Os 'Capitães-Generais' e os 'Capitães-Políticos'*, Lisbon, 1976.

Carrilho, Maria, *Forças Armadas e Mudança Política em Portugal no Século XX*, Lisbon, 1985.

Carvalho, Otelo Saraiva de, *Alvorada em Abril*, Lisbon, 1977.

Cerqueira, Henrique, *Acuso! O Crime* (2 vols.), Lisbon, 1976–77.

Delgado, Humberto (Tenente Aviador), *Da pulhice do 'Homo Sapiens' (Da Monarquia de vigaristas, pela República de bandidos à Ditadura de papa)*, Lisbon, 1933.

Delgado, Humberto da Silva, *A Marcha para as Indias*, Lisbon, 1954.

—— *The Memoirs of General Delgado*, London, 1964.

—— *28 de Maio*, Lisbon, 1939.

Dimas, Vítor, *Humberto Delgado: o Homem e Três Épocas*, Lisbon, 1977.

Galvão, Henrique, *Carta Aberta ao Dr. Salazar*, Lisbon, 1975.

Garcia, Manuel, e Lourdes Maurício, *O Caso Delgado*, Lisbon, 1977.

Lourenço, Cap. Vasco, *No Regresso Vinham Todos*, Lisbon, n.d.

Porch, Douglas, *The Portuguese Armed Forces and the Revolution*, London, 1977.

Praça, Afonso, *et. al.*, *25 de Abril: Documento*, Lisbon, 1974.

Raby, D. L., 'Populism and the Portuguese Left: From Delgado to Otelo', in Lawrence S. Graham & Douglas L. Wheeler (eds.), *In Search of Modern Portugal*, Madison, Wis., 1982, pp. 61–80.

Rodrigues, Avelino, Cesário Borga e Mário Cardoso, *O Movimento dos Capitães e o 25 de Abril*, Lisbon, 1974.

Romero-Robledo, Mariano Robles, e José António Novais, *Humberto Delgado: Assassinato de um Herói*, Lisbon, n.d.

Sertório, Manuel, *Humberto Delgado: 70 Cartas Ineditas*, Lisbon, 1978.

Spínola, António de, *Portugal e o Futuro*, Lisbon, 1974.

Wheeler, Douglas L., 'The Military and the Portuguese Dictatorship, 1926–74: 'The Honor of the Army'', in Lawrence S. Graham & Harry M. Makler (eds.), *Contemporary Portugal*, Austin, Texas, 1979, pp. 191–219.

Index

abono de família, 71
Abrantes, 97
Abreu, Rodrigo de, 201
Academia Militar, 202, 245
ADS (*Acção Democrato-Social*),
234–5, 238
Africa, 7, 56, 158, 208, 211, 213,
219–23, 227, 231, 243, 244–8
Agence France-Presse, 178
Albania, 93, 133, 257, 258
Alcácer do Sal, 142–3
Alegre, Manuel, 243
Alentejo, 52, 76, 77, 86, 94, 95,
109, 121, 124–9, 138, 141–4,
194, 211, 255
Alfeite, 194
Algarve, 52, 109, 194, 211, 242
Algeria, 134, 209, 227
Algiers, 116, 227–33, 243
Alhandra, 76, 81
Alhos Vedros, 77
Alianza Democrática (Chile), 12, 14,
261
Aljube gaol, 29, 108
Aljustrel, 128–9, 143
Almada, 77, 78, 79, 139–41, 144,
194, 199
Almeida, António de, 108
Almeida, Dinis de, 246, 249
Almeida, Francisco Vieira de, 178,
189, 200
Almeida, Pedro Ramos de, 229
Alpiarça, 126, 139

Alvarenga, Luís Sá Viana de, 202
Alverca, 199
Alves, Mário de Lima, 23–5
America (USA), 20, 62, 163, 166,
168, 170, 221, 222, 244, 262
Amnesty: of 1940, 47, 49; of 1945,
91
Amora, 78
anarchists & anarcho-syndicalists,
8, 12, 18, 41, 42, 45, 61, 65, 66,
69, 225
Andrade, Artur, 170, 189, 206
Angola, 2, 19, 30, 135, 140,
143–4, 152, 153–5, 190, 208,
209, 219–21, 245, 247
Angra do Heroismo (Azores), 46,
47
ANP (*Acção Nacional Popular*),
238–9
Antunes, Carlos Carneiro, 243
Antunes, Ernesto Melo, 248
ARA (*Acção Revolucionária
Armada*), 233, 243
Araguaia River (Brazil), 264
Araújo, Alberto, 46
Araújo, Alvaro de, 91
Areeiro, 184
Argentina, 2, 12, 91, 157, 207,
262–3, 266
Arriaga, Kaúlza de, 247
Arrifana, 80
Asia, 158
ASP (*Acção Socialista Portuguesa*),

232–4
Associação Académica de Coimbra,
138
Aveiro, 38, 129, 166, 238, 244
Avenida Aeroporto (Lisbon), 184
Avenida Brasil (Lisbon), 184
Avenida da Liberdade (Lisbon), 142
Avenida de Roma (Lisbon), 184
Avenida Infante Dom Henrique
(Lisbon), 183
Avenidas Novas district (Lisbon),
185
Axis (in World War II), 19, 22, 58,
62, 67, 72, 73, 87, 163
Azores, 20, 46, 62, 92, 162–3,
221, 246

Badajoz, 232
Badoglio, Marshal, 22, 91
Bakongo, 219
Baleizão, 126–7
Balsemão, Francisco Pinto, 239
Baptista, António Alçada, 235
Barbosa, Col. Tamagnini, 152
Barbosa, Plácido, 201
Barreiro, 48, 76, 77, 140, 141, 144,
210
Barroso, Maria, 238
Basto, Ludgero Pinto, 46
Batista dictatorship (Cuba), 266
Bayo, Alberto, 208
BBC (British Broadcasting
Corporation), 89
Beja, 16 (n. 1), 27, 51, 124, 126,
134, 143, 197, 203, 204,
208–13, 220, 225, 233, 242,
248–9, 256
Belas, 109–10
Ben Bella, Ahmed, 228, 230
Bevan, Aneurin, 200
Blancos (Uruguay), 265
Braga, 75, 129, 166, 188–9, 221,
238
Braga, Luís de Almeida, 186
Bragança, 74
Brandão, Carlos Cal, 180
Brandão, Mário Cal, 26
Brazil: military regime, 10, 13,

236, 263–5, 266; fall of Vargas
(1945), 22, 91; exiles in, 28, 35,
157, 201, 204, 207–8, 213, 222,
227–8, 230, 232
Brigadas Revolucionárias, 197, 233,
242–3
Britain, 20, 62, 92, 162, 163–5,
166, 200, 221, 222
Browder, Earl, 90; Browderism,
90, 116
Buenos Aires, 157
Bulgaria, 232

Cabeçadas, José Mendes, 28–29,
152, 234
Cabeçadas, Rui, 228, 232
Cabora Bassa, 220, 245
Cabral, Amílcar, 5
Cacilhas, 70, 187, 199
Caetano, Marcelo, 19, 137, 223,
234, 237–44
Cais dos Soldados (Lisbon), 183
Caixa de Crédito Agrícola, 87
Caixa Geral de Depósitos, 87
Calafate, Luís Cesariny, 202, 204,
207
Calapez, Major, 212
Caldas da Raínha, 109, 247
Câmara, Helder, 236
Camões High School (Lisbon), 185
Camões, Luis de, 118
Campino, Joaquim António, 95
Campolide, 109
Canada, 170, 222
Cape Verde Islands, 2, 42, 61, 95
Capilé, Cândido, 140
Caraça, Bento de Jesús, 18, 21, 27
Caracas, 157
Caramujo, 78
Carmona, António Oscar de
Fragoso, 28, 30, 36
Carneiro, Francisco de Sá, 239–40
Carrajola, Lt, 126–7
Carrillo, Santiago, 261
Carvalho, Guilherme da Costa,
121–2
Carvalho, Mário de, 231
Carvalho, Otelo Saraiva de, 246,

248, 249, 260
Carvalho, Vasco de, 46, 47, 50–1,
  54, 61
Casablanca, 210
Casa dos Estudantes do Império,
  135
Casas do Povo, 6, 9, 56, 125
Castelhano, Mário, 65
Castelo Branco, 135
Castro, Fidel, 204, 208
Castro, José Guilherme de Melo e,
  238
Castro, Mário de, 25, 26
Cathedral conspiracy (*Revolta da
  Sé*), 133, 143, 197, 198, 201–4,
  233
Catholic church: and Salazar
  regime, 2, 6; conservative
  influence of, 123–4; progressive
  Catholics and the opposition,
  18, 57, 134, 197, 201–3,
  233–7; PCP attitude towards,
  66; students' and workers'
  associations, 135, 201; in
  Delgado campaign, 134, 197
Caxias, 131–2, 207, 223
CDE (*Commissão Democrática
  Eleitoral*), 238–9
Centro Republicano Almirante
  Reis (Lisbon), 24
Cerqueira, Henrique, 231
CEUD (*Commissão Eleitoral de
  Unidade Democrática*), 238–9
CGT (*Confederação Geral de
  Trabalhadores*), 18, 42, 65
Champalimaud (industrial &
  financial group), 5
Chave d'Ouro café (Lisbon), 178,
  179
Chaves, 189
Chile, 2, 3, 9, 10, 12, 13, 14, 207,
  236, 258, 261–2, 266
China, 231, 257, 258
Christian Democrats, 261–2
Ciudad Rodrigo, 166
CMLP (*Comité Marxista-Leninista
  Português*), 224–5, 231
Coimbra, 28, 30, 94, 135–9, 205,

232, 240–1
Coimbrão, 108
Colorados (Uruguay), 265
Comiberlant, 243
Comintern, 3, 18, 42, 43, 47
Comisiones Obreras (Spain), 9
Communist Party: see PCP
Cortesão, Jaime, 166, 167–8, 171,
  200, 205
Costa, Carlos, 133
Costa, Francisco Inácio da, 95–7
Costa, Francisco Ramos da, 227,
  232, 233
Costa, Fernando dos Santos, 28,
  130, 132, 188, 190–2, 198, 199
Couço, 139
Coutinho, António Rosa, 260
Couto, 80
Cova da Piedade, 199
Covilhã, 128, 139, 191, 242
Covina glassworks, 76
Cristo, Francisco Homem, 159
Cuba, 134, 204, 208–9, 227, 243,
  266
Cuba (Alentejo), 125
CUF (*Companhia União Fabril*), 70,
  76–7, 89, 140
Cunene (warship), 243
Cunha, Joaquim da Luz, 247
Cunhal, Adelino, 49, 112
Cunhal, Alvaro: personal life, 42,
  49–50; political line in 1938,
  44–6; and 1941 PCP
  reorganisation, 41, 49–54; and
  1943 PCP Congress, 22, 55–7,
  60, 63–8; and 1944 strikes, 82;
  and 1946 PCP Congress, 91, 93,
  98–100; arrest (1949), 108–12,
  255; escape from gaol (1960),
  130–1; criticism of 'right-wing
  deviation', 123, 131–3,
  199–200, 223, 256; leaves
  Portugal (1962), 133, 223; on
  student movement, 139;
  analysis of 1961–2 protests,
  143–4; on Cathedral plot and
  Beja, 199, 200, 207, 213; and
  Marxist-Leninist schism,

224–6; and FPLN, 227–31
Curto, Ramada, 18
CUT (*Confederación Unica de Trabajadores*, Chile), 9
Czechoslovakia, 113

Damão, 35, 210
D-Day, 23
DDS (*Directório Democrato-Social*), 129, 166–8, 171, 187
Delgado, Humberto da Silva, 7, 9, 12, 15, 116, 134, 143, 153, 157, 255; and Norton de Matos, 30, 31; childhood & early career, 159–60; fascist tendencies, 160–2; Anglophilia, 162–5; origins of Presidential candidacy, 168–73; election campaign, 130, 177–97, 249, 257; plans for revolt, 190–3, 200–1; influence on Cathedral plot, 202; on Programme for the Democratisation of the Republic, 206; exile activities, 207–13, 226–32, 242; populist appeal, 258–60, 268
Democratic Party: *see* Republicans
D'Epinay, Rui, 224
DGS (*Direcção Geral de Segurança*), 238, 241, 263
Dimitroff, Georgi, 3, 5
Diniz, Alfredo, 52, 70, 82, 95, 96
Diniz, Armelim Moura, 18
Diu, 35, 210
Domingues, Manuel, 109–10, 112, 115
DRIL (*Directório Revolucionário Ibérico de Libertação*), 208
Duarte, Manuel, 19
Duke of Edinburgh, 166

Eanes, Ramalho, 246
EEC (European Economic Community), 221–2
EFA-ACEC Company, 194
EFTA (European Free Trade Association), 220, 222
El Salvador, 266

Emissora Nacional (National Radio), 153
Ermidas, 142
ERP (*Ejército Revolucionario del Pueblo*, Argentina), 262
Escoural, 126
Espírito Santo (industrial & financial group), 5
Estado Novo (New State), 3, 23, 26, 37, 68, 137, 143, 151–2, 154, 159, 177, 179, 187, 189, 192, 208, 237, 244
Estado Social, 244
Estoril, 55, 175 (n. 47)
Eufémia, Catarina, 126–7
Eurocommunism, 123, 261
Evora, 124, 126, 142, 212, 246

Falkland Islands, 262
FAO (Food & Agriculture Organisation of the United Nations), 227
FAP (*Frente de Acção Popular*), 197, 224–5, 231
Faro, 142, 210
fascism, 3–6
Feijões, 73
Fernandes, Pastor, 202
Fernando Pó, 208
Ferraz, Beleza, 192
Ferreira do Alentejo, 125
Ferreira, Georgette Oliveira, 108
Ferreira, José Medeiros, 138
Ferreira, Mário, 112
Ferreira, Mercedes de Oliveira, 108
Ferreira, Sofia de Oliveira, 108
Figueira da Foz, 242
Figueiredo, João Baptista de Oliveira, 263
Flores, 221
Fogaça, Júlio, 42, 48, 49, 52–3, 71, 90–1, 113, 114–15, 117, 120–1
Fonseca, Alvaro Duque da, 61, 95
Fonseca, Dalila Duque da, 95–6
FPLN (*Frente Patriótica de Libertação Nacional*), 116, 209, 227–33,

236, 242–3
França, Olívio, 26
France, 23, 91, 152, 166, 220, 225, 232, 240, 258
Franco, Francisco, 46, 119, 163, 166, 260–1
Freemasons, 18, 54, 97, 152, 205
Freitas, Albuquerque de, 209
FRELIMO (*Frente de Libertação de Moçambique*), 245
Frente Amplio (Uruguay), 265
Frente Patriótico Manuel Rodríguez (Chile), 262

GACs (*Grupos Anti-fascistas de Combate*), 20–1, 93
Gaia, 73
Galtieri, Leopoldo, 263
Galvão, Henrique Carlos Mata, 133, 134, 143, 152–9, 170–3, 204, 207–8, 210, 242, 255
Germany, 2, 5, 19, 72, 220–1, 232, 235
Giro, Estevão, 141
GNR (*Guarda Nacional Republicana*), 64, 73, 80, 85, 87, 108, 125–7, 141, 143, 183–5, 188, 191, 212, 240
Goa, 35, 134, 143, 210
Godinho, José Magalhães, 18–19, 21, 25
Godinho, José Marques, 28–9
Gomes, Francisco da Costa, 247
Gomes, João Varela, 203, 211–13, 248
Gomes, Mário de Azevedo, 27, 35, 36, 166, 200, 205
Gomes, Ruy Luís: and MUD, 26; and MND, 33, 35; Presidential campaign, 36–7, 151; in Delgado campaign, 185; in exile, 229
Gomes, Soeiro Pereira, 83–4, 113
Gomes, Teixeira, 167
Gonçalves, Armindo, 51
Gonçalves, Bento, 9, 42, 43, 45, 50, 54, 57, 60, 65, 90, 100 (n. 1)
Gonçalves, Cansado, 46, 47

Gonçalves, José, 95
Gonçalves, Vasco dos Santos, 203, 248, 260
Gramsci, Antonio, 4
Grândola, 139, 142, 219, 248
Greece, 93, 118
Gregório, José, 41, 50, 52, 53, 54, 91, 113, 116, 117, 122
grémios (employers' associations), 6, 72, 74, 80, 120
Grilo, Vélez, 46, 47, 50–1, 61
Grupelho Provocatório (PCP dissidents), 46, 47, 49, 50–1, 61–3
Guedes, Manuel, 46, 50, 52, 53, 54, 57–9, 62, 64, 113
Guerreiro, Emídio, 231
Guevarism, 134, 197, 233
Guimarães, 189
Guiné (Portuguese Guinea/ Guinea-Bissau), 2, 5, 144, 219, 230, 245–7

Hitler, Adolf, 4, 18, 92, 131
Huila (Angola), 152

Iberian Pact, 119
Inácio, Hermínio da Palma, 28–9, 197, 210, 242
India, 153, 210
Instituto Superior Técnico, 135, 241
Intendência Geral dos Abastecimentos, 74
International Civil Aviation Authority, 162
International Women's Day, 140
Intersindical, 242
Italy, 2, 5, 14, 19, 91, 232, 234, 266

Japan, 19
Jardim, Jorge, 245
JOC (*Juventude Operária Católica*), 201
Jorge, Joaquim Pires, 46, 48, 52–3, 62, 71, 88, 91, 95–7, 113, 133
JUC (*Juventude Universitária*

Católica), 201
Junta Revolucionária Portuguesa, 229–32
juntas de lavoura, 74
Junta Patriótica Central, 205–7, 211, 227–8, 232
Juntas Patrióticas, 204–7, 211, 228

Karamanlis, Constantine, 118
Khruschev, Nikita, 117
King Juan Carlos, 261
Korean War, 117

Labour Party, 200
Lacerda, Armanda Forjaz de, 97
Lacerda, Miguel Pereira Forjaz de, 52–3, 88, 97
Lamas, Maria, 34
Lambretta Company, 184
Lamego, 128
Lavradio, 77
Leal, Francisco Cunha, 36, 38, 155, 167–9, 186, 197, 234, 238
Legião Portuguesa (Portuguese Legion), 3, 67, 160, 188, 189, 193, 201
Leiria, 108, 109
Leitão, Júlio César, 42
Leixões, 242
Lenin, 62
Lesser, Bruno, 72
Lima, Alfredo Dias de, 126
Lima, Armando Cristofaretti da Costa, 156–7
Lima, Lino, 37
Lisbon: May 1945 demonstrations in, 23; MUD activities in, 24–5, 27, 29; and 1946 revolt, 28; in Norton de Matos campaign, 32; in 1953 parliamentary elections, 38; strikes in, 48, 69–70, 76–9, 81, 89–90, 128, 193–4, 242; PCP activities in, 83, 96–7, 108–9; wartime shortages in, 72, 73; Penitentiary, 111–12; economic conditions in, 123; student movement in, 135–8, 232, 237, 240–1; 1961–62

protests, 139–44; in Delgado's campaign, 178–9, 183–5, 190; and Beja revolt, 212; migration to, 221; Marxist-Leninists in, 225; Catholics in, 237; sabotage in, 243; and MFA, 246, 247, 268
Lisbon Telephone Company, 70, 140
Lisbon Tramways (*Carris*), 70, 140
Lobo, Maria Teresa, 239
Lopes, António Bastos, 108
Lopes, Higínio Craveiro, 36, 166, 190
Loureiro, Pinto, 51
Lourenço, António Dias, 52–3, 82, 84, 108, 133, 255
Lourenço, Guy, 95
Lourenço, Vasco, 246, 260
Lousã, 94
Luanda, 219
LUAR (*Liga de Unidade e Acção Revolucionária*), 29, 197, 242–3
'Lula', 264
Luso, 108
Luxembourg, 242
Luxemburg, Rosa, 61

Macau, 153, 231
Macedo, Costa, 192
Macedo, H., 72
Machado, António de Barros, 26
Macinhata do Vouga, 73, 108
Magro, José, 109, 115, 133, 255
Maia, 96
Malvinas Islands, 262
Manifesto of the 101, 235–6
Marighela, Carlos, 264
Marinha Grande, 108, 109, 193
Marques, Francisco Ferreira, 48, 53, 85, 108
Martins, José Augusto da Silva, 108, 112
Martins, Rogério, 239
Marxist–Leninists, 54, 68, 93, 113–14, 117, 133, 134, 197, 223–6, 231, 232, 235, 236–7, 241, 243, 255–7, 263–4
Matos, José Mendes Ribeiro

Norton de: and MUNAF, 19, 21, 28, 152; administration in Angola, 19, 30; in First World War, 19, 30; Presidential campaign (1949), 29–32, 134, 155, 205, 268; personal background, 30; relations with PCP, 108, 114; differences with Cunha Leal, 167
Matos, Manuel Pires de, 18
Matosinhos, 128, 242
May Day, 141–2
MDB (*Movimento Democrático Brasileiro*), 264
MDP (*Movimento Democrático Popular*), 237
MDP (*Movimiento Democrático Popular*, Chile), 12, 262
Mealhada revolt (1946), 27–8
Meireles, Manuel Quintão, 36–7, 155
Melo, Jorge de (industrialist), 5
Menano, Hermínio Duarte Borges, 184
MES (*Movimento da Esquerda Socialista*), 237
Mesquita, Mário, 109
Mexico, 208
MFA (*Movimento das Forças Armadas*), 2, 159, 203, 213, 244–9, 254, 259–60
Miguel, Firmino, 246
Miguel, Francisco, 46, 130, 255
Minho, 109
MIR (*Movimiento de la Izquierda Revolucionaria*, Chile), 262
MMI (*Movimento Militar Independente*), 200, 202
MND (*Movimento Nacional Democrático*), 33–8, 116, 119
Mocidade Portuguesa (Portuguese Youth), 3, 6, 135, 160
Monarchists, 18, 62, 129, 151, 163, 186, 202, 205
Monção, 95
Moniz, Egas, 34
Moniz, Jorge Botelho, 77, 78, 80, 85

Moniz, Júlio Botelho, 25, 134, 192, 200, 204, 209–10, 220
Monte Carlo Café (Lisbon), 185
Montemor-o-Novo, 126–7, 194
Montoneros (Argentina), 262
Montreal, 162
Morais, Manuel Tito de, 227–9, 232, 233
Moreira, José, 109
Morgado, José, 34, 35, 37
Morocco, 207, 210–13, 232
Moscavide, 183
Moscow, 42, 43, 47
Moura, Francisco Pereira de, 235, 237
Moura, Virgínia, 33, 36, 37, 185
Mozambique, 2, 144, 190, 219, 220, 222, 245, 247, 248
MPLA (*Movimento Popular pela Libertação de Angola*), 219
MUD (*Movimento de Unidade Democrática*): formation, 23–4; submission of membership lists to authorities, 24–5; activities 1946–49, 26–9; mentioned, 30, 31, 205, 259; and PCP, 93, 94, 107, 114–15, 116
MUD Juvenil, 27, 63, 84, 93, 107
MUNAF (*Movimento de Unidade Nacional Anti-Fascista*): origins & structure, 17–19, 205; and armed struggle, 19–22, 27–9; and MUD, 24, 27, 29, 259; and PCP, 54, 60, 66, 85, 94, 97, 114–5
Mussolini, Benito, 4, 22, 163

National Construction Company, 70
National Labour Statute (1933), 8
NATO (North Atlantic Treaty Organisation), 33, 34, 162, 166, 210, 243
Nazi-Soviet Pact, 61
Neto, Francisco Lino, 238
Neves, Tancredo, 264
Nicaragua, 266
Nogueira do Cravo, 80

Obidos, 246
Odemira, 142
Oeiras, 243
Olhão (Algarve), 27
Oliveira de Azeméis, 73
Oliveira, Francisco Paula de, 43
Oporto: February 1927 uprising
    in, 15 (n. 1); in 1945 coup
    attempt, 21; MUD committee in,
    26; in 1946 revolt, 28; MND
    trial, 35; Rio Tinto incident, 37;
    in 1953 parliamentary elections,
    38; anarchists in, 65; labour
    unrest in region, 80, 128,
    193–4, 198, 242; PCP activity
    in, 88, 95–7, 111, 223;
    opposition in, 129, 166–7, 170,
    172, 205; student movement,
    135, 137, 140–1, 241; 1962
    demonstrations, 140–2, 144;
    Colonial Exhibition (1934),
    152–3; and Delgado, 179–82,
    185, 190, 191, 201, 213, 257;
    migration to, 221; Bishop of
    Oporto, 233, 238; sabotage in,
    243; and MFA, 246
ORA (*Organização Revolucionária
    da Armada*), 42, 63
Ota, 97
O Tempo e o Modo, 234–5

PAIGC (*Partido Africano pela
    Independência de Guiné e Cabo-
    Verde*), 245
Pais, Sidónio, 152
Pampilhosa da Serra, 128
Paris, 227, 231, 242
Parry & Sons shipyard, 70, 140,
    193–4
Pato, Octávio, 63, 84–5, 109, 113,
    133
Patuleia, José, 126
PCB (*Partido Comunista Brasileiro*),
    264
PC do B (*Partido Comunista do
    Brasil*), 263–4
PCP (*Partido Comunista Português*),
    6, 8, 11, 12, 254–60, 268; early

history, 41–7; relations with
    MUNAF, 17–22; reorganisation
    of 1941, 47–55; strategy of mass
    insurrection, 20–22, 132, 197,
    255–7; and Republicans, 65–6;
    3rd Congress (1st Illegal), 22,
    47, 50, 55–68; in Norton de
    Matos campaign, 32; and MND,
    34, 36, 38; Communist Youth,
    63, 115; and Catholicism, 66;
    and labour movement, 68–90,
    241–2; relations with
    peasantry, 86–8, 94, 121,
    124–7, 258; 'strategy of
    transition', 90–100, 114–15;
    4th Congress (2nd Illegal), 93,
    94–5, 98–100; numerical
    strength, 94–5; crisis of
    1949–51, 108–16; 5th
    Congress (3rd Illegal), 117,
    120–3; relations with Spanish
    party, 119–20; 'peaceful
    solution' line, 117–23, 195;
    'right-wing deviation', 131–3,
    199–200, 256; and students,
    136, 139; role in 1962 protests,
    141–4; and Cunha Leal, 167–9,
    197; and Delgado, 168–9,
    186–7, 193–5, 197–200; and
    Cathedral plot, 201–3; and
    Juntas Patrióticas, 205–7, and
    Beja revolt, 213; Marxist–
    Leninist schism, 223–6; and
    FPLN, 226–33, 243; organises
    ARA, 243; and MFA, 248–9
Penafiel, 97
Penedo Gordo, 127
Peniche, 91, 112, 113, 129,
    130–1, 170, 172, 223, 242
Peronists (Argentina), 12, 262
Pias, 124
Pinochet, Augusto, 261–3
PIDE (*Polícia Internacional e de
    Defesa do Estado*), 23, 26, 32, 48,
    67, 85, 94, 95–7, 108–12, 116,
    125, 126, 138, 156–7, 184–5,
    188–9, 193, 194, 201, 204, 205,
    206, 212, 223, 231, 232, 238,

241, 263
Pintado, Xavier, 239
Ponte de Lima, 30
Popular Front, 43–4
Portel, 125
Portela, Lelo, 152
Portuguese Geographical Society,
    153
Póvoa de Santa Iria, 76, 81
Póvoa do Varzim, 88
PPD (*Partido Popular Democrático*),
    239
PPM (*Partido Popular Monárquico*),
    202
Praça da Liberdade (Oporto), 140,
    179
Praça de Saldanha (Lisbon), 185
Praça do Comércio (also *Terreiro do
    Paço*), Lisbon, 141, 142, 183
Pragma, 235
Prague, 228–30
PRP (*Partido Republicano
    Português*): *see* Republicans
PRP (*Partido Revolucionário do
    Proletariado*), 233, 243
PSP (*Polícia de Segurança Pública*),
    138, 141, 183, 188
PVDE: *see* PIDE

Queen Elizabeth II, 166
Queiroga, Fernando, 21, 28

Radical Party (Argentina), 12
Rádio Club Português, 154
Rádio Renascença, 248
Rapazote, António Gonçalves, 239
Rato chapel, 237
Recife, 208, 236
Redol, António Alves, 83
Régua, 75
Reis, Câmara, 36, 168
Republican Congress (of
    Democratic Opposition): First
    (1957), 129, 166; Second
    (1969), 238; Third (1973),
    243–4
Republicans, 11, 13, 14, 18;
    military strategy, 20–2, 27–9,

259, 268; and suspension of
    MUD's public meetings, 25; in
    Norton de Matos's campaign,
    30, 32; break with Communists,
    32–3; PCP relations with, 65–6,
    97, 107–8, 129–30, 140; and
    the military, 150–2; and
    Cathedral plot, 201, 204; and
    Juntas Patrióticas, 205–6;
    deficiencies, 213; and colonial
    question, 220; in exile, 231; in
    1960s, 233–4, 236; Republican
    Congresses, 129, 166, 238, 243–
    4
Ribatejo, 52, 58, 59, 63, 76, 81,
    83–5, 87, 94, 124, 126, 128,
    141, 143–4, 194, 198, 242
Ribeiro, Aquilino, 123, 186
Ribeiro, Helder, 180
Ribeiro, Militão, 71, 108–14
Rio Tinto, 37
Roberto, Holden, 219
Rocha, Alberto, 19
Rodrigues, Francisco Martins,
    49–50, 94, 133, 223–4, 226
Rodrigues, João, 90–1, 116
Rodrigues, Luisa, 108
Romba, Captain, 190
Rome, 227, 228, 231
Rossio Square (Lisbon), 183
Rotterdam, 242
RRS (*Resistência Republicana e
    Socialista*), 233–4
Ruívo, Mário, 227, 229

Saboga, António, 109
SACOR (State petrol company),
    193
Sacramento, Mário, 129
Salazar, António de Oliveira: and
    regime, 1, 2, 4, 18, 55, 118–9,
    130, 195, 198, 207, 244, 248,
    259, 267–8; reshuffles Cabinet
    (Sept. 1944), 19; promises free
    elections (1945), 23, 91;
    wartime policies, 62, 71; car
    presented by Hitler, 131;
    relations with monarchists,

151; attacked by Henrique Galvão, 157–8; and Anglo-Saxon powers, 163–4; meetings with Franco, 166; and Delgado, 177–82, 192; survives Botelho Moniz coup, 209–10; and Goa, 210; disablement, 223, 237; and Catholic critics, 233–6
Saldanha, Marshal, 150, 186
Salgueiro, João, 239
Salgueiro, Prestes, 32
Santa Apolónia station (Lisbon), 183–4
Santa Clara military court, 156
Santa Maria hijacking, 134, 208–9
Santa Maria hospital (Lisbon), 156–7, 204
Santarém, 74, 238
Santo António da Charneca, 243
Santos, Almeida, 202–3
Santos, Fernando Piteira, 19, 52–3, 95, 97, 115–16, 207, 211, 227–9, 232, 243
Santos, João Lopes dos, 96
Santos, José Adelino dos, 126, 194
Santos, Miguel dos, 21, 28
Santos, Vasco da Costa, 202
São Bento station (Oporto), 179
São João da Madeira, 80
São João do Estoril, 237
São Martinho do Campo, 182
São Paulo, 156, 264
São Romão do Coronado, 95–6
São Tomé, 208, 234
Sarney, José, 264
Seara Nova, 168, 234
Sebastianismo, 151
SEDES (*Sociedade para o Estudo do Desenvolvimento Económico e Social*), 239
Seixal, 78, 79
Selvagem, Carlos, 154
Sérgio, António, 35, 36, 168, 170, 200
Serra da Estrela, 128
Serra, Jaime dos Santos, 108
Serra, Manuel, 198, 201–4, 207, 211–13, 233, 255

Sertório, Manuel, 169, 186–7, 196, 207, 226, 227–31
Setúbal, 128, 142, 143, 221, 242
Silva, António Guedes da, 52–3
Silva, Casimira da, 108
Silva, F. F. Joaquim Pereira da, 72
Silva, José, 37
Silva, Lopes da, 192
Silva, Manuel Rodrigues da, 91, 109
Silva, Orlando Juncal da, 95, 97
Silva, Vassalo e, 210–11
Simão, José Veiga, 239
Simões, Jacinto, 19
Sindicatos nacionais (official unions), 6, 56, 57, 60, 68–9, 71, 81, 117, 241–2
Sines, 142
Sintra, 28, 210
Sisyphus, 266
Skapinakis, Nikias, 207
Soares, João, 28
Soares, Mário: and MUD, 24, 25, 29; and Norton de Matos, 30, 32; and Alvaro Cunhal, 49; and PCP, 63, 84, 110, 115; and Delgado, 164, 230, 234; on Cathedral plot, 201; in creation of Socialist Party, 233–4; deportation, 234, 237–8; in Government after 1974, 138, 243; and Maria Barroso, 238; and Palma Inácio, 242
Soares, Pedro, 48, 53, 71, 90–91, 229
Socialist International, 234
Socialist Party (founded 1973), 232, 234, 242–3, 249, 268
Socialist Party (SPIO – *Secção Portuguesa da Internacional Operária*), 18
Somoza regime (Nicaragua), 266
SONAP (State petrol company), 193
Sousa, Américo de, 133
Sousa, Augusto de, 108
Sousa, José de, 42, 45, 55, 60–1
Soviet Union (USSR), 62, 90, 115,

117, 120, 133, 256
Spain: Republic & Civil War, 42, 46, 63, 65, 154, 260; opposition to Franco, 207, 208, 260–1; Franco regime, 2, 3, 12, 13, 260–1; trade with, 72; trade unions, 9; PCP & Spain, 52, 119–20, 258; Post-Franco changes, 14, 91, 182, 261, 266; Portuguese independence from, 47; Delgado in, 213, 232
Spínola, António de, 247–8
Stalin, 60, 62, 117
strikes, 48, 69–71, 75–86, 89–90, 124–9, 135–44, 193–5
student movement: Communist influence in (1934), 42; 1947 protests, 27; 1956–61 developments, 135; 1962 conflicts, 135–9; 1968–73 protests, 240–1
Suárez, Adolfo, 261
Sweden, 222
Switzerland, 232, 234

Tagus Cement Company, 84
Tancos, 243
Tangier, 210
TAP (*Transportes Aéreos Portugueses*), 134, 210, 242
Tarrafal, 2, 15 (n. 1), 42, 47, 49, 50, 60, 61, 65, 89, 90, 91, 100, 114, 115, 234
Tavares, Francisco Sousa, 202
Teixeira, Fernando Blanqui, 223
Terreiro do Paço (Lisbon): *see Praça do Comércio*
Thatcher, Margaret, 263
Timor, 19
Tomar, 28, 74
Tomás, Admiral Américo, 178, 190, 209, 235, 239, 240, 243
Torres Novas, 159
Tortozendo, 128
Trafaria, 156
Trás-os-Montes, 75, 88
Trevões, 73

Trotskyism, 47, 50, 57, 62, 197, 226, 231, 233, 243
Tupamaros, 265

UDP (*União Democrática Popular*), 237
UDP (*União Democrática Portuguesa*), 35
União Nacional, 178, 189, 193, 238–9
União Socialista, 18–19
United Nations, 26, 94, 166, 171
UPA (*União das Populações de Angola*), 219
Uruguay, 10, 265–6

Vale do Vargo, 124–5
Valente, João Pulido, 224
Vargas, Getúlio, 91
Vasconcelos, Perestrelo de, 203
Vatican, 236
Veiga, José Augusto, 126
Venezuela, 207, 208
Veríssimo, Alexandrino Inácio, 126
Vicente, Arlindo, 151, 169–70, 179, 186–8, 205
Vidigal, Germano, 108, 126–7
Vietnam, 244, 258
Vila do Conde, 88
Vila Franca de Xira, 48, 81, 83, 84, 85, 97
Vila Real, 75
Vila Viçosa, 126
Vilarigues, Sérgio, 52–3, 63, 113
Vilhena, Colonel, 204
Vital, António Lobão, 34, 36, 37, 186
Voz da Liberdade, 228
Voz do Operário (Lisbon), 27, 32

Washington, 162, 170, 172
Wiriyamu, 245

Yugoslavia, 93

Zenha, Francisco Salgado, 63